# Learn Visio® 2000 for the Advanced User

**Ralph Grabowski**

Wordware Publishing, Inc.

**Library of Congress Cataloging-in-Publication Data**

Grabowski, Ralph.
     Learn Visio 2000 for the advanced user   /   by Ralph Grabowski.
          p.     cm.
     Includes index.
     ISBN  1-55622-711-6 (pbk.)
     1.  Computer graphics.      2.  Visio.      I.  Title.
     T385.G69275     2000                                99-057151
     006.6'869--dc21                                     CIP


© 2000 Wordware Publishing, Inc.

All Rights Reserved

2320 Los Rios Boulevard
Plano, Texas 75074

No part of this book may be reproduced in any form or by any means
without permission in writing from Wordware Publishing, Inc.

Printed in the United States of America

ISBN 1-55622-711-6
10 9 8 7 6 5 4 3 2
   01



All inquiries for volume purchases of this book should be addressed to Wordware Publishing, Inc., at the
above address. Telephone inquiries may be made by calling:

(972) 423-0090

# Contents

# *Introduction*

Visio is known for its drag-and-drop simplicity. To create a drawing, you simply drag a shape from a stencil into the drawing page, connect the shapes with lines, add some text, and print out your drawing. You're done—in just a couple of minutes.

Many people use Visio 2000 in just that way—straight out of the box, with no modification. But this is just one of the ways Visio was designed to be used. Specifically, you can customize Visio, and you can program Visio. This book is all about customizing Visio; no programming knowledge is required to learn from this book.

## About This Book

In this book, *Learn Visio 2000 for the Advanced User,* you learn:

- How to create and customize shapes, groups, masters, stencils, and template drawings
- The purpose of the ShapeSheet, the meaning of sections and cells, and the unique features of the Custom Properties section
- How to export Visio data to an external database file and set up a two-way link between the drawing and database file
- Dozens of tips and tricks for creating better Visio drawings.

Step-by-step tutorials guide you through several techniques for customizing Visio. By the end of this book, you should be able to customize the Visio workspace, have a thorough understanding of the importance of ShapeSheet sections, and be able to set up a link between your Visio drawing and an external database file.

Little or no programming knowledge is required. If you can write a formula in a spreadsheet, then you can handle the very small amount of programming introduced by this book. In fact, you should not attempt to program Visio until you have a thorough understanding of the ShapeSheet, as described by this book.

This book does not teach you how to program Visio using VBA (Visual Basic for Applications, the programming language included with Visio), Visual Basic, or C++. To learn to program Visio, you may wish to obtain one of the other fine books produced by Wordware Publishing.

# Acknowledgments

First of all, I must thank Judy Lemke for the thorough technical edit she performed on the manuscript. Her keen eye and deep experience with Visio made this a much better, more accurate book.

I'd like to thank Scott Campbell of Visio Corp. for helping out. Thanks to Jim Hill ("How is the book coming?") of Wordware Publishing for believing in the potential of these Visio books. Also, a big thank you to the patience of my wife, Heather ("Time for lunch!"), and the enthusiasm of my children, Stefan, Heidi, and Katrina ("How'd you draw that?"). Last, but not least, thanks to Him who makes all things possible.

# About the Author

Ralph Grabowski has been writing about software for fifteen years. He began his magazine career in 1985 as the technical editor for *CADalyst* magazine, the first magazine for AutoCAD users; later, he became the magazine's senior editor. Ralph is now a contributing editor with *Cadence* magazine; the launch editor for *Technical Design Solutions* magazine for Visio Technical and IntelliCAD users; and is a regular contributor to *AutoCAD User* magazine. He has contributed irregularly to a dozen other computer magazines. Ralph is also the editor of *upFront.eZine*, the weekly CAD newsletter sent by e-mail.

Ralph is the author of over fifty books about CAD, graphics, and the Internet. This is his fifth book about Visio software and his thirteenth book for Wordware Publishing. Ralph has written books and manuals for AutoCAD, AutoCAD LT, Generic CADD, FelixCAD, HTML and VRML, IntelliCAD, MicroStation, TurboCAD, and VDraft.

You can contact Ralph by e-mailing him at ralphg@xyzpress.com or visiting his web site at http://www.upfrontezine.com.

# Section I

# Customizing Visio

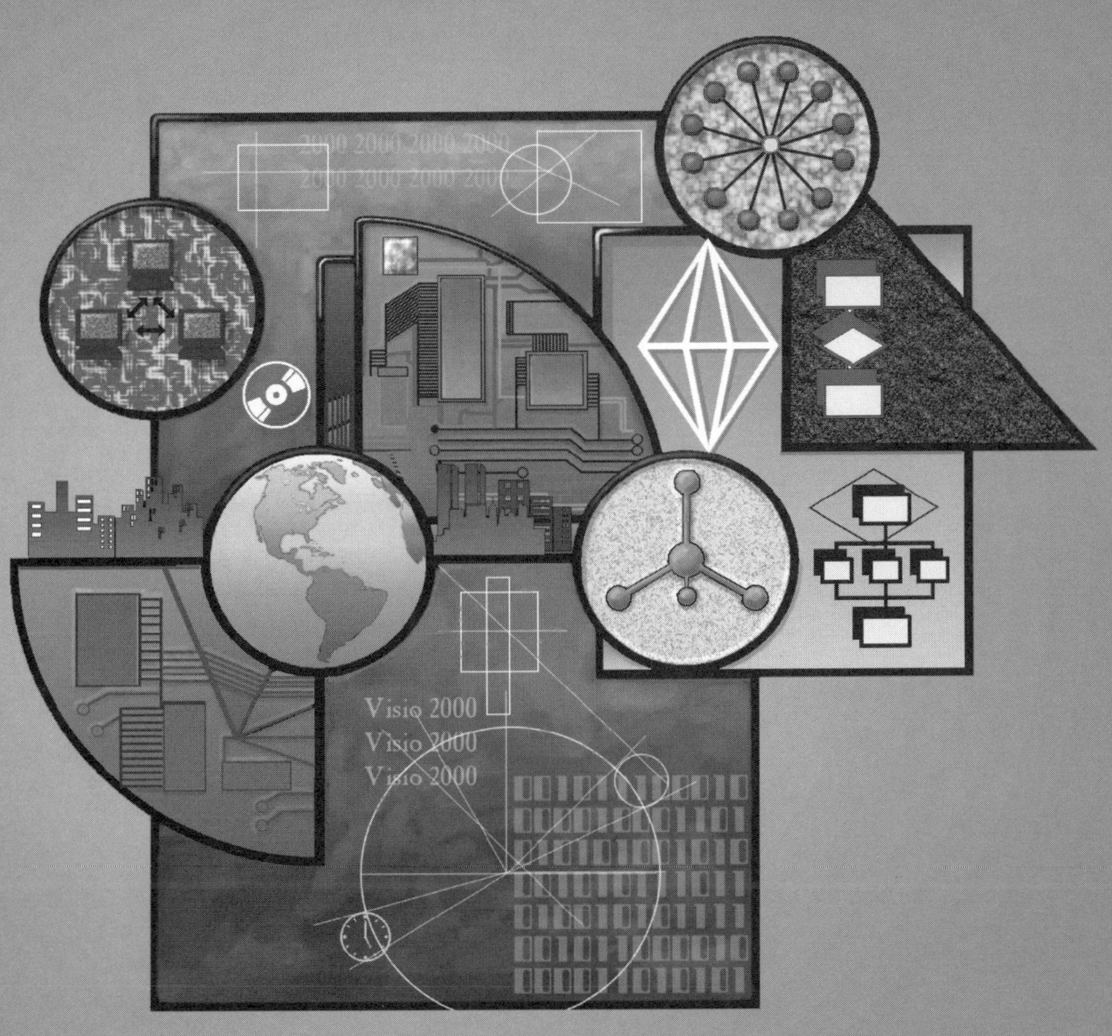

# Chapter 1

# *Introduction to Shapes*

To create a drawing with Visio, you drag a shape from a stencil onto the drawing page. Many people use Visio in that way—straight out of the box, with no modification. But there are other ways to use Visio.

You can customize Visio. *Customize* means to make it your own. By customizing Visio, you take ownership of Visio. You make Visio work more closely to the way you work.

In this chapter, you learn about:

➤ Reasons for customizing Visio

➤ Selecting shapes

➤ The Visio toolbox of customizing and programming

➤ Shape coordinates

By the end of this chapter, you should be familiar with eight different ways to customize Visio, and understand Visio's coordinate system.

## Why Customize Visio?

There are many reasons for customizing Visio and its drawings. Your firm or agency may want to have a uniform look to all of its diagrams. Visio includes thousands of shapes, but you may want to create shapes specific to your discipline. You might be someone who exchanges drawings with CAD users, and wants Visio to mimic the drawing properties of the CAD drawings. You may want to draw more quickly, and don't want to be wasting your time tweaking the look of lines, text, and shapes. You find yourself using several commands frequently, but the commands are not quickly accessed.

You can customize many areas of Visio to suit your needs, such as:

➤ Creating new shapes, and changing existing shapes

➤ Making your new shape available to other Visio drawings by turning it into a master shape

➤ Collecting your shapes into stencils

➤ Defining standardized drawings via templates

➤ Customizing Visio's linetypes, arrowheads, colors, fill patterns, and other areas

➤ Creating custom toolbars with the commands you use most frequently

These aspects of customizing Visio require absolutely no programming knowledge.

## Basic Shape Control

Visio has several ways to let you select more than one object in the drawing. The easiest method is to press **Ctrl+A**. Use this keyboard shortcut to select all objects in the drawing. Notice that all objects are surrounded by thin dashed rectangles.

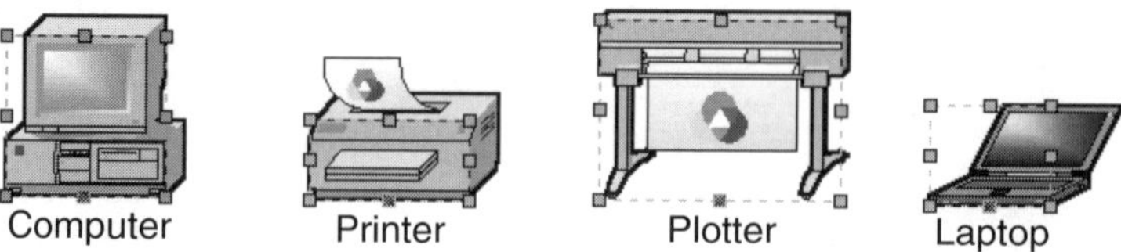


To select a single object, make sure you are using the pointer tool (looks like the standard Windows pointer) and click to select. To *click* means to press the left mouse button.

Another selection method is to *window* the objects: click and drag. To *drag* means to move the mouse while holding down the button. Notice that Visio draws a rectangle from your click point to where the cursor is. Only objects whose alignment box is completely within the selection rectangle are selected.

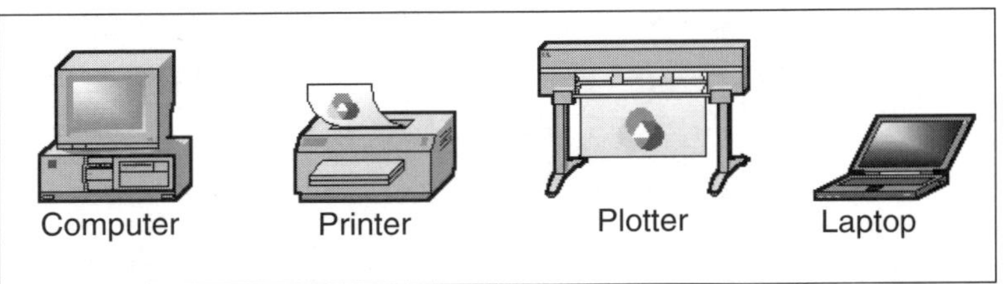


To select more than one object, select one object, then hold down the **Shift** key and select additional objects. Notice that the first object you pick has green handles; the second and subsequent objects have cyan (light blue) handles.

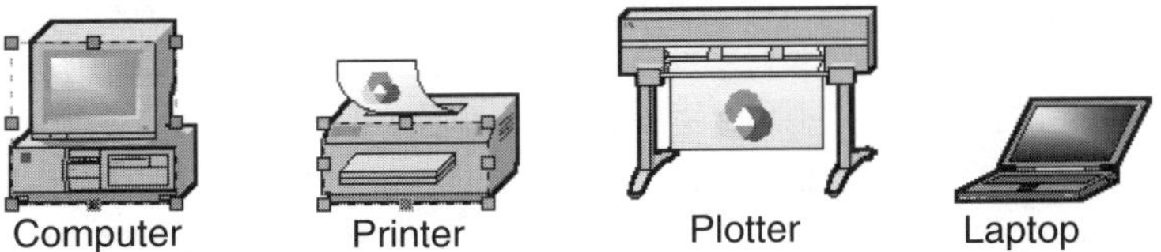


To remove an object from the selection, select it a second time while holding down the **Shift** key and the handles disappear.

To deselect all objects, simply click anywhere in the drawing away from all shapes.

To move a shape, drag it. On the status bar, you see the word **Move**.

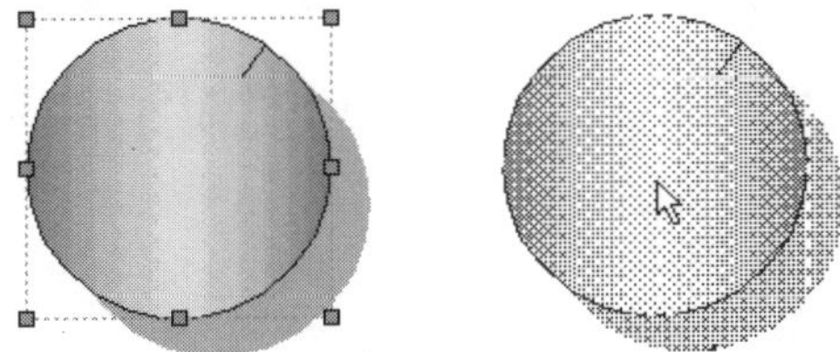

To copy a shape, hold down the **Ctrl** key while dragging the shape. Notice the small plus sign (+) that appears next to the cursor. It confirms that you are copying, not moving. On the status bar, you see the word **Copy**.

For multiple copies of a shape spaced equally from one another, simply press **F4** or select **Edit | Repeat** from the menu bar. Each time you press **F4**, Visio places another copy at the same distance from the previous copy.

If you make a mistake moving or copying, press **Ctrl+Z** or select **Edit | Undo** from the menu bar. You can undo the last ten "mistakes."

# Visio's Customization Toolbox

Visio is so easy to use that it is tempting to not bother trying to change anything. Yet, there is great power in customization.

For this reason, I present to you Visio's "customization toolbox." Just like a mechanic's toolbox that contains specialized tools that help him efficiently repair your automobile, Visio contains a toolbox of tools, ranging from simple screwdrivers and shims, to powerful analyzing scopes and computer interfaces. I've divided the Visio toolbox into eight drawers:

Drawer 1: Drawing geometry.

Drawer 2: Applying styles, as described in Chapter 2 of this book.

Drawer 3: Selecting commands, as discussed extensively in *Learn Visio 2000* (Wordware Publishing).

Drawer 4: Saving to VSD, VSS, and VST files, as summarized in Chapter 3 of this book.

Drawer 5: Creating customized toolbars, described in Chapter 4.

Drawer 6: Uncovering ShapeSheets, as exhaustively expanded on in Section II.

Drawer 7: Linking to databases, as delineated in detail by Section III.

Drawer 8: Automating Visio via programming, not included in this book.

This chapter gives you an overview of the Visio toolbox. In the following chapters, you learn how to use the tools found in each drawer. The sole exception is Drawer 8, automating (programming) Visio. The topic of automation is too large and too advanced to be included in this book.

# Drawer 1. Drawing Geometry

The first drawer in the Visio toolbox contains the tools with which you draw geometry. (*Geometry* is Visio's term for objects or entities.) Any time you draw in Visio, you draw with one of seven basic geometries: line, infinite line, arc, elliptical arc, ellipse, polyline, and spline.

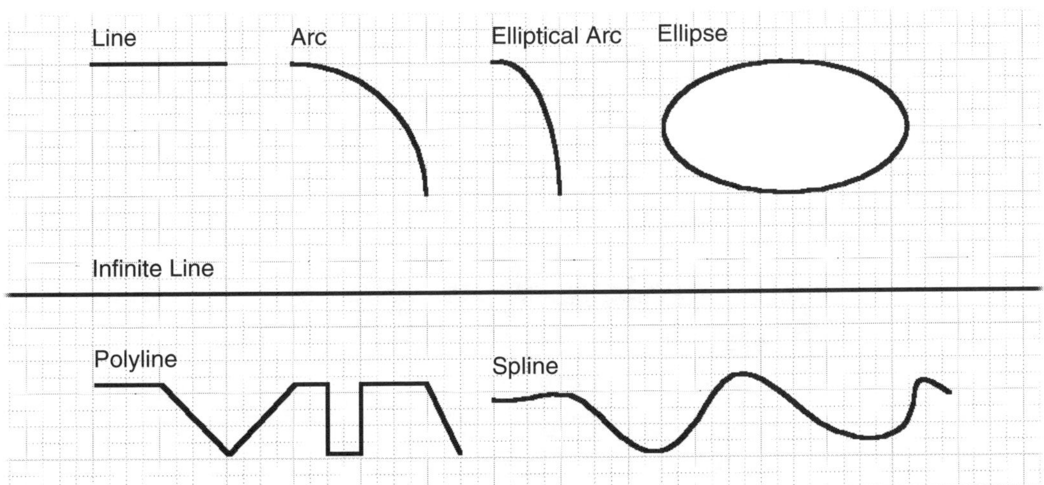


You can call these the "fundamental seven." Every shape you see in Visio, from the simplest line to the most complex shape and intelligent connector, contains at least one of these seven.

I lied; most shapes are actually drawn with one or two or three fundamental geometries—line, elliptical arc, and ellipse.

Of the other four, the infinite line, ellipse, and polyline are new to Visio 2000. Because they are new, most shapes included with Visio 2000's stencils do not make use of them. The spline is rarely used in shapes. (Note that Visio 2000 changes the spline geometry from a NUBS to a NURBS—from a non-uniform B-spline to a non-uniform rational B-spline.)

It turns out an arc is almost never used in Visio, because the arc is rather limited. Attempting to stretch an arc results in unexpected clover and hourglass shapes. The elliptical arc is more adaptable, since it stretches predictably and can mimic circular arcs. So, whenever Visio's printed and online documentation speaks of arcs, it really means elliptical arcs.

## The Drawing Tools

"But what about text?" you protest. "And the rectangle?" Looking at the buttons on the **Standard** toolbar, there seem to be tools for drawing seven kinds of geometry. The geometry tools are Text, Pencil, Freeform, Line, Arc, Rectangle, and Ellipse.

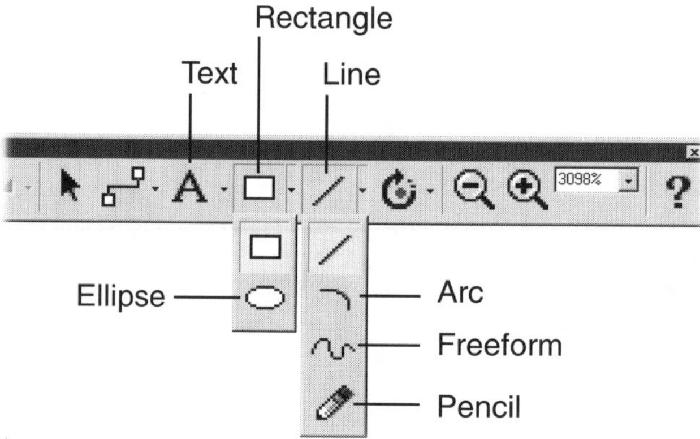


The truth is that the tool bar is a disguise. Come with me as we uncover the masquerade and see what is really happening behind the scenes when you click a button and draw with its tool:

➤ **Text tool** draws a text block within an invisible rectangle made of four lines. *Text block* is the term Visio gives to the text that you can type on top of every shape.

➤ **Pencil tool** draws a line or an elliptical arc, depending on how the cursor moves.

➤ **Freeform tool** draws a spline. Technically, the spline is a NURBS (short for *non-uniform rational B-spline*), similar to that found in computer-aided design software and other drawing programs. NURBS should not be confused with the NUBS (short for *non-uniform B-spline*) used in earlier versions of Visio. In NURBS, all weights are equal; in NUBS, weights can be unequal. By the way, the B in NUBS and NURBS refers to Carl de Boor's B-splines and not Bezier, as commonly held.

➤ **Line tool** draws a line. Hold down the **Shift** key to constrain the line to 45- and 90-degree angles.

➤ **Arc tool** draws a 90-degree elliptical arc (one quarter of an ellipse). It would be more accurate to call this tool the Elliptical Arc tool. Unlike the other tools, holding down the **Shift** key does not draw a circular arc.

➤ **Rectangle tool** draws a rectangle out of four lines. Hold down the **Shift** key to draw a square, also made of four lines.

➤ **Ellipse tool** draws an ellipse. Hold down the **Shift** key to draw a circle, also made from an ellipse. (The ellipse geometry is new in Visio 2000. Earlier versions of Visio created the ellipse and circle shapes from two elliptical arcs.)

Missing from the list are the arc, infinite line, and polyline geometries. As an end user, you cannot create an arc or a polyline directly; the geometries can be created by the ShapeSheet or VBA programming. The infinite line is created when you drag a guide from the ruler onto the page.

In summary, four of the tools draw *native* geometries (line, elliptical arc, NURBS, and ellipse); the other tools on the toolbar draw *derivative* objects.

## The Secret Revealed

You may have noticed there seem to be other drawing tools, such as the **Connector** tool. This may lead you to wonder, "How is it possible to draw a line with the Line tool, and then create something that acts different when drawing a line with the Connector tool?" Even if you weren't wondering, here is the one-word answer: ShapeSheet.

When I invited you to come with me behind the disguise, I was making a veiled reference to the ShapeSheet. I won't go into much detail here, except to say that it is the ShapeSheet that determines how a shape acts. In this case, the line's ShapeSheet determines whether it acts like a line or like a smart connector. It is the ShapeSheet of the four line objects that make them look like a solid rectangle.

Every shape owes its existence to the ShapeSheet. The ShapeSheet tells you everything you need to know about the shape. There are, however, a couple of exceptions. The most notable is that you cannot access the text block from the ShapeSheet (you can by automation); this shortcoming may be corrected in a future version of Visio.

You learn more about ShapeSheets in Section II of this book—in greater detail than you ever thought possible.

## Visio Objects

In addition to shapes and geometries, Visio has *objects*. Although the definition varies widely of what an object is, here I refer to those that are represented by the ShapeSheet:

| Object | Meaning |
| --- | --- |
| **Page** | The page object is what you draw on, although you can draw off the edges of the page, too. (The area outside the page is called the *pasteboard*.) A drawing can contain up to 200 pages. The page object is not printed; it specifies visual aids, such as the limits of the printable area, the drawing scale, the layer structure, the grid, and the snap. |

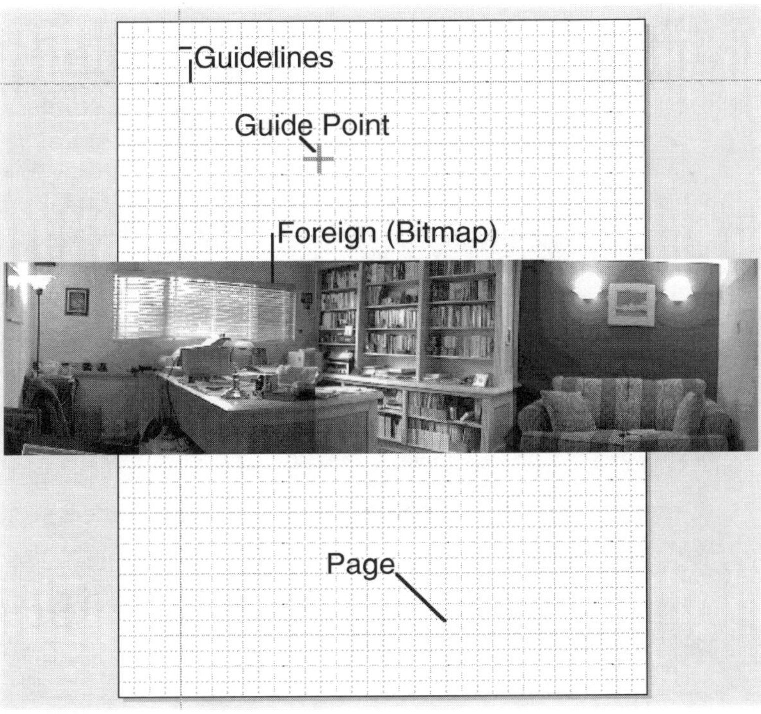





| Object | Meaning |
| --- | --- |
| **Group** | The group object is a collection of shapes and geometries, treated as a single object. Many "shapes" you drag from a stencil onto the page are actually groups. (More about groups in Chapter 2.) |
| **Shape** | The shape object is a collection of geometries treated as a single object. The ShapeSheet gives shapes their intelligence. |
| **Style** | The style object represents styles defined in the drawing. Styles are created with **Format | Define Styles**, and are applied to shapes and text. |
| **Guide** | The guide object comes in two forms: the guideline and guide point, which help you position shapes in the drawing. They are like *construction lines* in computer-aided design software. Indeed, Visio 2000 changes the definition of guides to that of the infinite line. Until Visio 2000, your printer could not print them; now an option in **Format | Behavior** lets you print guides. |

| Object | Meaning |
| --- | --- |
| **Foreign** | The foreign object is the result of using the **Insert \| Picture, Insert \| Object** , and **Edit \| Paste** commands to insert a file or an object created by another program, or pasted from the Clipboard. Visio recognizes the following foreign objects: Metafile, Bitmap, OLE Link Object, OLE Embedded Object, and Control. Prior to Visio 2000, this object was called the *image* object. |
| **Document** | The document object defines the preview quality, summary, and output format, which are set by **File \| Properties**. |

# Drawer 2. Apply Styles

Once you've drawn some geometry and placed some shapes, you can change their look. You can customize the:

- ➤ Color of the lines, arcs, and splines making up the shape
- ➤ Color and style of fill and the optional drop shadow
- ➤ Pattern of the lines, arcs, and splines
- ➤ Width of the lines, arcs, and splines
- ➤ Line ends, known as *arrowheads* in computer-aided design software
- ➤ Line caps, whether squared off or rounded
- ➤ Layer association
- ➤ Text block, including its font, size, color, and justification

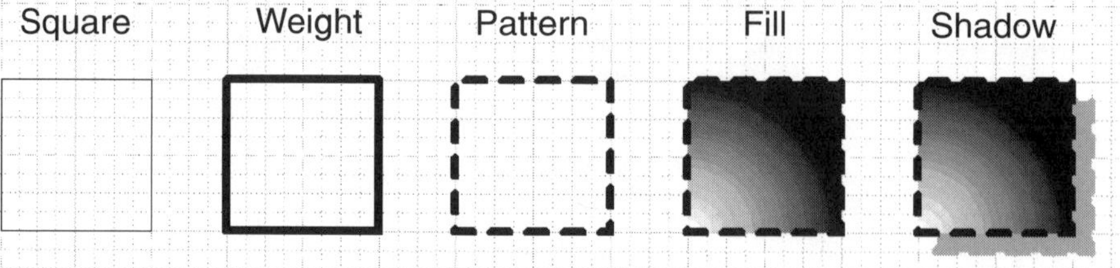


To customize shapes with styles, use the **Format \| Define Styles** command, as described in Chapter 2, "Creating Masters and Styles."

# Drawer 3. Select Commands

With the shape drawn and the properties applied, you can use many of Visio's editing commands to further customize things to your liking. The **Shape** menu lists most of the shape manipulation commands, with the remaining commands listed in the **Tools** menu.

For in-depth coverage of using Visio's commands, you may wish to consult *Learn Visio 2000* from Wordware Publishing.

# Drawer 4. VSD, VSS, and VST Files

You save your Visio drawings as VSD files, short for ViSio Drawing. To store your customized shapes, you convert them into masters and save the masters in stencil (VSS) files. Template (VST) files let you customize the entire Visio environment.

Masters, stencils, and templates are covered in Chapter 3, "Creating Stencils and Templates."

# Drawer 5: Customized Toolbars

Until Visio 2000, you could not customize the toolbar, except via programming. With Visio 2000, you can create and modify toolbars as easily as in most other Windows applications.

Customizing toolbars is described in Chapter 4, "Tailoring Toolbars and Menus."

# Drawer 6. ShapeSheets

I've been mentioning ShapeSheets as the secret behind the object. Let me give you a brief look here. The rest of the details will have to wait for Section II of this book.

The ShapeSheet looks very much like a spreadsheet, hence the name. To see the ShapeSheet for yourself, follow these steps:

1. Draw a rectangle in the drawing.

2. Select the rectangle. Visio surrounds it with eight, small, green squares, called *selection handles*, to show you that the rectangle is selected.

3. From the menu bar, select **Window**, then click **Show ShapeSheet**. Notice that Visio splits the screen in half, displaying the drawing in one window and the ShapeSheet in the second window.

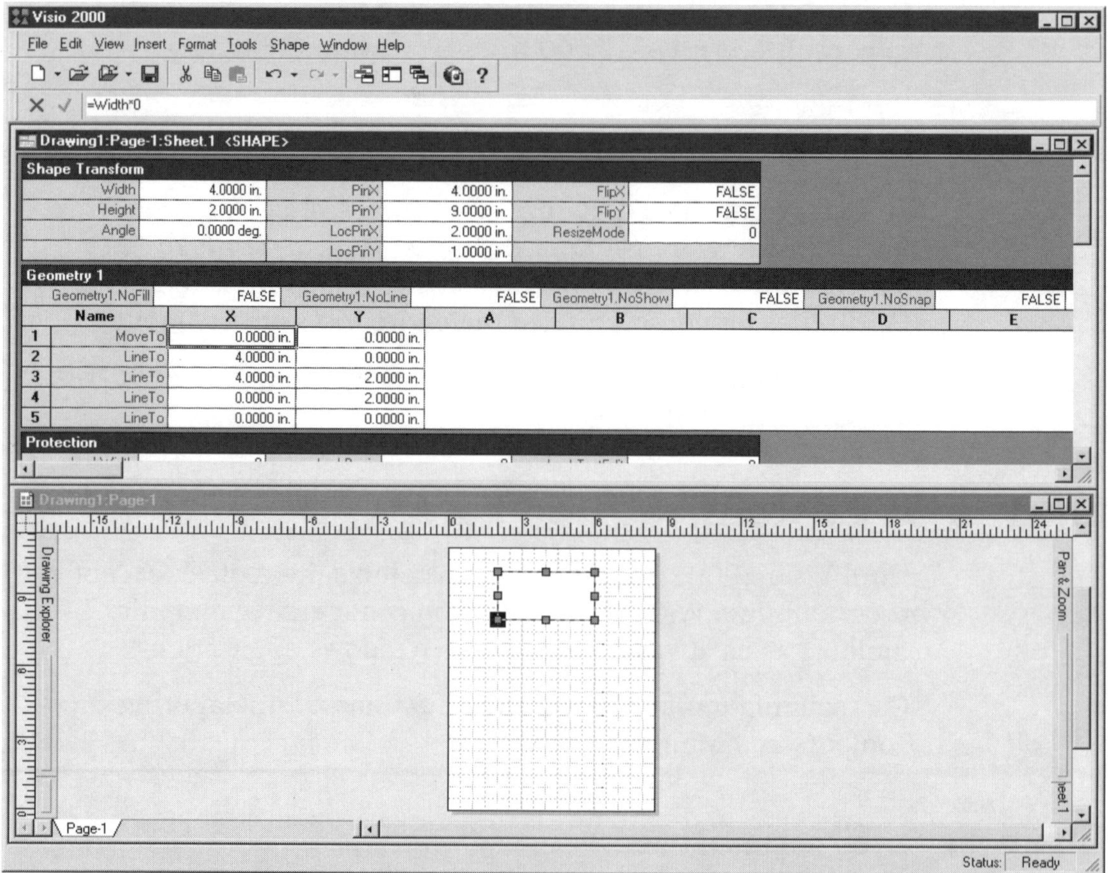

4. Examine the ShapeSheet. There is one ShapeSheet for every object. Notice the spreadsheet format: rows and columns. If all you see are headings (white text on blue background), click a heading to expand it.

5. Look at the column under the Geometry 1 heading. You see the words **MoveTo**, **LineTo**, **LineTo**, **LineTo**, and **LineTo**. There you have it: the four lines that make up the rectangle.

6. Close the ShapeSheet window by clicking the close button (looks like **x**).

The ShapeSheet contains much data, which may at first seem overwhelming to you. You cannot, however, hope to write programs for Visio, or even link drawings with database information, without a thorough understanding of the ShapeSheet, its sections, and their cells. For that reason, the most important part of this book is Section II, *Customizing ShapeSheets*.

# Drawer 7. Database Links

There is more to Visio than drawing. It can also be used to store and access data in three ways. First, to store data inside the drawing, you use custom properties, which are discussed in Section II of this book.

Second, data can be exported and imported to and from the drawing. Third, Visio uses ODBC drivers (short for *open database connectivity*) to link the drawing with database files.

## *Custom Properties*

Custom properties let you store any kind of data with a shape. For example, in an office drawing, you have desks, chairs, and computers. With each desk shape, you can include the inventory number and owner data (Visio lets you change the custom properties associated with any shape). To access custom properties, right-click a shape and select **Properties** from the shortcut menu. If the shape contains custom properties, then Visio displays a dialog box with the shape's custom properties. (If not, Visio offers to let you create custom properties for the shape.)

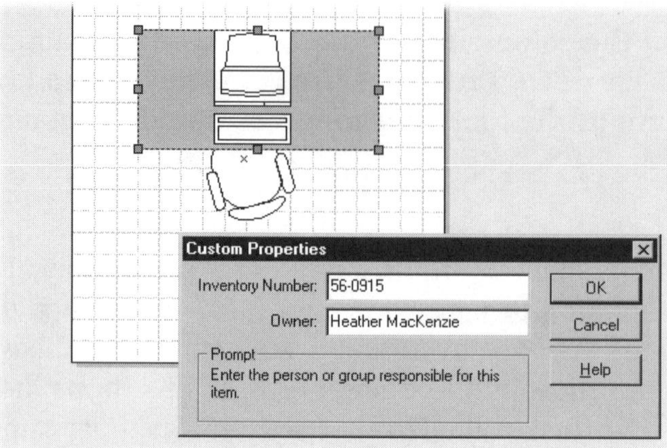



"Custom properties" is, in my humble opinion, a terrible term for describing data stored with a shape. "Custom data" or "User-definable data" may have been better. Among computer-aided design software, the equivalent to Visio's custom properties are known as "attributes" by IntelliCAD and AutoCAD, and as "tags" by MicroStation.

## Data Export and Import

The data stored in custom properties can be summarized by a table in the drawing. Alternatively, it can be exported to a spreadsheet file. The **Property Reporting** wizard performs both of these functions. To run the wizard, select **Tools | Property Report**.

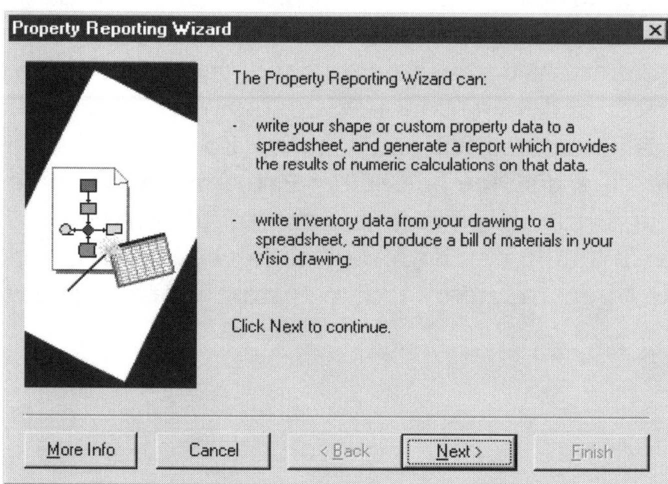

The reverse is possible. You can write a text file using records and fields in a CSV format (short for *comma-separated values*). Visio imports the file and converts the data into a drawing. See Chapter 11, "Creating Drawings from Text Files."

## Linking with ODBC Databases

Visio includes two wizards that take care of the details of reading and writing external database files via ODBC. The best part is that you don't need a database or spreadsheet program; Visio itself creates the files in the native format of several database programs. Via ODBC, Visio reads and writes files used by Access, dBase, Excel, FoxPro, Oracle, Paradox, and SQL Server, as well as plain text files using tabs or commas as field separators.

The **Database** wizard exports data contained in ShapeSheet cells of selected shapes to a file in one of the file formats listed above. Complete details can be found in Chapter 10, "Exporting Drawings to Database Files."

The Database wizard goes further by creating a two-way link between the database file and the shapes in the drawing. Once the link is set up, truly amazing things happen. Make a change to the drawing and Visio automatically updates the database file; make a change to the database file and ODBC automatically updates the Visio drawing. Complete details can be found in Chapter 12, "Linking Drawings with Databases."

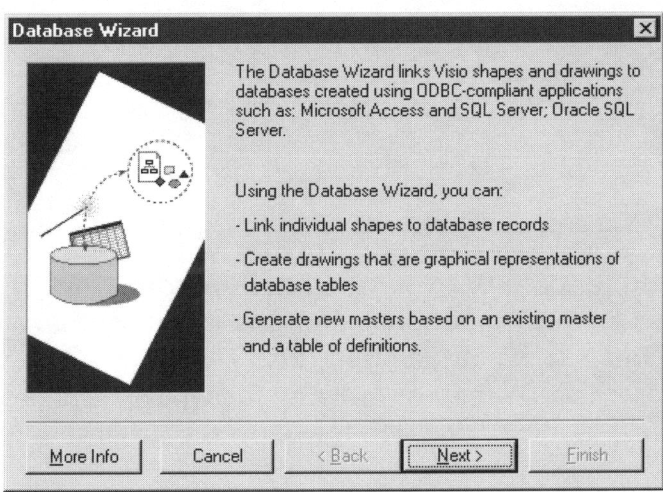

# Drawer 8. Automation

You can write programs that work with Visio. This is often referred to as *automation* by Microsoft Corp. Visio itself includes a programming language called Visual Basic for Applications, or VBA for short. VBA is found in a number of other applications, such as Word and Excel from Microsoft, IntelliCAD from Visio, and AutoCAD from Autodesk. The advantage is that if you can learn to program VBA in one of these programs, the skill is easily transferred.

VBA is available in all editions of Visio 2000—Standard, Technical, Professional, and Enterprise. To access the VBA Editor, select **Tools | Macros | Visual Basic Editor** or press **Alt+F11**. The Visual Basic Editor opens as an independent application.

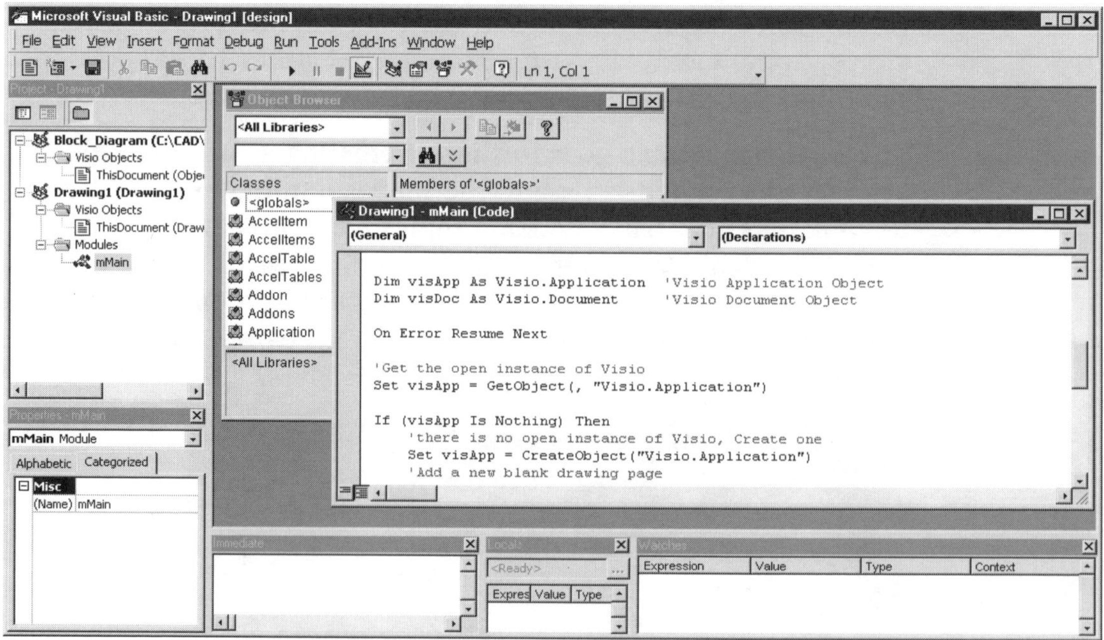


In addition to VBA, you can write programs in C, C++, Visual Basic, and any other programming language that supports automation. It is via automation (also known as ActiveX) that Visio exposes itself—shapes, drawing files, pages, shapes, layers, menus, toolbars, and windows—to the programming language.

Automation is the only means (currently) to access text in the drawing. It is how you customize the user interface, such as the menus and toolbars.

The topic of automation is so extensive that it needs its own book. Hence, the topic is not discussed in this book.

# The (Rather Dry) Subject of Coordinate Systems

Before leaving this chapter, we need to discuss the all-important topic of how things get measured. Visio is a two-dimensional *vector* program, which means it deals with shapes that have length and direction, and are fixed in a *plane* (a.k.a., the page). This means that Visio knows the size of a shape, whether it is rotated, and where it is located.

To know the size and position of a shape, Visio has to measure it from somewhere. That somewhere is called the *origin*. In Visio, the origin is (usually) located at the lower-left corner of the page.

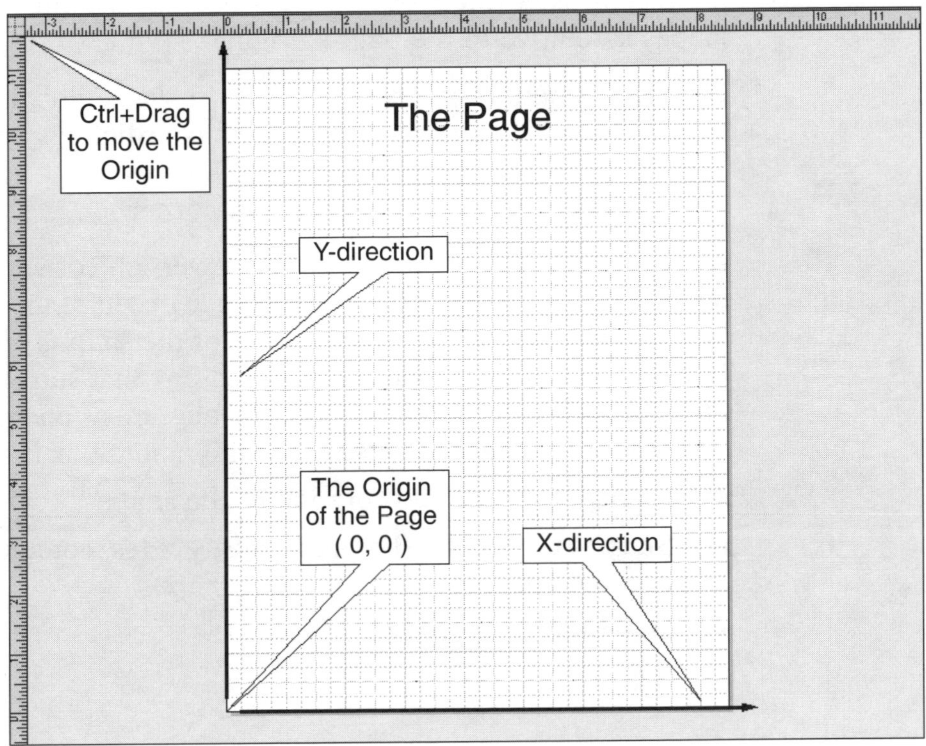

You are probably familiar with the origin from your days in geometry class. Technically, the origin is where the x- and y-coordinates are both 0. The x-direction measures things horizontally. The y-direction measures things vertically.

I say that the origin is usually at the lower-left corner because you can move Visio's origin. Hold down the **Ctrl** key, then drag the cursor from the intersection of the two rulers. When you let go of the mouse button, Visio repositions the origin (0,0) at that point. (Unlike some other drawing programs, you cannot move the rulers themselves.)

To return the origin to its original (a.k.a. default) position, double-click the intersection of the two rulers. The origin moves back to the lower-left corner of the page.

## Shape Coordinates

So far, I have been speaking of the page's coordinate system. You can call it the *global* coordinate system because the position of all shapes is relative to the page's origin.

The complement to global is *local*, as in "Page globally, shape locally." Every shape has its own local coordinate system, sometimes called *shape coordinate system*. Like the page origin, the origin of the shape is at its lower-left corner.

But what if the shape doesn't have a lower-left corner, such as a circle? We need to be more accurate; the origin of the shape's coordinates is at the lower-left corner of the shape's *alignment box*. The alignment box is that green dotted box that surrounds a shape when you select it. In many ways, the alignment box is more important than the shape itself. The alignment box is used to:

➤ Change the size and rotation of the shape

➤ Snap and glue the shape to grids, guides, connection points, and the alignment box of other shapes

➤ Determine the origin of the shape

➤ Position the text block

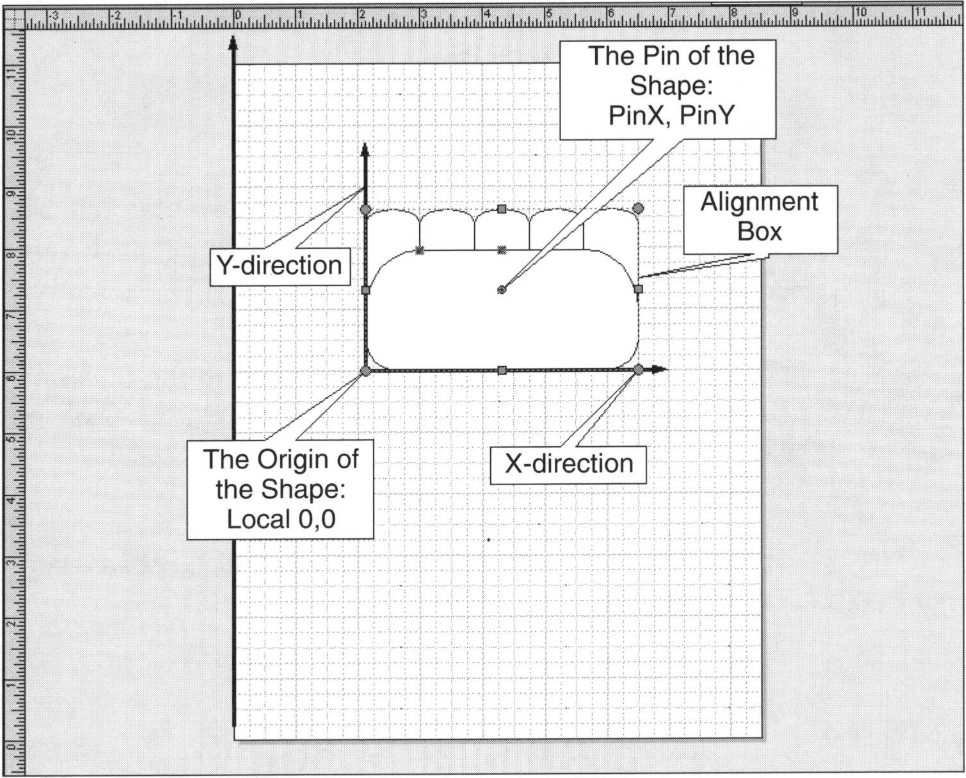




# The Relationship Between Page and Shape Coordinates

Visio measures the position of the shape on the page via the **PinX** and **PinY** positions (found in the ShapeSheet). Think of them as sticking a pin through a telephone message into a corkboard. Now measure the x- and y-distances from the lower-left corner of the corkboard to the pin hole. That's how Visio does it.

The location of the pin is called the *center of rotation*. When you rotate a shape, it is rotated about the x,y-coordinates defined by PinX and PinY. To see the pin location, select the shape with the **Rotation** tool. The small, green circle with the dot in the middle indicates the center of rotation (or pin location).

Most often, Visio uses a simple formula to determine the location of the center of rotation:

**PinX = Width/2**
**PinY = Height/2**

The **Width** and **Height** in those two formulae refer to the width and height of the alignment box. By dividing each value by two, Visio places the center of rotation at the precise center of the alignment box.

It is possible to stick that pin anywhere in the telephone message. You might stick the pin in the upper corner of the message, or right though its center. In the same way, the Visio PinX and PinY position can be located anywhere on that shape—even outside the shape (try that with the telephone message!). For that reason, Visio provides the **LocPinX** and **LocPinY** coordinates to determine the location of the pin.

**Caution:**

In some cases, there may be more than two coordinate systems. Consider a shape within a group on a page. The coordinates of the shape are relative to the position of the group. And the coordinates of the group are relative to the page. For this reason, we don't say the coordinates of a shape are relative to the page. Instead, we use another word: *parent*.

We say the shape's coordinates are *relative* to its parent's. *Parent* is a generic term used by Visio to mean the group, or the page, or even the group within another group to which the shape belongs.

If you think about it, this has some serious implications down the road. You might be working with the coordinates of a shape, thinking they're relative to the page. *Careful*: the coordinates might be relative to a group, giving you an unexpected result.

There is much more on the topic of alignment boxes and shape coordinates in Section II, *Customizing ShapeSheets.*

# Chapter Review

In this chapter, you were introduced to the Visio toolbox and its eight drawers full of tools. You learned about the object that shapes are made of and how to apply the properties of shapes. You received a brief overview of commands for editing shapes; saving your work to drawing, stencil, and template files; the power hidden in ShapeSheets; linking to external databases; and programming Visio through automation. At the end of the chapter, you learned how Visio measures things.

In the next chapter, you use the toolbox to create customized shapes, grouping shapes together, making a master of your custom shapes, and adding masters to stencils.

# Chapter 2

# *Creating Masters and Styles*

After creating custom shapes and properties, you'll probably want to use them in other drawings and may want to share them with other users. You could use the Clipboard to copy shapes from one drawing and paste them into another. The better approach is to create a master, which is stored in a stencil file. In the same way, custom line patterns and arrowheads are stored in the stencil file.

In this chapter, you learn about:

- ➤ Grouping shapes
- ➤ Saving masters in stencil files
- ➤ Editing the master's icon
- ➤ Designing a custom color, fill and drop shadow pattern, line pattern and width, line end and cap, text block, and layer

By the end of this chapter, you should know how to group shapes, create masters, and create customized properties and styles.

## Grouping Shapes Together

A shape sometimes consists of a single object, such as a simple rectangle that represents a desk. More often, though, many objects make up a shape. When it comes time to copy or move the shape, you can select all the objects that make up the shape, but there is an easier way.

When you know that you want a selection of objects to represent a single shape, group them. Select the objects that make up the shape, then press **Ctrl+G** or select **Shape | Grouping | Group** from the menu bar. Visio indicates the group by placing a single alignment box that encompasses all shapes in the group. The figure shows the individual shapes that were grouped together to create the PS/2 shape.

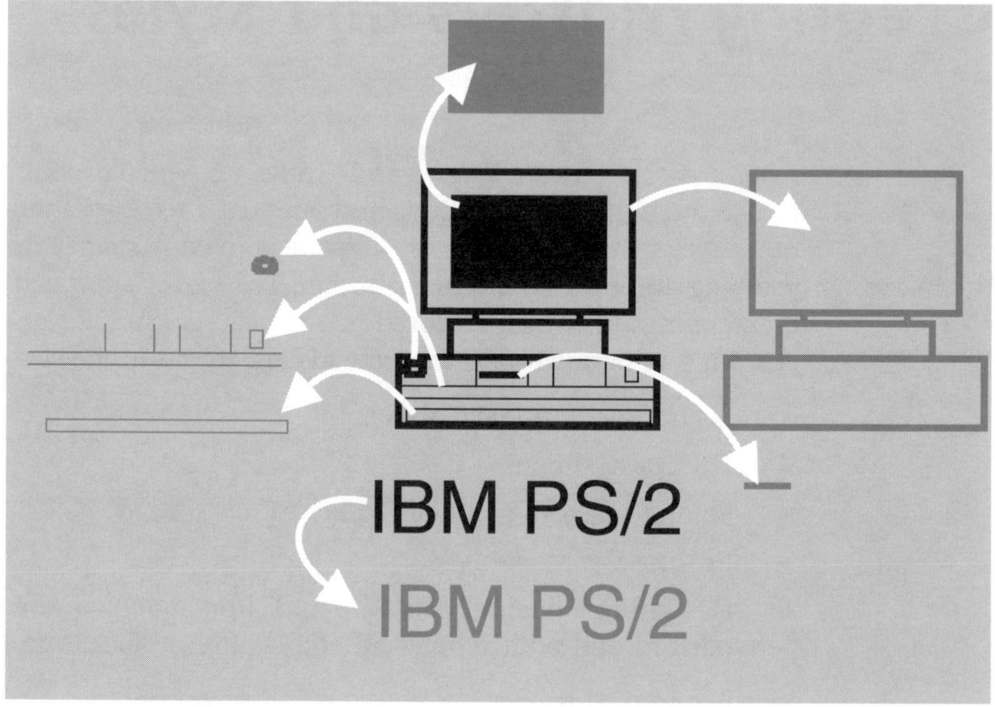


When the **Add shape to groups on drop** option is turned on in the Behavior dialog box, you can add a shape to a group by dragging the shape onto the group. Visio 2000 provides a way to add geometry to a group:

1. Choose the geometry tool, such as **Line**, **Arc**, or **Ellipse**.
2. Select the group.
3. Hold down the **Ctrl+Shift** keys, then draw the new geometry.

**Caution:**

When the group is selected, formatting and editing commands apply to every shape in the group. If you select a yellow fill, then all shapes in the group change to the yellow fill. In previous versions of Visio, you could format individual shapes only after the shapes were ungrouped; as of Visio 2000, it is possible to format shapes individually while within the group.

The Behavior dialog box (select from the menu bar **Format | Behavior**) allows you to decide how a group is picked (new in Visio 2000). You have three choices for selecting a group:

➤ The first pick selects the group; the second pick selects a member (this is the default option).

➤ The first pick selects the group only; additional picks cannot select a member of the group.

➤ The first pick selects a member; the second pick selects the group.

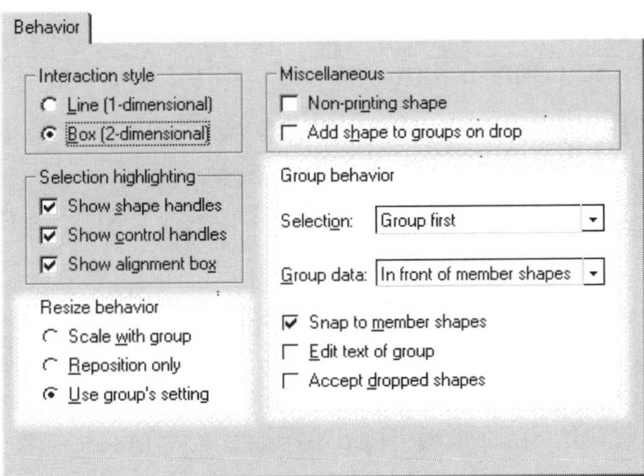

You add shapes to and remove shapes from an existing group with the **Shape | Grouping | Add to Group** and **Remove from Group** commands.

The **Ungroup** command disbands the group into individual shapes.

**Caution:**

When you use the Ungroup command on a shape dragged from a stencil, Visio severs the link between the shape and its originating master. If the group is locked, then you cannot ungroup it.

The **Convert to Group** command is of interest when you work with objects that have been inserted from other applications using the **Edit | Paste Special** command or **Insert | Object** command. If the inserted object is in WMF or EMF formats (a vector-like format), Visio converts the object into a group. (If the inserted object contains bitmaps, they are not converted.) You can then use the Ungroup command to edit the individual lines and text within the group.

New to Visio 2000 is the ability to specify the display order of the geometry making up the group. Visio refers to *group data* as the text and geometry you've created with drawing tools.

➤ **Hide** hides the group data; the group's connection points and control handles are still visible.

➤ **Behind member shapes** displays the group data behind shapes.

➤ **In front of member shapes** displays the group data in front of shapes.

The **Group** command is useful for rounding up shapes and corralling them. On their own, however, groups cannot be used to share your customized shapes with other drawings and other users. For that, you need to turn to masters.

# Making a Master Out of a Shape

We saw how the Group command lets you work with two or more shapes as if they were a single shape. To use your customized shape with other drawings, you need to turn the group into a *master*. The term "master" sounds to me as if the shape needs to travel through seven levels of colored belts to achieve "master status." Fortunately, the process is trivial—almost too simple for such an exalted designation.

1. Select **File | Stencils | New Stencil** to create a new stencil file. Notice that Visio opens a stencil that is green and blank.

2. Hold down the **Ctrl** key, and drag the shape into the stencil file. (If you don't hold down the **Ctrl** key, the shape is *moved* from the page to the stencil, instead of being *copied*.) Visio creates a small icon of the shape and gives it the generic name **Master.0**.

> **Tip:**
> Click the stencil icon on the stencil's title bar, and then choose **Save** to save the stencil, or click the diskette icon on the stencil's title bar to save the stencil file to disk.

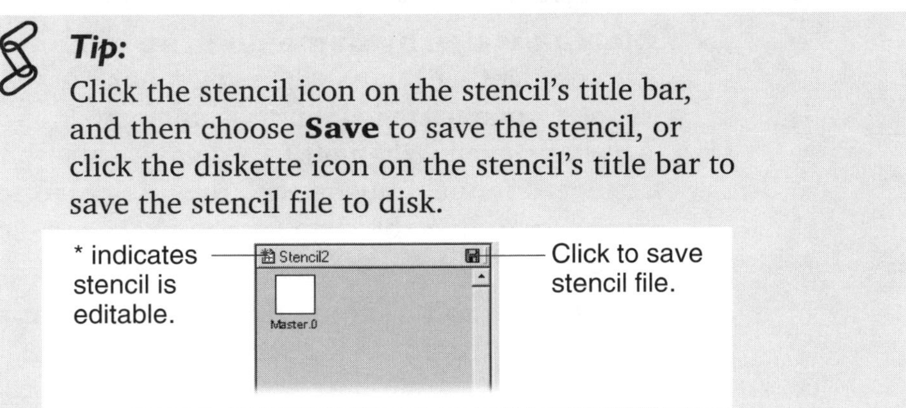


3. To change the name of the master, right-click the **Master.0** icon and select **Master Properties** from the shortcut menu. Notice that the Master Properties dialog box lets you specify the look of the icon:

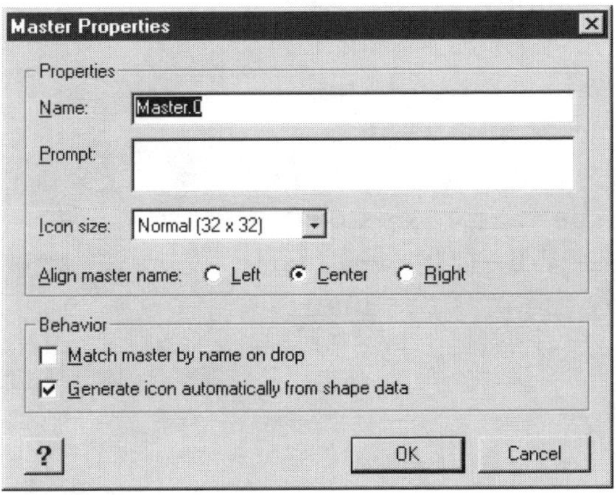

➤ **Name** changes the name you see below the master's icon.

➤ **Prompt** displays a helpful ScreenTip and status bar text when you pause the cursor over the icon.

➤ **Icon size** resizes the icon: normal (default), tall, wide, and double in both width and height.

➤ **Align master name** changes the alignment of the master's name below its icon: left, center (default), or right.

➤ **Match master by name on drop** controls the conflict that occurs when you modify a shape from one stencil, but it is unmodified in another stencil. When off (the default), the shape is instanced in the drawing with the original formatting. When on, Visio formats the shape according to the changes you have made.

➤ **Generate icon automatically from shape data** creates an icon based on the shape geometry, when on (the default).

4. Type a descriptive name in the **Name** field, such as "Knob - Round, Aluminum" to replace the generic Master.*n* name.

5. (*Optional*) Type a descriptive sentence in the **Prompt** field, such as "Standard aluminum round knob with label." The prompt is displayed on the status line and in the tooltip, when the cursor is paused over the master. When this field is left blank, only the master's name is displayed.

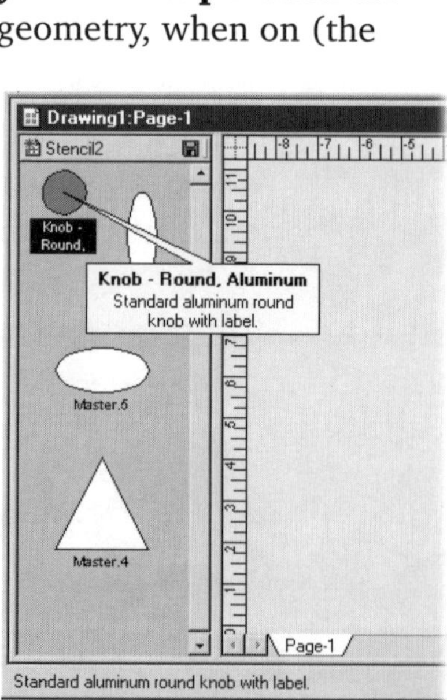

6. Click **OK**. Notice that the name under the icon changes. When you pass the cursor over the icon, notice the help line in the tooltip and on the status bar.

7. Click the stencil icon on the stencil's title bar, and then choose **Save** to save the stencil.

# Alternatives to Master Creation

There are several ways to create a master in Visio:

➤ Drag a shape into the stencil file, as described above

➤ Copy and edit an existing master

➤ Develop a new master from scratch

➤ Create a shortcut master (new to Visio 2000)

I'll briefly describe the remaining three methods.

## *Edit an Existing Master*

An alternative method to creating a new master is to make a copy of an existing master, then edit the copy. Follow these steps:

1. Drag a few shapes onto the drawing page.

2. Select **Window | Show Document Stencil**. Notice that Visio opens a stencil called **Document Stencil**. This holds all the masters used in the current drawing.

3. Right-click the master you wish to edit and select **Duplicate** from the shortcut menu. Notice that Visio creates a copy of the master, with a dot-number suffix (such as Feature on/off.9) to differentiate it from the original master.

**Tip:**
You can quickly copy a shape onto a stencil by dragging the shape while you hold down the **Ctrl** key.

4. Right-click the copied master, and select **Master Properties**. Fill out the Master Properties dialog box and click **OK**.

5. Right-click the copied master, and select **Edit Master**. Notice that Visio opens the master in a new window.

6. You may now edit the copied master using all the shape editing tools normally available.

7. Click the **Close** button in the upper right-hand corner of the window. If Visio displays a dialog box asking if you want to update the master, click **Yes**.

8. Be sure to save the stencil file.

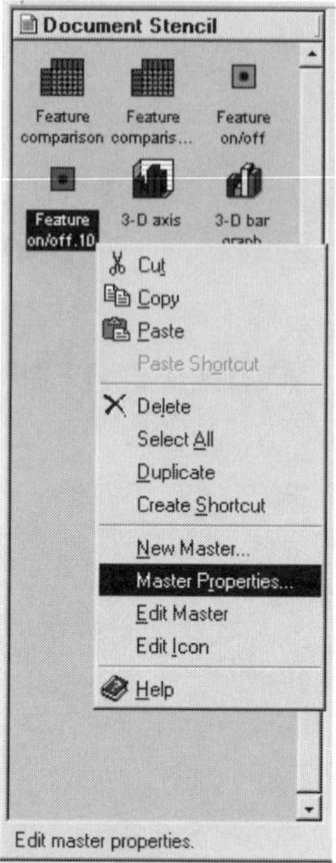

**Caution:**

If you do not make a copy of the master, you are editing the original. Editing the original may have unintended consequences: Visio will update all instanced shapes of that master, changing the look of your drawing. Note that this is a valid technique for updating shapes in a drawing, but must be exercised with care.

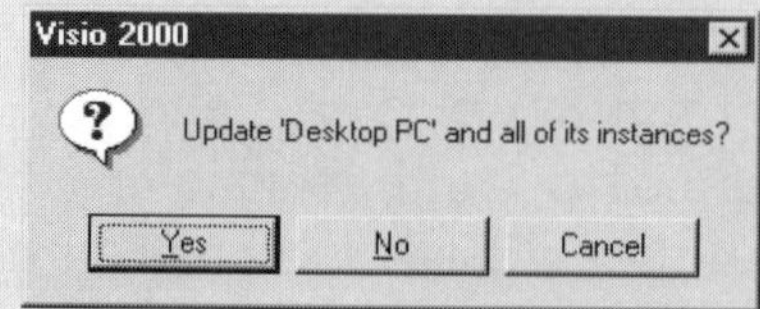


## Develop a New Master From Scratch

The third method for creating a master is to start from scratch:

1. Create a new stencil. From the menu bar, select **File | Stencils | New Stencil**.

2. Right-click the green area in the stencil window, and from the shortcut menu select **New Master**.

3. Fill out the **New Master** dialog box, and click **OK**.

4. Double-click the new master on the stencil to open a window in which you draw the master. Use the drawing tools, such as Line and Rectangle, to draw the master.

5. When finished, click the **Close** button in the upper-right corner of the master window. When Visio asks, "Update *mastername*?", choose **Yes**. Notice that the master's icon automatically updates to reflect your drawing activity.

## Create a Shortcut to a Master

Another method is to create a *shortcut* to a master. You are probably familiar with shortcuts from the Windows desktop: the shortcut is an icon that is linked to (or points to) the actual file. You can differentiate a shortcut by the addition of the small boxed arrow icon, as well as the default wording "Shortcut to."

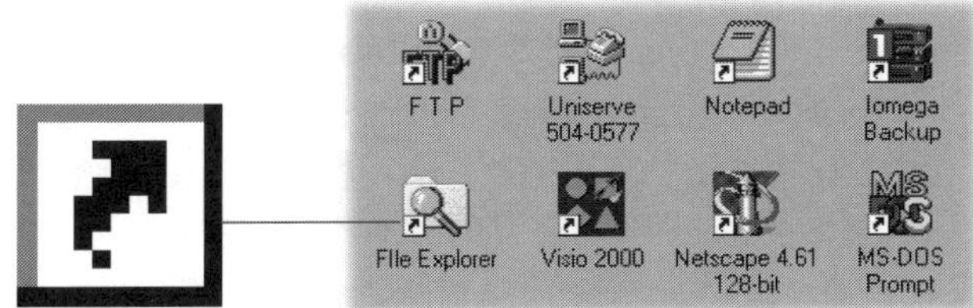


Visio 2000 introduced the concept of creating shortcuts to masters. Shortcuts have several advantages:

➤ Shortcuts save file space, since the entire master is not saved; instead, a pointer to the master is saved.

➤ Shortcuts save time maintaining masters; update the master, and the shortcuts are also updated.

➤ Shortcuts allow instances to behave and appear different from the master.

**Caution:**

> Before you can create a shortcut to a master, the stencil must have been saved. You cannot create shortcuts in a brand-new, never-saved stencil. (The method for creating master shortcuts described in Visio's user documentation works only when you are working with two stencils opened as read-only. You need to change both to editable stencils; then you can **Ctrl+Shift**+drag to create the shortcut.)

To create a shortcut of a master, right-click a master, and select **Create Shortcut** from the menu. Notice that Visio creates an identical icon with the shortcut arrow, and the name "Shortcut to *n*", where *n* is the name of the master. The shortcut can be moved and copied into other documents.

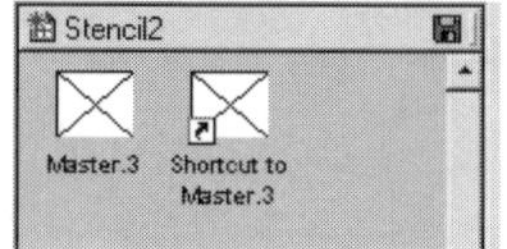

To modify the properties of the shortcut, right-click the shortcut and select **Master Shortcut Properties**. The dialog box is similar to the Master Properties dialog box, except for the addition of two sections:

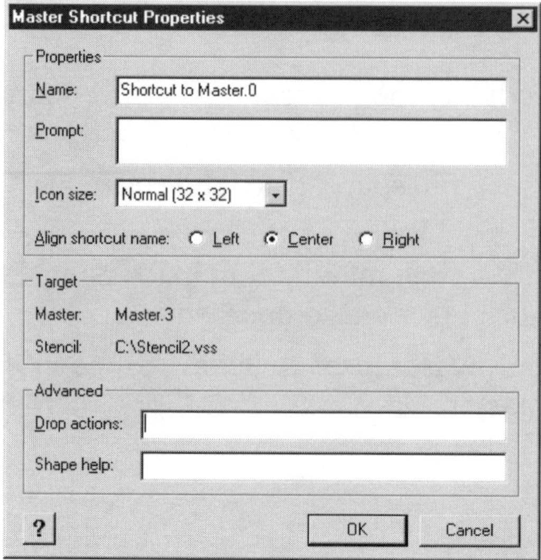

**Drop actions** specifies the drop action to apply when the master shortcut is droped on the page. A *drop action* defines a value or formula to be assigned to a ShapeSheet cell in the new shape. Drop actions are defined by the shortcut, not the master. Thus, you can have several shortcuts, each of which produces a different effects when dropped on the page. The Drop actions field can be blank, can define a single action, or can define a series of actions, each separated by a semicolon.

The action consists of the name of a cell, an equals sign, and the formula to apply to the cell. An example given by the Visio documentation is:

User.SubType=3;FillForegnd=7;Sheet2!Width=(ThePage!PageWidth / 2 - 4cm)

**Shape help** contains text to call a help file; leave the field blank to use the master's help text. Here is the syntax for calling up help from a file: *filename*.chm!*keyword* or *filename*.chm!*#number* where *filename* is the name of the compiled HTML help file, *keyword* is the index term, and *number* is the numeric ID for the help section.

# Editing the Master Icon

You may have noticed that some of the masters provided with Visio have icons that are much more colorful than the shape itself. I find that irritating; I want to know ahead of time what the shape will look like, and not be surprised upon instancing.

On the other hand, the automatically generated icon can be difficult to understand. You may want to change the look of the icon to make it more legible. Here's how:

Right-click the master and select **Edit Icon** from the shortcut menu. Notice that Visio opens a window with an enlarged view of the icon. Notice also that the toolbar changes to show color options and editing tools.

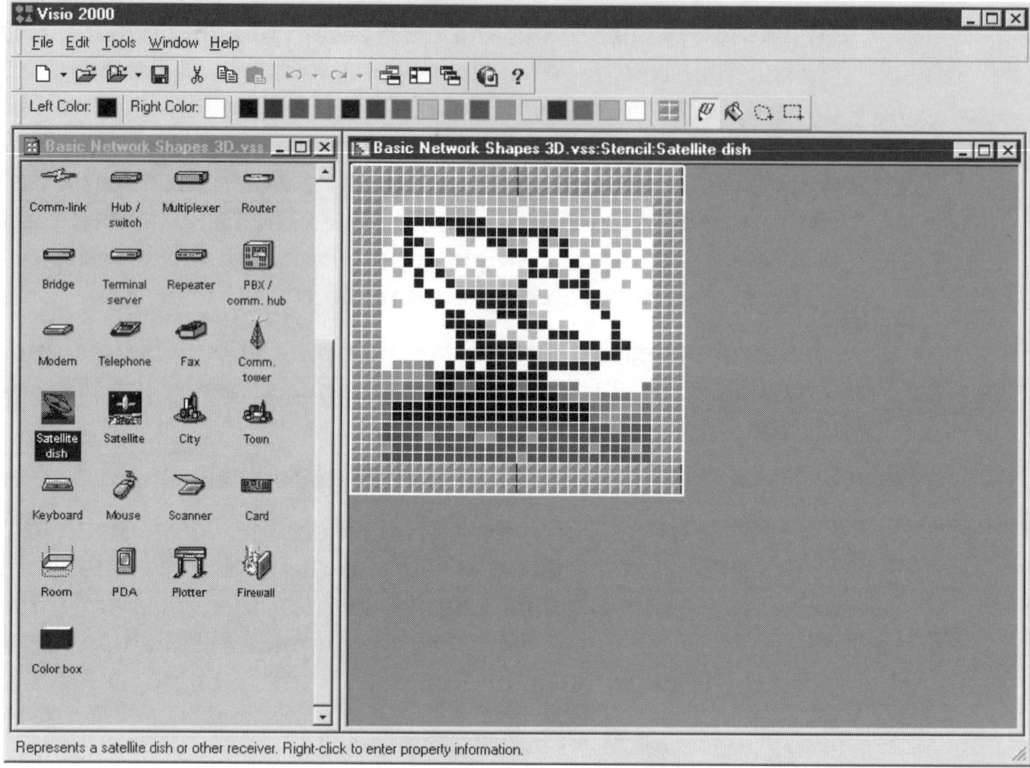

The first two color buttons, labeled **Left Color** and **Right Color**, are the colors that will be applied when you click the left and right mouse buttons, respectively. You select one of the 16 colors by clicking the left or right mouse button over the color sample. The last color, which looks like a green pattern, is a transparent color. It lets the color of the underlying stencil window show through. The remaining buttons are the editing tools:

➤ **Pencil Tool** colors a single pixel at a time.

➤ **Bucket Tool** colors all touching pixels of the same color.

➤ **Lasso Tool** selects an irregular area, which can be dragged to a new location.

➤ **Selection Net Tool** selects a rectangular area, which can be dragged to a new location.

In addition to the toolbar, you can use the commands in the **Edit** menu: **Undo**, **Cut**, **Copy**, **Paste**, **Clear**, and **Select All**.

As you edit the icon, the changes are immediately reflected in the **Stencil** window. There is no need to save the changes. Click the **Close** button in the upper right-hand corner of the editing window to close it.

# Customizing Shape Formats

To change the look of a shape, you can makes its lines thicker, add a colored fill, a drop shadow, and so on. In other software programs, these are called *properties*. If you created a new property (such as a new fill pattern), it would be called a *custom property*. The problem is, Visio uses the term "custom property" for something entirely different, as you learn in Section II of this book. As much as I would have liked to, I can't call this part of the chapter "Customizing Properties." Hence, I came up with "Customizing Shape Formats," which sounds awkward but is accurate.

In all, Visio provides ten formats, some of which can be customized by you. The ones that can be fully customized are:

➤ Line pattern (a.k.a. *linetype* or *line style* in other software)

➤ Line end (a.k.a. *arrowhead*)

➤ Fill pattern (a.k.a. *patterning* or *hatching*)

➤ Text style

For the remainder of this chapter, you learn how to customize the four formats. The other six formats cannot be customized or have a very low customization possibility. These are color, weight, round corners, line cap, drop shadow, and layer. In brief:

**Color**   Visio comes with twenty-four predefined colors and shades of gray, numbered 0 to 23. To customize a color, scroll down the list of colors to the very end and select **Custom**. You specify the hue-saturation-luminosity or the red-green-blue components from the Windows Edit Color dialog box.

> **Tip:**
>
> When it seems that the only custom color you can select is black, move the luminosity slider up (the narrow, colorful slider in the Edit Color dialog box). The custom color you select appears as an unnumbered color sample at the end of the Color list box of appropriate dialog boxes.

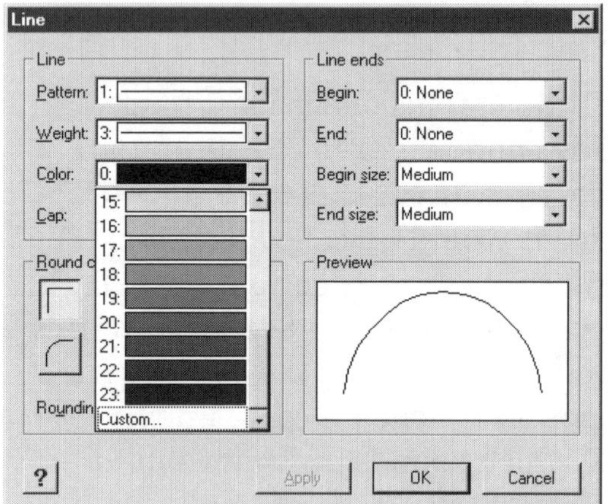

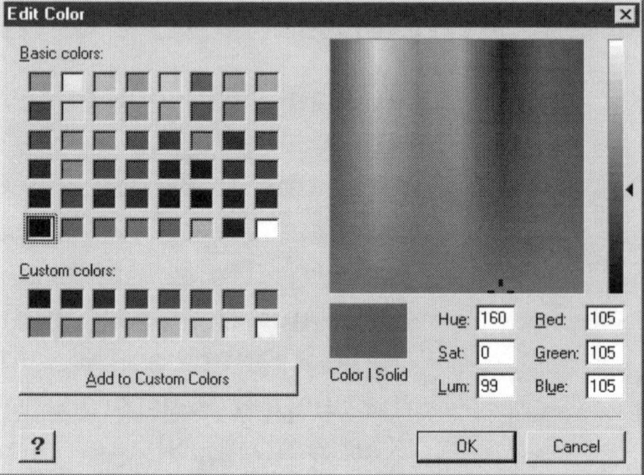

**Weight**   Visio comes with six weights numbered 1, 3, 5, 9, 13, and 17. (In some other software programs, weight is call *linewidth*.) The numbers refer to the width of the weight measured in hundreds of inches. For example, weight 1 creates a weight 0.01" wide, while weight 17 creates the weight 0.17" wide.

To customize a line weight, scroll down the list of weights to the very end and select **Custom**. You specify the width of the line in the Custom Line Weight dialog box. For units, you can use **in** for inches, **mm** for millimeters, **pt** for points, etc. (The complete list of units is provided in Chapter 8, "The Complete ShapeSheet Section Reference" in this book.)

**Tip:**

The custom weight you specify does not appear in the Weight list box for future use, except when you have selected an object with that custom weight.

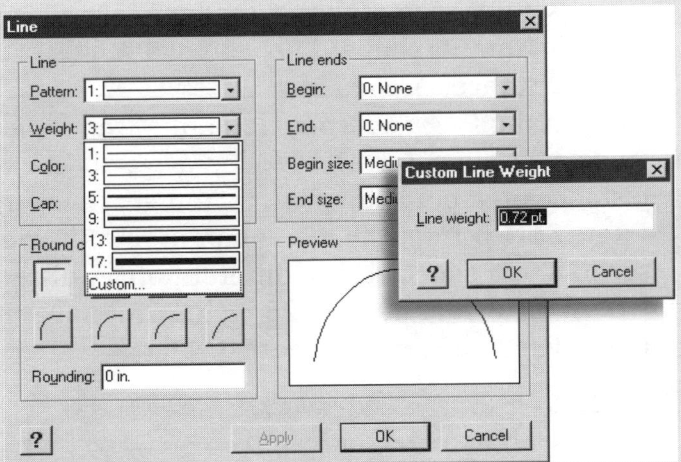

**Round Corners**   Visio can round the corner between two connecting lines. Not surprisingly, Visio calls this a "round corner"; CAD software calls it a *fillet*. Visio predefines round corners ranging from 0 inches (no rounding) to 0.4375 inches. You specify your own rounding value by selecting **Format | Corner** and entering a value in the **Rounding** field of the Corners dialog box.

**Cap**   You cannot create custom caps. Visio gives you two choices: round (the default) and square (which I think should be the default).

**Drop Shadow**   Visio creates the drop shadow effect by copying the shape by an offset distance, then making all elements of the copied shape gray (or whatever color you select). The drop shadow has five parameters that you can change. Three of the parameters—pattern, foreground color, and background color—are specified by the Shadow dialog box (select **Format |**

**Shadow** from the menu bar). Fortunately, those lovely gradient fills are available for drop shadows.

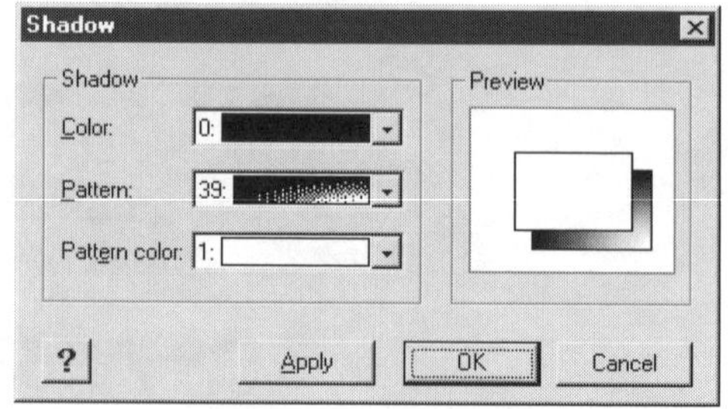

The other parameters specify the offset distance of the shadow from its shape. The offset distances are hidden away in the **Page Properties** tab of the Page Setup dialog box (the offset distances are "hidden away" because you can't set the distance on a per-shape basis). You get there by selecting **File | Page Setup** from the menu bar. In the **Shape Shadow Offset** section, you can specify a different offset distance for **Right** and **Down**. The default is 0.125 inches. To make the shadow offset to the left or up, enter negative values.

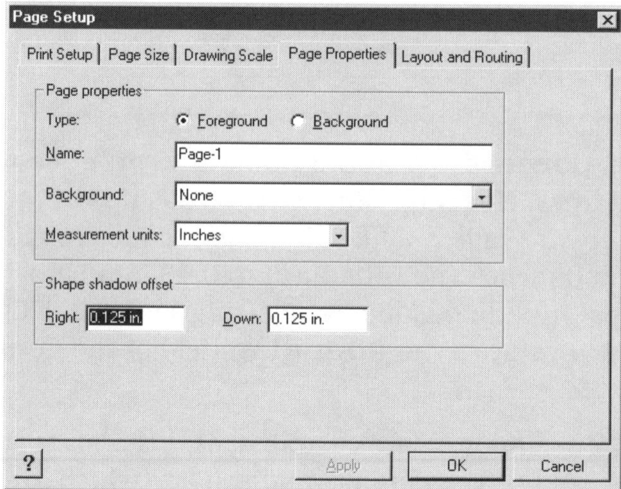

*Tip:*

The one **Shape Shadow Offset** setting affects all shapes on the page; you cannot have a different offset distance for different shapes on the same page. The workaround is to use one or more background pages, each with a different shadow offset.

**Layer**   Visio uses *layers* to organize shapes into categories. This is different from the concept of layers (a.k.a. *levels*) in other software, which uses layers to *segregate* objects from one another. Visio allows you to assign a shape to more than one layer. By assigning shapes to one or more layers, you can selectively view, print, and lock layers, as well as control whether shapes on a layer can be snapped to or glued to.

By default, all shapes are drawn on no layer (in earlier versions of Visio, layer 0 was the default). Some masters have predefined layers. To place a shape on a layer takes two steps: (1) create the layer; and (2) assign the shape to the layer.

To create layers in a drawing, select **View | Layer Properties** from the menu bar. The Layer Properties dialog box is usually empty in a new drawing. Click **New** to create a new layer (giving a name to the layer creates it), and then name it in the New Layer dialog box. The name can be up to 31 characters long. Each layer has eight properties:

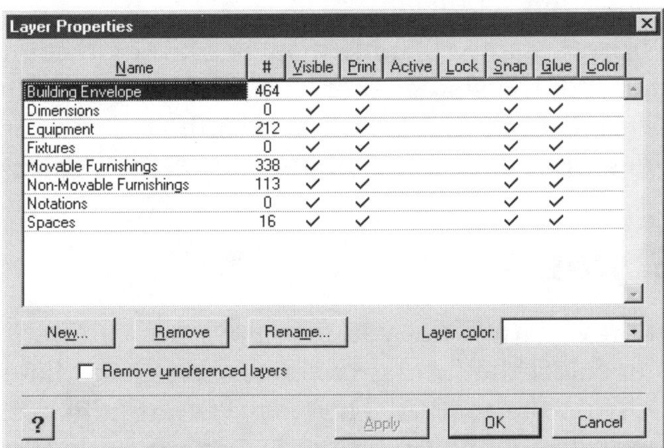

➤   **#**   Number of shapes assigned to the layer. Click **#** to show the number of shapes. This column is usually empty until you click the **#** header; Visio then counts the shapes.

➤   **Visible**   Shapes on a layer are usually visible. Uncheck to hide the layer. When unchecked, the shapes are hidden and are not displayed.

➤ **Print**   Shapes on a layer are usually printed. When unchecked, the shapes are displayed but are not printed.

➤ **Active**   Shapes are normally assigned to layer 0 or their own preassigned layer. When checked, shapes are assigned to the active layer. Visio can have more than one active layer, meaning that newly added shapes are assigned to all active layers.

➤ **Lock**   Shapes can usually be selected. When checked, shapes cannot be selected, and other layer properties cannot be changed.

➤ **Snap**   Shapes usually snap to other shapes. When unchecked, other shapes cannot be snapped to shapes on this layer; shapes on this layer, however, can still snap to other shapes not on this layer.

➤ **Glue**   Shapes usually glue to other shapes. When unchecked, other shapes cannot be glued to shapes on this layer; shapes on this layer, however, can still glue to other shapes not on this layer.

➤ **Color**   Shapes usually display their own colors. When checked, the shape colors are overridden by this color, selected from the Layer color list box. The property overrides—but does not change—the shape's colors.

# Masters vs. Styles

As you draw with Visio, you may have noticed that there are two places to select the format of shapes: one is in dialog boxes, the other is from the toolbar. The two are mutually exclusive—much to my surprise, when I first learned about formatting shapes. Here's where the split occurs:

➤ Dialog boxes display customized formats created via masters: **Line Pattern**, **Line End**, and **Fill Pattern**. (I'm leaving out text, because you cannot create a font from scratch with Visio.)

➤ Toolbars display customized formats created via styles: **Text**, **Line**, and **Fill**. Note that a line style includes line patterns and line ends. (By default, Visio does not display all of its toolbars. To do so, right-click any toolbar and select a toolbar name from the shortcut menu.)

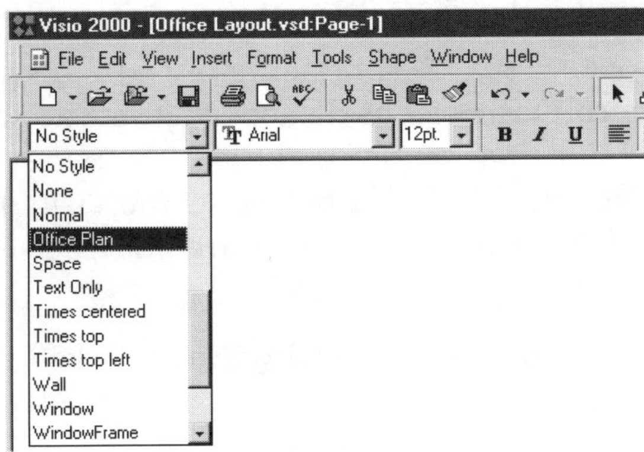

The distinction between masters and styles became clear to me once I understood the difference: masters create formats from scratch; styles create formats from existing elements.

It takes two steps for a custom line pattern to appear in the **Line** list box of the toolbar: (1) create a master from scratch; and (2) create the style from the master. The converse is not possible—a style cannot appear in a formatting dialog box, other than in the dialog box displayed by the **Format | Style** command.

In summary, then, masters are used to create line patterns, line ends, and fill patterns. Styles are made from those formats, plus the default formats that already exist in Visio. Text styles are based only on existing formats. The table shows the relationship:

| Master | Style |
|---|---|
| Line Pattern - - - - - - -> | Line |
| Line End - - - - - - - - -> | Line |
| Fill Pattern  - - - - - -> | Fill |
| ... | Text |

# The Master Gotcha

When I created my first line pattern via a master, I hit a road-block. I'd save the stencil file; the next time I brought the stencil file back into Visio, the line pattern master was gone! This exercise in futility repeated itself, until I learned the reason.

When I open a stencil containing line and fill patterns, the custom pattern master icons disappear from the stencil file (unless I open the stencil as an original file). The patterns appear instead in the Line and Fill dialog boxes. As the Visio documentation states, "This is because patterns are not true shapes, but attributes that you apply to shapes."

With that important peculiarity firmly tucked into the recesses of your mind, let's now create some custom patterns.

# Designing a Custom Line Pattern

A line pattern affects the look of the lines making up a shape. In traditional drafting, the line pattern consists of a repeating pattern of dashes, gaps, and dots. For example, drafters use — — — (the dash-gap pattern) to indicate a hidden line. The —— — —— — pattern (long dash, gap, short dash) pattern is used to indicate a center line. Line patterns are known as *linetypes* and *line styles* in other drawing programs.

Visio comes with 24 line patterns numbered 0 through 23. Pattern #0 is no line at all (invisible), while pattern #1 is the solid or continuous line (the default).

It takes two steps to create a custom line pattern—this procedure is drastically changed from earlier versions of Visio: (1) specify the pattern parameters; then (2) draw the pattern.

**Notes:**

While you can include text in the pattern, such as ———— GAS ———— GAS ————, Visio does not display it later when you apply the pattern. The restriction may be lifted in a future version of Visio.

Custom line patterns cannot use a gradient fill (it will display as solid fill), a bitmap, or a metafile (a.ka. a picture pasted from the Clipboard).

A line pattern is limited to displaying 1,000 pattern instances along the line.

When designing the custom line pattern, use a weight of 0. This allows the pattern to inherit the shape's weight.

To create a custom line pattern, follow the steps in this tutorial, which creates a parallel-line pattern.

1. Select **View | Windows | Drawing Explorer** from the menu bar. Notice that Visio opens the Drawing Explorer window.

2. Right-click **Line Patterns** and select **New Pattern**. Notice the New Pattern dialog box.

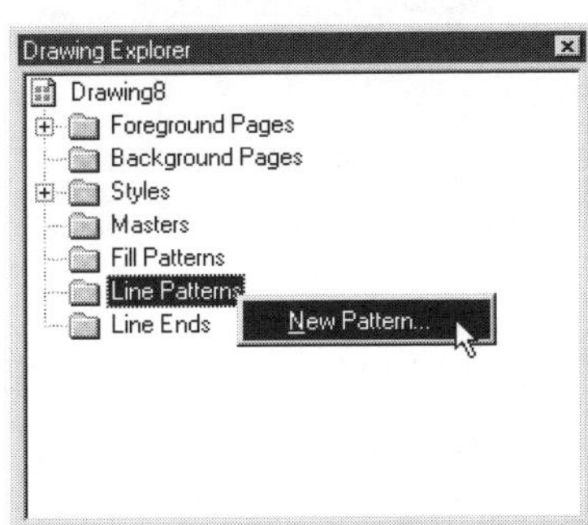
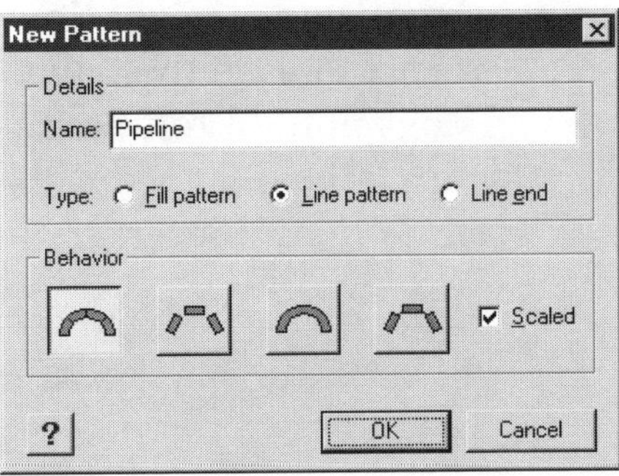

3. Enter the following data in the New Pattern dialog box:

   ➤ **Name**:          Pipeline

   ➤ **Type**:          Line pattern

➤ **Behavior**:  First icon

➤ **Scaled**:  On/checked. Checking the **Scaled** option means the pattern grows when you resize the shape.

The **Behavior** section specifies how the line pattern behaves when applied to lines that are not straight. From left to right, the four icons represent the following behavior:

➤ Apply the pattern along the curve; the original line is not visible.

➤ Approximate the pattern with straight segments along the curve; the original line is not visible.

➤ Stretch out the pattern along the entire length of the curve; the original line is not visible.

➤ Approximate the pattern with straight segments along the curve; unlike the second option, the original line is visible.

4. Click **OK**. Open the **Line Patterns** folder. Notice the Pipeline pattern.

5. Right-click **Pipeline**, and select **Edit Pattern** from the shortcut menu. Notice that a new window appears, with a page and a green pasteboard.

6. Draw two straight lines with the **Line** tool on the page. The length does not matter; an inch or so long is fine. The distance between the two lines does matter: try an 1/8-inch or so.

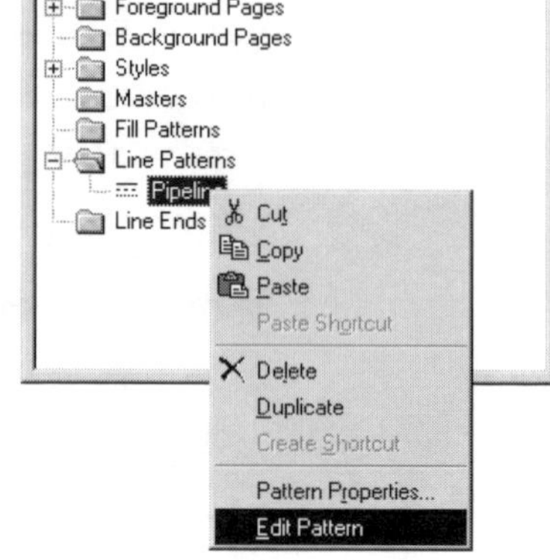


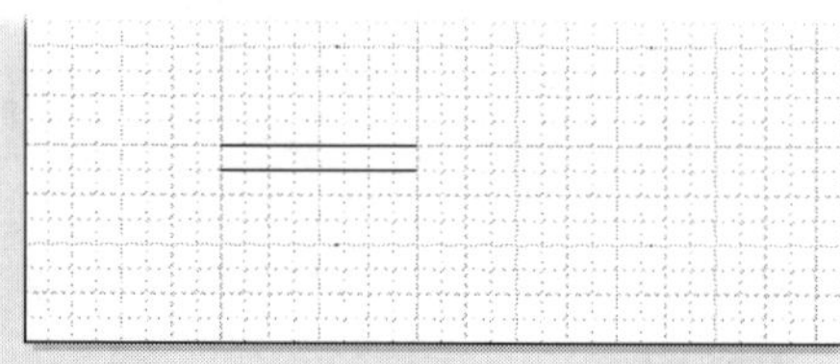

7. Click the **x** on the stencil design window's title bar. When Visio asks, "Update 'Pipeline' and all shapes that may be using it as a pattern?" choose **Yes**.

# Applying a Custom Line Pattern

You can now begin using the parallel line pattern. To see it at work:

1. Draw a curvy path with the Freeform tool.

2. Select **Format | Line**.

3. In the **Line** section of the Line dialog box, click the **Pattern** list box. Scroll right down to the end, and select **Pipeline**.

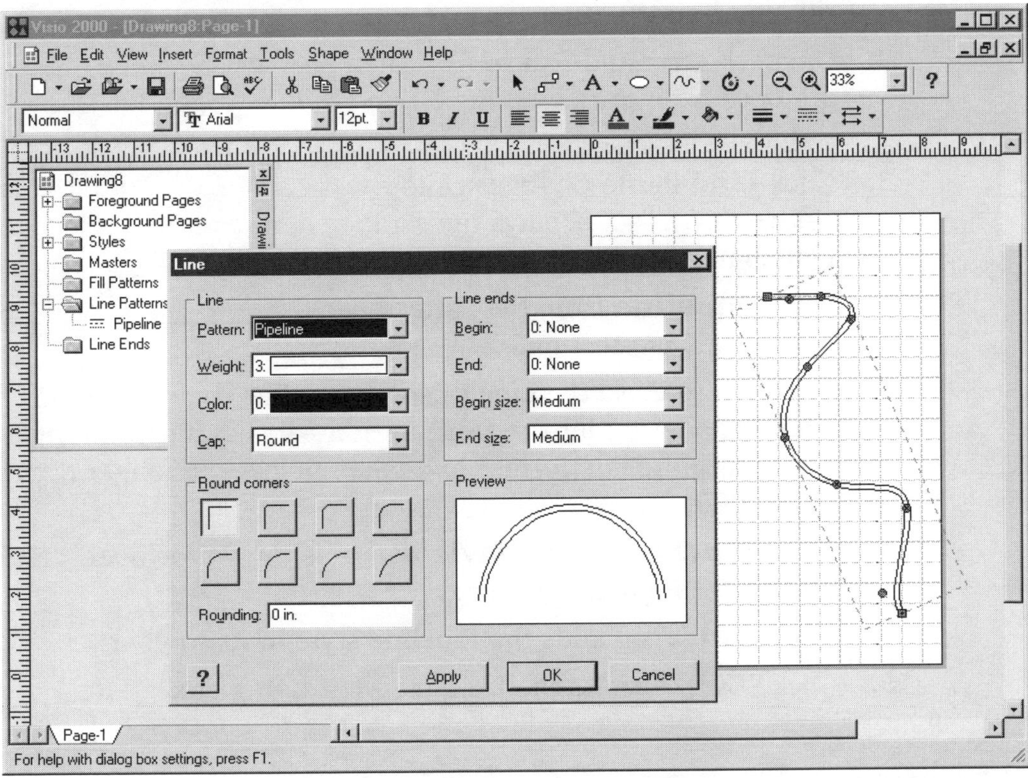

4. Click **Apply**. Notice that the ellipse changes from a single line to a double line.

5.  Click **Cancel**. The dialog box goes away and the ellipse returns to its former single-line self. We'll bring back the double-line version in the next section.

# Defining a Custom Line Style

The parallel line pattern exists only in the Line format dialog box. It would be nice to select it directly from the toolbar. To do this, you must create a style. Before starting, ensure no objects are selected.

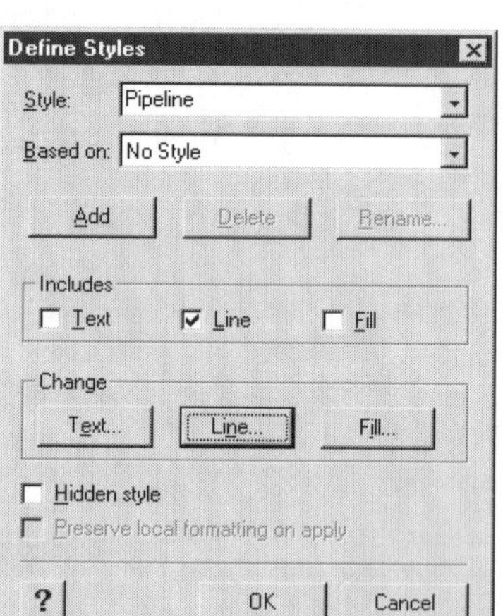

1.  From the menu bar, select **Format | Define Styles**. Notice the Define Styles dialog box lets us define text, fill, and line styles.

2.  Uncheck **Text** and **Fill** to turn them off, because we are creating a line style.

3.  Click **Line** in the Change section. Notice that Visio displays the same Line dialog box as we visited earlier.

4.  Select **Pipeline** from the Pattern list box in the Line section.

5.  Click **OK** to close the Line dialog box. (The thick green line that would appear under the **Line** button—to remind you that changes to the line format had taken place—no longer occurs in Visio 2000).

6.  Enter **Pipeline** for the **Style** name—simply type over **<New style>** in the text entry box.

7.  Click **Add**. Visio adds the Pipeline style to its toolbar.

8.  Click **OK** to dismiss the Define Styles dialog box.

# Applying a Custom Line Style

You've created a line style. Let's test it!

1. Right-click any toolbar, and select **Format Shape** from the shortcut menu. Notice the Format Shapes toolbar.

2. Select the spline shape on the drawing page.

3. Click the **Line Style** list box found at the left end of the Format Shape toolbar.

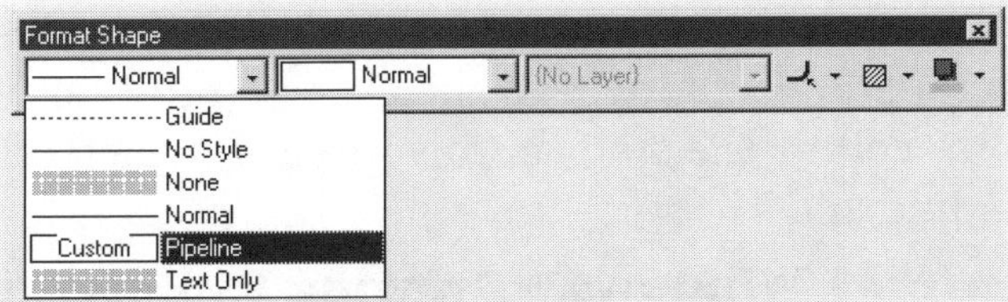


4. Select **Pipeline**. Notice that Visio does not display a sample of the line style, but prints the word **Custom**. The spline changes from a single line to a double line.

There you have it. You created a custom line pattern, which appears in format dialog boxes. You then created a style from the master, which appears in the toolbar list box. A similar process works for creating custom line ends and fill patterns, as we see in the following sections.

Make sure to choose the Basic line style again. When you try to complete the upcoming exercises that call for a line, you need to use the Basic line style, not the Pipeline style.

# Designing a Custom Line End

Line ends are used for callouts, leaders, and dimensions. The line end is known as an *arrowhead* in computer-aided design software.

Visio comes with forty-six line patterns numbered 0 through 45. Pattern #0 is no line end at all, the default. The other line ends are arrows, dots, diamonds, lines, and combinations.

The line end affects the look of the end of an *open* object, such as a line, arc, or spline. Visio does not apply line ends to closed shapes, such as the four lines that make up a rectangle.

To create a custom line end: (1) specify the line end parameters; then (2) draw the line end—this procedure is drastically different from earlier versions of Visio. Visio comes with so many different line ends, it's hard to think of one it doesn't have yet. After some head scratching, I thought of the architectural tick, a thick diagonal slash. Follow the steps in this tutorial, which creates the custom line end:

1. Select **View | Windows | Drawing Explorer** from the menu bar. Notice that Visio opens the Drawing Explorer window.

2. Right-click **Line Ends** and select **New Pattern**. Notice the New Pattern dialog box.

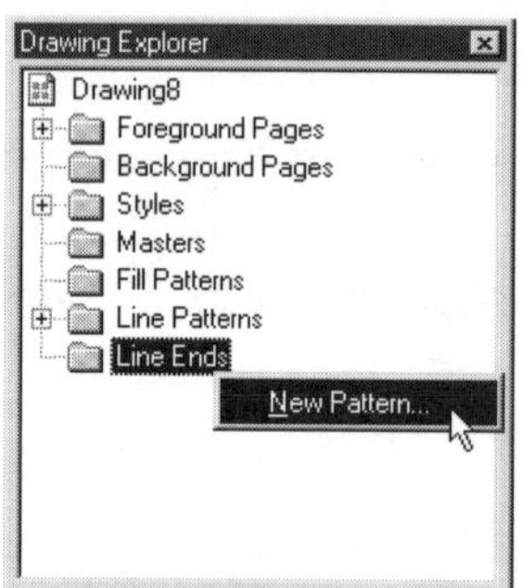
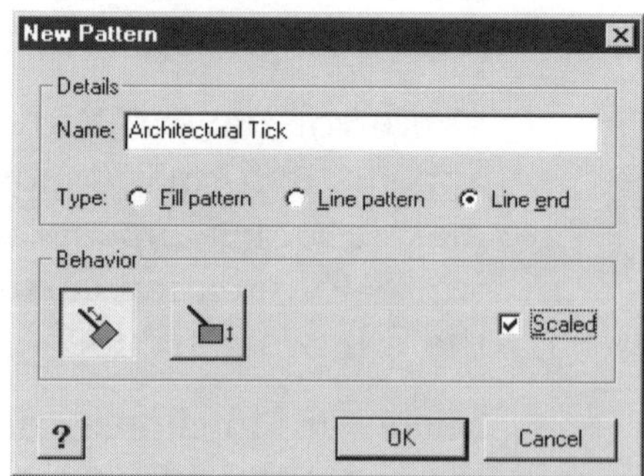

3. Enter the following data in the New Pattern dialog box:

   ➤ **Name**:       Architectural Tick

   ➤ **Type**:       Line end

   ➤ **Behavior**:   First icon

   ➤ **Scaled**:     On/checked. Checking the **Scaled** option means the pattern grows when you resize the shape.

The **Behavior** section specifies how the line ends behave when applied to lines that are at an angle. From left to right, the two icons represent the following behaviors:

➤ Apply the line end at the same angle as the line

➤ Keep the line end horizontal

4. Click **OK**. Open the **Line Ends** folder. Notice that **Architectural Tick** appears in the Drawing Explorer window, under **Line Ends**.

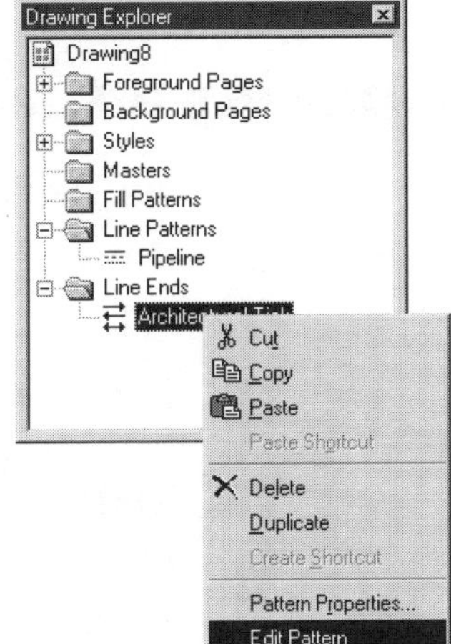

5. Right-click **Architectural Tick**, and select **Edit Pattern** from the shortcut menu. Notice that a new window appears, with a page and a green pasteboard.

6. Draw a tick mark as follows: Use the **Line** tool to draw a 1/4-inch-long line at 45 degrees. Use the **Format | Line** command to change the width to **13**, and give the line **Square** line caps.

7. Draw a short, horizontal line from the center of the thick line to the left (see illustration). The short segment connects the tick with the end of the line. If the segment is not there, or if the segment runs to the right, there will be a gap between the tick and the end of the line.

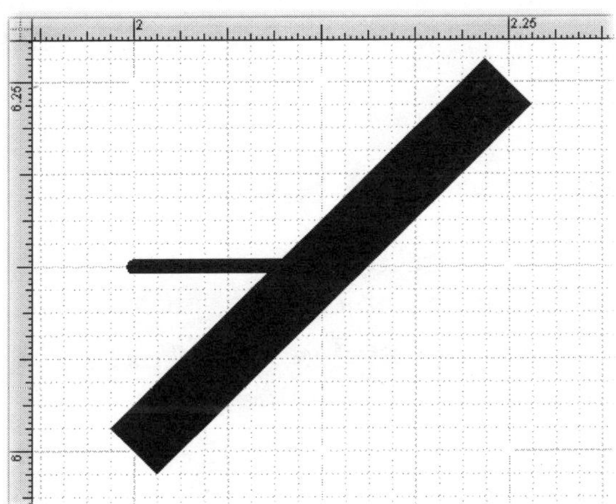

8. Click the **x** on the stencil design window's title bar. When Visio asks, "Update 'Architectural Tick' and all shapes that may be using it as a pattern?" choose **Yes**.

# Applying a Custom Line End

You can now begin using the new line end. To see it at work:

1. Draw a line, or any other open shape, at an angle.

2. Select the shape, and then select **Format | Line**.

3. In the Line Ends section of the Line dialog box, click the **Begin** list box. Scroll right down to the end and select **Architectural Tick**. Repeat for the End list box.

4. Click **Apply**. Notice that the line changes from no line end to thick tick marks.

5. Click **Cancel**. The dialog box goes away and the line returns to its former no-end self. We'll bring back the line ends in the next section.

# Defining a Custom Line End Style

To select the line end directly from the toolbar, create a style. Before starting, ensure no objects are selected.

1. Select **Format | Define Styles**. Click **Text** and **Fill** to turn them off since we are creating a line style.

2. Click **Line** in the Change section. Notice that Visio displays the same Line dialog box we visited earlier.

3. Select **Architectural Tick** from the Begin and End list boxes in the Line End section.

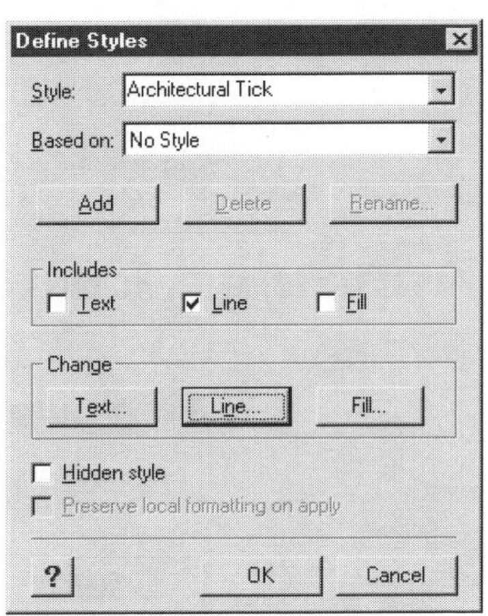



4. Click **OK** to close the Line dialog box.

5. Enter **Architectural Tick** for the Style name.

6. Click **Add**. Visio adds the Architectural Tick style to its toolbar.

7. Click **OK** to dismiss the Define Styles dialog box.

To test the new style, select the line. From the Format Shape toolbar, click the **Line Style** list box. Select **Architectural Tick**. The line's ends change to the tick marks.

# Designing a Custom Fill Pattern

Fill patterns are used to fill a closed shape. They are known as *hatch patterns*, *poching*, and *patterning* in other drawing programs.

Visio comes with forty-one fill patterns numbered 0 through 40. Pattern #0 is no fill pattern; pattern #1 is white fill, the default. Patterns 25 through 40 are gradient fills. Other than the solid color fills, you need to specify two colors for a fill pattern, called the *color* and the *pattern color* (in earlier versions of Visio, these were known as the *foreground* and *background* color, respectively).

**Note:**

Custom fill patterns cannot use a gradient fill (it will be displayed as solid fill), a bitmap, or a metafile (a.k.a. a picture pasted from the Clipboard). A fill pattern is limited to displaying a 200x200 grid (maximum of 40,000 instances).

To create a custom fill pattern: (1) specify the pattern parameters; then (2) draw the pattern—this procedure is a reversion to earlier versions of Visio. Follow the steps in this tutorial, which creates the grass fill pattern:

1. Select **View | Windows | Drawing Explorer** from the menu bar. Notice that Visio opens the Drawing Explorer window.

2. Right-click **Fill Patterns** and select **New Pattern**. Notice the New Pattern dialog box.

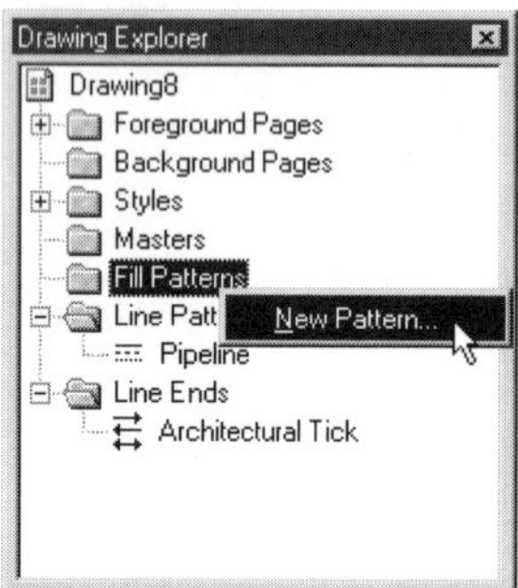
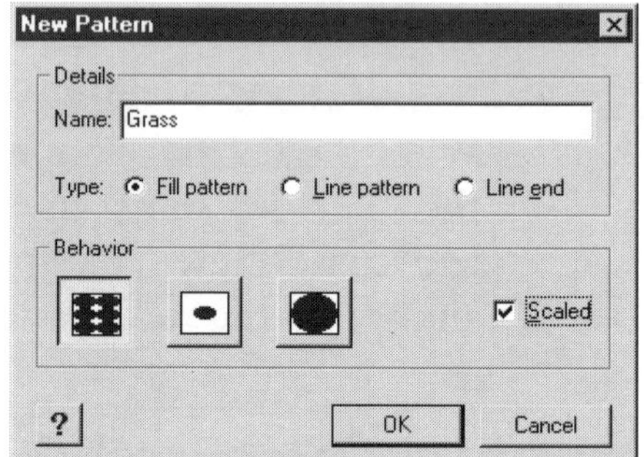

3. Enter the following data in the New Pattern dialog box:

   - **Name**:      Grass
   - **Type**:      Fill Pattern
   - **Behavior**:   First icon
   - **Scaled**:    On/checked. Checking the **Scaled** option means the pattern grows when you resize the shape.

The **Behavior** section specifies how the fill pattern behaves. From left to right, the three icons represent the following behaviors:

   - Apply the pattern at its original size, using as many copies as are needed to fill the area.

   - Apply a single pattern, making it large enough to fill the entire area.

   - Apply a single pattern at its original size.

4. Click **OK**. Notice the open Fill Patterns folder. **Grass** appears in the Drawing Explorer window, under **Fill Patterns**.

5. Right-click **Grass**, and select **Edit Pattern** from the shortcut menu. Notice that a new window appears, with a page and a green pasteboard.

6. Draw the pattern as shown in the figure: (1) draw a vertical line about 1/4-inch tall; (2) make two copies; (3) rotate the copies to 45 degrees; and (4) move the bottom ends together.

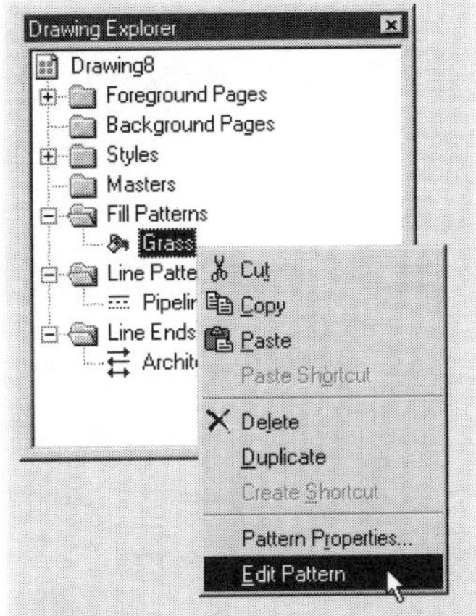

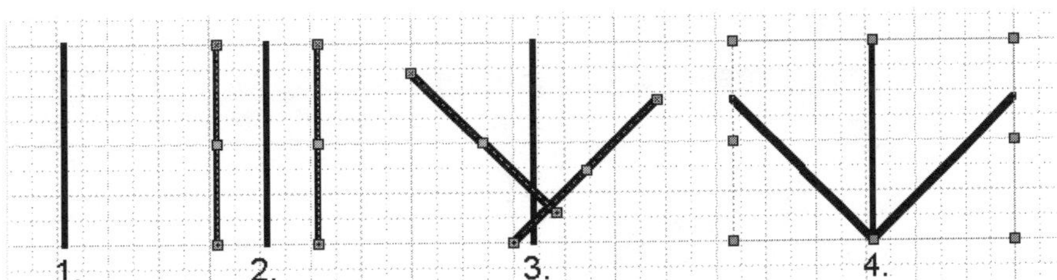

If we were to use these three lines as the fill pattern, the repeating pattern would abut each other, creating something that looks like a connected series of Ws with vertical lines running through. The grass pattern, however, is supposed to look random: a tuft of grass here, another tuft over there.

7. Draw a large rectangle. Change its format to no line and no fill; that makes the rectangle invisible, which acts as a "spacer" to keep the pattern from repeating too closely. Copy the grass pattern three lines over and down, as shown in the figure.

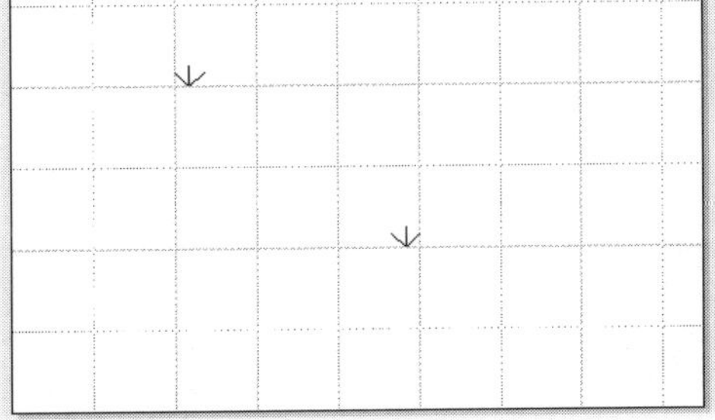

8.  Click the **x** on the stencil design window's title bar. When Visio asks, "Update 'Grass' and all shapes that may be using it as a pattern?" choose **Yes**.

# Applying a Custom Fill Pattern

You can now begin using the new fill pattern. To see it at work:

1.  Draw an ellipse, or any other closed shape that is as big as the entire page.

2.  Select **Format | Fill**.

3.  In the Fill section of the Fill dialog box, scroll down the **Pattern** list box and select **Grass**.

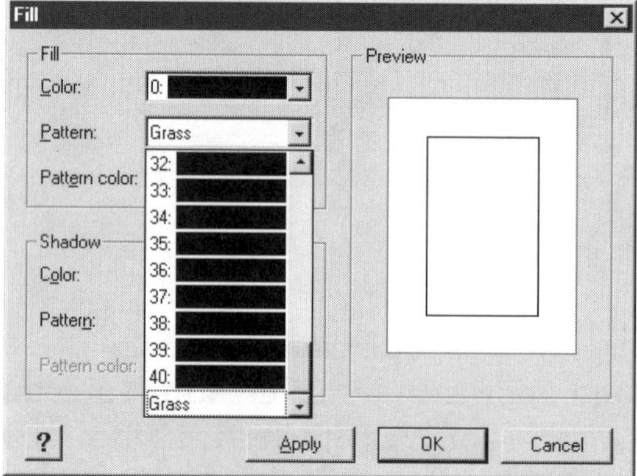

4.  Click **Apply**. Notice that the ellipse's fill changes from white to widely-separated grass tufts.

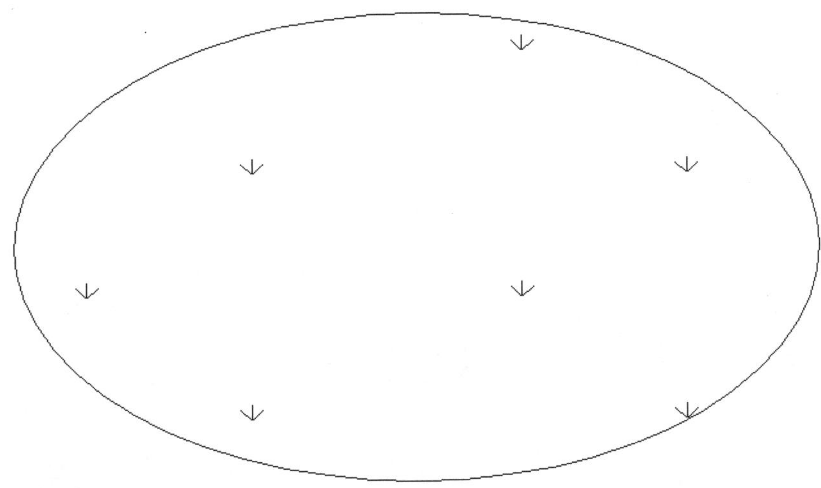

5. Click **Cancel**. The dialog box goes away and the ellipse returns to its former white-filled self. We'll bring back the grass in the next section.

# Defining a Custom Fill Style

To select the fill pattern directly from the toolbar, create a style:

1. Select **Format | Define Styles**. Click **Text** and **Line** to turn them off, because we are creating a fill pattern.

2. Click **Fill** in the Change section. Notice that Visio displays the Fill dialog box.

3. Select **Grass** from the Pattern list box in the Fill section.

4. Click **OK** to dismiss the Fill dialog box.

5. Enter **Grass** for the Style name.

6. Click **Add**. Visio adds the Grass fill style to its toolbar.

7. Click **OK** to dismiss the Define Styles dialog box.

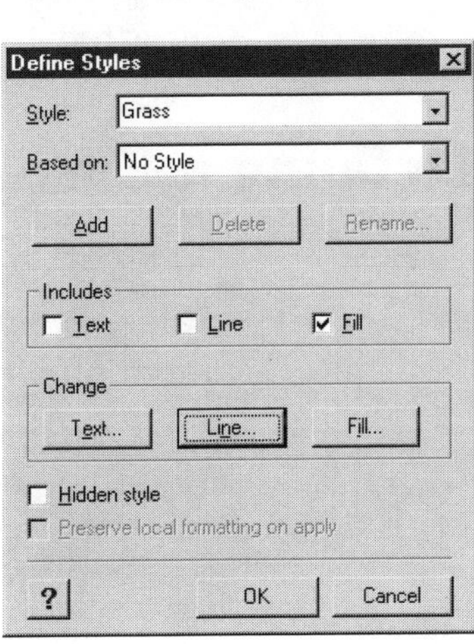

To test the new style, select the ellipse. Click the **Format Shape** toolbar's Fill Style list box. Select **Grass**. The ellipse changes to the grass fill pattern.

# Designing a Custom Text Style

A text style lets you combine all possible text formats into a single selection. And, boy, are there a lot of format options for text. To see for yourself, type some text in the drawing, and then select **Format | Text** from the menu bar.

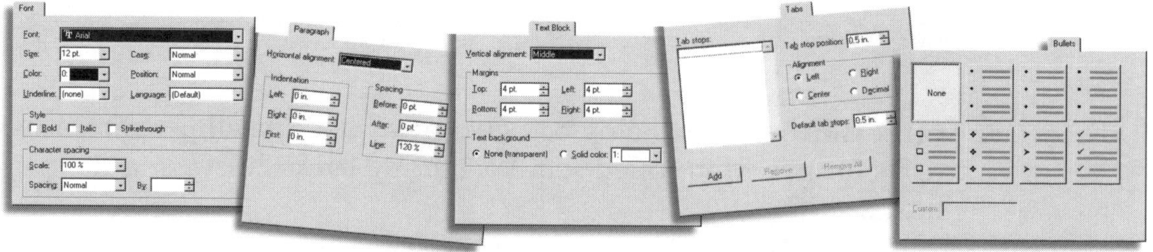

There are so many options that the Text dialog box needs five tabs: **Font**, **Paragraph**, **Text Block**, **Tabs**, and **Bullets**. I count a total of twenty-eight options. Your mileage may vary.

Text is the only one of the four formats that is not created via a master. That's because you cannot create a font in Visio. Fonts are provided by your computer system, which can number in the hundreds.

# Defining a Custom Text Style

To create a custom text style, follow these steps:

1. Select **Format | Define Styles**. Click **Fill** and **Line** to turn them off since we are creating a text style.

2. Click **Text** in the Change section. Notice that Visio displays the Text dialog box.

3. Select the parameters you wish to customize. A common example is to select a font, a size, and its justification.

4. Click **OK** to dismiss the Text dialog box.

5. Enter **Custom** for the Style name.

6. Click **Add**. Visio adds the Custom text style to its toolbar.

7. Click **OK** to dismiss the Define Styles dialog box.

To test the new style, select some text. From the Text Style list box, select **Custom**. The text changes to the new format.

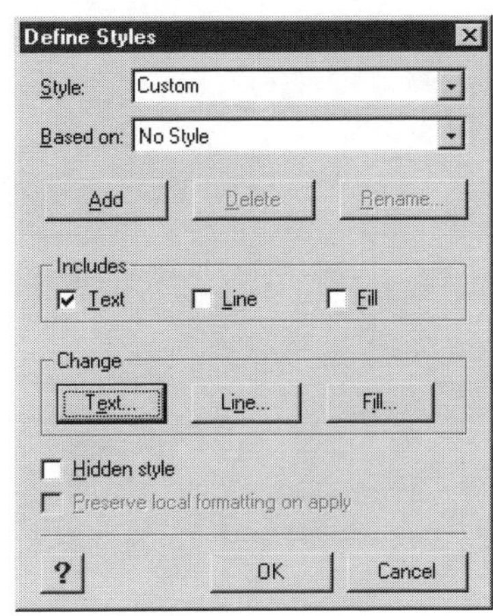



**Customizing Visio**

# Chapter Review

In this chapter, you learned how to make a master of your custom shapes by adding the master to a stencil file and editing the master icon. You also learned to customize patterns and styles that are applied to shapes.

In the next chapter, you put together what you've learned in the last two chapters and create a template file.

# Chapter 3

# *Creating Stencils and Templates*

After that hard work creating shapes, custom formats, and masters, you need a way to save them to a file on disk. That way, you can share the shapes and patterns with other users.

In this chapter, you learn about:

➤ Creating a VSS stencil file

➤ Customizing the page

➤ Creating a VST template file

➤ Creating a VSW workspace file

By the end of this chapter, you should know how to save and edit stencil files, and customize pages as templates and workspaces.

## *Visio File Types*

| Extension | Meaning |
|-----------|---------|
| VSD | Visio drawing file |
| VSS | Visio stencil file |
| VST | Visio template file |
| VSW | Visio workspace file |

# Creating a Stencil

The stencil contains masters of shapes, line patterns, line ends, and fill patterns. A master is a shape stored in the stencil. When you drag the master shape from the stencil to the page, you create an *instance* of the master.

A stencil can be made to open at the same time you open a new drawing, via opening a template VST file (more about this later in the chapter).

Until Visio 2000, the following coloring scheme was used to differentiate between shapes: a gray background meant a 2D shape, while a yellow background indicated a 1D shape (connector). The color coding disappeared with Visio 2000, which is unfortunate.

# Opening a Stencil File for Editing

Because the stencil file is so important and shouldn't be mucked about with, Visio automatically locks the stencil by making it read-only. *Read-only* means that Visio opens the file, but cannot make changes to the file. Ergo, neither can you.

Still, because you are the vice president in charge of Visio Customization at your firm, you need to edit the patterns and shapes from time to time. Here's how (but *shhhhhhh*... don't tell any of your co-workers!):

1. Make sure the stencil you want to open as editable is not open. From the menu bar, select **File | Stencils | Open Stencil**. Notice the Open Stencil dialog box. If necessary, navigate to the folder that holds the stencil file.

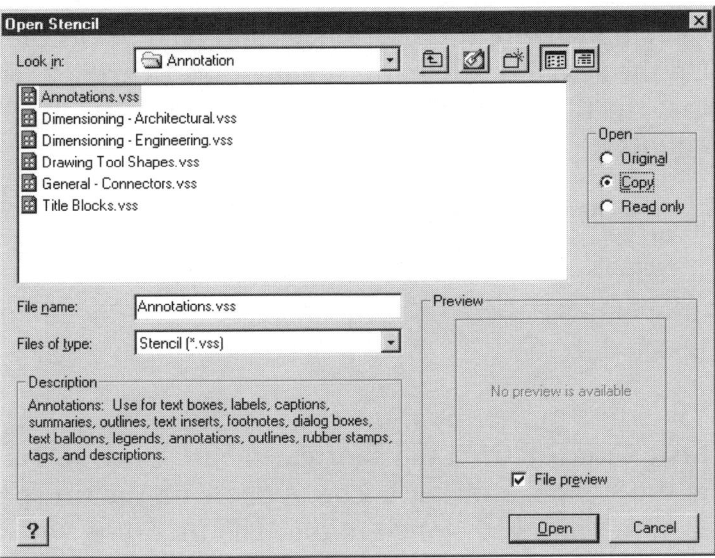



2.  Take a close look at the **Open** area, located to the right of the Open Stencil dialog box—an area you may have ignored until now. The **Open** area has three options:

    ➤ **Original** opens the stencil as a read-write VSS file. This option allows you to revise the original stencil.

    ➤ **Copy** makes a copy of the stencil, and opens it as a read-write VSS file. This option is useful when you plan to make huge revisions to the stencil, or when you want to give the stencil a different filename. Visio makes a copy of the stencil file and gives it a generic name, such as **Stencil2**. It is up to you to give it a more descriptive name when you use the **Save As** command.

    ➤ **Read-only** opens the stencil as a read-only VSS file; the default. This option prevents you from making changes to the contents of the stencil file, such as adding masters and editing patterns.

3.  Select a **VSS** file.

4.  Select the **Copy** radio button.

5.  Click the **Open** button. Notice that Visio opens the stencil file. On the stencil's title bar is a name like **Stencil2**. Notice, too, that the title bar has a red asterisk ( * ): it means the stencil is editable.

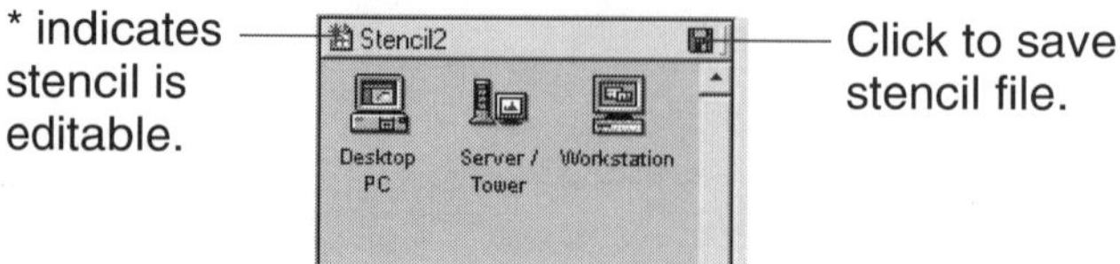


6.  You edit a master by right-clicking the master, then selecting **Edit Master** from the shortcut menu. Once you make a change to the stencil, a diskette icon appears on the title bar: click it to save the changed stencil to file. The first time you do this, Visio displays the Save As dialog box; this gives you a chance to rename the stencil, from its generic Stencil2 name to a more descriptive name.

**Tips:**

Editing a master in the Document stencil changes the look of all instanced shapes. This is an effective method of updating shapes.

When you edit the masters in a stencil, the changes don't affect the shapes already on the page.

# Customizing the Page

So far in this book, I have been emphasizing customization of the shape. The page itself can be customized in many ways. You can think of customizing as *preformatting*.

It might be better to say, "customize the drawing" because a drawing contains one or more pages. But, as it turns out, each page can be customized on its own, independent of other pages in the drawing.

There are two primary reasons why you would want to customize the page: to make it faster and better.

➤ **Faster**   When you start with a drawing that is preformatted, you don't have to fuss over details, such as the size, scale, and orientation of the page. If these and other parameters have been preset, that saves you time. When you save time, you get your work done faster. When you get your work done faster, you can rest more. Or, you can do more work and get paid more.

➤ **Better**   By preformatting a drawing, you can ensure your firm's standards are being upheld. For example, your firm probably has a unique logo, a specific typeface for text, and a restricted list of paper sizes. When these and other parameters are preset, your work looks consistent.

There are so many parameters that can be set for a page that I won't show them via tutorials. Instead, I'll list them and show you where they are located in dialog boxes. (In Section II of this book, you get to see where these parameters are set in the page's ShapeSheet.)

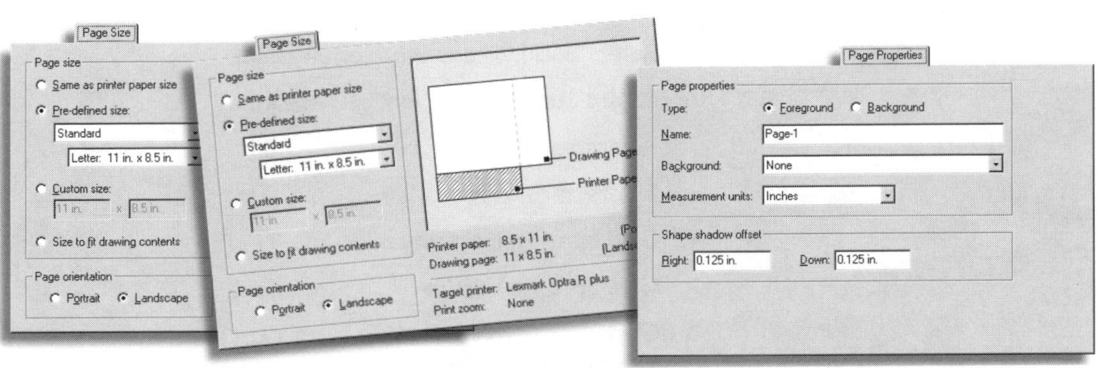

| Command to Access Dialog Box | Page Property | Default Value |
| --- | --- | --- |
| **File \| Page Setup \| Setup** | | |
| | Printer Paper Size | 8.5"x11" |
| | Printer Paper Orientation | Portrait |
| | Adjust to | 100% of normal size |

| Command to Access Dialog Box | Page Property | Default Value |
| --- | --- | --- |
| | Fit to | 1 sheet across by 1 sheet down |
| **File \| Page Setup \| Page Size** | | |
| | Page Size | Same as printer |
| | Orientation | Not available when the Same As Printer option is chosen |
| **File \| Page Setup \| Drawing Scale** | | |
| | Drawing Scale | No scale (1:1) |
| **File \| Page Setup \| Page Properties** | | |
| | Type | Foreground |
| | Name | Page-1 |
| | Background | None |
| | Measurement units | Inches |
| | Shadow Offset X | 0.125 in. |
| | Shadow Offset Y | 0.125 in. |
| **Tools \| Ruler & Grid** | | |
| | Rulers Subdivisions Horizontal | Fine |
| | Rulers Subdivisions Vertical | Fine |
| | Rulers zero Horizontal | 0 in. |
| | Rulers zero Vertical | 0 in. |
| | Grid Spacing Horizontal | Fine |
| | Grid Spacing Vertical | Fine |
| | Grid Minimum spacing Horizontal | 0 in. |
| | Grid Minimum spacing Vertical | 0 in. |
| | Grid origin Horizontal | 0 in. |
| | Grid origin Vertical | 0 in. |
| **View \| Layer Properties** | | |
| | Layers | none |

In addition, you can add these items to the custom page:

➤ Styles for text, line patterns and ends, and fill patterns via **Format | Define Styles**.

➤ Snap and glue settings via **Tools | Snap & Glue**.

➤ Standard title block and drawing border.

➤ Printer settings via **File | Properties | Output Format**

➤ Instructions for working with the drawing.

# Creating Templates

When you create a custom shape or custom pattern, you store it in a stencil file to reuse and share with other drawings. When you create a custom page, you store it in a *template* file to reuse with other drawings.

There is nothing special about a template file over a drawing file, except for one point: when you open a template file, Visio opens a *copy* of the file and gives it a generic name, such as **Drawing2**. In this way, you cannot (accidentally or otherwise) write over the template, destroying the original in the process.

For example, say you opened the **Home Plan.Vst** template file (found in Visio 2000 Technical Edition's **\Visio 2000\Solutions\Building Architecture** folder). Notice from Visio's title bar that the drawing has been given the generic name of **Drawing2**. The template includes these features:

➤ Ten stencil files are automatically opened, such as **Cabinets** and **Electrical and Telecom**.

➤ The page is set up for A-size in landscape format (see File | Page Setup | Page Size).

➤ The scale is preset to 1/4"=1", a common architectural scale (see File | Page Setup | Drawing Scale).

Layers and styles are defined in the masters; these appear in the drawing once you start dragging masters onto the page:

> ➤ Layers are set up, such as **Fixtures**, **Building Envelope**, and **Dimensions** (see View | Layer Properties)

> ➤ Line styles are predefined, such as **Building** and **Dim-Architecture** (see Format | Style).

To save a drawing as a template file, follow these steps:

1. Select **File | Save As** from the menu bar.

2. Select **Template (*.vst)** from Save as type. If necessary, change to the appropriate folder.

3. Type a meaningful name in File name.

4. Click **Save**.

5. Notice that Visio displays the Properties dialog box. You can fill it out, if you like. You may want to click the **Contents** tab, which displays a summary of the contents of the drawing.

6. Click **OK**. Visio saves the drawing as a VST template file.

## Editing a Template File

The next time you open the VST file, notice that Visio gives you no choices in the Open section of the Open dialog box. **Original**, **Copy**, and **Read-only** are grayed out. Unlike the stencil file, you cannot open a template file for editing.

Fortunately, there is a workaround:

1. Open the template file you wish to edit. Notice that Visio opens a copy of the template.

2. Make your editing changes.

3. Select **File | Save As** from the menu bar.

4. Navigate to the folder that contains your template.

5. Select **Template (*.vst)** from Save as type. Your template appears in the Save As dialog box. Double-click it to replace it.

6. Notice that Visio asks if you are sure you want to replace the existing template file. Click **Yes**.

The template file has been edited and is safely stored back on disk.

# Creating Workspaces

There is one variant on the template file of which you should be aware. Called the *workspace,* this VSW file simply saves the names and window positions of the currently open drawings.

Saving the workspace is useful when you have two or more drawing files and stencils open at one time. When you open the workspace file, Visio returns the drawings and stencils to their saved state.

**Caution:**

The workspace file does not save the drawing(s). You must save each drawing individually. Technically, the VSW file contains pointers to the files, not the files themselves.

To save a multiple drawing display:

1. Save every drawing. Click on the drawing's title bar, and then select **File | Save** from the menu bar. (To see all drawings at once, select **Window | Tile**.)

2. Select **File | Save As** from the menu bar.

3. Type a name for the workspace in File name, and then check **Workspace** under Save.

4. Click **Save**.

To open the workspace, use the **File | Open** command, then select a file with the VSW extension.

# Chapter Review

In this chapter, you learned how to save and edit stencil files, and customize pages, and save drawings as templates and workspaces.

In the next chapter, you learn how to customize toolbars.

# Chapter 4

# *Tailoring Toolbars and Menus*

Before Visio 2000, you could not easily change the toolbars and menus. The only option available to you, as an end user, was to turn on and off the visibility of the toolbars. Creating a new toolbar or menu required knowing how to program with VBA (Visual Basic for Applications).

With Visio 2000, you can fully customize the toolbars and menus. That means you can change the look of the toolbars, create one or more new toolbars, edit a toolbar or menu to hold almost any Visio command, and delete toolbars and portions of the menu. All this is done by right-clicking any toolbar, then selecting **Customize** from the shortcut menu.

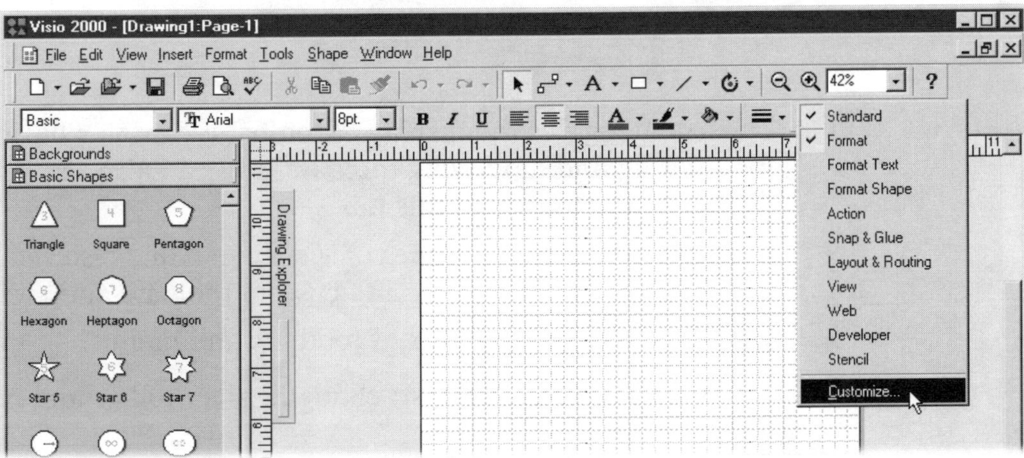

In this chapter, you learn about:

➤ Changing toolbar and menu options

➤ Creating a new toolbar

➤ Sharing the new toolbar and menu with other users

When you right-click a toolbar, Visio displays a shortcut menu with the names of all toolbars. The checkmark next to a toolbar name means the toolbar is currently visible. Selecting a toolbar name toggles its visibility.

The Customize dialog box has three tabs: **Toolbars**, **Commands**, and **Options**.

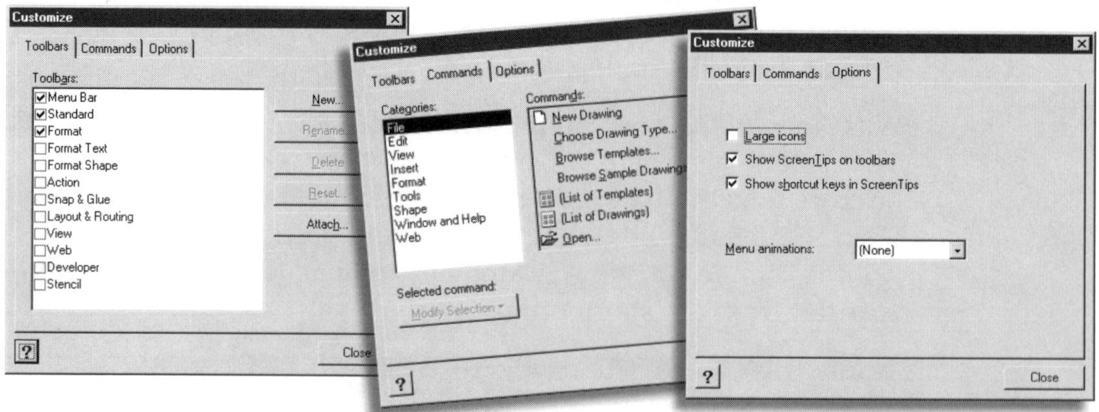

➤ **Toolbars** toggles the display of toolbars; contains buttons for creating and modifying toolbars. You can also reset the display of the menus in this tab.

➤ **Commands** lists the names of Visio commands, sorted by menu names; used for creating custom toolbars and menus.

➤ **Options** changes the look of toolbars and menus.

We'll work with the last tab first: changing the toolbar and menu options.

**Tip:**
One toolbar is missing from the list of toolbars displayed by the shortcut menu. The missing toolbar is listed in the Toolbars tab of the Customize dialog box: it is called **Menu Bar**. That's right—you can toggle the display of the menu bar. When customizing the Visio user interface, you might want to turn off the menu bar so that users can only access commands via modified toolbars. This allows you to limit access to specific commands.

# Changing Toolbar and Menu Options

The Options tab of the Customize dialog box allows you to change the look and feel of Visio toolbars and menus.

1. Select **View | Toolbars | Customize** from the menu bar. (As an alternative, you can right-click any toolbar, and select **Customize** from the shortcut menu.) Notice the Customize dialog box.

2. Select the **Options** tab.

3. Change any of the options:

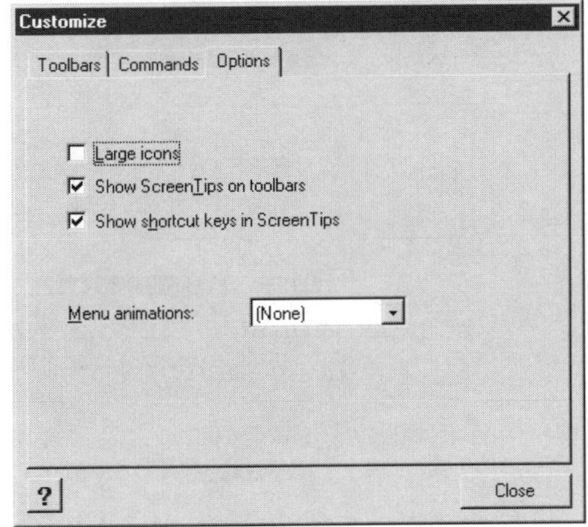

   **Large icons** When on, displays toolbar icons at twice their normal size. The default (smaller) size is 16x16 pixels, whereas the large size is 32x32 pixels. Selecting the larger size makes the icons easier to see, especially on high-resolution screens. Selecting the smaller size allows you to see more buttons per toolbar, and takes up less screen real estate. When customizing a toolbar, you can create your own icons.

**Show ScreenTips on toolbars** When on, Visio displays a tooltip when the cursor lingers over a toolbar button (Visio follows Microsoft's convention and calls them ScreenTips). The tooltip describes the name of the toolbar button. ScreenTips with shortcut keys are useful enough to always keep turned on. When customizing a toolbar, you can specify the wording of the tooltip.

**Show shortcut keys in ScreenTips** When on, the tooltip also displays the shortcut keystroke (those that begin with Ctrl), if one is available for the tool. When customizing a toolbar, you cannot specify the Ctrl shortcut key, but you can specify the Alt shortcut key for menu items.

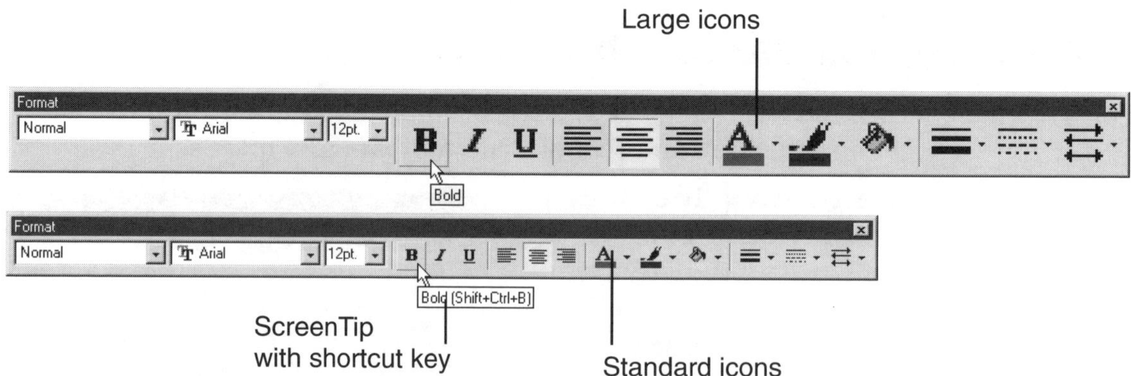


**Menu animations**: Determines how the menus open. On a fast computer, menu animations are not noticeable; even so, I find them annoying and keep this feature set to None. The options are:

➤ **None** The menu opens normally.

➤ **Random** The menu opens by unfolding or sliding.

➤ **Unfold** The menu opens by sliding open sideways and downwards.

➤ **Slide** The menu opens by sliding down.

4. Click **Close** to see the effect of the options you changed.

# Creating a New Toolbar

Use the following procedure to create a new toolbar:

1. Select **View | Toolbars | Customize** from the menu bar. Notice the Customize dialog box.

2. Click **New**. Notice the New Toolbar dialog box.

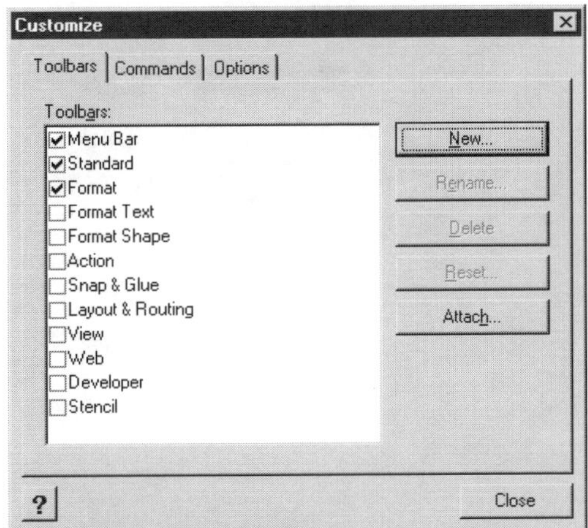
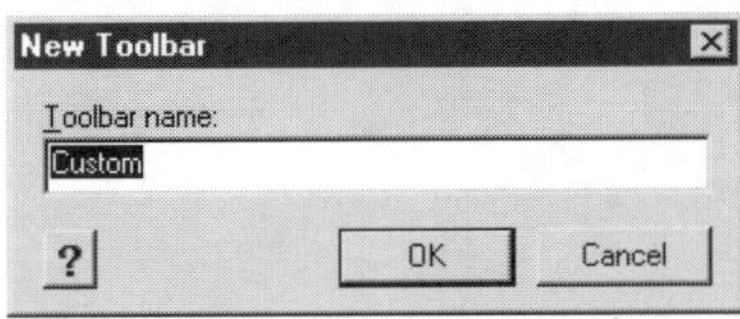

3. Enter a descriptive name for the toolbar; the default is "Custom." This name will appear on the toolbar's title bar, as well as on the list of available toolbars.

4. Click **OK**. Notice the new, empty toolbar. (Drag the toolbar away from the Customize dialog box so it doesn't disappear when you click another tab in the Customize dialog box.) You now fill the empty toolbar with buttons of your choice.

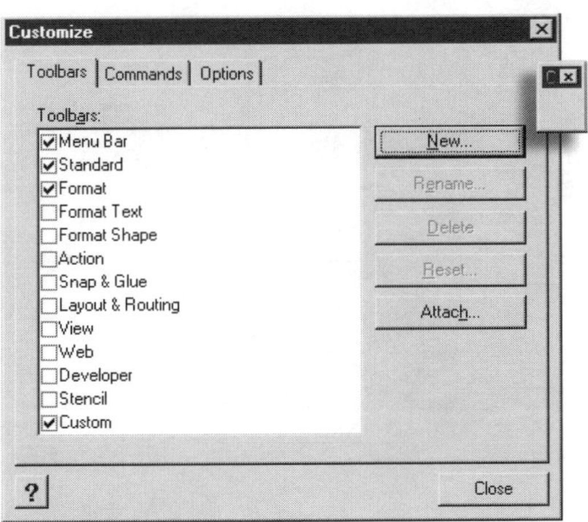

5. To fill the toolbar with buttons, you drag icons onto it. Select the **Commands** tab of the Customize dialog box. Notice that all of Visio's commands are sorted by menu name. For example, the **File** category lists all file related commands.

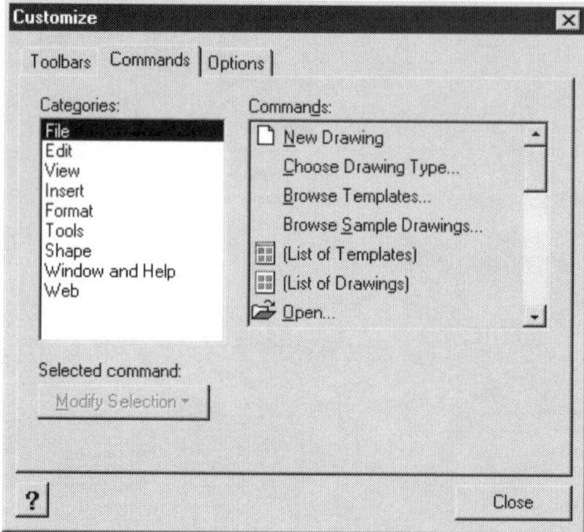

6. Drag a command from the Customize dialog box onto the new toolbar. For example, under Categories, select **Edit**. Under Commands, drag **Select All** to the new toolbar.

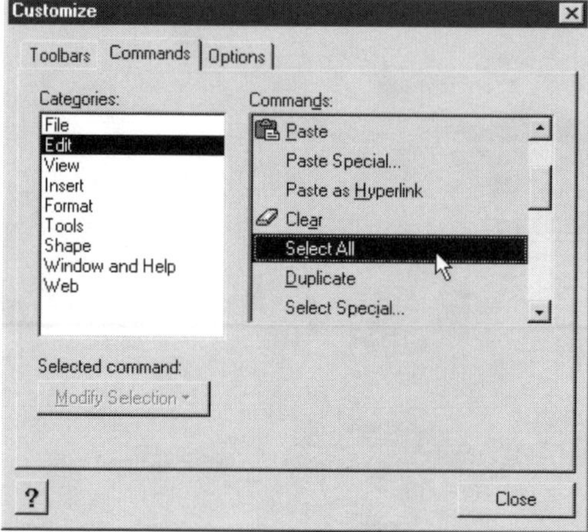

**7.** To change the properties of the new button, right-click the button. Notice the shortcut menu.

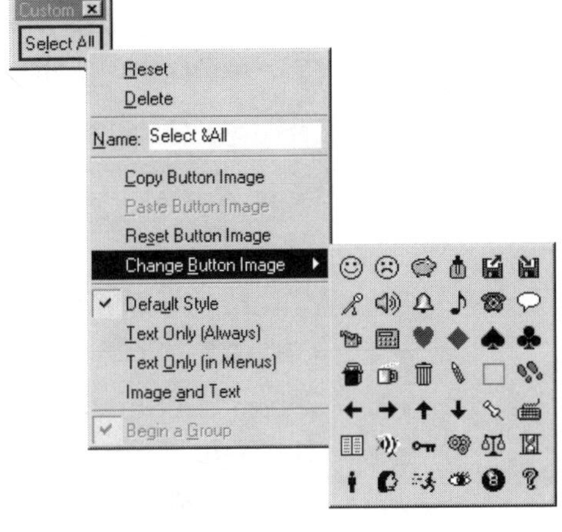

**Reset** resets the button's options.

**Delete** removes the button from the toolbar.

**Name** specifies the name displayed by the ScreenTip and in the menu. To change the name, click the name, edit the text, and then press **Enter**.

**Tip:**

The ampersand (&) prefixes the underlined character in menus, such as **Select All**. The underlined character is used with the **Alt** key for shortcut keystrokes. This allows you to create Alt-based shortcut keys.

**Copy Button Image** copies the button's image to the Windows Clipboard.

**Paste Button Image** pastes an image from the Clipboard onto the button. This allows you to create a custom image in a paint program, such as PaintShop Pro. Remember to keep the size to 16x16 pixels.

**Reset Button Image** changes the image back to its original form.

**Change Button Image** selects an alternative image for the icon from the popout menu.

**Default Style** displays an icon on a toolbar, or an icon and text on a menu.

**Text Only (Always)** displays text only in the toolbar and on a menu.

**Text Only (In Menus)** displays text only in menus and, despite the name, in toolbars as well.

**Image and Text** displays icon image and text.

**Begin a Group** inserts a vertical (or horizontal) line to separate visually a group of buttons.

8. When you are finished creating the custom toolbar, click the **Toolbars** tab on the Customize dialog box.

9. Select the customized toolbar name in the Toolbars list. Notice that you can now rename and delete the toolbar with the **Rename** and **Delete** buttons. (The **Reset** button resets the properties of the toolbars provided with Visio; the properties are reset back to their default settings. The **Attach** button is discussed later in this chapter.)

10. Click **Close** to exit toolbar customization. You can now test your new toolbar.

**Tip:**
When you drag a toolbar near the edge of the Visio window, the toolbar automatically docks. To prevent the toolbar from docking, hold down the **Ctrl** key while dragging the toolbar.

## Adding Items to a Menu

While you cannot create a new menu, you can add commands to existing menus. (A menu is **File**, **Edit**, **View**, etc.) For example, you can add the **Strikethrough** command to the **Format** menu; this allows you to format text more quickly than bringing up the Text dialog box.

1. From the menu bar, select **View | Toolbars | Customize**.

2. When the Customize dialog box appears, select the **Commands** tab.

3. In the Categories list, select a menu name. For example, select **Format**. Notice the list of formatting commands in the Commands list.

4.  Drag a command to a Visio menu on the menu bar. For example, drag **Strikethrough** to **Format** on the menu bar. Notice that the **Format** menu drops down.

5.  Drag the command to the position at which you want the command. Notice that Visio displays a heavy line that shows you where the command will end up.

6.  Let go of the mouse button. Notice that the command is placed in the menu.

7.  You can now edit the look and feel of the command. You can change the text and the Alt shortcut, add an image, or place a separator line. Right-click the menu item. Notice the same shortcut menu:

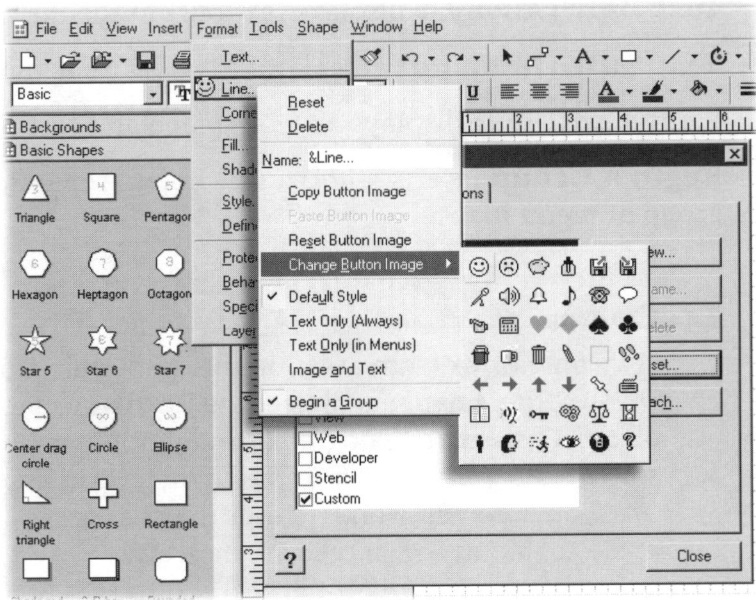

**Reset** resets the menu's options.

**Delete** removes the item from the menu.

**Name** specifies the name displayed by the menu. To change the name, click the wording and edit the text.

**Copy Button Image** copies the menu item's image to the Windows Clipboard.

**Paste Button Image** pastes an image from the Clipboard onto the menu item. This allows you to create a custom image in a paint program, such as PaintShop Pro. Remember to keep the size to 16x16 pixels.

**Reset Button Image** changes the image back to its original form.

**Change Button Image** selects an alternative image for the menu item from the popout menu.

**Default Style** displays an icon and text on a menu.

**Text Only (Always)** displays text only in the menu.

**Text Only (In Menus)** displays text only in menus, as well.

**Image and Text** displays an icon image and text.

**Begin a Group** inserts a horizontal line to separate visually a group of menu items.

**Caution:**

You can easily delete an entire menu by selecting Delete. If this happens, select the **Toolbars** tab on the Customize dialog box. Under Toolbars, select **Menu Bar**. Click **Reset**. When Visio asks, "Are you sure you want to reset the changes made to 'Menu Bar' toolbar?" click **OK**.

8.  When you are finished editing the menu, click **Close** to exit toolbar customization. You can test your new menu. Unlike toolbars, you cannot give the menu bar a new name, nor delete the menu bar.

# Sharing the New Toolbar and Menu with Others

After customizing a toolbar or the menu, the menu or toolbar is available only on your computer until you share it. To make customized toolbars available anywhere the current drawing is opened, the toolbar must be attached to the drawing file. This is done with the **Attach** button on the Toolbars tab in the Customize dialog box.

1. Select **View | Toolbars | Customize** from the menu bar. Notice the Customize dialog box.

2. Select the **Toolbars** tab, and click **Attach** to attach the toolbar to the drawing file. Notice that Visio displays the Attach Toolbars dialog box. The dialog box lists all customized toolbars.

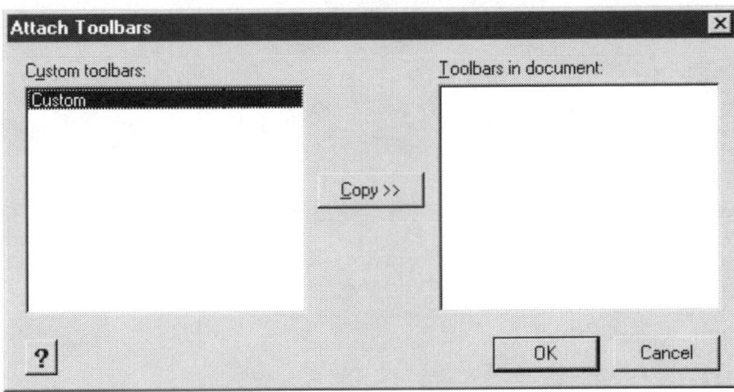

3. Select the toolbar name, then click **Copy**.

4. Click **OK** to close the Attach Toolbars dialog box.

5. Click **Close** to close the Customize dialog box.

# Chapter Review

In this chapter, you learned how to create, edit, and share toolbars and menus.

In the next section of the book you learn about the ShapeSheet and the role it plays in customizing and programming Visio.

# Customizing ShapeSheets

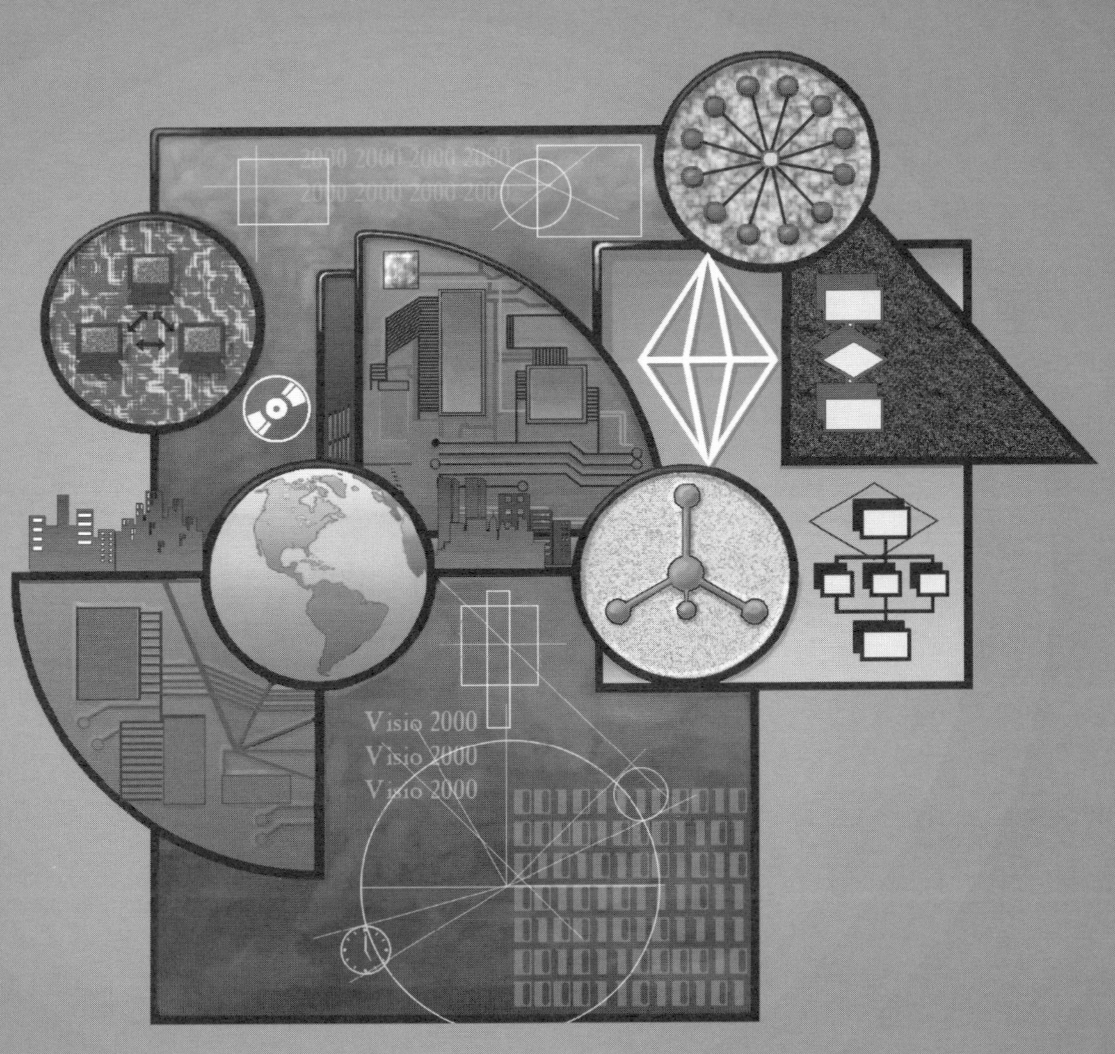

# Chapter 5

# Introduction to ShapeSheets

Visio stores everything in a *ShapeSheet* (try saying ShapeSheet three times fast!). Every aspect of every page, shape, object, and guide is stored in the ubiquitous ShapeSheet. As a Visio user, you probably never saw a ShapeSheet; as an advanced user, you must become intimate with the ShapeSheet.

Each object has its own ShapeSheet. By understanding the format and content of the ShapeSheet, you gain a huge amount of control over how to make shapes act and react—with little or no programming!

In this chapter, you learn about:

➤ What the ShapeSheet is, and why it is important to Visio drawings

➤ Understanding the sections, rows, and cells that make up the ShapeSheet

➤ Discovering the ShapeSheet behind pages and shapes

➤ Making simple changes to cells in the ShapeSheet

By the end of the chapter, you should be able to view the ShapeSheet, understand its format, and make simple changes to its cells.

## The ShapeSheet is a Spreadsheet

The ShapeSheet defines two facts: (1) what every shape looks like; and (2) how shapes react when you move, copy, stretch, and otherwise interact with shapes. The ShapeSheet is very important in Visio because the ShapeSheet makes shapes intelligent. You could say, "Behind every great shape lies a ShapeSheet." An understanding of the ShapeSheet is crucial to learning how to customize Visio; indeed, you cannot program Visio without first understanding the ShapeSheet.

As the name suggests, the ShapeSheet looks like a spreadsheet, such as that created by Quattro Pro or Excel. There is one ShapeSheet for every object in the drawing.

The ShapeSheet consists of several sections. Each section contains a title bar, and one or more rows, columns, and cells. (Some sections contain a single cell; others contain multiple cells, but no rows.) The figure below shows one section of a ShapeSheet.

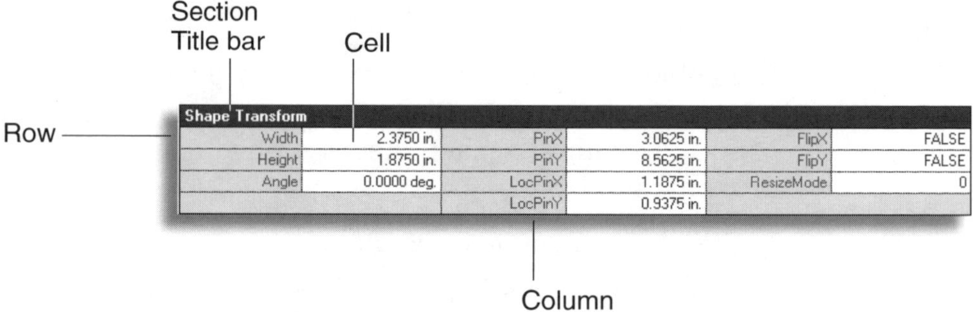


Unlike the name suggests, ShapeSheets are not limited to just shapes. You will find a ShapeSheet behind every page, group, shape, style, guide, and document, and even objects inserted from other applications. There are ShapeSheets *everywhere* controlling every aspect of Visio.

## Title Bar

Every section has a title bar, such as **Shape Transform** in the figure above. The title bar describes the function of the section. The title bar also performs a second function: it lets you expand and contract the section. A ShapeSheet usually consists of more sections than can be displayed on the screen. While you can scroll through the ShapeSheet, it is convenient to collapse sections you are not working with. To collapse the section, click the title bar. To expand the section, click the title bar a second time.



## Cells

Below the title bar are one or more cells, usually organized in rows. Some cells and rows contain descriptive titles, such as **Width** and **PinX** in the Shape Transform section. The titles are gray and have red text; after the value of a cell is changed, the text changes to blue. In some rare cases, such as in the **User-defined cells** and **Custom Properties** sections, you can change the name of the title of the row.

Other cells contain data and formulae, such as **0.75 in.** and **Width*0.5**. The data cells are white and have black text. (Black text means the cell contains original data, while blue text means the cell contains data that was modified.).

To change the value of a data cell, click it. The ability to change data and formulae directly in the cell is new in Visio 2000. As an alternative, the *formula bar* (located below the Visio toolbar) looks just like the formula bar in a spreadsheet: use it to type new data. Click the green check mark (or press **Enter**) to make the change; click the red X to retain the original data (or press **Esc**).



There is one other visual effect to observe when you click on a cell. When it makes sense, Visio highlights the associated portion of the shape. In the figure below, I clicked cell **X2** in the **Connection Points** section, which caused Visio to place a heavy black box around the shape's related connection point (located at the top of the shape).

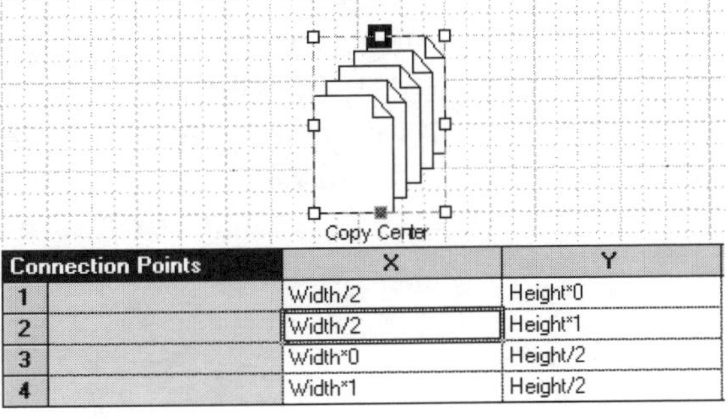


| Connection Points | X | Y |
|---|---|---|
| 1 | Width/2 | Height*0 |
| 2 | Width/2 | Height*1 |
| 3 | Width*0 | Height/2 |
| 4 | Width*1 | Height/2 |

## Layout

The layout of sections in the ShapeSheet is inconsistent. Some sections have alternating columns of title and data cells, as in the **Shape Transform** section. Other sections consist of a single column of titles and a row of column titles, as in the **Custom Properties** section illustrated below.

| Custom Properties | Label | Prompt | Type | Format | |
|---|---|---|---|---|---|
| Prop.Cost | "Cost" | "Enter the cost associated with this process." | 2 | "$###,###.00" | |
| Prop.Duration | "Duration" | "Enter the duration of this step." | 2 | No Formula | |
| Prop.Resources | "Resources" | "Enter the number of people required to complete t | No Formula | No Formula | |

The column titles describe the cells in the column, such as **Label**, **Prompt**, and **Type** in the figure above.

Again, Visio is not consistent. The column titles in some sections are descriptive; in other sections, the column titles are generic, such as **A**, **B**, **C**, and **D**. In this case, you need to refer to Chapter 8, "The Complete ShapeSheet Reference," which describes every aspect of the ShapeSheet.

In one case, the section consists of a single cell. This is found in the **Layer Membership** section, which lists the layer numbers to which the shape belongs.

| Layer Membership |
|---|
| "0" |

## Sections

Visio has a total of thirty-four sections that can be found in a ShapeSheet; no ShapeSheet, however, contains all sections since some are specific to the object. The following table lists the names of sections. The asterisk (*) indicates sections that were added to Visio 2000. Some section names changed with Visio 2000; the old name is in parentheses. Also note that older versions of Visio had a Guide Info section, which no longer exists in Visio 2000.

<table>
<tr><td>1-D Endpoints</td><td>Layers</td></tr>
<tr><td>Actions</td><td>Line Format</td></tr>
<tr><td>Alignment</td><td>Miscellaneous</td></tr>
<tr><td>Character</td><td>Page Layout *</td></tr>
<tr><td>Connection Points</td><td>Page Properties</td></tr>
<tr><td>Controls</td><td>Paragraph</td></tr>
<tr><td>Custom Properties</td><td>Protection</td></tr>
<tr><td>Document Properties *</td><td>Ruler & Grid</td></tr>
<tr><td>Events</td><td>Scratch</td></tr>
<tr><td>Fill Format</td><td>Shape Layout *</td></tr>
<tr><td>Foreign Image Info (Image Info)</td><td>Shape Transform</td></tr>
<tr><td>Geometry</td><td>Style Properties *</td></tr>
<tr><td>Glue Info</td><td>Tabs *</td></tr>
<tr><td>Group Properties *</td><td>Text Block Format</td></tr>
<tr><td>Hyperlinks (Hyperlink)</td><td>Text Fields</td></tr>
<tr><td>Image Properties *</td><td>Text Transform</td></tr>
<tr><td>Layer Membership</td><td>User-defined cells</td></tr>
</table>

# ShapeSheet Pros and Cons

I have been making parallels between the ShapeSheet and the spreadsheet. In fact, the earliest Visio prototype, created in 1990, actually was an Excel spreadsheet, which contained formulae that drove a drawing engine.

The power of the ShapeSheet is that it makes shapes perform complicated actions without needing to write code with advanced programming languages. If you can write a formula in Excel, such as **=B1*C1**, then you'll have no problem programming ShapeSheet cells.

The drawback to ShapeSheet is that there are many ShapeSheet cells behind every shape, even a simple line. For that reason, it can get confusing navigating among ShapeSheets and sections and cells. Although the ShapeSheet contains a lot of information, not everything is accessible. Some data must be accessed using programming, such as Visual Basic for Applications (included with Visio). For example, even though shapes can contain text, that text cannot be accessed in the ShapeSheet; instead, you must use the **GetName** and **SetName** methods found in VBA.

# A Visual Tour of the ShapeSheet

When you work with a ShapeSheet, Visio commonly looks like the screen shot illustrated below. Notice that Visio's menu and toolbar change, depending on whether the focus is in the drawing window or the ShapeSheet window.

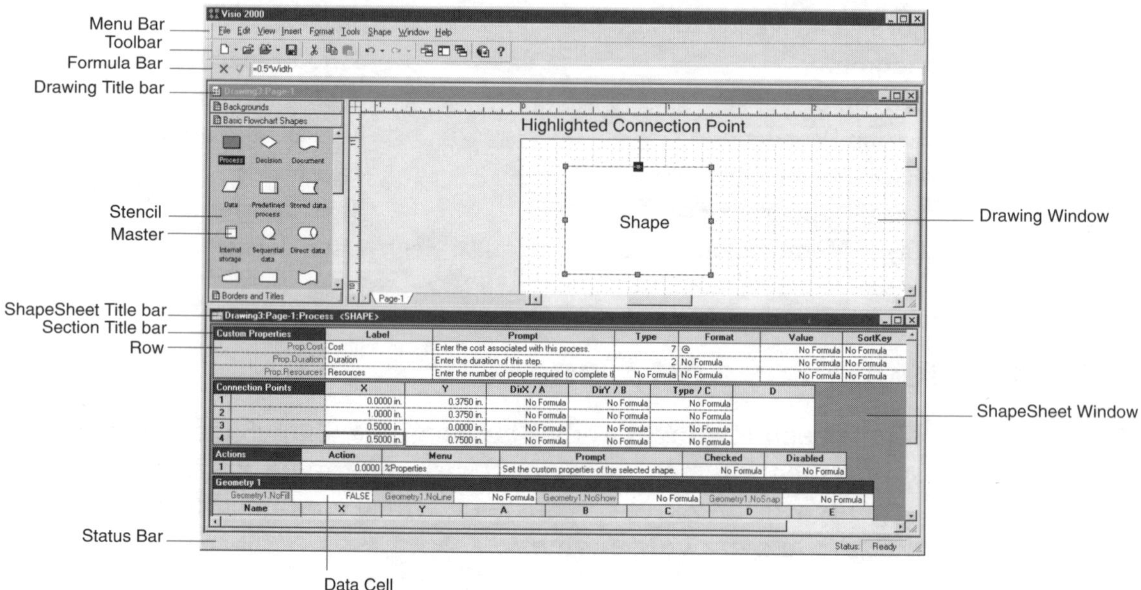

# Displaying the ShapeSheet

Start Visio with the **Basic Diagram.VST** stencil, found in the **\solutions\block diagram** folder. Notice that Visio starts with a single blank page.

Look at the Visio title bar. Part of it reads **Drawing1:Page-1**. That nomenclature is more than a pair of generic names. It is how Visio identifies the drawing and page you are looking at (a drawing can contain up to 200 pages). The identification of a page is important for customizing and programming purposes.

The name of the drawing file is **Drawing1**, at least until you save the drawing by another name. Initially, a drawing contains a single page named **Page-1**. Although the page looks blank to you (except for the grid lines), Visio stores a bunch of information about the page in—you guessed it!—a ShapeSheet. Let's now look at the ShapeSheet of a page.

From the menu bar, select **Window | Show ShapeSheet**. (The vertical bar (|) separates menu picks. In this case, you select **Window** from the menu bar, then select the **Show ShapeSheet** item.)

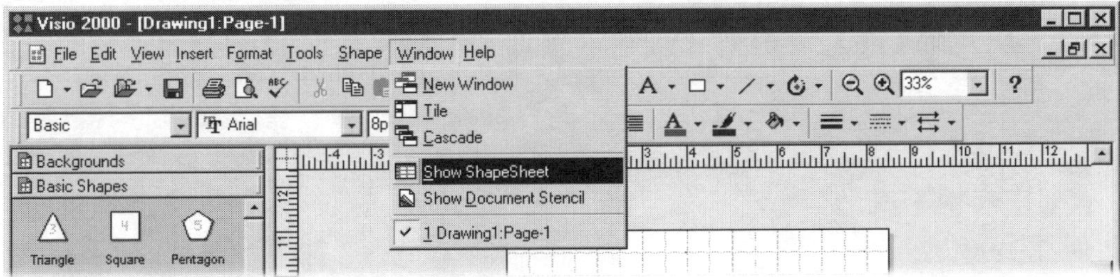

Visio splits the drawing window in half, showing the drawing in one half, and the ShapeSheet in the other half. In this case, you are looking at the ShapeSheet of the page, because no object was selected. This is an example of a ShapeSheet that is linked to something (a page) that isn't a shape.

Look at the ShapeSheet. The title bar reports whose sheet this is: **<Page>**. At the top are two sections, **Page Properties** and **Page Layout**. If the sections are compressed, meaning only the title bar is showing, click on each title bar to expand the sections.

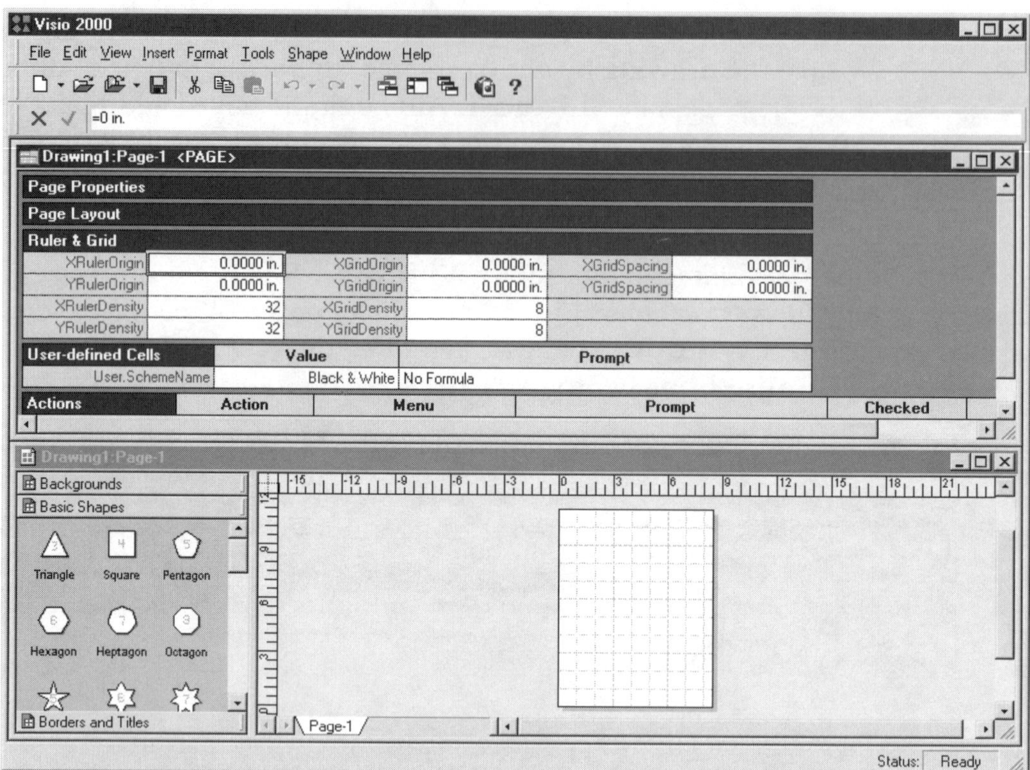

# The ShapeSheet Behind a Page

Let's take a look at how the ShapeSheet controls the page. Along the way, I'll throw in some tips that help make it easier to use ShapeSheet. Unfortunately, I don't have any tips on making ShapeSheet easier to pronounce!

The **Page Properties** section contains a number of cells that describe the properties of a page, such as its size, scale, and the drop shadow. For example, the **PageWidth** cell contains the width of the page, 8.5 in. in this case.

| Page Properties | | | | | |
|---|---|---|---|---|---|
| PageWidth | 8.5000 in. | PageScale | 1.0000 in. | ShdwOffsetX | 0.1250 in. |
| PageHeight | 11.0000 in. | DrawingScale | 1.0000 in. | ShdwOffsetY | -0.1250 in. |
| DrawingSizeType | 0 | DrawingScaleType | 0 | InhibitSnap | FALSE |

In the **PageWidth** field, replace 8.5 in. with **11 in.**, as follows:

1. Click the **PageWidth cell**.

2. Type **11** and press **Enter**. The data cell now contains **11 in.** Notice that Visio changes the width of the page to 11 inches.

   Congratulations! You have now used the ShapeSheet to control the Visio drawing. This is an example of the ShapeSheet controlling an object, which, in this case, happens to be the page.

## Keyboard Shortcuts and Dialog Boxes

The ShapeSheet is not the only way to control a Visio drawing, of course. You are probably already familiar with Visio's keyboard shortcuts and dialog boxes. But you probably didn't realize that the changes you make in the dialog boxes were being reflected in the ShapeSheet. Let's look at this interactivity now.

Visio lets you interactively change the size of the page:

1. Click on the page in the drawing window.

2. Hold down the **Ctrl** key and drag the edge of the page with the cursor (the cursor should change from the pointer to a double-headed arrow). Change the width of the page, say to double its previous width.

3. Looking at the ShapeSheet, notice that the **PageWidth** updates to reflect the new width of your page.

   That was an example of how a change to the object is reflected by a change in its ShapeSheet.

   The third way to change the page size and the contents of the ShapeSheet is via dialog boxes. The **File | Page Setup** command displays a dialog box that lets you specify the size of the page, including its width. Whatever number you type in for the **Page Size** is recorded in the page's ShapeSheet. If you go look at the **Page Setup** dialog box now (after having stretched the page), you'll see the page width reflects the changes you made.

So, there you have it. You can:

➤ Change the page properties using the ShapeSheet

➤ Change the ShapeSheet by modifying the page

➤ Change the page properties by using the Page Setup dialog box

# The ShapeSheet Behind a Shape

I showed you the ShapeSheet behind a page, because the page has a less intimidating collection of ShapeSheet sections. The exercise was a bit of a detour to show you that a ShapeSheet is not always attached to a shape. Let's now look at an actual *shape* ShapeSheet.

First, though, get rid of the page's ShapeSheet by clicking the small **x** at the upper-right corner of its window frame. Otherwise, the Visio window gets pretty crowded with too many windows open.

1. Drag the **Triangle** shape from the **Basic Shapes** stencil, and drop it on the page.

2. Hold down the **Ctrl** and **Shift** keys and zoom into the rectangle shape (you zoom in with a click-drag motion, windowing the shape). That gives you a clearer view of the triangle.

3. Click the shape to select it. Notice that the triangle has green handles surrounding it. That tells you Visio has selected the object.

4. From the menu bar, select **Window | Show ShapeSheet**. Notice that Visio opens the ShapeSheet window.

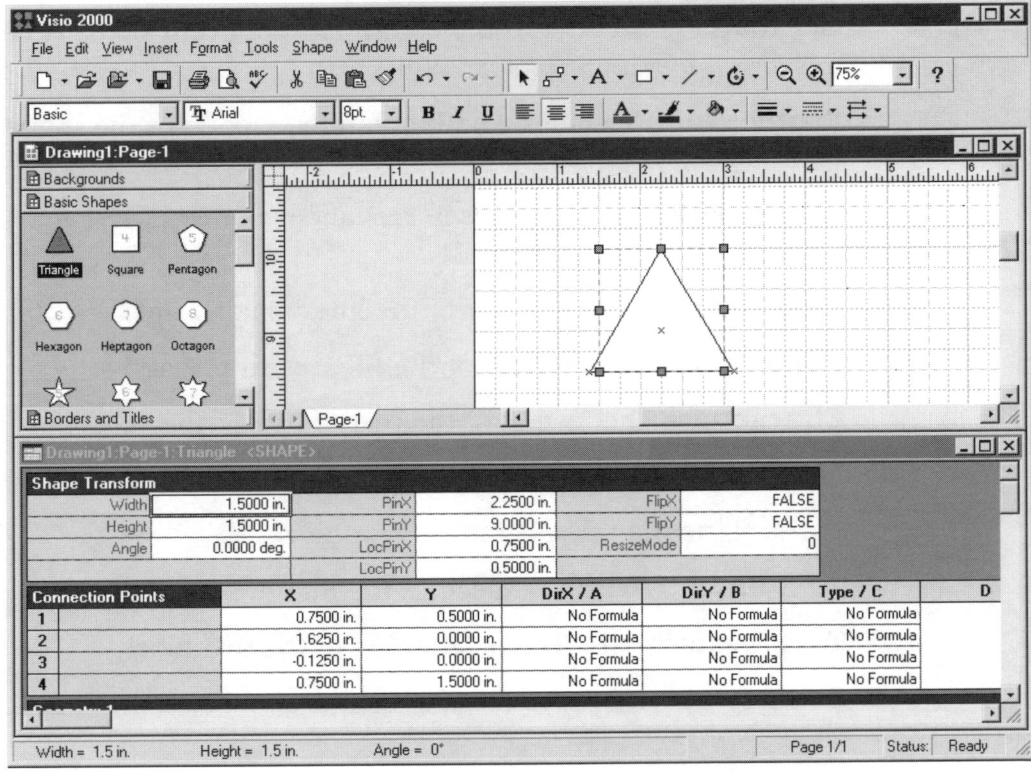



| Shape Transform | | | | | | |
|---|---|---|---|---|---|---|
| Width | 1.5000 in. | PinX | 2.2500 in. | FlipX | FALSE | |
| Height | 1.5000 in. | PinY | 9.0000 in. | FlipY | FALSE | |
| Angle | 0.0000 deg. | LocPinX | 0.7500 in. | ResizeMode | 0 | |
| | | LocPinY | 0.5000 in. | | | |

| Connection Points | X | Y | DirX / A | DirY / B | Type / C | D |
|---|---|---|---|---|---|---|
| 1 | 0.7500 in. | 0.5000 in. | No Formula | No Formula | No Formula | |
| 2 | 1.6250 in. | 0.0000 in. | No Formula | No Formula | No Formula | |
| 3 | -0.1250 in. | 0.0000 in. | No Formula | No Formula | No Formula | |
| 4 | 0.7500 in. | 1.5000 in. | No Formula | No Formula | No Formula | |



Like I said, shapes have more sections than pages. Here you see a whole bunch of sections. You may need to use the vertical scroll bar to see all the sections.

I'm not going to get into the nitty-gritty details about the contents of the sections (you can find that in Chapter 8), so here is an overview of the 12 sections behind the simple triangle:

**Shape Transform**  Position information about the shape, such as its width and height.

**Connection Points**  The position of connection points on the shape.



**95**

**Geometry 1**   The x- and y-coordinates of every shape (lines, in this case), making up the triangle.

**Protection**   Specifies whether various aspects of the shape can be changed.

**Miscellaneous**   Specifies miscellaneous properties, such as whether the shape is printed.

**Line Format**   The format of the lines making up the rectangle.

**Fill Format**   The format of the fill and drop shadow.

**Character**   The format of the text, if any, in the shape.

**Paragraph**   The positioning of paragraphs of text.

**Tabs**   Lists the tabs set for the text block.

**Text Block Format**   Specifies the margins, text direction, etc.

**Text Transform**   The positioning of the text block.

**Events**   Specifies whether an event occurs when the shape changes.

**Image Properties**   Changes the quality of bitmap images.

**Glue Info**   Specifies how the shape is glued to a connector.

**Shape Layout**   Controls how shapes are laid out automatically.

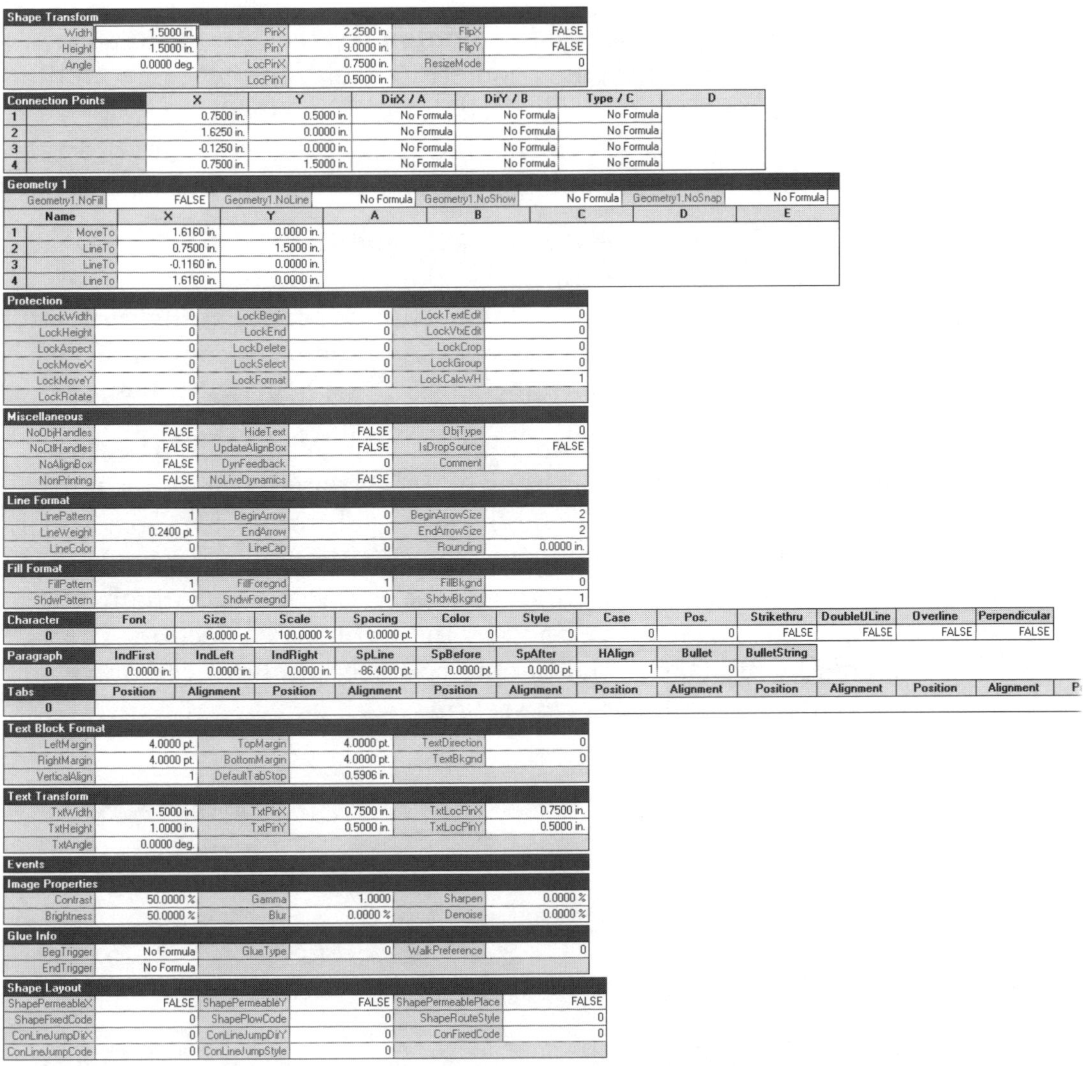

**Shape Transform**

| | | | | | |
|---|---|---|---|---|---|
| Width | 1.5000 in. | PinX | 2.2500 in. | FlipX | FALSE |
| Height | 1.5000 in. | PinY | 9.0000 in. | FlipY | FALSE |
| Angle | 0.0000 deg. | LocPinX | 0.7500 in. | ResizeMode | 0 |
| | | LocPinY | 0.5000 in. | | |

**Connection Points**

| | X | Y | DirX / A | DirY / B | Type / C | D |
|---|---|---|---|---|---|---|
| 1 | 0.7500 in. | 0.5000 in. | No Formula | No Formula | No Formula | |
| 2 | 1.6250 in. | 0.0000 in. | No Formula | No Formula | No Formula | |
| 3 | -0.1250 in. | 0.0000 in. | No Formula | No Formula | No Formula | |
| 4 | 0.7500 in. | 1.5000 in. | No Formula | No Formula | No Formula | |

**Geometry 1**

| Geometry1.NoFill | FALSE | Geometry1.NoLine | No Formula | Geometry1.NoShow | No Formula | Geometry1.NoSnap | No Formula |
|---|---|---|---|---|---|---|---|

| | Name | X | Y | A | B | C | D | E |
|---|---|---|---|---|---|---|---|---|
| 1 | MoveTo | 1.6160 in. | 0.0000 in. | | | | | |
| 2 | LineTo | 0.7500 in. | 1.5000 in. | | | | | |
| 3 | LineTo | -0.1160 in. | 0.0000 in. | | | | | |
| 4 | LineTo | 1.6160 in. | 0.0000 in. | | | | | |

**Protection**

| | | | | | |
|---|---|---|---|---|---|
| LockWidth | 0 | LockBegin | 0 | LockTextEdit | 0 |
| LockHeight | 0 | LockEnd | 0 | LockVtxEdit | 0 |
| LockAspect | 0 | LockDelete | 0 | LockCrop | 0 |
| LockMoveX | 0 | LockSelect | 0 | LockGroup | 0 |
| LockMoveY | 0 | LockFormat | 0 | LockCalcWH | 1 |
| LockRotate | 0 | | | | |

**Miscellaneous**

| | | | | | |
|---|---|---|---|---|---|
| NoObjHandles | FALSE | HideText | FALSE | ObjType | 0 |
| NoCtlHandles | FALSE | UpdateAlignBox | FALSE | IsDropSource | FALSE |
| NoAlignBox | FALSE | DynFeedback | 0 | Comment | |
| NonPrinting | FALSE | NoLiveDynamics | FALSE | | |

**Line Format**

| | | | | | |
|---|---|---|---|---|---|
| LinePattern | 1 | BeginArrow | 0 | BeginArrowSize | 2 |
| LineWeight | 0.2400 pt. | EndArrow | 0 | EndArrowSize | 2 |
| LineColor | 0 | LineCap | 0 | Rounding | 0.0000 in. |

**Fill Format**

| | | | | | |
|---|---|---|---|---|---|
| FillPattern | 1 | FillForegnd | 1 | FillBkgnd | 0 |
| ShdwPattern | 0 | ShdwForegnd | 0 | ShdwBkgnd | 1 |

**Character**

| | Font | Size | Scale | Spacing | Color | Style | Case | Pos. | Strikethru | DoubleULine | Overline | Perpendicular |
|---|---|---|---|---|---|---|---|---|---|---|---|---|
| 0 | 0 | 8.0000 pt. | 100.0000 % | 0.0000 pt. | 0 | 0 | 0 | 0 | FALSE | FALSE | FALSE | FALSE |

**Paragraph**

| | IndFirst | IndLeft | IndRight | SpLine | SpBefore | SpAfter | HAlign | Bullet | BulletString |
|---|---|---|---|---|---|---|---|---|---|
| 0 | 0.0000 in. | 0.0000 in. | 0.0000 in. | -86.4000 pt. | 0.0000 pt. | 0.0000 pt. | 1 | 0 | |

**Tabs**

| | Position | Alignment | Position | Alignment | Position | Alignment | Position | Alignment | Position | Alignment | Position | Alignment | P |
|---|---|---|---|---|---|---|---|---|---|---|---|---|---|
| 0 | | | | | | | | | | | | | |

**Text Block Format**

| | | | | | |
|---|---|---|---|---|---|
| LeftMargin | 4.0000 pt. | TopMargin | 4.0000 pt. | TextDirection | 0 |
| RightMargin | 4.0000 pt. | BottomMargin | 4.0000 pt. | TextBkgnd | 0 |
| VerticalAlign | 1 | DefaultTabStop | 0.5906 in. | | |

**Text Transform**

| | | | | | |
|---|---|---|---|---|---|
| TxtWidth | 1.5000 in. | TxtPinX | 0.7500 in. | TxtLocPinX | 0.7500 in. |
| TxtHeight | 1.0000 in. | TxtPinY | 0.5000 in. | TxtLocPinY | 0.5000 in. |
| TxtAngle | 0.0000 deg. | | | | |

**Events**

**Image Properties**

| | | | | | |
|---|---|---|---|---|---|
| Contrast | 50.0000 % | Gamma | 1.0000 | Sharpen | 0.0000 % |
| Brightness | 50.0000 % | Blur | 0.0000 % | Denoise | 0.0000 % |

**Glue Info**

| | | | | | |
|---|---|---|---|---|---|
| BegTrigger | No Formula | GlueType | 0 | WalkPreference | 0 |
| EndTrigger | No Formula | | | | |

**Shape Layout**

| | | | | | |
|---|---|---|---|---|---|
| ShapePermeableX | FALSE | ShapePermeableY | FALSE | ShapePermeablePlace | FALSE |
| ShapeFixedCode | 0 | ShapePlowCode | 0 | ShapeRouteStyle | 0 |
| ConLineJumpDirX | 0 | ConLineJumpDirY | 0 | ConFixedCode | 0 |
| ConLineJumpCode | 0 | ConLineJumpStyle | 0 | | |

# The Interconnectedness of Sections

At first glance, the list of section names seems random. Staring at the list a bit longer, out of apparent chaos comes some sort of order. The first sections define the shape's geometry; the next sections format the shape and its text; the final sections are more esoteric in nature.

To end this chapter, let's pay attention to two sections in particular: Shape Transform and Geometry 1 (refer to the figure on the previous page). Prepare yourself, for we now enter a world where nothing is as it appears. Indeed, we will encounter rectangles that don't exist, and numbers that mean other things.

The first time we came across the Shape Transform section (earlier in this chapter), it controlled the width and height of the page: 8.5 in wide and 11 in high. That was fairly straightforward. This time, the Shape Transform section seems to control the width and height of the triangle: 1.5 in wide and 1 in high.

I use the word *seems* because, in fact, the **Width** and **Height** values do not determine the size of the triangle—at least, not directly. Instead, they define the size of the *alignment box*. This is the green dashed rectangle you see surrounding a selected object. Changing Width in the Shape Transform section affects the triangle, which is defined by the Geometry 1 section. The changes you make in the Geometry 1 section, however, don't affect the Shape Transform section.

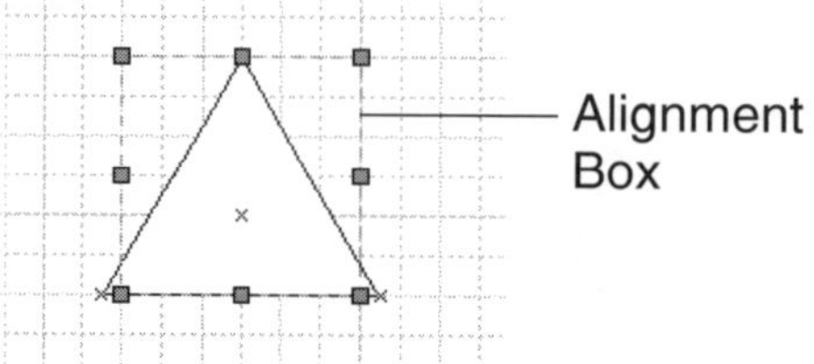


The green dashed square surrounding the circle is its alignment box. Here is an important rule to remember: *The alignment box does not have to coincide with its shape.* Most of the time, it does. Once in a while, you'll find it better that it doesn't.

To relate the alignment box to the triangle, the ShapeSheet connects the data in the Shape Transform cells with the cells in the Geometry 1 section. It does this using formulae, something you have not yet encountered.

To display the formulae, right-click anywhere in the ShapeSheet window, and select **Formulas** from the shortcut menu. Notice that the X and Y cells of the first two sections in the Geometry 1 section contain formulae:

| Geometry 1 | X | Y |
| --- | --- | --- |
| MoveTo | Width*1.0774 | Height*0 |
| LineTo | Width*0.5 | Height*1 |

We will call the first cell **MoveTo.X**, because it lies in the inter-section of the **MoveTo** row and the X column (the MoveTo row was called **Start** in earlier versions of Visio). The cell contains the formula **Width*1.0774**. Now, if you recall your algebra, you might guess that width is the name of a variable of some sort. That would be a very good guess, but wrong. Visio does not use variables in its ShapeSheet (the nearest thing to a variable are the **Scratch** and **User-defined cells** sections).

Instead, words like width and height refer to the names of cells. In this case, width refers to the Width cell in the Shape Trans-form section. There is no possibility of confusion, since only the Shape Transform section contains a cell called width. So, what we have here is that MoveTo.X takes the width of the alignment box and multiplies it by 1.0774: **Width*1.0774**. Similarly, the MoveTo.Y cell contains a formula that multiplies the alignment box height by 0: **Height*0**.

Now, what happens when you multiply something by 0? It equals zero. Thus, the triangle starts at X=1.0774 and Y=0. (Why 1.0774? I have no idea. It seems to me that this is an error, and should be X=1.)

In the **LineTo** row, you see similar formulae, except that the Width is multiplied by 0.5. What happens when you multiple something by 0.5? It is half of itself. Thus, the triangle is drawn up to its apex at X=1.5 and Y=0.

The illustration shows the path Visio takes to draw the triangle, from 1 to 2, to 3, to 4. All of the triangle's dimensions in the ShapeSheet are relative to the alignment box.

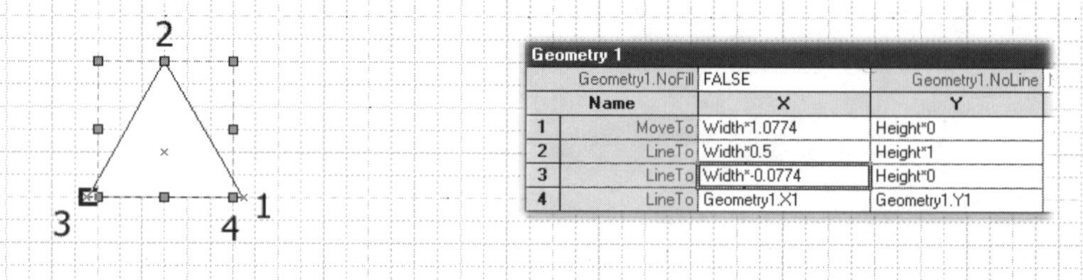

| Geometry 1 | | | |
|---|---|---|---|
| Geometry1.NoFill | FALSE | | Geometry1.NoLine |
| **Name** | **X** | **Y** | |
| 1 | MoveTo | Width*1.0774 | Height*0 |
| 2 | LineTo | Width*0.5 | Height*1 |
| 3 | LineTo | Width*-0.0774 | Height*0 |
| 4 | LineTo | Geometry1.X1 | Geometry1.Y1 |

It is at this point that I must unmask another seeming certainty: there are no triangles in Visio. All shapes in Visio are drawn from lines, arcs, elliptical arcs, ellipses, infinite lines, polylines, or spline curves. It is for this reason that there are four rows in the Geometry 1 section: each row defines the endpoints of three lines that make up the triangle. (For the triangle to be a *closed* shape, the last endpoint must be identical to the first endpoint.)

To see the interconnectedness of ShapeSheet sections, make a small, seemingly insignificant, change to the ShapeSheet:

1. Double-click the **MoveTo.X** cell of the Geometry 1 section. Notice that it contains **Width*1.0774**.

2. Replace the number **1.0774** with **2**, and then press **Enter**.

3. Notice what happens to the triangle—it has become longer and the alignment box stays the same width.

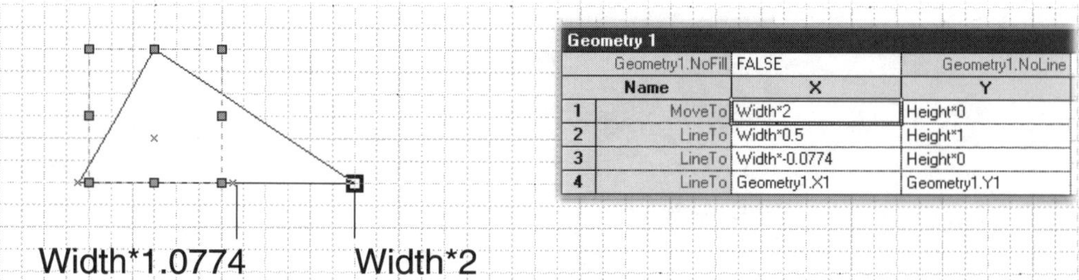


| Geometry 1 | | | |
|---|---|---|---|
| Geometry1.NoFill | FALSE | | Geometry1.NoLine |
| **Name** | **X** | **Y** | |
| 1 | MoveTo | Width*2 | Height*0 |
| 2 | LineTo | Width*0.5 | Height*1 |
| 3 | LineTo | Width*-0.0774 | Height*0 |
| 4 | LineTo | Geometry1.X1 | Geometry1.Y1 |

4. Click the **Height** cell of the Shape Transform section. Notice it contains **1.5 in.**

5. Type **2** to replace the number, and then press **Enter** to make the change, and watch the triangle become taller.

6. From the menu bar, select **File | Exit** and answer **No** to the question about saving changes to the drawing.

You have now seen how formulae connect sections in the ShapeSheet.

# Chapter Review

In this chapter, you learned that Visio stores everything in ShapeSheet. For this reason, you have a huge amount of control over how shapes act and react—with little or no programming—by simply changing the content of the ShapeSheet cells. You learned about the sections, rows, and cells that make up the ShapeSheet and how to make simple changes to cells.

In the next chapter, you learn more about ShapeSheet cells. In particular, you learn Visio's commands for the ShapeSheet, how to type formulas in cells, and how to add sections and rows to a ShapeSheet.

**Customizing ShapeSheets**

# Chapter 6

# *Controlling the ShapeSheet*

In this chapter, you learn more about ShapeSheet cells. In particular, you learn how to:

➤ Add sections and rows to a ShapeSheet

➤ Find and use Visio's commands for ShapeSheets

➤ Print the ShapeSheet

By the end of the chapter, you should be able to navigate around the ShapeSheet section with ease.

## Controlling the ShapeSheet

As noted in the previous chapter, there is one ShapeSheet per object—shape, connector, guide, image, page, and so on. To display the ShapeSheet of an object, you must first select the object. The sole exception to this is the page; to view the ShapeSheet of a page, make sure nothing is selected.

To select an object, click it with the Pointer tool (looks like the standard Windows arrow cursor). Visio lets you know which object is selected by surrounding it with a thin, green, dotted line (called the *alignment box*) and small, green squares (called *handles*).

When you select more than one object, Visio shows the ShapeSheet of the first selected object. The first selected object is the one with the green alignment box and handles; the second and other selected objects have cyan (light blue) or purple alignment boxes and handles. The exception is the page. When no object is selected, Visio displays the ShapeSheet of the page.

You open the ShapeSheet by selecting **Window | Show ShapeSheet** from the menu bar. The ShapeSheet opens in its own window. Typically, Visio *tiles* all open windows so that you see a portion (albeit a smaller portion) of every window. To maximize the ShapeSheet window, double-click its title bar.

# Shortcuts to the ShapeSheet

When you find yourself accessing the ShapeSheet often, Visio provides two shortcuts to access the ShapeSheet faster with fewer screen selections.

The **Developer** toolbar includes an icon to display the ShapeSheet. To open the **Developer** toolbar, right-click anywhere on the toolbar (or select **View | Toolbars** from the menu bar). Select **Developer** from the menu. The fourth button from the left displays the ShapeSheet of the selected object. The usual selection rules apply: when no object is selected, Visio displays the ShapeSheet for the page.

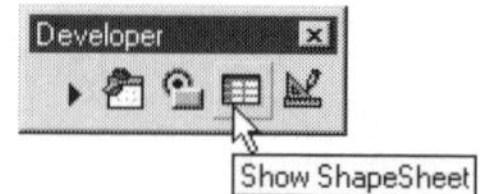


That icon on the Developer toolbar saves you two menu picks (**Window | Show ShapeSheet**). But you still need to select the object first. When you find you are working a lot with the ShapeSheet of a few specific shapes, you may want to change the *double-click behavior* of those shapes. Double-click behavior is a six-syllable term for a simple concept: Visio lets you specify what happens when you double-click a shape.

You can display the ShapeSheet menu on the shortcut menu for an object, page, style, or drawing (click a drawing or style in the Drawing Explorer window). Choose **Format | Behavior**, and click the **Advanced** tab. Under **Developer Settings**, select **Run In Developer Mode**. When you now right-click an object, page, drawing, or style, the **Show ShapeSheet** command appears on the shortcut menu.

The **Format | Behavior, Double Click** tab command presents a list of events that can occur when you double-click a shape. One of the options is **Open Shape's ShapeSheet**. When you double-click a shape, Visio opens its ShapeSheet. That's more efficient than clicking the icon on the Developer toolbar.

You can also assign the behavior on a shape-by-shape basis. While you can assign double-click behavior to shapes, connectors, guides, and images, it does not work with pages. Here are the steps you take to assign double-click behavior to a shape:

1. Select the shape. (You may select more than one shape.)

2. Select **Format | Behavior** from the menu bar. Notice the Behavior dialog box.

3. Select the **Double-Click** tab.

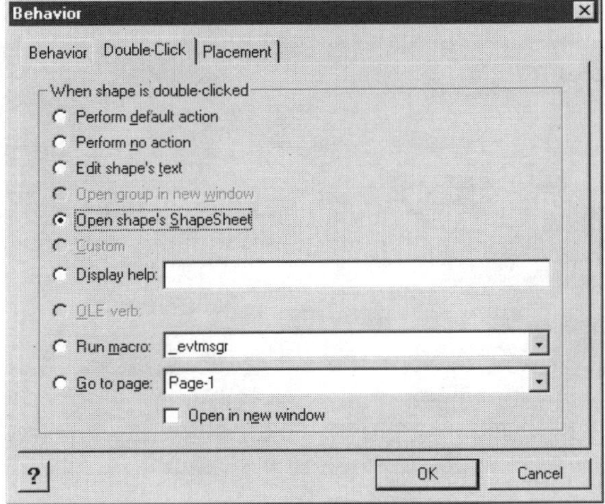


4. Click **Open shape's ShapeSheet**.

5. Click **OK**. The behavior is assigned to the shape.

6. Double-click the shape to test its behavior. Notice that the shape's ShapeSheet window opens.

7. With the ShapeSheet open, take a look at the **Events** section. When you make the selection on the Double-Click tab, Visio made a change to the shape's ShapeSheet. The value of

**EventDblClick** changed from **0** to **OPENSHEETWIN()** in the Events section.

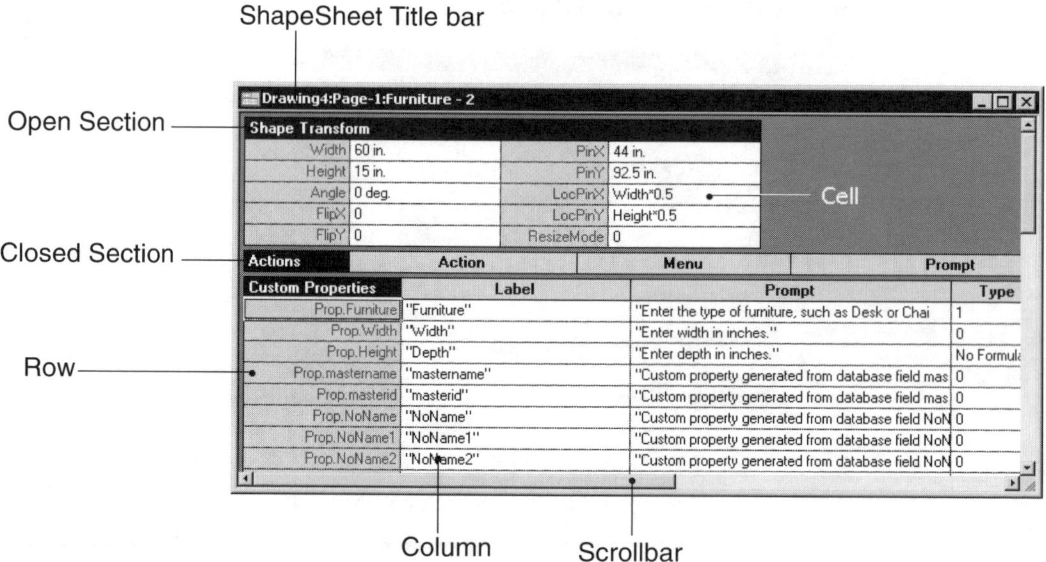

# Opening and Closing Sections

The ShapeSheet window contains one or more (usually more!) *sections*. A section consists of a title bar, and then one or more rows, columns, and cells. Sections look like mini-spreadsheets. For details on the meaning of all ShapeSheet sections and cells, see Chapter 8, "The Complete ShapeSheet Section Reference."

Very often, the ShapeSheet is larger than its window. For this reason, Visio provides two controls for letting you concentrate on specific sections.

You can collapse an unneeded section down to just its title bar:

1. Move the cursor to the title bar of a section. Notice that the cursor changes to a minus sign.

2.  Click the title bar. Notice that the section collapses, except for the title bar. The section is closed.

3.  Notice the cursor is now a plus sign.

4.  Click the title bar and the section expands.

| Shape Transform | | | | | | | |
|---|---|---|---|---|---|---|---|
| Width | 1.5 in. | PinX | 1.75 in. | FlipX | FALSE |
| Height | 1.5 in. | PinY | 7.25 in. | FlipY | FALSE |
| Angle | 0 deg. | LocPinX | Width*0.5 | ResizeMode | 0 |
| | | LocPinY | Height*0.3333 | | |

Some sections can become very wide, such as the Tabs section. When you cannot see the entire width of a section, click the horizontal scroll bar to move the contents in the window.

New to Visio 2000 is the ability to change the width of section columns, just as you can in a spreadsheet.

## Closing the ShapeSheet

To close the ShapeSheet window, click the Close button located in the right corner of the ShapeSheet's title bar.

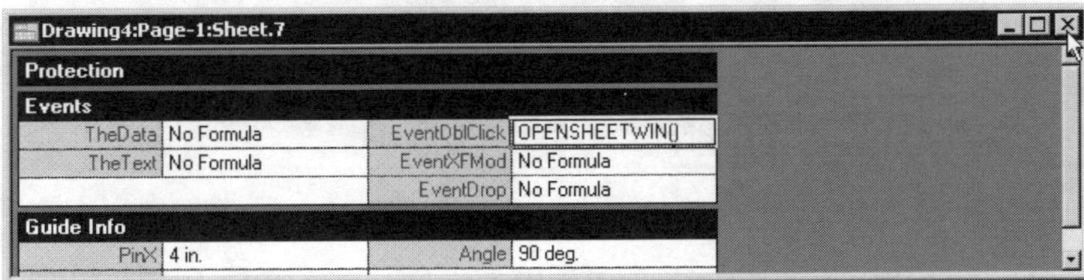

# ShapeSheet Commands

Visio has commands for the ShapeSheet in two locations. Commands are accessed from the menu bar, or by right-clicking to display the shortcut menu.

When you open a ShapeSheet window, notice that the Visio menu bar and toolbar change. The menu bar contains commands specific to working with the ShapeSheet. The toolbar consists of generic buttons that are of no importance to ShapeSheets.

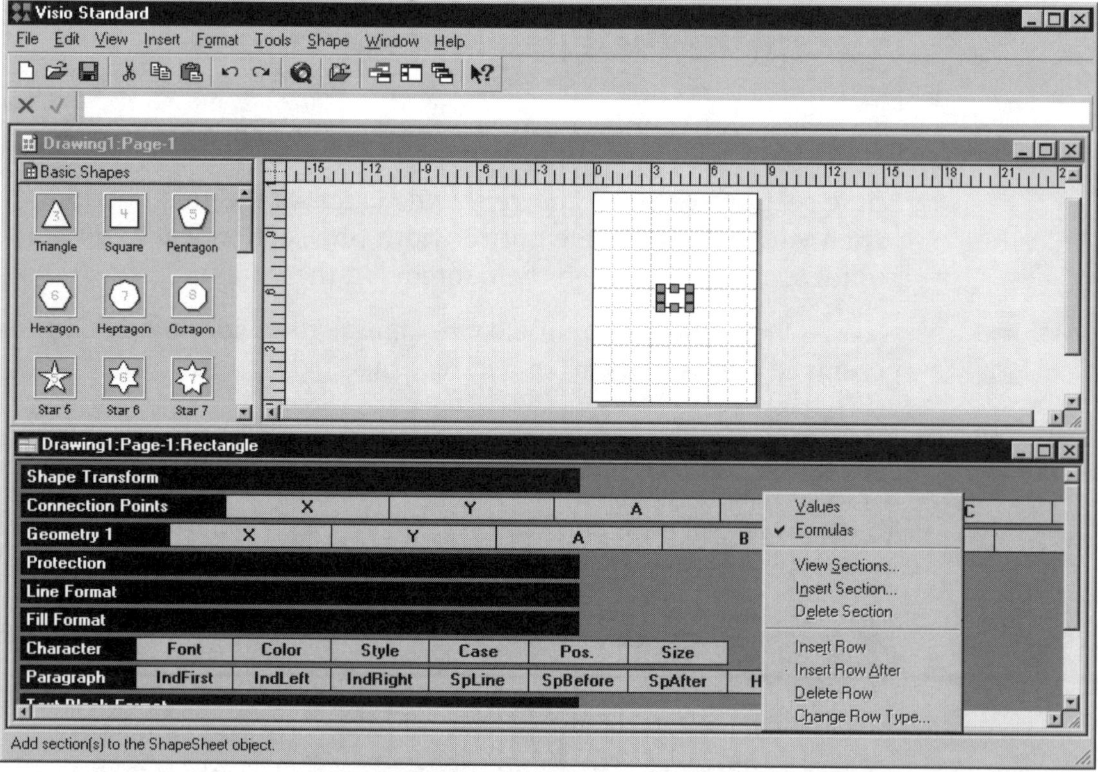

Right-click anywhere in the ShapeSheet to display the shortcut menu. As with the menu bar, the commands on the shortcut menu are specific to the ShapeSheet. The shortcut menu contains all but three of the commands found on the menu bar.

The ShapeSheet commands found on the menu bar and the shortcut menu are:

| Command | Menu Bar | Shortcut Menu |
| --- | --- | --- |
| Action | Edit | ... |
| Change Row Type | Edit | Change Row Type |
| Delete Row | Edit | Delete Row |
| Delete Section | Edit | Delete Section |
| Formulas | View | Formulas |
| Function | Insert | ... |
| Name | Insert | ... |
| Row | Insert | Insert Row |
| Row After | Insert | Insert Row After |
| Section | Insert | Insert Section |
| Show Sections | View | View Sections |
| Values | View | Values |

## Action

Menu bar: **Edit | Action**

Shortcut menu: *none*

Displays the Action dialog box. Specifies an action for a shape, which appears as a command on the shape's shortcut menu. Before you can use the Action command, you must highlight a row in the Action section of the ShapeSheet.

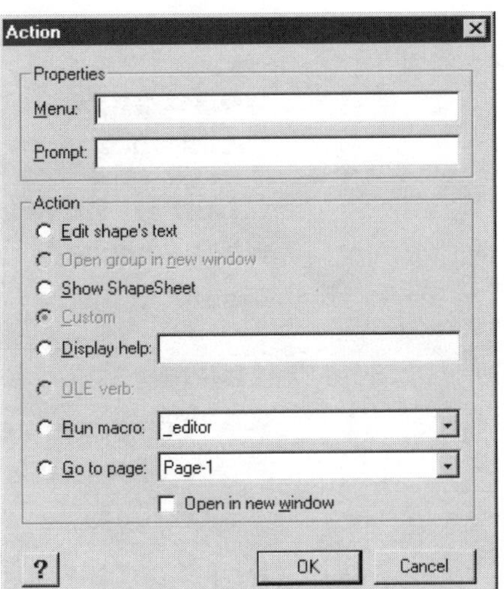


### Command Options

**Menu** specifies the wording that appears on the shortcut menu; usually consists of one or two words.

**Prompt** specifies the wording on the status bar; usually consists of a sentence describing the action.

**Edit shape's text** edits the shape's text block.

**Open group in new window** opens the group in the Group window. Valid only if the shape is part of a group.

**Show ShapeSheet** opens the ShapeSheet window of the object.

**Custom** performs custom action. You enter the formula for this action directly in the Action section of the ShapeSheet spreadsheet.

**Display help** displays an online help topic; uses the following syntax:

> *filename.***hlp!***keyword*
> or
> *filename.***hlp!***#number*

**OLE verb** activates OLE options, such as Edit, when an OLE object is double-clicked.

**Run macro** runs a macro, which you select from the list box.

**Go to page** displays the specified page, which you select from the list box.

**Open in new window** displays the page in a new window when checked; displays the page in the current window when unchecked.

### Tips

➤ The Action dialog box is similar to the **Format | Behavior** dialog box's Double-Click tab, but adds the Menu and Prompt fields.

➤ You may specify only one action per shape.

➤ Insert an Actions section, and then choose Edit | Action.

### Related ShapeSheet Command

*none*

## Change Row Type

Menu bar: **Edit | Change Row Type**

Shortcut menu: **Change Row Type**

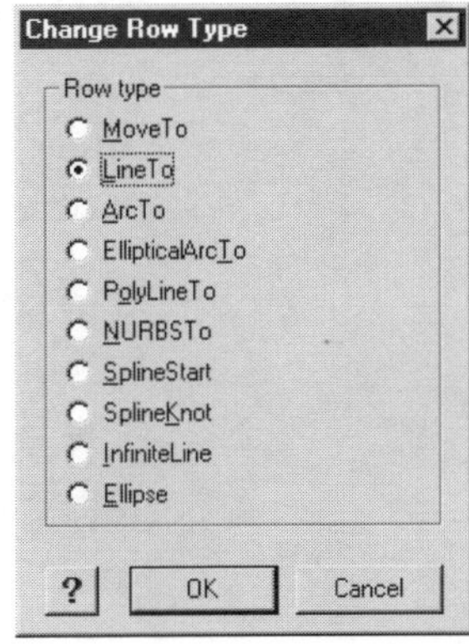

Opens the **Change Row Type** dialog box. This command works only when you have selected a row in the Geometry or Connections section. When a row in the Geometry section is selected, the command lets you change the type of geometry, such as a line to an arc.

### Command Options

**MoveTo** specifies the x,y-coordinates of the first vertex of the shape. Can also be used to move to a point without drawing a line—draws a gap. (New in Visio 2000; replaces the Start cell.)

**LineTo** changes the geometry into a line. The X and Y cells define the endpoint of the line.

**ArcTo** changes the geometry into a circular arc. The X and Y cells define the endpoint of the arc; the A cell defines the bow of the arc.

**EllipticalArcTo** changes the geometry into an elliptical arc. The X and Y cells define the endpoint of the arc; the A and B cells define the coordinates of the arc's control point; the C cell defines the orientation angle; the D cell defines the ratio of the major to minor axis.

**PolyLineTo** changes the geometry into a polyline. The X and Y cells define the x,y-coordinates; cell A contains a polyline formula. (New in Visio 2000.)

**NURBSTo** changes the geometry into a NURBS (non-uniform rational B-spline). The X and Y cells contain the x,y-coordinates; the A cell contains the position of the second-to-last knot; the B cell contains the position of the last weight; the C cell contains the position of the first knot; the D cell contains the position of the first weight; the E cell contains the formula for the non-uniform rational B-spline. (New in Visio 2000.)

**SplineStart** changes the geometry into a spline start. The X and Y cells define the spline's second control point; the A, B, and C cells define the spline's first, second, and last knots; the D cell defines the degree of the spline.

**SplineKnot** changes the geometry into a spline knot. The X and Y cells define the control point; the A cell defines the spline knot.

**InfiniteLine** changes the geometry to an infinite line. The X and Y cells define the x,y-coordinates of two points on an infinite line.

**Ellipse** changes the geometry to an ellipse. The X and Y cells define the x,y-coordinates of the ellipse's center point; the A and B cells contain the coordinates of the first additional point, and the C and D cells contain the coordinates of the second additional point.

### Tips

➤ This command only applies to rows in the Geometry and Controls sections.

➤ You must select a row in a Geometry or Controls section before you can use this command.

➤ Use this command to convert an elliptical arc to a circular arc.

### Related Command

*none*

## Delete Row

Menu bar: **Edit | Delete Row**

Shortcut menu: **Delete Row**

Deletes a row in the ShapeSheet section. You must select a row for this command to work.

## Command Options

*none*

## Tips

➤ You restore the deleted row with the **Edit | Undo** command.

➤ When you delete a row, the shape's behavior may change.

## Related Commands

Insert Row

Insert Row After

# Delete Section

Menu bar: **Edit | Delete Section**

Shortcut menu: **Delete Section**

Deletes the ShapeSheet section. You must select a section before using this command.

## Command Options

*none*

## Tips

➤ You restore the deleted section with the **Edit | Undo** command.

➤ When you delete a section, the shape's behavior may change.

## Related Command

Insert Section

# Formulas

Menu bar: **View | Formulas**

Shortcut menu: **Formulas**

Displays formulas in cells, instead of values.

## Command Options

*none*

## Tips

➤ Normally, you want to see formulae in the ShapeSheet cells. To have Visio evaluate the formulae, select **View | Values**.

➤ The illustration shows formulae (left) and values (right):

| Geometry 1 | | |
|---|---|---|
| Geometry1.NoFill | FALSE | Geometry1.NoLine |
| **Name** | **X** | **Y** |
| 1 MoveTo | Width*1.0774 | Height*0 |
| 2 LineTo | Width*0.5 | Height*1 |
| 3 LineTo | Width*-0.0774 | Height*0 |
| 4 LineTo | Geometry1.X1 | Geometry1.Y1 |

| Geometry 1 | | |
|---|---|---|
| Geometry1.NoFill | FALSE | Geometry1.NoLine |
| **Name** | **X** | **Y** |
| 1 MoveTo | 1.6160 in. | 0.0000 in. |
| 2 LineTo | 0.7500 in. | 1.5000 in. |
| 3 LineTo | -0.1160 in. | 0.0000 in. |
| 4 LineTo | 1.6160 in. | 0.0000 in. |

## Related Command

Values

# Function

Menu bar: **Insert | Function**

Shortcut menu: *none*

Displays the Insert Function dialog box, which lists the names of all functions that work in Visio cells. This command is not available until the cursor is in the formula bar.

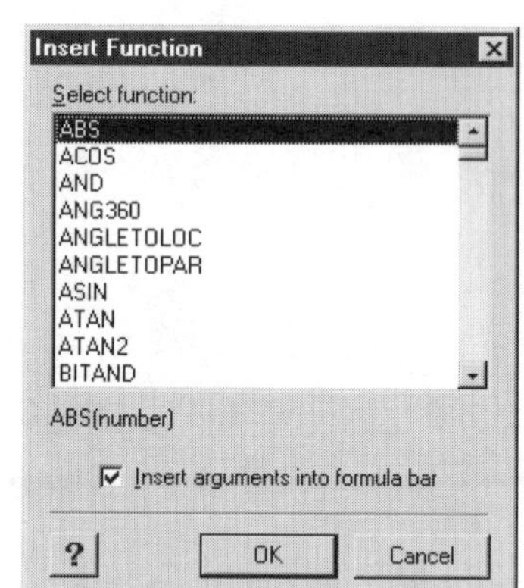


## Command Options

**Select function** lists the names of functions Visio provides for use in ShapeSheet cells.

**Insert arguments into formula bar** inserts the function name and the names of its arguments, when checked, such as:

**DATE(year, month, day)**

You must enter the appropriate values of the arguments yourself. When unchecked, only the function name and its parentheses are inserted, such as:

**DATE()**

## Tips

➤ This command works only when the cursor is in the formula bar.

➤ Functions can be used in any ShapeSheet cell.

➤ The most common function is to reference another cell, such as:

**= Width**

## Related Commands

Name

Section

# Name

Menu bar: **Insert | Name**

Shortcut menu: *none*

Displays the dialog box, which lists the names of all cells found in the ShapeSheet. This command is not available until the cursor is in the formula bar.

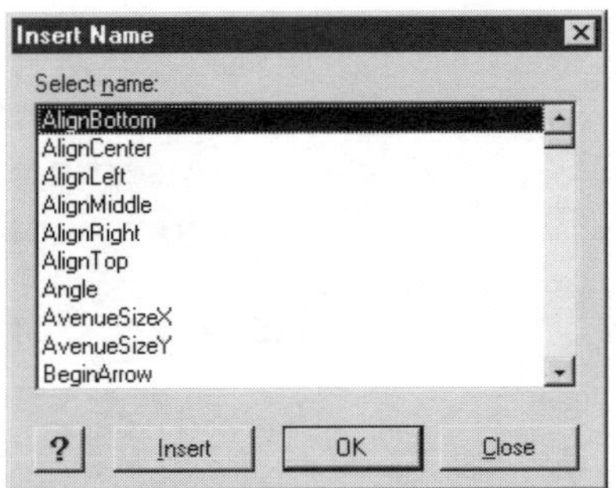


## Command Option

**Select name** lists the names of cells in the ShapeSheet.

## Tips

➤ This command works only when the cursor is in the formula bar.

➤ To insert more than one cell name, click the **Insert** button instead of the **OK** button.

➤ To simply reference another cell, use the equal sign:

**= Height**

### Related Command

Function

Row

## Row

Menu bar: **Insert | Row**

Shortcut menu: **Insert Row**

Inserts a row before the selected row in a section. This command does not work until you select a row.

### Command Options

*none*

### Tips

➤ Before you can use this command, you must select a row.

➤ This command inserts a row before the selected row; to insert a row after the selected row, use the **Row After** command.

### Related Command

Row After

Delete Row

## Row After

Menu bar: **Insert | Row After**

Shortcut menu: **Insert Row After**

Inserts a row after the selected row in a section. This command does not work until you select a row.

## Command Options

*none*

## Tips

➤ Before you can use this command, you must select a row.

➤ This command inserts a row after the selected row; to insert a row before the selected row, use the **Row** command.

## Related Command

Row

Delete Row

# Section

Menu bar: **Insert | Section**

Shortcut menu: **Insert Section**

Displays the Insert Section dialog box to add sections to a ShapeSheet. Visio does not display all sections that apply to the shape. This dialog box lets you insert sections that are not already displayed. Section names that are grayed out are already inserted or may not be inserted by this shape.

The illustration shows the Insert Section dialog boxes for a shape (left) and a page (right).

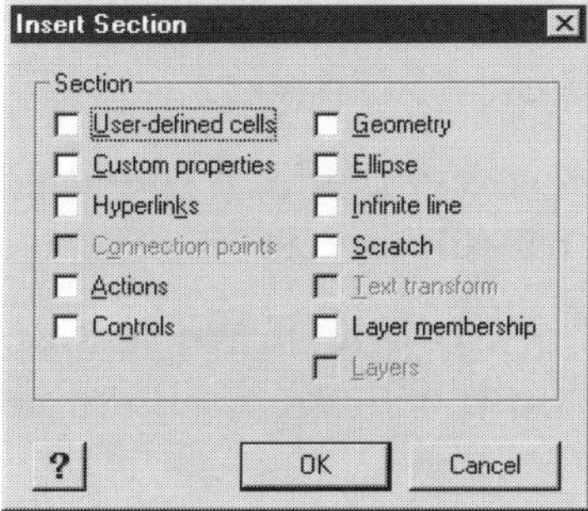


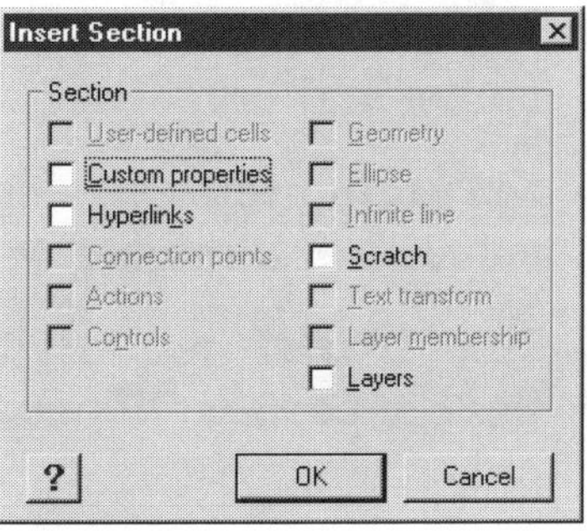

## Command Options

**Actions** inserts the Action section, which lets you specify an action for the object. Valid for all objects.

**Connection points** inserts the Connection Points section, which specifies the x,y-coordinates for connection points on the object. Valid for all shapes and images.

**Controls** inserts the Controls section, which specifies the x,y-coordinates, behavior, and anchor point for control handles on the object's alignment box. Valid for all shapes and images.

**Custom properties** inserts the Custom Properties section, which specifies the custom properties of the object. Valid for all objects.

**Ellipse** inserts a new Geometry section with an Ellipse row (new in Visio 2000).

**Geometry** inserts the Geometry *n* section, which specifies the vertices for the path of a shape. You may insert more than one Geometry section. Valid for all shapes and images.

**Hyperlinks** inserts the Hyperlinks section, which specifies the filenames and URLs of linked documents (new in Visio 2000).

**Infinite line** inserts a new Geometry section with an **InfiniteLine** row (new in Visio 2000).

**Layer membership** inserts the Layer Membership section, which specifies the name(s) of the object's layer assignment. Not available for pages.

**Layers** inserts the Layers section, which specifies the layer names and properties. Valid only for pages.

**Scratch** inserts the Scratch section, which specifies user-defined values and formulae. Valid for all objects.

**Text transform** inserts the Text Transform section, which specifies the position of text within the shape's alignment box. Valid only for shapes.

**User-defined cells** inserts the User-defined cells section, which specifies user-defined data. Valid for all objects.

## Tips

➤ The **Geometry** section can be inserted more than once. Additional sections are labeled **Geometry 2**, **Geometry 3**, etc.

➤ Sometimes a section is inserted but not visible. Before using the **Insert Section** command, make all sections visible with the **Show Sections** command.

➤ To remove a section, use the **Delete Section** command. Some sections cannot be removed.

➤ To insert a row in a section, use the **Row** command.

## Related Commands

Show Sections

Delete Section

Row

## Show Sections

Menu bar: **View | Sections**

Shortcut menu: **View Sections**

Displays the **View Sections** dialog box, which lets you display additional sections in ShapeSheet. Visio does not display all sections that apply to the shape. This dialog box lets you show sections that are not already displayed.

A check mark means the section is displayed. No check mark means the

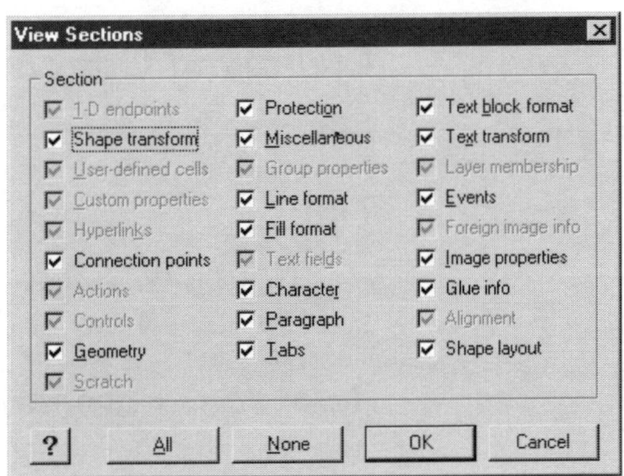

section is not displayed. A section name is grayed out when it is not valid for this shape.

## Command Options

**All** displays all valid ShapeSheet sections.

**None** hides all valid ShapeSheet sections.

## Tips

➤ These options are different when you view each object: shape, page, drawing, and style.

➤ Before using this command, use the **Sections** command to insert the needed section. The **View Sections** command will not display sections that have not yet been inserted.

➤ When a section name is grayed out in the View Sections dialog box, it is not a valid section for the object.

➤ Click the section title bar to collapse and expand a section.

## Related Command

Sections

# Values

Menu bar: **View | Values**

Shortcut menu: **Values**

Displays values in cells, instead of formulae.

## Command Options

*none*

## Tip

➤ Normally, you want to see formulae in the ShapeSheet cells. To have Visio evaluate the formulae, select **View | Values**.

## Related Command

Formula

# Printing the ShapeSheet

The **Tools | Macros | Visio Extras | Print ShapeSheet** command lets you print out a copy of the ShapeSheet on a printer connected to your computer. Optionally, you can redirect the ShapeSheet printout to the Windows Clipboard or to a file on disk.

The **Print ShapeSheet** command prints the ShapeSheet for selected objects. When no object is selected, the command prints the ShapeSheet for the current page. This command is similar to the List and DbList commands in IntelliCAD.

This command is available from the menu bar displayed only with the drawing window. The command displays the Print ShapeSheet dialog box.

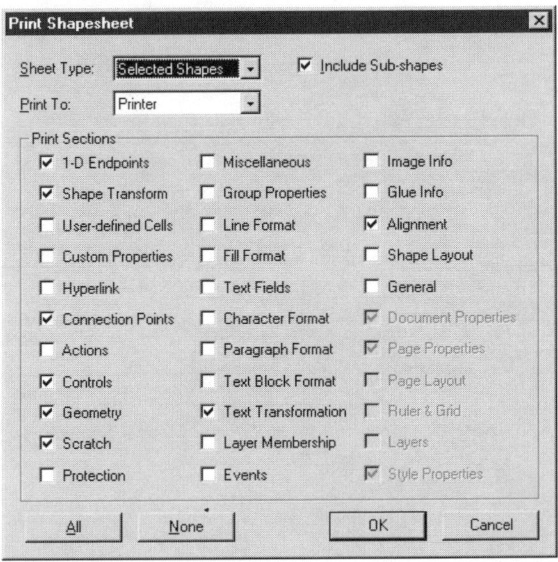



In the **Print Sections** area, you can select the sections you want printed. A check mark means the section will be printed, such as **1-D Endpoints**, in the figure. No check mark means the section will not be printed, such as **Miscellaneous**. If a section name is grayed out, the section does not exist with the selected object, such as **Document Properties**.



**Customizing ShapeSheets**

The **Include Sub-shapes** option prints reports for all related shapes.

By default, Visio automatically places a check mark next to all sections displayed in the ShapeSheet. To select all sections, click the **All** button; conversely, click the **None** button to deselect all section names.

The **Print To** list box sends the ShapeSheet report to the printer, a file on disk, or to the Windows Clipboard. Clicking the **OK** button with **Printer** option selected brings up the standard Windows Print dialog box, which lets you select the printer and its settings. The **File** option displays the Save As file dialog box, which lets you select a folder and specify the filename. The file will have the .TXT extension. The Clipboard data can be pasted in a word processor or a spreadsheet.

```
SHAPESHEET : TRIANGLE SHEET.1
Start Section : 1-D ENDPOINTS
End Section : 1-D ENDPOINTS   (CELLS TOTAL : 0)

Start Section : SHAPE TRANSFORM
Cell      Value    Formula
Width    1.5000 in.        1.5 inches
Height   1.5000 in.        1.5 inches
Angle    0.0000 deg.       0 degrees
PinX     1.7500 in.        1.75 inches
PinY     7.2500 in.        7.25 inches
LocPinX  0.7500 in.        Width*0.5
LocPinY  0.5000 in.        Height*0.33333333333333
FlipX    FALSE    FALSE
FlipY    FALSE    FALSE
ResizeMode       0         0
End Section : SHAPE TRANSFORM   (CELLS TOTAL : 10)

Start Section : CONNECTION POINTS
Cell      Value    Formula
Connections.X1   0.7500 in.       Width*0.5
Connections.Y1   0.5000 in.       Height*0.33333333333333
Connections.X2   1.6250 in.       Width*1.0833333333333
Connections.Y2   0.0000 in.       Height*0
Connections.X3   -0.1250 in.      Width*-0.08333333333333
Connections.Y3   0.0000 in.       Height*0
Connections.X4   0.7500 in.       Width*0.5
Connections.Y4   1.5000 in.       Height*1
End Section : CONNECTION POINTS   (CELLS TOTAL : 8)

Start Section : CONTROLS
End Section : CONTROLS   (CELLS TOTAL : 0)
```

# Chapter Review

In this chapter, you learned how to find and use Visio's commands for ShapeSheets, and how to add sections and rows to a ShapeSheet.

In the next chapter, you learn how to use the ShapeSheet sections to control shapes, pages, and the drawing.

**Customizing ShapeSheets**

# Chapter 7

# *Customizing and Programming ShapeSheets*

The most powerful, yet simple, method for making Visio work for you is by customizing the ShapeSheet. In this chapter, you learn how to change some sections of the ShapeSheet. In particular, the exercises in this chapter work with the Custom Properties section. It is through custom properties that Visio lets you add your own data to a shape, such as pricing information or model number.

This book does not attempt to teach you how to program Visio with a programming language, such as Visual Basic for Applications (included with Visio), Visual Basic, or C++. (For programming Visio, get the book *Visio 2000 Developer's Guide: Software Patterns*, ISBN 1-55622-738-8, from Wordware Publishing.) In this chapter, however, you are introduced to typing simple formulae in ShapeSheet cells.

In this chapter, you learn about:

➤ Creating a custom property

➤ Adding a command to a shape's shortcut menu

➤ Making a master from the shape

➤ Writing ShapeSheet formulae

➤ Referencing section names

By the end of this chapter, you should be able to create custom properties and have an understanding of writing simple formulae in ShapeSheet cells.

# Introduction to Custom Properties

A *custom property* is a piece of data attached to a shape, such as the inventory number of a piece of furniture. Custom properties are the same as attributes found in AutoCAD and IntelliCAD, or tags in MicroStation.

A shape can have none, one, or more custom properties. Many of the shapes included with Visio contain one or more custom properties.

You can easily create new custom properties and edit existing ones. Once the custom properties are set up, you can enter data, change the data, and export the data to a spreadsheet.

**To add custom properties:** When a shape does not have custom properties, you add them by selecting **Shape | Custom Properties**. New in Visio 2000 is a helpful dialog box that asks "No custom properties exist. Would you like to define custom properties now?" Select **Yes**, and Visio displays the Define Custom Properties dialog box.

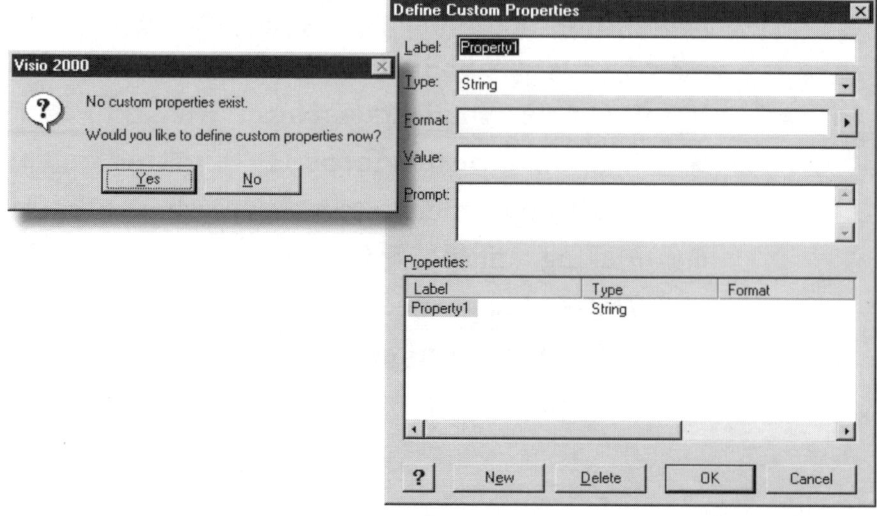

If you find the Define Custom Properties dialog box intimidating, the **Custom Properties Editor** (select **Tools | Macros | Custom Properties Editor** from the menu bar) is a wizard-style interface that leads you through the steps of creating a custom property.

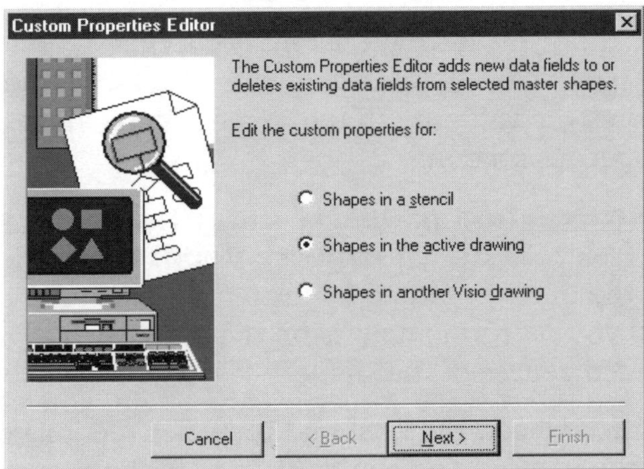



Another alternative is to insert the Custom Properties section in the shape's ShapeSheet, then define the properties and values. We study this approach in this chapter as a way of learning how the ShapeSheet works.

**To edit custom property values:** There are several ways you can enter (or edit) custom property values. Each of these displays the Custom Properties dialog box. This assumes the shape already has custom properties:

➤ Right-click the shape in the drawing, and select **Properties**.

➤ Select **Shape | Custom Properties** from the drawing and shapes menu bar.

➤ Select **Shape | Actions | Properties** from the drawing menu bar.

➤ In some cases, the Custom Properties dialog box pops up automatically when you drag the shape from the stencil into the drawing. This is controlled by the **Ask** cell of the Custom Properties section.

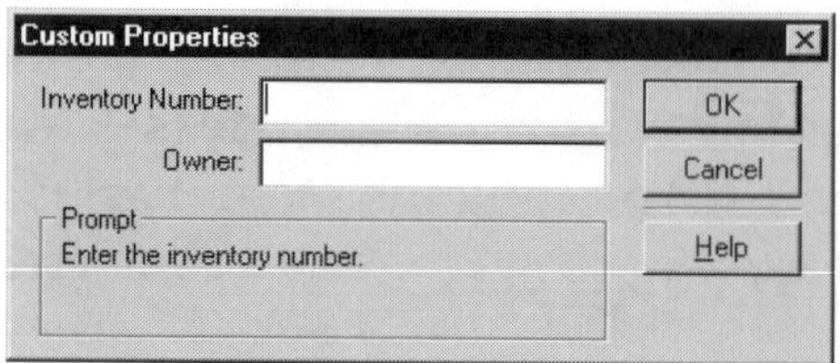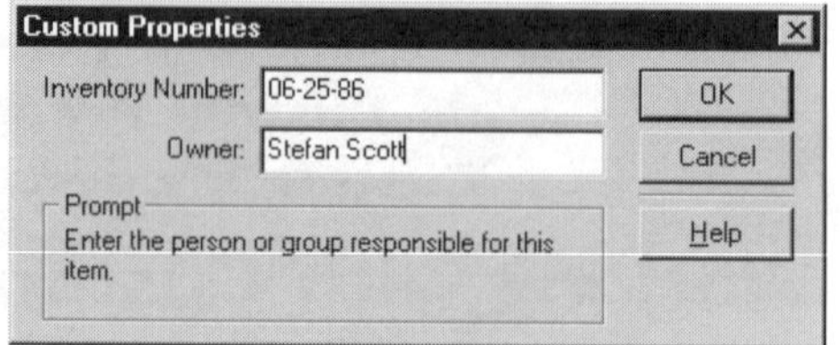

The first time you see the Custom Properties dialog box, it usually has blank values. Once you enter values and press **Enter**, Visio stores the values with the shape's ShapeSheet in the Custom Properties section.

**To export custom property data:** The Property Reporting Wizard (select **Tools | Property Report** from the menu bar) exports the data contained in custom properties to a spreadsheet. This lets you perform analysis on the data, such as simply counting all occurrences of the shape.

In the spreadsheet, the Custom Properties section contains cells that do the work of associating data with the shape. Later in this chapter, you learn the meaning of every cell in the section.

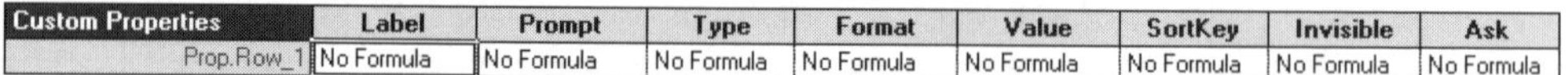

| Custom Properties | Label | Prompt | Type | Format | Value | SortKey | Invisible | Ask |
|---|---|---|---|---|---|---|---|---|
| Prop.Row_1 | No Formula | No Formula | No Formula | No Formula | No Formula | No Formula | No Formula | No Formula |

When you compare the ShapeSheet section with the Custom Properties dialog box, you can see corresponding ShapeSheet cells and dialog box options.

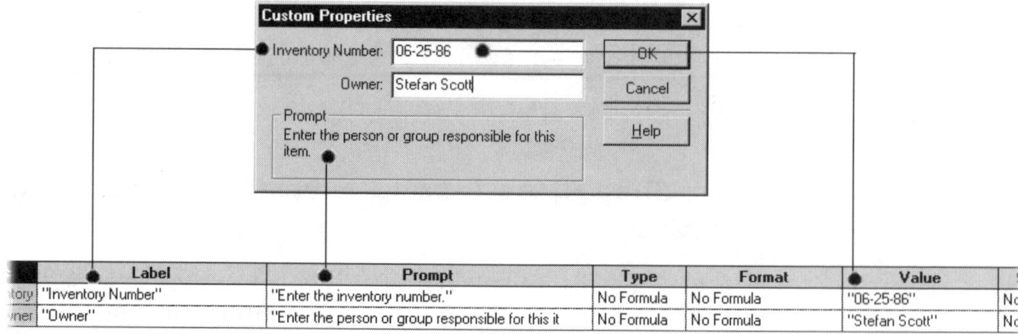

| | Label | | Prompt | Type | Format | | Value | |
|---|---|---|---|---|---|---|---|---|
| tory | "Inventory Number" | | "Enter the inventory number." | No Formula | No Formula | | "06-25-86" | No |
| ner | "Owner" | | "Enter the person or group responsible for this it | No Formula | No Formula | | "Stefan Scott" | No |

You can add custom properties to the following Visio objects: 1D and 2D shapes, pages, inserted objects, guides, etc.

# Working with Custom Properties

To explore the power that custom properties have, we'll work through a tutorial. In the tutorial, you create a desk shape from a rectangle shape. Then, you add custom properties to the desk shape that describe it, such as size, location, model number, and purchase date. The tutorial includes these general steps:

➤ Creating the Custom Properties section

➤ Seeing the link between the section and the dialog box

➤ Understanding the purpose of each cell in the Custom Properties section

➤ Adding text to the shape

## *Creating the Custom Properties Section*

A shape doesn't have custom properties until you (or someone else) add them. In the following steps, you add the Custom Properties section to a rectangle shape.

1. Start Visio with a new drawing.

2. Open the **Basic Shapes** stencil, found in the **\Visio 2000\Solutions\Block Diagram** folder.

3. Drag the **Rectangle** shape from the stencil into the drawing.

4. Open the ShapeSheet with **Window | Show ShapeSheet**.

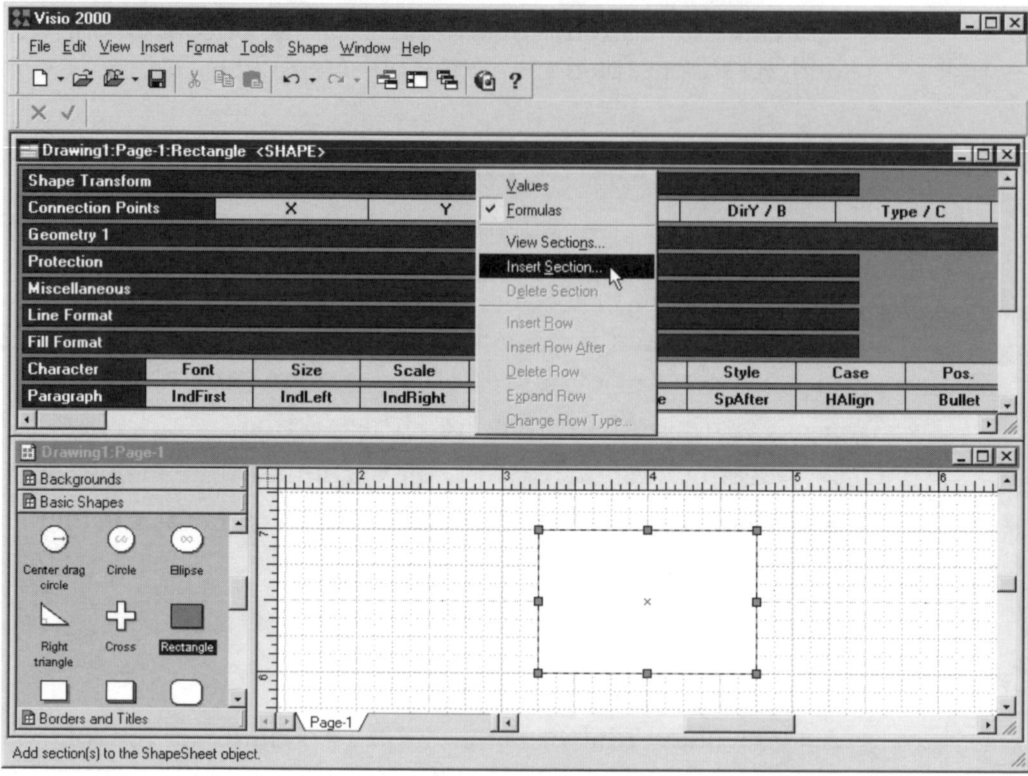

5.  Look through the ShapeSheet sections. Notice that there is no section for custom properties.

6.  To add the Custom Properties section, right-click anywhere in the ShapeSheet window. Select **Insert Section** from the shortcut menu. Notice that the Insert Section dialog box displays section names in two colors: black and gray. The black section names, such as User-defined cells and Custom Properties, are ones that may be added to the rectangle shape. The gray section names, such as Connection Points and Layers, are not appropriate for this shape or are already present in the ShapeSheet.

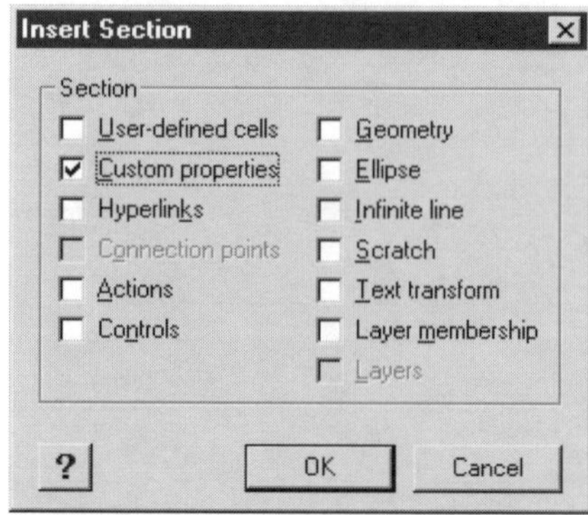

7.  Select **Custom Properties** and click **OK**. Notice that Visio adds the Custom Properties section to the ShapeSheet. The section has a single row called **Prop.Row_1** with every value set to **No Formula**.

| Custom Properties | Label | Prompt | Type | Format | Value | SortKey | Invisible | Ask |
|---|---|---|---|---|---|---|---|---|
| Prop.Row_1 | No Formula | No Formula | No Formula | No Formula | No Formula | No Formula | No Formula | No Formula |

## Seeing the Link between the Section and the Dialog Box

The Custom Properties dialog box presents a friendly interface to the data contained in the cells of the Custom Properties ShapeSheet section. In the following steps, you display the Custom Properties dialog box and enter the value.

1.  To see why this is so, select **Shape | Custom Properties** from the menu bar. Visio displays the Custom Properties dialog box: the label is **Row_1** and the prompt area is blank.

2.  Type **Desk**.

3.  Click the **OK** button to dismiss the Custom Properties dialog box. In the ShapeSheet section, notice that the cell under **Value** changes from **No Formula** to **Desk**. That little exercise showed you that the Custom Properties dialog box is directly linked to the **Custom Properties** ShapeSheet section.

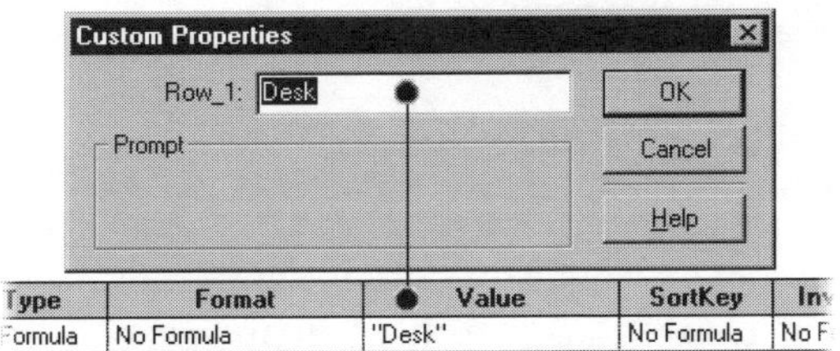

## Understanding the Purpose of Each Cell

### Label Cell

When the **Label** cell contains **No Formula**, Visio displays the row name as the label in the dialog box, such as Row_1. The purpose of the Label cell is to let you change the text to something less generic and more meaningful.

In the following steps, you change the label:

1. Double-click the cell below Label, which contains **No Formula**.
2. Type the word **Furniture**.
3. Press **Enter**. Notice that the cell changes to **"Furniture"** and that the text color is blue.

   Also notice the word has quotation marks ("") surrounding it. Visio automatically adds the quotation marks because it knows that Furniture is a text string. (If there were no quotation marks, Visio would try to treat the word as a variable.)

   Finally, notice that the word Furniture is in blue. This is how Visio indicates changed cells; unchanged cells have black text.

4. Select **Shape | Custom Properties** to bring up the Custom Properties dialog box. Notice that the label has changed from **Row_1** to **Furniture**.

5. Click **OK** to dismiss the dialog box.

### Prompt Cell

It may be that the Label is enough of a prompt to assist the user in filling in the value. Nevertheless, Visio provides context-sensitive help via the **Prompt** cell. It specifies the text that appears in the **Prompt** section of the Custom Properties dialog box.

In the following steps, you create the label:

1. Click the cell below Prompt, which contains **No Formula**.

2. Type the sentence **Enter the type of furniture, such as Desk or Chair**.

3. Press **Enter**. Notice that the cell changes to **"Enter the type of furniture, such as Desk or Chair"**. As with the label, the sentence is surrounded by quotation marks and is colored blue.

4. Select **Shape | Custom Properties** to bring up the Custom Properties dialog box. Notice that the prompt area is no longer blank but filled in.

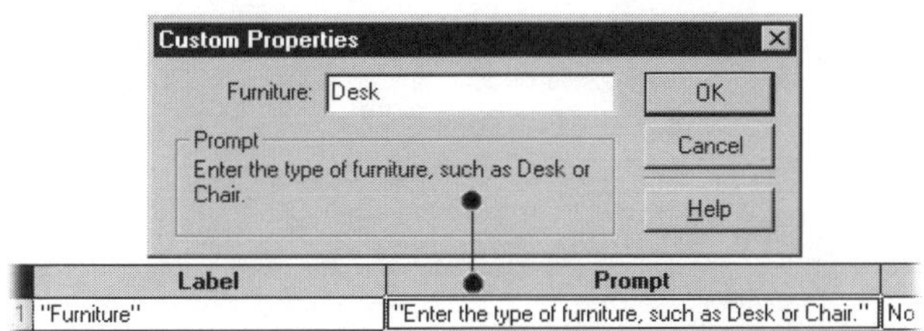


5. Click **OK** to dismiss the dialog box.

### *Invisible Cell*

We are going to skip over some cells and leave them for later, since they are more complex. We'll move on to the **Invisible** cell, which determines whether or not the Custom Properties dialog box displays a row.

Normally, rows are displayed. By making the row invisible, the **Value** cell cannot be changed from the dialog box. Invisible cells provide a low level of security; a knowledgeable user can always edit the ShapeSheet, just as you are doing right now!

In the following steps, you see the effect of this cell and are introduced to the formula bar.

1. Double-click the cell below Invisible, which contains **No Formula**. Notice the equal sign (=). This means that Visio is expecting a formula. Don't worry about formulae now. You may need to scroll to view the Invisible cell.

2. Type the number **1** and press **Enter.** Notice that the cell changes to **TRUE** without quotation marks. When a word or a number is not surrounded by quotation marks, Visio treats it as a number. If the cell contained **"TRUE"**, Visio would treat that as text, not a number. As with the other cells you changed, the number is colored blue.

   This cell is called a *toggle* cell because it can contain only two kinds of value: on or off, just like a light switch. Visio has several ways in which it recognizes on and off values, as shown in the following table:

| Yes | No |
|---|---|
| TRUE | FALSE |
| 1 | 0 |
| Non-0 | No Formula |

   To make this row invisible, you can enter **true**, **1**, or any value other than **false** or **0** (that's the meaning of *non-0*). To make the row visible, you can enter **false** or **0**. It seems that only Visio can enter the value of **No formula**.

3. Select **Shape | Custom Properties** to bring up the Custom Properties dialog box. Visio says "No custom properties exist!" But we know the truth: setting the **Invisible** cell to **1** (or any other value that isn't zero) makes it *appear* as if a custom property does not exist.

 **Note:**
When the Custom Properties section contains more than one row, and one row is made invisible, then Visio would display the Custom Properties dialog box with the visible rows.

4. Click **No** to dismiss the dialog box.

5. Change the **Invisible** cell to **0** and open the Custom Properties dialog box. Notice that the dialog box shows the custom property. Click **OK** to dismiss the dialog box.

### *Ask Cell*

**Ask** determines whether the Custom Property dialog box is displayed automatically under two conditions: (1) when the shape is dragged from the stencil onto the page; or (2) when the shape is copied. (If you do not see the Ask cell in the ShapeSheet, you need to click the horizontal scroll bar.)

Like Invisible, Ask is a toggle cell. To turn on the feature, enter **true** or **1** in the cell. Ask works in conjunction with Invisible. When all rows are invisible, then there is nothing to ask! So the setting of Ask has no effect when all Custom Properties rows are invisible.

In the following exercise, you add two more rows to the Custom Properties section to see the effect of the Ask cell.

1. Right-click the first row in the Custom Properties section (not the title bar).

2. Select **Insert Rows** from the shortcut menu. Notice that the second row receives the generic name of **Prop.Row_2**.

3. Repeat steps 1 and 2 to add a third row. Notice that Visio fills each cell with **No Formula**. It would be nice if Visio would optionally copy all the values from the previous row. That would make life easier for us hard-working programmers!

| Custom Properties | Label | Prompt | Type | Format | Value | SortKey | Invis |
|---|---|---|---|---|---|---|---|
| Prop.Row_1 | "Furniture" | "Enter the type of furniture, such as Desk or Chair." | No Formula | No Formula | "Desk" | No Formula | 0 |
| Prop.Row_2 | No Formula | No Formula | No Formula | No Formula | No Formula | No Formula | No For |
| Prop.Row_3 | No Formula | No Formula | No Formula | No Formula | No Formula | No Formula | No For |

4. Enter the following data into the two new rows:

| Row | Label | Prompt | Value | Invisible | Ask |
|-----|-------|--------|-------|-----------|-----|
| Prop.Row_2 | Width | Enter width in inches | 36 in. | 1 | 1 |
| Prop.Row_3 | Depth | Enter depth in inches. | 24 in. | 0 | 0 |

***Tip:***

You can use the arrow keys on your keyboard to move from one cell to another cell. The names of the rows, such as Prop.Row_2, can be renamed.

| Custom Properties | Label | Prompt | Type | Format | Value | SortKey | Invisible | Ask |
|-------------------|-------|--------|------|--------|-------|---------|-----------|-----|
| Prop.Row_1 | "Furniture" | "Enter the type of furniture, such as Desk or Chai | No Formula | No Formula | "Desk" | No Formula | 0 | 1 |
| Prop.Row_2 | "Width" | "Enter width in inches." | No Formula | No Formula | 36 in. | No Formula | 1 | 1 |
| Prop.Row_3 | "Depth" | "Enter depth in inches." | No Formula | No Formula | 24 in. | No Formula | 0 | 0 |

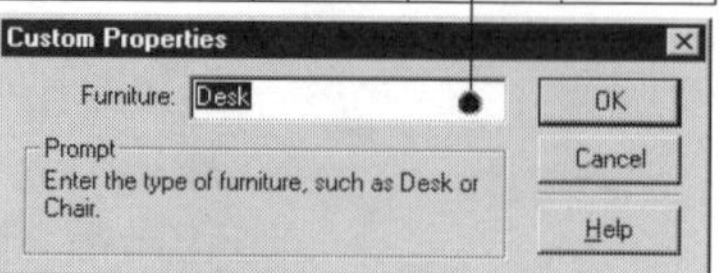


5. Click the drawing window. Make a copy of the rectangle shape (hold down the **Ctrl** key and drag the rectangle to make a copy). When you let go, notice that the Custom Properties dialog box displays only the **Furniture** custom property. That's because row 2 is turned off by **Invisible = 1**; row 3 is turned off by **Ask = 0**.

6. Click **OK** to dismiss the dialog box.

7. Select **Shape | Custom Properties** from the menu bar. Notice that the dialog box now displays two rows, **Furniture** and **Depth**. That's because row 2 is turned off by **Invisible = 1**. The Ask cell does not affect the display of the Custom Properties dialog box when it appears via the menu bar. Ask comes into effect only when you copy the shape.

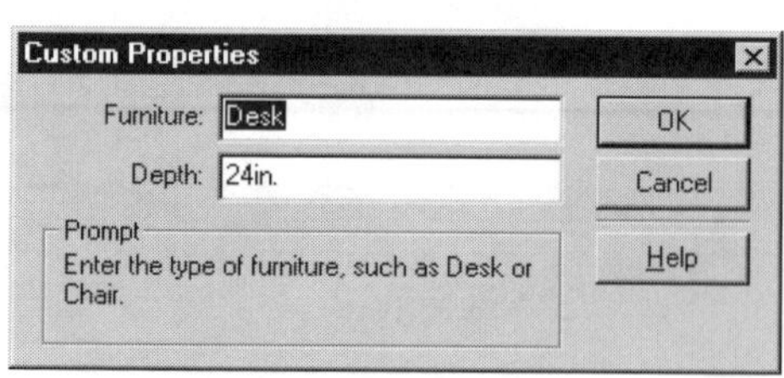

8.  Back in the ShapeSheet, set all three Invisible cells to 0 and all three Ask cells to 1. That ensures that their dialog box always displays all three rows of custom properties in the Custom Properties dialog box and when you copy the shape.

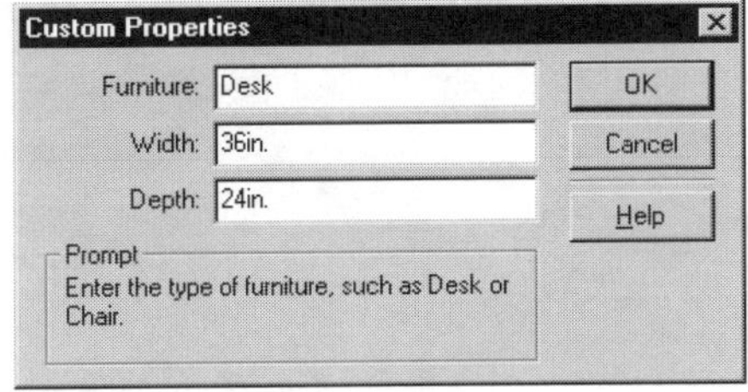

### SortKey Cell

Visio normally displays the custom properties in the order they appear in the section rows. The **SortKey** cell lets you change the order, by specifying the order in which items should be listed in the dialog box.

The sort is locale specific, case insensitive, and ascending. Locale specific means that Visio takes into account the language your computer is operating under. Case insensitive means Visio ignores the difference between uppercase and lowercase. Ascending means that the sort order is 1 to 9, and A to Z.

It may seem strange that the sort key is a string, and not a number. The string allows you to use words for the sort order. For example, you could use the words "first," "second," "third," and "fourth." Visio automatically encloses the "numbers" in quotation marks. In the following exercise, you change the display order of the custom properties:

By the way, can you guess how Visio would sort "first," "second," "third," and "fourth?" The answer is at the end of this section.

1.  We want the Depth listed before the Width. Enter the following values in the **Sort** cells:

| Row | Label | Sort |
| --- | --- | --- |
| Prop.Row_1 | Furniture | 1 |
| Prop.Row_2 | Width | 3 |
| Prop.Row_3 | Depth | 2 |

2.  Select any of the rectangle shapes. Select **Shape | Custom Properties** from the menu bar. Notice that the dialog box

displays the three items in the order you specified: Depth before Width. Click **OK**.

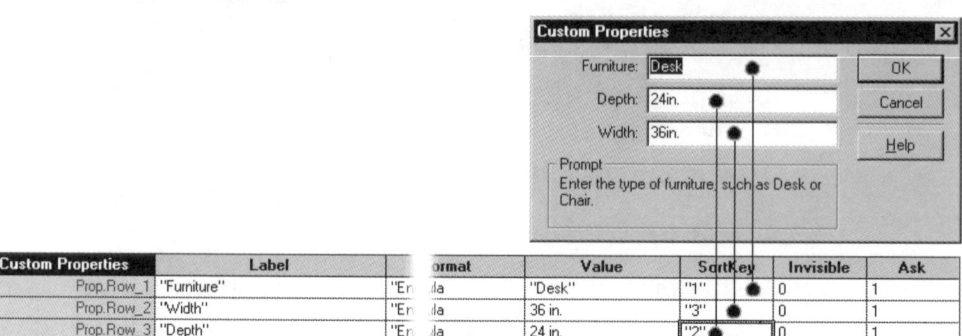

| Custom Properties | Label | | ormat | Value | SortKey | Invisible | Ask |
|---|---|---|---|---|---|---|---|
| Prop.Row_1 | "Furniture" | | "En  la | "Desk" | "1" | 0 | 1 |
| Prop.Row_2 | "Width" | | "En  la | 36 in. | "3" | 0 | 1 |
| Prop.Row_3 | "Depth" | | "En  la | 24 in. | "2" | 0 | 1 |

The answer to the quiz question: Visio would sort in the order of "first," "fourth," "second," and "third." That's because "fourth" comes in the dictionary before "second."

## *Value Cell*

We touched upon the **Value** cell earlier. It contains the values the user enters. Or, it can contain a default value that you specify via the ShapeSheet. Be careful, though, because whatever you have stored in the Value cell will be overwritten by the value entered by the user. Visio does have a **Guard()** function to guard cells against changes, but the function does not protect the contents Value cell.

When you created the Width and Depth rows, you entered arbitrary values (though standard values for a desk). It would be cool if the rectangle shape could change its size according to the values entered by the user.

From Chapter 6 in this book, you know that the size of the Rectangle shape is controlled by the Shape Transform section. The section contains two cells, Width and Height, that specify the size of the rectangle. To make the shape change its size according to its custom properties, you use the following formula:

=Prop.Row_2

Let's examine what this stuff means, with its weird punctuation:

**=**   If you have ever typed a formula in a spreadsheet, then you know that the = prefix signals the start of a formula.

**Prop**   This is shorthand notation for the Custom Properties section. It describes the section that owns the cell. Think of this as being the name of the parent.

**.**   The dot is a separator. It separates the section name from the cell name.

**Row_2**   This refers to the row name, depending on the section. Think of this as being the name of the child. In a *section.cell* name the surname comes before the given name. The names are separated by a dot: Prop.Row_2 refers to row #2 of the (*Custom*) Prop(*erties*) section.

In the case of the Custom Properties section, the row number is a special case. **Row_n** always refers to the Value cell: Visio retrieves the data stored in the Value cell. To refer to other cells in a Custom Properties row, add the specific cell name as a suffix, such as **Prop.Row_2.Formula**.

In summary, the formula =**Prop.Row_2** means that the cell takes on the same value as found in row 2 of the Custom Properties section. (We get more into Visio's formulae later in this chapter.)

In the following exercise, you link one cell to another by a simple formula:

1. If necessary, open the Shape Transform section by clicking on its title bar. Ensure that you can see both the Shape Transform and Custom Properties sections in the ShapeSheet window.

2. Double-click the data cell next to **Width** in the Shape Transform section.

3. Delete the text in the cell.

4. Click row 2 of the Custom Properties section. Notice that Visio automatically fills in the *section.cell* reference for you: Prop.Row_2.

**5.** Press **Enter**. Notice the rectangle cell immediately changes its width to reflect the value stored in the Value cell.

**6.** Repeat steps 2 and 3 for the **Height** cell in the Shape Transform section. Then click row 3 of the Custom Properties section. Press **Enter**, and watch Visio resize the rectangle. The reason that the rectangle is so much larger than the page is that the (default) scale is 1:1. The 24"x36" rectangle (table) overwhelms the 8.5"x11" page.

**7.** Let's now use the Custom Properties dialog box to change the size of the desk. Select **Shape | Custom Properties** from the menu bar.

**8.** When the dialog box appears, enter:

       Width     3.6"
       Depth     2.4"

Notice that the shape resizes ten times smaller and that the Custom Properties section updates to reflect the new values. There is a great interconnectedness between the shape, the dialog box, the Shape Transform section, and the Custom Properties sections.

## Type and Format Cells

Until now you have been typing whatever values we like: text, numbers, dimensions. The **Type** cell lets you restrict the type of value acceptable for each row of the Custom Properties section. The default (No Formula) specifies string data, where everything is surrounded by quotation marks. You can, however, force Visio to only accept numbers, or a date value, or some other format of data.

You specify the type via a number between 0 and 7, as described by the table.

| Type | Meaning | Format Cell |
|------|---------|-------------|
| 0 | String of text | Formats the text using format pictures. |
| 1 | Fixed list; single item selection | Items stored as a string, with semicolon delimiters. For example, **"Small; Smaller; Smallest"**. |
| 2 | Number | Formats the number using format pictures. For example, **# #/4 uu"** displays a fraction to the nearest 1/4-inch, such as **5 1/4 inches**. The number may be an integer, dimension, angle, date, time, duration, or currency. |
| 3 | Boolean list box | Format cell has no effect. Choice is either **TRUE** or **FALSE**. |
| 4 | Variable list | Items stored as a string, with semicolon delimiters. For example, **"Small; Smaller; Smallest"**. Note that one item may be selected from the list, or the user may type a different value. |
| 5 | Date or time value | Formats the date or time using format pictures. For example, **DateTime("8/25/56 12:34"),"C"** displays **Saturday, September 25, 1956 12:34:00 PM**. |
| 6 | Duration (elapsed time) | Formats the duration using format pictures. For example, **[d]** displays elapsed days. |
| 7 | Currency value | Formats the currency using a format picture. For example, **UUU** results in the currency's three-letter abbreviation, such as **99.00 USD**. |

The **Type** cell works together with the **Format** cell, which specifies what the data should look like. Most of the time, you format the value with *format pictures*, a term Visio uses to describe the combination of characters and letters that specify formats. For example, the format picture "**#.##u**" displays **25.78in.** In this example, the **#.##** specifies two decimal places; the **u** specifies

**Customizing ShapeSheets**

abbreviated, lowercase units. The complete list of format pictures is provided in Chapter 8.

In the following exercise, you use the Type and Format cells to create a selection of furniture, and restrict the dimensions to inches with no decimal places:

1.  In the ShapeSheet window, click the **Type** cell of row 1 in the Custom Properties section.

2.  Change the **No Formula** to **1**. This specifies a fixed list.

3.  Click **Format** cell of row 1. Here you specify the items that should appear in the list.

4.  Type **"Desk;Chair;Rug;Couch"** (include the quotation marks) and press **Enter**.

5.  To see the effect of these changes, select **Shape | Custom Properties**. Notice the dialog box now contains a list box.

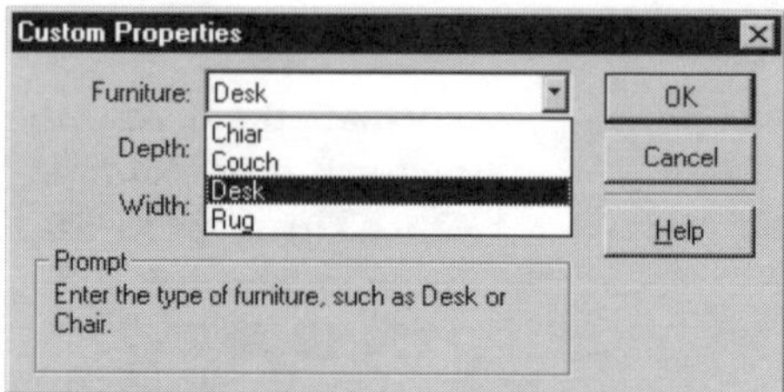


6.  Click the list box to see the choices. Select **Rug** and click **OK**. The ShapeSheet changes the Value cell of row 1 to **"Rug"**.

7.  We now specify the type and format of the Width and Depth cells. Enter the following values:

| Row | Type | Format |
| --- | --- | --- |
| Prop.Row_2 | 2 | "#.##U" |
| Prop.Row_3 | 2 | "# uu" |

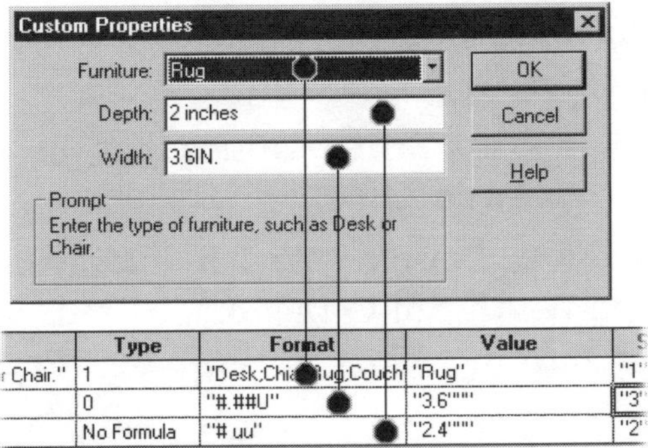



| | Type | Format | Value | S |
|---|---|---|---|---|
| r Chair." | 1 | "Desk;Chia Rug;Couch" | "Rug" | "1" |
| | 0 | "#.##U" | "3.6"" | "3" |
| | No Formula | "# uu" | "2.4"" | "2" |

Let's examine the result of these two format pictures. (Recall that the Sort cells are reversing the display order of row 2 and 3.) The format picture "**#.##U**" displays **3.6IN.** The **#.##** restricts decimals to two places, without zero padding. The **U** specifies uppercase, abbreviated units.

The format picture "**# uu**" displays **2 inches**. The **#** forces the display of whole numbers. The lack of the dot removes the display of the decimal point. The space (between # and uu) forces the display of the space; note that it is lacking in the earlier format picture. The **uu** specifies lowercase, fully spelled out units.

Notice that the format pictures affect the display only in the dialog box; they do not affect the accuracy of the number stored in the Value cells. Although the Custom Properties dialog box displays **2 inches**, the Value cell contains **2.4"**.

### *Prop.Row_n Cell*

Finally, we arrive at the very first cell. The row name cell specifies the name of the row. Initially, Visio gives it a generic name, such as **Prop.Row_1**. You may, however, give the row a more descriptive name of up to thirty-one characters long. The name may contain letters, numbers, and the underscore character ( _ ) but no spaces.

In the following exercise, you rename the rows:

1. In the ShapeSheet window, click the row name cell **Prop.Row_1** in the Custom Properties section. Notice that Visio shows **Row_1** in the formula bar. That's because the **Prop.** portion of the name

will remain, so that everyone knows the row belongs to the Custom Properties section.

2.  Type **Furniture** and press **Enter**. Notice that the name of the row changes to **Prop.Furniture**.

3.  Repeat step 2 for row 2, but type **Width** and press **Enter**. Notice that the referenced Width cell in the Shape Transform section changes its formula, from **=Prop.Row_2** to **=Prop.Width**.

4.  Repeat step 2 for row 3, but type **Height** and press **Enter**. Again, Visio automatically updates the ShapeSheet.

## Adding Text to the Shape

You've now created this lovely desk shape—or maybe it's a rug… a couch… a chair? You really can't tell the identical-looking white rectangles apart. One way to tell the chair from the rug from the desk is to give them different line and fill properties. The chair could have rounded corners. The rug could have a gray fill pattern. The desk could have thicker lines.

Another method is to simply label the desk with "Desk," the rug with "Rug," and so on. A flaw in Visio, however, is that there is no Text section. When you click on a shape and type some text, those words are not accessible via the ShapeSheet. Text is, however, available via automation (i.e., VBA programming). This limitation may be overcome with the next release of Visio.

There is, fortunately, a workaround. In the following exercise, you use the **Insert | Field** command to add a text label to each shape. The nice thing about Visio's Field is that it automatically updates the text when you change the custom property, say from rug to desk.

1.  Select the desk shape.

2.  Select **Insert | Field** from the menu bar. Notice that Visio displays the Field dialog box, which has three columns of options: **Category**, **Field**, and **Format**. The Field area lists options for each category item; the Format list lets you select the formatting for the text or numbers. Some of the fields of the **Date/Time** category automatically update themselves, such as **Current Date**.

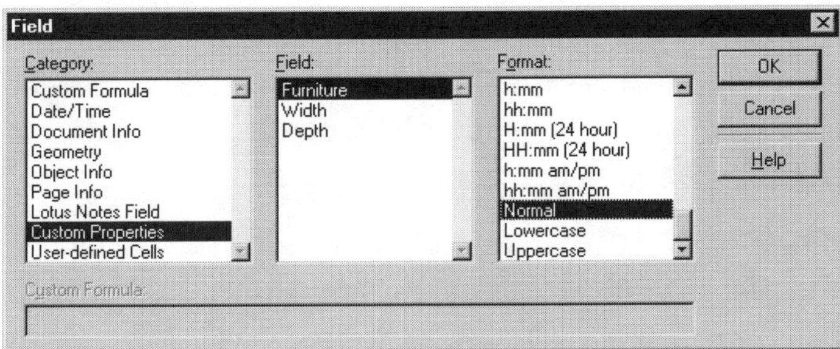

3. Select **Custom Properties** from the first column, Category. Notice that the **Field** column now lists the names of the three custom properties you defined: **Furniture**, **Width**, and **Depth**.

4. Select **Furniture** from the second column, Field.

5. Select **Normal** from the third column, Format. For text, there are three options in the Format column: **Normal**, **Lowercase**, and **Uppercase**. All other format options apply to units, dates, and times.

6. Click **OK**. Notice that Visio instantly adds the text **Rug** to the rectangle shape. You may need to zoom in to see the text.

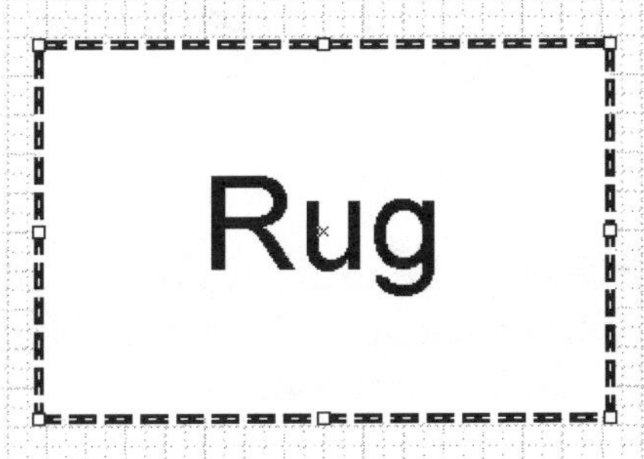


7. Depending on the size of the rectangle, you may need to change the size of the font. The default size is 8 pt, about 0.1" tall. Select the shape and select a different size, such as 36 pt (half-inch tall). If you like, you can change the font itself; the default is Arial, which is not the prettiest font in the world.

**Customizing ShapeSheets**

8.  Finally, prove to yourself that the text updates itself automatically. Select **Shape | Custom Properties**. Select a different value for **Furniture**, such as **Couch**. Click **OK**. Notice that Visio instantly changes the text to **Couch**.

To add another field, such as the Width and Depth properties, enter the text mode, click an insertion point, and insert another field.

# Applying Custom Properties

Now that you have created custom properties, there are several things Visio lets you do with them:

➤ Add the Properties command to the shortcut menu, so that you can easily access the custom properties.

➤ Create a master, so that you can easily pass on the shape and its custom properties to other drawings.

➤ Edit the master's custom property via a wizard, so that you can easily make changes to the data.

➤ Prepare a property report to easily summarize custom properties in the drawing or export the data in a spreadsheet format.

## *Add the Properties Command*

Until now, you have accessed the custom properties via the ShapeSheet or by selecting **Shape | Custom Properties** from the menu bar. There is a faster method.

In the following exercise, you make the custom properties available via the shortcut menu. The only problem with this method is that it must be applied to each shape, on a one-by-one basis.

1.  In the ShapeSheet window, right-click and select **Insert Section** from the shortcut menu.

2.  Select **Actions** from the Insert Section dialog box and click **OK**. Notice that Visio adds the Actions section to the ShapeSheet. The

Actions section has five cells but you only deal with two: Action and Menu.

| Actions | Action | Menu | Prompt | Checked | Disabled |
|---|---|---|---|---|---|
| 1 | DOCMD(1312) | "Properties" | "" | 0 | 0 |

3. Type the following function in the **Action** cell:

   =DoCmd(1312)

4. Type the following in the **Menu** cell:

   =Properties

5. Right-click the desk shape. Notice that the shortcut menu now includes the Properties command at the top of the list. Select it and the Custom Properties dialog box appears.

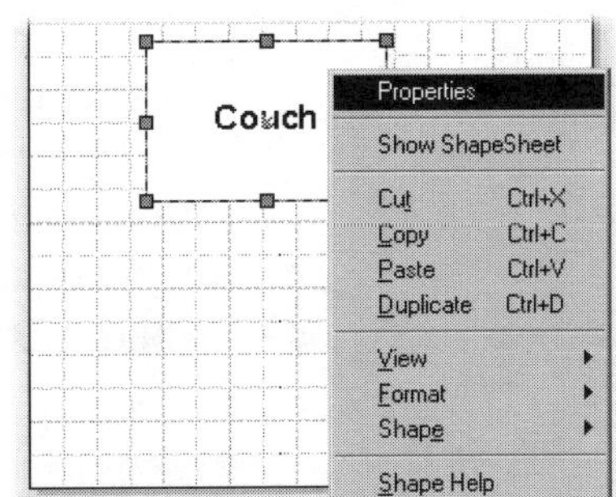


## Create a Master

You have learned how to create custom properties to store data in a desk shape. But the custom properties only apply to that one shape. Sure, you can make copies of the desk shape within the drawing. You can use the Copy and Paste commands to make the desk shape available in other Visio drawings. But, ideally, the desk shape with its custom properties should be stored in a stencil.

The shapes that you drag from the stencil into the drawing are called *instances*. The dictionary definition of instance is "something representative of a group." In the case of Visio, the "group" is the original shape on the stencil. That shape is called the *master*. Masters are stored in stencil files.

In the following exercise, you turn your desk shape into a master and store it in a new stencil file.

1. Close the ShapeSheet window. Select **Window | Show Document Stencil** (called **Master Shapes** in earlier versions of Visio). Notice that Visio opens a green stencil window. This window displays the masters of shapes used in the drawing. The window should have at least one shape called **Rectangle**. (If you dragged other masters into the drawing, they also show up.) The Rectangle master appears because that's the shape from which you created your desk shape.

2. Hold down the **Ctrl** key and drag the desk shape onto the master shape window. Notice that the master is represented by an icon that looks like the desk shape and is named **Master.1** (or similar number). If you like, you can change the name and the icon, as described next.

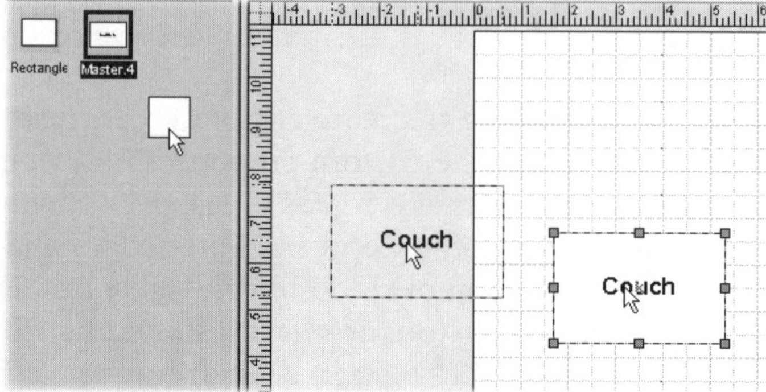

3. Right-click the **Master.1** icon to display the shortcut menu.

4. Select **Master Properties** from the shortcut menu. Notice that Visio displays the Master Properties dialog box.

5. Change the **Master Name** from **Master.1** to **Furniture**. This label will appear under the icon.

6.  Type in the **Prompt** area: **Generic furniture shape for Chair, Couch, Desk, or Rug.** This is the text that appears on the status line when you click the icon.

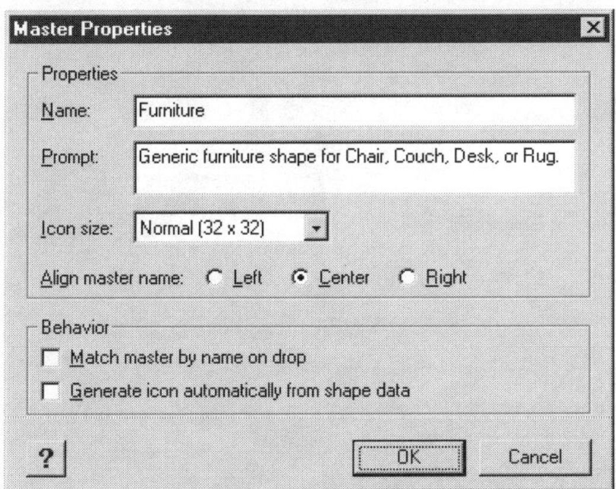

7.  Leave all other options as they are and click **OK**. Notice that Visio changes the name under the icon from **Master.1** to **Furniture**.

8.  If you want to change the icon, right-click the icon. Select **Edit Icon**. Notice that Visio opens a new window with a greatly enlarged version of the icon. Notice also that the toolbar changes to show colors and some icon editing tools. As you make your changes, notice that the icon in the stencil window is updated at the same time. There is no need to save the changed icon. Make a mistake? Select **Edit | Undo Change Icon**. When done, close the icon editing window.

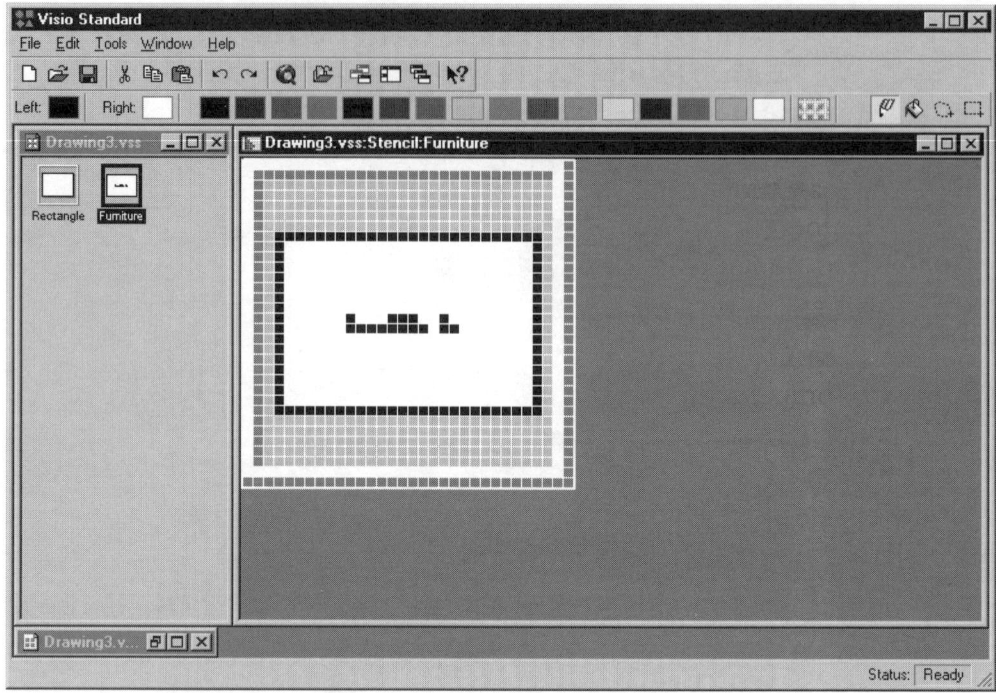

9. You don't need to save the document stencil. It is saved with the drawing.

10. Try using the new master. Drag the **Furniture** master into the drawing. As you do, the Custom Properties dialog box appears. Make your selection of furniture and sizes. Watch with pleasure as Visio draws the rectangle to the size you specified, and labels the shape automatically.

# Export the Data

So far, you have learned how to store custom data in shapes. You can view the data stored in individual shapes. But Visio is holding the data captive, so to speak. Ideally, you should be able move that data out of the drawing and into another application, such as a spreadsheet or database. Once in the spreadsheet, you can sort the data, add up numbers, print out summaries, and so on.

You can take a couple of approaches, which I do not elaborate on in this book:

➤ Create a bill of material from the custom properties with the Property Report wizard (**Tools | Property Report**). The Property Report wizard creates a report of the shapes in your drawing. If the shapes have custom properties, these are summarized by the report. The wizard produces two formats of its report: (1) as a bill of material table in the Visio drawing; or (2) export in a format that can be read into a spreadsheet program.

➤ Link the custom properties with records in a database file. Database linking is discussed in Chapter 9.

# Writing ShapeSheet Formulae

A formula can contain numbers, coordinates, numbers with units, cell names, functions, operators, inherited formulas, and local formulas. You can type the formula into a cell or use the **Insert | Name** command to reference the formula in another cell.

ShapeSheet functions can be used in any ShapeSheet cell. The **Scratch** and **User-defined cells** sections, however, are particularly useful for carrying out calculations. The result can be transferred to any other cell, as required.

Visio groups its ShapeSheet functions into these groups: geometric, window management, color and pattern management, date and time, text, event, miscellaneous, statistical, mathematical, trigonometric, logical, and error handling functions. (A summary of all ShapeSheet functions is provided at the end of Chapter 8.)

There are far too many ShapeSheet functions (over a hundred) to work through an example of each. Instead, to show how they work, we'll work through the **Gravity** function, one of the more useful geometric functions.

Gravity orients text for readability in a shape that has been rotated. The format of the function is:

=Gravity(*angle* [, *limit1*, *limit2*])

It is used in the **TxtAngle** cell of the **Text Transform** section. The *angle* usually refers to the Angle cell of the Shape Transform section. The Gravity function returns 180 degrees when the *angle* is between *limit1* and *limit2*; that makes the text display upside-down, relative to the shape. Otherwise, Gravity returns 0 degrees. When you leave out *limit1* and *limit2*, Gravity uses 90 and 270 degrees, respectively.

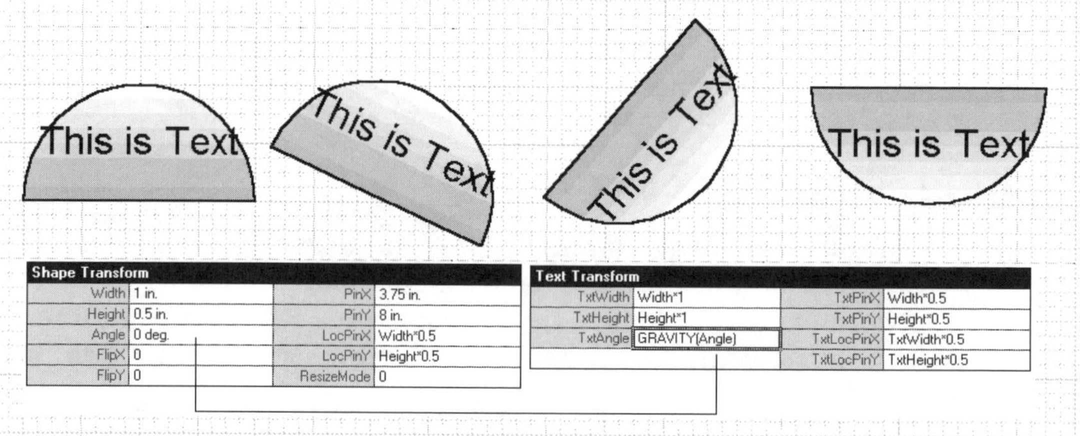


| Shape Transform | | | |
| --- | --- | --- | --- |
| Width | 1 in. | PinX | 3.75 in. |
| Height | 0.5 in. | PinY | 8 in. |
| Angle | 0 deg. | LocPinX | Width*0.5 |
| FlipX | 0 | LocPinY | Height*0.5 |
| FlipY | 0 | ResizeMode | 0 |

| Text Transform | | | |
| --- | --- | --- | --- |
| TxtWidth | Width*1 | TxtPinX | Width*0.5 |
| TxtHeight | Height*1 | TxtPinY | Height*0.5 |
| TxtAngle | GRAVITY(Angle) | TxtLocPinX | TxtWidth*0.5 |
| | | TxtLocPinY | TxtHeight*0.5 |

To help you out, use the Insert | Function command to display a list of function names. Similarly, the Insert | Name command displays a list of cell names. But be careful! These two commands only work in the correct context:

➤ Both commands are only available from the menu bar when you are working in the ShapeSheet window.

➤ Both commands work only when the cursor is in the formula bar.

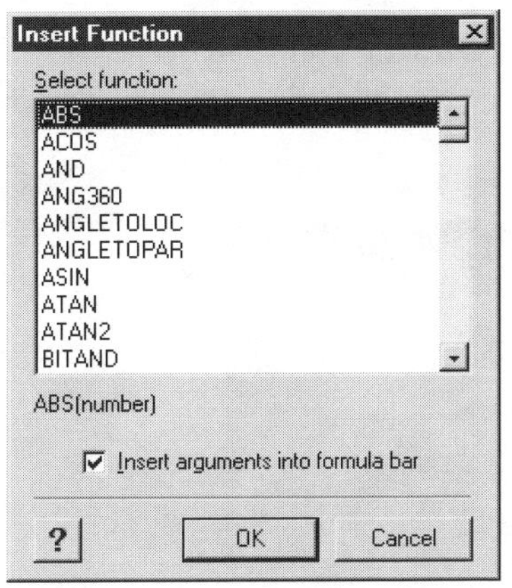

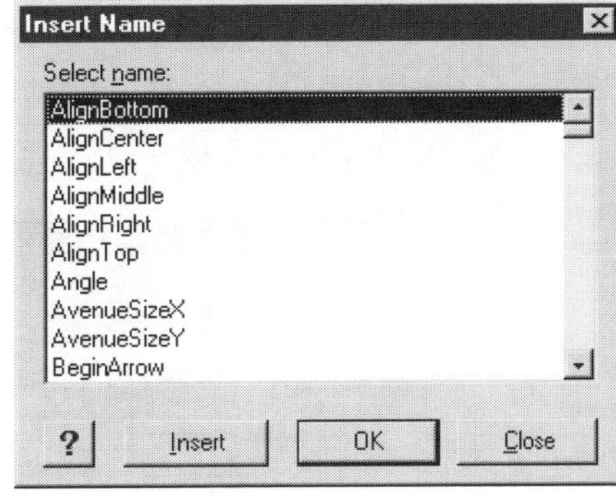

# ShapeSheet Cell Names



In a spreadsheet, you access a cell by its row-column coordinate, such as A1 or CB202. Visio's ShapeSheet doesn't have the perfectly rectangular structure of a spreadsheet, so Visio uses names to reference the cells. In the Gravity example, the function refers to another cell by its name, Angle.

Every cell of every row of every section has a unique name, such as the Angle cell of the Shape Transform section. When a section has one or more rows containing cells that might have the same name, the cell name is suffixed with an integer, such as the **Action.C1** and **Action.C2** cells of the Action section.

Functions can refer to the cells found in other shapes, groups, and guides by using the exclamation mark (!), also called *bang*, as follows:

shapename!cellname

When the drawing contains more than one copy of the same shape, then you need to resort to ID (short for identification) numbers, as follows:

shapename.ID!cellname

To find the ID number of a shape, select **Format | Special** from the menu bar. The ID number is displayed at the top of the dialog box. Visio assigns the ID number when the shape is created. The ID number does not change unless the shape is moved to another page or Visio document.

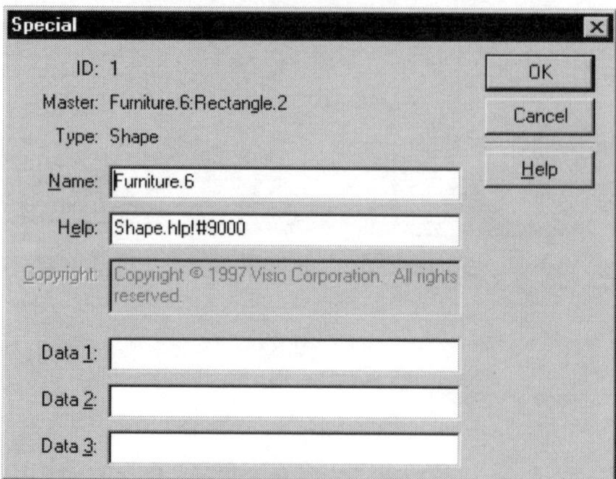

The table below lists in alphabetical order Visio's more than three hundred cell names. If you are not sure of the section that a cell belongs to, look across to the second column for the section name. For example, the Address cell is found in the Hyperlinks section. (Chapter 8 lists the cell names with each section.) The asterisk (*) indicates new cell and section names in Visio 2000. This list is more accurate than the list provided by Visio 2000's documentation.

| Cell Name | Found in Section(s) |
| --- | --- |
| A | Geometry |
| Action | Actions |
| Active | Layers |
| Address | Hyperlinks |
| AlignBottom | Alignment |
| AlignCenter | Alignment |
| AlignLeft | Alignment |
| Alignment | Tabs |
| AlignMiddle | Alignment |
| AlignRight | Alignment |

| Cell Name | Found in Section(s) |
| --- | --- |
| AlignTop | Alignment |
| Angle | Shape Transform |
| ArcTo | Geometry |
| Ask | Custom Properties |
| AvenueSizeX * | Page Layout * |
| AvenueSizeY * | Page Layout * |
| | |
| B | Geometry |
| BeginArrow | Line Format |
| BeginArrowSize * | Line Format |
| BeginX | 1-D Endpoints |
| BeginY | 1-D Endpoints |
| BegTrigger | Glue Info |
| BlockSizeX * | PageLayout * |
| BlockSizeY * | PageLayout * |
| Blur * | Image Properties * |
| BottomMargin | Text Block Format |
| Brightness * | Image Properties * |
| Bullet * | Paragraph |
| BulletString * | Paragraph |
| | |
| C | Geometry |
| Can.Glue | Controls |
| Case[n] | Character |
| Checked[n] | Actions |
| Color | Layers |
| Color[n] | Character |
| Comment * | Miscellaneous |
| ConLineJumpCode * | Shape Layout * |
| ConLineJumpDirX * | Shape Layout * |
| ConLineJumpDirY * | Shape Layout * |
| ConLineJumpStyle * | Shape Layout * |
| Contrast * | Image Properties * |
| CtrlAsInput * | PageLayout |
| | |
| D[n] | Connection Points, Geometry |

| Cell Name | Found in Section(s) |
| --- | --- |
| Default * | Hyperlinks |
| DefaultTabstop * | Text Block Format |
| Denoise * | Image Properties * |
| Description | Hyperlinks |
| DirX/A[n] | Connection Points |
| DirY/B[n] | Connection Points |
| Disabled[n] | Actions |
| DisplayMode * | Group Properties * |
| DontMoveChildren * | Group Properties * |
| DoubleULine * | Character |
| DrawingScale | Page Properties |
| DrawingScaleType | Page Properties |
| DrawingSizeType | Page Properties |
| DynamicsOff * | Page Layout * |
| DynFeedback | Miscellaneous |
| | |
| E | Geometry |
| EditMode | Text Fields |
| EllipticalArcTo | Geometry |
| EnableFillProps * | Style Properties * |
| EnableGrid * | Style Properties * |
| EnableLineProps * | Style Properties * |
| EnableTextProps * | Style Properties * |
| EndArrow | Line Format |
| EndArrowSize * | Line Format |
| EndTrigger | Glue Info |
| EndX | 1-D Endpoints |
| EndY | 1-D Endpoints |
| EventDblClick | Events |
| EventDrop | Events |
| EventXFMod | Events |
| ExtraInfo | HyperLinks |
| | |
| FillBkgnd | Fill Format |
| FillForegnd | Fill Format |
| FillPattern | Fill Format |

| Cell Name | Found in Section(s) |
| --- | --- |
| FlipX | Shape Transform |
| FlipY | Shape Transform |
| Font[n] | Character |
| Format * | Text Fields |
| Format | Custom Properties |
| Frame | HyperLinks |
| | |
| Gamma * | Image Properties * |
| Glue | Layers |
| GlueType | Glue Info |
| | |
| HAlign | Paragraph |
| Height | Shape Transform |
| HideForApply * | Style Properties * |
| HideText | Miscellaneous |
| | |
| ImgHeight | Image Info |
| ImgOffsetX | Image Info |
| ImgOffsetY | Image Info |
| ImgWidth | Image Info |
| IndFirst | Paragraph |
| IndLeft | Paragraph |
| IndRight | Paragraph |
| InhibitSnap * | PageProperties |
| Invisible | Custom Properties |
| IsDropSource * | Miscellaneous |
| IsDropTarget * | Group Properties * |
| IsSnapTarget * | Group Properties * |
| IsTextEditTarget * | Group Properties * |
| | |
| Label | Custom Properties |
| LayerMember | Layer Membership |
| LeftMargin | Text Block Format |
| LineAdjustFrom * | Page Layout * |
| LineAdjustFrom * | Page Layout * |
| LineAdjustTo * | Page Layout * |

| Cell Name | Found in Section(s) |
| --- | --- |
| LineAdjustTo * | Page Layout * |
| LineCap | Line Format |
| LineColor | Line Format |
| LineJumpCode * | Page Layout * |
| LineJumpFactorX * | Page Layout * |
| LineJumpFactorY * | Page Layout * |
| LineJumpStyle * | Page Layout * |
| LinePattern | Line Format |
| LineTo | Geometry |
| LineToLineX * | Page Layout * |
| LineToLineY * | Page Layout * |
| LineToNodeX * | Page Layout * |
| LineToNodeY * | Page Layout * |
| LineWeight | Line Format |
| Lock[n] | Layers |
| LockAspect | Protection |
| LockBegin | Protection |
| LockCalcWH | Protection |
| LockCrop | Protection |
| LockDelete | Protection |
| LockEnd | Protection |
| LockFormat | Protection |
| LockGroup | Protection |
| LockHeight | Protection |
| LockMoveX | Protection |
| LockMoveY | Protection |
| LockPreview * | Document Properties * |
| LockRotate | Protection |
| LockSelect | Protection |
| LockTextEdit | Protection |
| LockVtxEdit | Protection |
| LockWidth | Protection |
| LocPinX | Shape Transform |
| LocPinY | Shape Transform |
| Menu[n] | Actions |

| Cell Name | Found in Section(s) |
| --- | --- |
| MoveTo (Start) | Geometry |
| | |
| Name[n] | Layers |
| NewWindow | Hyperlinks |
| NoAlignBox | Miscellaneous |
| NoCtlHandles | Miscellaneous |
| NoFill | Geometry |
| NoLine * | Geometry |
| NonPrinting | Miscellaneous |
| NoObjHandles | Miscellaneous |
| NoShow | Geometry |
| NoSnap * | Geometry |
| NotLiveDynamics * | Miscellaneous |
| | |
| ObjBehavior | Miscellaneous |
| ObjInteract | Miscellaneous |
| ObjType | Miscellaneous |
| OutputFormat * | Document Properties * |
| Overline * | Character |
| | |
| PageHeight | Page Properties |
| PageLineJumpDirX * | Page Layout * |
| PageLineJumpDirY * | Page Layout * |
| PageScale | Page Properties |
| PageWidth | Page Properties |
| PinX | Shape Transform |
| PinY | Shape Transform |
| PlaceDepth * | Page Layout * |
| PlaceStyle * | Page Layout * |
| Pos[n] | Character |
| Position | Tabs |
| PreviewQuality * | Document Properties * |
| PreviewScope * | Document Properties * |
| Print[n] | Layers |
| Prompt | Actions, Custom Properties, User-defined cells |
| Prop.name.Invisible | Custom Properties |

| Cell Name | Found in Section(s) |
| --- | --- |
| Prop.name.Label | Custom Properties |
| Prop.name.Prompt | Custom Properties |
| Prop.name.SortKey | Custom Properties |
| Prop.name.Type | Custom Properties |
| Prop.name.Value | Custom Properties |
| Prop.Row_n | Custom Properties |
| | |
| ResizeMode | Shape Transform |
| ResizePage * | Page Layout * |
| RightMargin | Text Block Format |
| Rounding | Line Format |
| RouteStyle * | Page Layout * |
| | |
| Scatch cells | Scratch |
| SelectMode * | Group Properties * |
| ShapeFixedCode * | Shape Layout * |
| ShapePermeablePlace * | Shape Layout * |
| ShapePermeableX * | Shape Layout * |
| ShapePermeableY * | Shape Layout * |
| ShapePlowCode * | Shape Layout * |
| ShapeRouteStyle * | Shape Layout * |
| Sharpen * | Image Properties * |
| ShdwBkgnd | Fill Format |
| ShdwForegnd | Fill Format |
| ShdwOffsetX | Page Properties |
| ShdwOffsetY | Page Properties |
| ShdwPattern | Fill Format |
| Size[n] | Character |
| Snap[n] | Layers |
| SortKey | Custom Properties |
| Spacing * | Character |
| SpAfter[n] | Paragraph |
| SpBefore[n] | Paragraph |
| SpLine[n] | Paragraph |
| SplineStart | Geometry |
| StrikeThru * | Character |

| *Cell Name* | *Found in Section(s)* |
| --- | --- |
| Style[n] | Character |
| SubAddress | HyperLinks |
| | |
| TextBkgnd | Text Block Format |
| TextDirection * | Text Block Format |
| TheData | Events |
| TheText | Events |
| Tip | Controls |
| TopMargin | Text Block Format |
| TxtAngle | Text Transform |
| TxtHeight | Text Transform |
| TxtLocPinX | Text Transform |
| TxtLocPinY | Text Transform |
| TxtPinX | Text Transform |
| TxtPinY | Text Transform |
| TxtWidth | Text Transform |
| Type * | Text Fields |
| Type | Custom Properties |
| Type/C[n] | Connection Points |
| | |
| UICategory * | Text Fields |
| UICode * | Text Fields |
| UIFormat * | Text Fields |
| UpdateAlignBox | Miscellaneous |
| User.Row_n | User-defined cells |
| | |
| Value | Custom Properties, User-defined cells |
| Value[n] | Text Field |
| VerticalAlign | Text Block Format |
| Visible[n] | Layers |
| WalkPreference | Glue Info |
| Width | Shape Transform |
| | |
| X Behavior[n] | Controls |
| X Dynamics[n] | Controls |
| X[n] | Connection Points, Controls |

| Cell Name | Found in Section(s) |
| --- | --- |
| XGridDensity | Ruler & Grid |
| XGridOrigin | Ruler & Grid |
| XGridSpacing | Ruler & Grid |
| Xn | Geometry |
| XRulerDensity | Ruler & Grid |
| XRulerOrigin | Ruler & Grid |
| Y Behavior[n] | Controls |
| Y Dynamics [n] | Controls |
| Y[n] | Connection Points, Controls |
| YGridDensity | Ruler & Grid |
| YGridOrigin | Ruler & Grid |
| YGridSpacing | Ruler & Grid |
| Yn | Geometry |
| YRulerDensity | Ruler & Grid |

# Chapter Review

In this chapter, you learned how to create a custom property, add commands to the shape's shortcut menu, and make a master from the shape. You received an introduction to simple programming of Visio with cell functions and learned how to reference cells by name.

The next chapter presents a complete reference to ShapeSheet sections.

# Chapter 8

# *The Complete ShapeSheet Section Reference*

This chapter contains a reference that lists all sections found in the ShapeSheet and the formulae you can use in cells. The first part of the chapter consists of the ShapeSheet sections listed in alphabetical order.

The second part of the chapter groups together the ShapeSheet formulae.

## ShapeSheet Types

Visio has eight specific ShapeSheet types, as shown by the table. The asterisk (*) indicates a type new in Visio 2000.

| ShapeSheet Type | To Access the ShapeSheet |
| --- | --- |
| 1-D Shape | Select the shape; from the menu bar select Window \| Show ShapeSheet. |
| 2-D Shape | Select the shape; from the menu bar select Window \| Show ShapeSheet. |
| Document * | In the Drawing Explorer, right-click the drawing filename and select Show ShapeSheet. |
| Foreign | Select the object; from the menu bar select Window \| Show ShapeSheet. |
| Group * | Select the group; from the menu bar select Window \| Show ShapeSheet. |

| ShapeSheet Type | To Access the ShapeSheet |
| --- | --- |
| Guide | Select the guide; from the menu bar select Window \| Show ShapeSheet. |
| Page | Select nothing; from the menu bar select Window \| Show ShapeSheet. |
| Style * | In the Drawing Explorer, right-click a style name and select Show ShapeSheet. |

As an alternative, you can right-click a name, such as the name of a shape, in the Drawing Explorer, and select Show ShapeSheet.

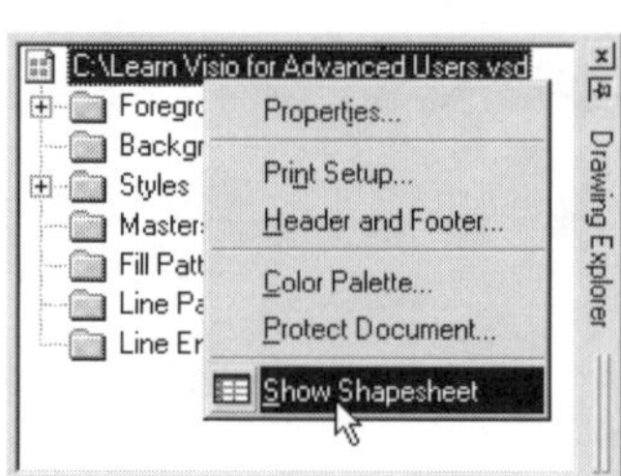


# Visio 2000 Changes

The following sections are new to Visio 2000:

➤ Document Properties

➤ Group Properties

➤ Image Properties

➤ Page Layout

➤ Shape Layout

➤ Style Properties

➤ Tabs

The Tabs section is not new; rather, it is for the first time visible in the ShapeSheet with Visio 2000. These sections changed names in Visio 2000:

➤ Character Format is renamed **Character**.

➤ Hyperlink is renamed **Hyperlinks**.

➤ Image Info is renamed **Foreign Image Info**.

➤ Paragraph Format is renamed **Paragraph**.

In addition, a number of cells changed names with Visio 2000.

The **Guide Info** section was removed from Visio 2000; it has been replaced by the **InfiniteLine** row of the **Geometry** section.

# Invisible Sections and Cells

There are some sections and cells that do not appear in the ShapeSheet. Other sections appear under specific situations only:

The "no name" section has two sections: **HelpTopic** and **Copyright**. It does not appear in the ShapeSheet, but can be accessed via VBA.

The **Alignment** section appears only when a shape is glued to a guide.

The **Char.Locale** cell of the **Character** section does not appear in the ShapeSheet, but can be accessed via VBA.

The **Foreign Image Info** section appears only for linked and embedded OLE objects.

The **Image Properties** section appears only for bitmap foreign images.

Earlier versions of Visio allowed you to insert the **Text Fields** section; Visio 2000 no longer allows this. The workaround is to insert a text field from the menu bar (**Insert | Field**) or via VBA.

# ShapeSheet Jargon

There are some terms used by the ShapeSheet that should be clarified:

**Not 0** means you can enter any value other than 0.

**Origin** is located at the lower-left corner of either the page, the group, or the selection rectangle of the shape. The x,y-coordinates of the origin are 0,0; it cannot be relocated. The origin is important because many of the shape's dimensions are measured from 0,0.

**Parent** of a shape is either: (1) the page that the shape resides on; or (2) the group containing the shape. The location of the parts of the shape, such as **BeginX** and **BeginY**, are measured from the origin of the parent.

**Pin** of a shape is its rotation point. Think of sticking a pin in a sheet of paper on a bulletin board, then spinning the paper about the pin.

# ShapeSheet Sections

## *1-D Endpoints*

Contains the x- and y-coordinates of the start and ending points of a 1D (short for *one-dimensional*) shape. A 1D shape has only two endpoints, and *behaves* like a line but needs not be a line; 1D shapes are used primarily as connectors.

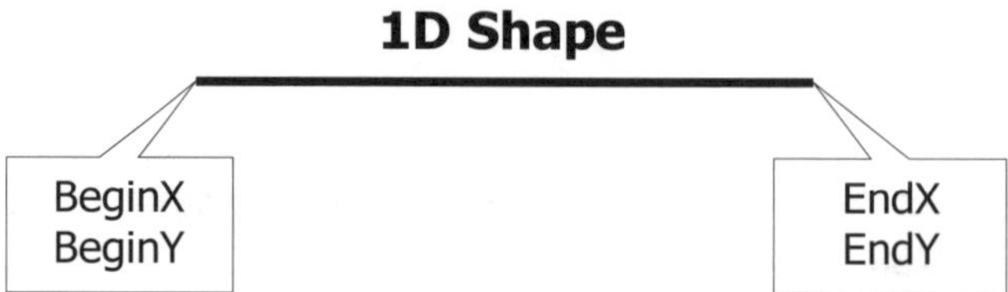


## *Cells*

| 1-D Endpoints | | | |
|---|---|---|---|
| BeginX | 2.25 in. | EndX | 5.375 in. |
| BeginY | 9.75 in. | EndY | 5.5 in. |

**BeginX** specifies the x-coordinate of the beginning point of the 1D shape. The distance is relative to the origin of the shape's immediate parent, such as the page or its group. For example, 1 in. means the shape starts 1 inch to the right of the lower-left corner

**BeginY** specifies the y-coordinate of the beginning point of the 1D shape.

**EndX** specifies the x-coordinate of the endpoint of the 1D shape.

**EndY** specifies the y-coordinate of the endpoint of the 1D shape.

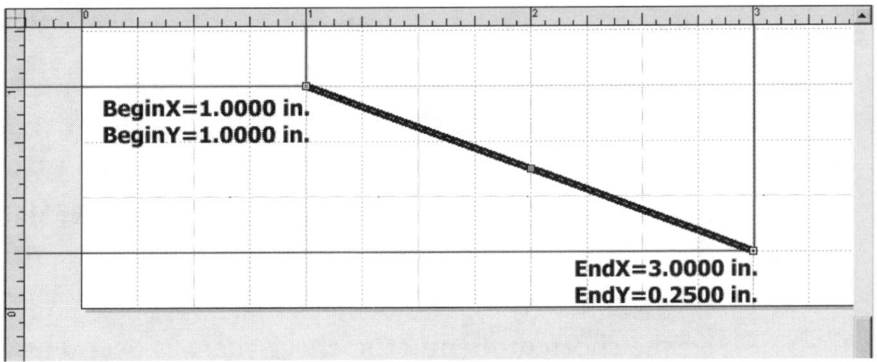


## Tip

> ➤ Visio marks the Begin point with a small x, and the End point with a small +.

## Actions

Contains a list of one or more command names that appear on the shortcut (right-click) menu of a shape or page. For example, when right-clicking the shape shown in the figure below, Visio displays a shortcut menu giving you the option of a filled, hollow, or no circle.

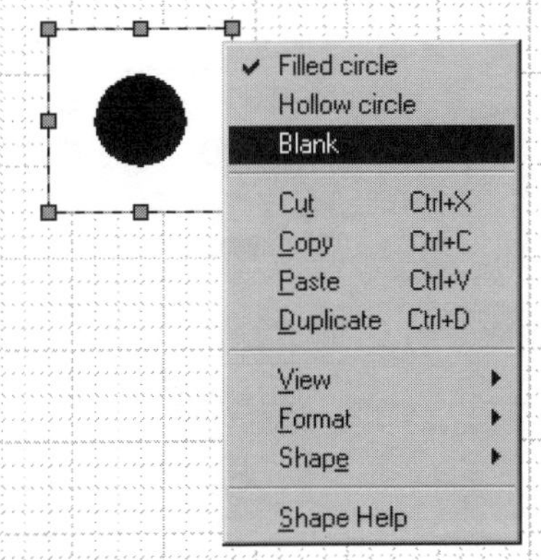


## Cells

**Action** (default =0) specifies a formula executed when you choose the command defined by the **Menu** cell next door. This

| Actions | Action | Menu | Prompt | Checked | Disabled |
|---|---|---|---|---|---|
| 1 | 0 | "" | "" | 0 | 0 |

cell is evaluated when the action occurs; it does not execute when you enter the formula.

**Menu** (default ="") specifies the command name appearing on the shape or page's shortcut menu (accessed by right-clicking the object).

**Prompt** (default ="") specifies the prompt text that appears on the status bar when the command is selected.

**C** (default =0) toggles a check mark (✓) next to the command on the shortcut menu. The check mark is useful as an indicator that an option has been selected. (This cell was called Checked in previous versions of Visio.)

| C | Meaning |
|---|---|
| 0 | Check mark is not displayed |
| not 0 | Check mark is displayed |

**D** (default =0) toggles highlighting (gray or black text) of the command on the shortcut menu. The gray version of the name is useful as an indicator that an option is not available. (This cell was called Disabled in previous versions of Visio.)

| D | Meaning |
|---|---|
| 0 | Black text (command is enabled) |
| not 0 | Gray text (command is disabled) |

## Tips

➤ To display a separator line above the command name, prefix the name in the Menu cell with the underscore character (_).

➤ To display the command at the bottom of the shortcut menu, prefix the name with a percent character (%).

➤ You can combine the two metacharacters, for example: _%Make Department.

## Alignment

Contains the alignment of the shape glued to a guide (or guide point). This section only appears in the ShapeSheet when a 2D shape is glued to one or more guides; it does not appear when 1D shapes are glued to a guide.

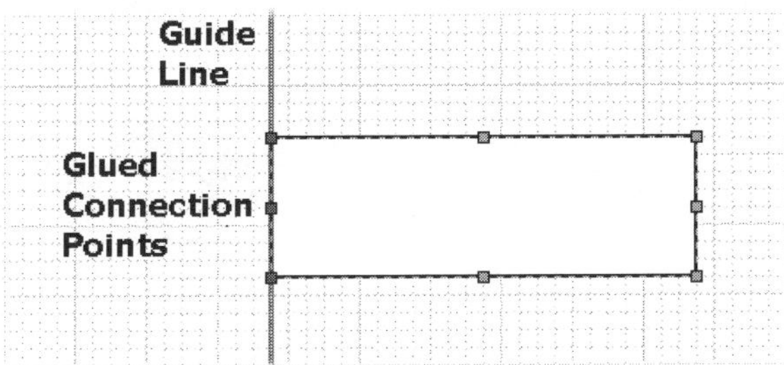


### Cells

| Alignment | | | |
| --- | --- | --- | --- |
| AlignLeft | INTERSECTX(Sheet.2!PinX,Sheet. | AlignCenter _MARKER(1) | AlignRight _MARKER(1) |
| AlignTop | _MARKER(1) | AlignMiddle INTERSECTY(Sheet.2!PinX,Sheet.2! | AlignBottom _MARKER(1) |

**AlignLeft** (default =MARKER_1) specifies the horizontal position of a vertical guide (or guide point) to which the shape's left border is aligned.

**AlignCenter** (default =MARKER_1) specifies the horizontal position of a vertical guide (or guide point) to which the shape's horizontal center is aligned.

**AlignRight** (default =MARKER_1) specifies the horizontal position of a vertical guide (or guide point) to which the shape's right border is aligned.

**AlignTop** (default =MARKER_1) specifies the vertical position of a horizontal guide (or guide point) to which the shape's top border is aligned.

**AlignMiddle** (default =MARKER_1) specifies the vertical position of a horizontal guide (or guide point) to which the shape's vertical center is aligned.

**AlignBottom** (default =MARKER_1) specifies the vertical position of a horizontal guide (or guide point) to which the shape's bottom border is aligned.

### Tips

➤ A formula in this section refers to the Shape Transform section of the guide to which the shape is glued.

➤ All of the alignment positions listed above are relative to the origin of the guide's parent.

➤ When a 2D shape is glued to a guide, the handles change from green to red.

## Character

Contains the format of the text in the shape, via a font number, color, style, case, position, and font size.

### Cells

| Character | Font | Size | Scale | Spacing | Color | Style | Case | Pos. | Strikethru | DoubleULine | Overline | Perpendicular |
|---|---|---|---|---|---|---|---|---|---|---|---|---|
| 0 | 0 | 8 pt. | 100 % | 0 pt. | 0 | 0 | 0 | 0 | FALSE | FALSE | FALSE | FALSE |

**Font** (default =0) specifies a number that specifies the font name. The number 0 represents the default font, which is Arial in most Windows systems; Font 2 is often Times New Roman.

**Caution:**

Font numbers are not consistent and will change, depending on the fonts installed on a particular computer system.

**Size** (default =10 pt.) specifies the height of the text.

6pt. text

12pt. text

## 24pt. text

# 48pt. text

# 72pt. text

(72 points = 1 inch)

| *Units of Measurement* | *Acceptable Abbreviations* |
| --- | --- |
| centimeters | centimeters, cm., cm |
| ciceros | ciceros, cicero, ci., ci, c |
| degrees | degrees, degree, deg., deg, ° |
| didots | didots, didot, di., di, d |
| feet | feet, foot, ft., ft, f, ' |
| inches | inches, inch, in., in, i, " |
| kilometers | kilometers, km., km |
| meters | meters, meter, metres, metre, m., m |
| miles | miles, mile, mi., mi |
| millimeters | millimeters, mm., mm |
| minutes | minutes, minute, min., min, ' |
| nautical miles | nm.,n.m.,nm |
| percent | % |
| picas | picas, pica, p |
| points | points, point, pt., pt |
| radians | radians, radian, rad., rad |
| seconds | seconds, second, sec., sec, " |
| yards | yards, yard, yds., yds, yd., yd |

**Scale** specifies the width of the font as a percentage of the default width (new to Visio 2000):

| Scale | Meaning |
| --- | --- |
| 1% – 99% | Text is narrower than default |
| 100% | Default width |
| 101% – 600% | Text is wider than default |

**Spacing** specifies the spacing between characters (new to Visio 2000). The amount can be specified in increments of 0.05".

**Color** (default =0) specifies a number representing the color of the shape's text.

| Color | Meaning |
| --- | --- |
| 0 | Black |
| 1 | White |
| 2 | Red |
| 3 | Green |
| 4 | Blue |
| 5 | Yellow |
| 6 | Magenta |
| 7 | Cyan |
| 8 | Dark Red |
| 9 | Dark Green |
| 10 | Dark Blue |
| 11 | Dark Yellow |
| 12 | Dark Magenta |
| 13 | Dark Cyan |
| 14 | Gray |
| 15-23 | Shades of gray, ranging from light to dark gray |
| 24 | A custom color specified by the RGB(r,g,b) function, such as RGB(64,128,128) |

**Style** (default =0) specifies a number that defines the formatting of the character. For example, 1 means the text is in boldface, while 5 (1 + 4) means the text is boldface and underlined.

| | |
| --- | --- |
| 0: | No Style |
| **1:** | **Bold** |
| 2: | Italic |
| 4: | Underline |
| 8: | SMALL CAPS |
| 15: | ALL STYLES |

| Style | Meaning |
|---|---|
| 0 | No style |
| 1 | Bold |
| 2 | *Italic* |
| 4 | Underline |
| 8 | SMALL CAPS |

**Case** (default =0) specifies the case of a shape's text if it was entered in lowercase; if the text was entered in uppercase, this cell has no effect.

> 0: Normal Case
> 1: UPPER CASE (ALL CAPS)
> 2: Title Case (initial  Caps)

| Case | Meaning |
|---|---|
| 0 | Normal case; text is displayed as typed. |
| 1 | Uppercase; text is converted to all capital letters. |
| 2 | Title case; the first letter of each word is capitalized, except when the word is prefixed by a number or a punctuation mark. |

**Pos** (default =0) specifies a number specifying the position of the text relative to the baseline.

> 0: Normal Case
> 1: Superscript text.
> 2: Subscript text.

| Pos | Meaning |
|---|---|
| 0 | Normal |
| 1 | Superscript |
| 2 | Subscript |

**Strikethru** specifies the text is stricken-through when set to TRUE (new to Visio 2000).

**DoubleULine** specifies the text is double underlined when set to TRUE (new to Visio 2000).

**Overline** specifies the text is overlined when set to TRUE (new to Visio 2000).

**Perpendicular** specifies the text is displayed perpendicular when set to TRUE (new to Visio 2000).

### Tips

➤ The size of text is independent of the scale of the drawing.

➤ Visio uses the (slightly different) value of 72 points to the inch; the correct value is 72.727272... points per inch.

➤ The Character section contains an invisible cell. Locale is not displayed by the ShapeSheet; you can only access it via VBA.

## Connection Points

Contains one row of cells for each connection point on the shape. A connection point is displayed by a small blue x.

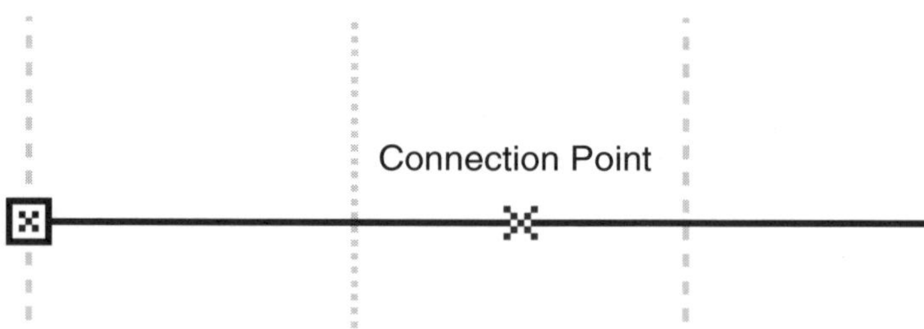


### Cells

| Connection Points | X | Y | DirX / A | DirY / B | Type / C | D |
|---|---|---|---|---|---|---|
| 1 | Width*0 | Height*0 | 0 in. | 0 in. | 0 | |

**X** specifies the x-coordinates of the connection point (default =Width*0).

**Y** specifies the y-coordinates of the connection point (default =Height*0).

**DirX/A** specifies the x-component of the alignment vector for a connection point; it can be used to orient the attached leg of a dynamic connector (this cell is renamed from **A** in earlier versions of Visio).

**DirY/B** specifies the y-component of the alignment vector for a connection point; it can be used to orient the attached leg of a dynamic connector (this cell is renamed from **B** in earlier versions of Visio).

**Type/C** specifies the type of connection point (this cell is renamed from **C** in earlier versions of Visio):

| Type/C | Meaning |
|---|---|
| 0 | Inward |
| I | Outward |
| 2 | Inward and outward |

**D** is a scratch cell that can be used for any purpose.

### Tips

➤ Visio measures the x,y-coordinates of connection points from the origin of the shape, not the parent.

➤ The cell names are normally blank, as shown by the figure above. Rename a cell with a unique name by selecting the cell and typing (or use the formula bar). Visio automatically names all cells in the Connection Points section by incrementing their names with an integer suffix, such as **Connections.Row_2** (see figure below). Named connection rows are new to Visio v5.0 and are lost when the drawing is exported to earlier versions.

| Connection Points | X | Y | A | B | C | D |
|---|---|---|---|---|---|---|
| 1 | Connections.Custom Width*0.515 | Height*0.25 | No Formula | No Formula | No Formula | No Formula |
| 2 | Connections.Row_2 Connections.Custom.X | Height*0.75 | | | | |
| 3 | Connections.Row_3 Controls.X1 | Controls.Y1 | No Formula | No Formula | No Formula | No Formula |
| 4 | Connections.Row_4 Controls.X2 | Controls.Y2 | | | | |
| 5 | Connections.Row_5 Controls.X3 | Controls.Y3 | | | | |
| 6 | Connections.Row_6 Controls.X4 | Controls.Y4 | | | | |
| 7 | Connections.Row_7 Controls.X5 | Controls.Y5 | | | | |
| 8 | Connections.Row_8 Controls.X6 | Controls.Y6 | | | | |

➤ To add a connection point to a shape, select the **Connection Point Tool** from the **Standard** toolbar, select the shape, then hold down the **Ctrl** key while clicking to make connection points.

➤ Select **View | Connection Points** from the drawing menu bar to toggle the display of connection points.

> ➤ Earlier versions of Visio had cells **A**, **B**, and **C** as scratch cells, available for your use to store constants and formulae; as of Visio 2000, these three cells now have a specific purpose.

## Controls

Contains data for each control handle defined for the shape.

### Cells

| Controls | X | Y | X Dynamics | Y Dynamics | X Behavior | Y Behavior | Can Glue | Tip |
|---|---|---|---|---|---|---|---|---|
| 1 | Width*0 | Height*0 | Controls.X1 | Controls.Y1 | 0 | 0 | TRUE | "" |

**X** (default =Width*0) specifies the x-coordinate of the shape's control handle.

**Y** (default =Height*0) specifies the y-coordinate of the shape's control handle.

**XDynamics** (default =Controls.X1) specifies the x-coordinate of the control handle's anchor point.

**YDynamics** (default =Controls.Y1) specifies the y-coordinate of the control handle's anchor point.

**XBehavior** (default =0) specifies a number describing the behavior that the control handle exhibits when moved in the x-direction—left and right.

**YBehavior** (default =0) specifies a number describing the behavior that the control handle exhibits when moved in the y-direction—up and down.

| X, YBehavior | Meaning |
|---|---|
| 0 | Control handle moves in proportion with the shape when stretched. |
| 1 | Control handle moves in proportion with the shape but the handle itself is locked. |

| X, YBehavior | Meaning |
| --- | --- |
| 2 | X: Control handle moves an offset, constant distance from the shape's left side.<br><br>Y: Control handle moves an offset, constant distance from the shape's bottom side. |
| 3 | Control handle moves an offset, constant distance from the shape's center. |
| 4 | X: Control handle moves an offset, constant distance from the shape's right side.<br><br>Y: Control handle moves an offset, constant distance from the shape's top side. |
| 5 | Control handle moves in proportion with the shape when stretched but is hidden (same as 0 but invisible). |
| 6 | Control handle moves in proportion with the shape but the handle itself is locked (same as 1 but invisible). |
| 7 | X: Control handle moves an offset, constant distance from the shape's left side (same as 2 but invisible).<br><br>Y: Control handle moves an offset, constant distance from the shape's bottom side (same as 4 but invisible). |
| 8 | Control handle moves an offset, constant distance from the shape's center (same as 3 but invisible). |
| 9 | X: Control handle moves an offset, constant distance from the shape's right side (same as 4 but invisible).<br><br>Y: Control handle moves an offset, constant distance from the shape's top side (same as 4 but invisible). |

**CanGlue** (default =TRUE) controls whether a control handle can be glued to other shapes.

| CanGlue | Meaning |
| --- | --- |
| 0 | Control handle cannot be glued |
| *not 0* | Control handle can be glued |

**Tip** (default ="") specifies an ASCII text string that appears as a tool tip when the user pauses the cursor over the shape's control handle.

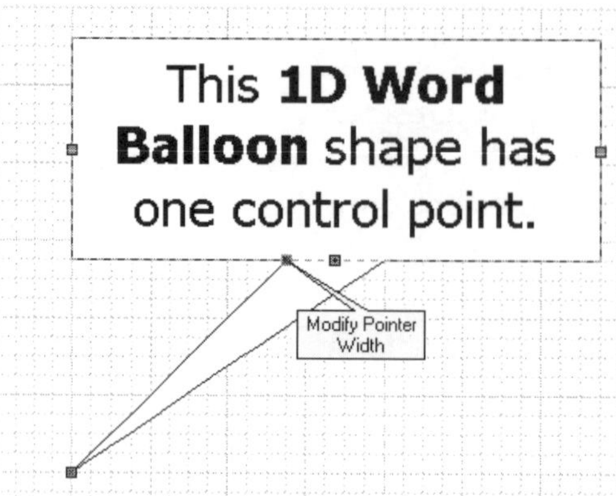



## Tips

➤ You add a control handle to a shape by adding the Controls section to the ShapeSheet.

➤ The *anchor point* of a control handle is used to display a rubber band image when the shape is moved.

## Custom Properties

Contains cells that allow you to associate data with the shape.

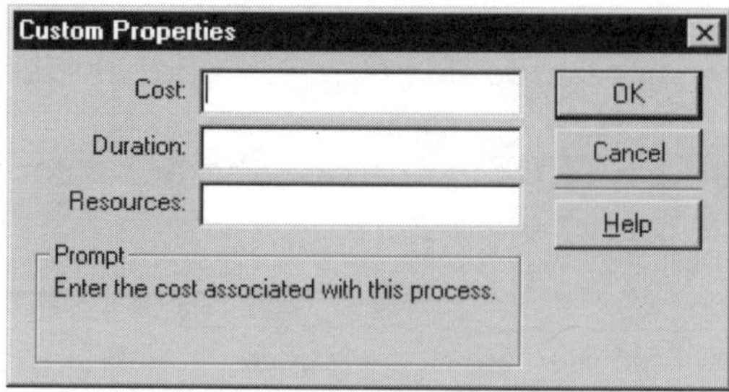

## Cells

| Custom Properties | Label | Prompt | Type | Format | Value | SortKey | Invisible | Ask |
|---|---|---|---|---|---|---|---|---|
| Prop.Row_1 | No Formula | No Formula | No Formula | No Formula | No Formula | No Formula | No Formula | No Formula |

**Prop.Row_**_n_ (default =Prop.Row_1) specifies the name of the row. When you refer to the row, Visio retrieves the data stored in the **Value** cell. To refer to other cells in the row, add the cell name as a suffix, such as **Prop.Row_1.Formula**.

**Label** (default =No Formula) specifies the text that prompts the user in the Custom Properties dialog box, such as **"Cost"** in the figures above. When **Label** is **No Formula**, Visio displays the row name in the dialog box, such as **Prop.Row_1**.

**Prompt** (default =No Formula) specifies the prompt text that appears in the **Prompt** section of the Custom Properties dialog box, such as "Enter the cost associated with this process" in the figure above.

**Type** (default =No Formula) specifies the data type.

| Type | Meaning |
|---|---|
| 0 | A string, which is text of up to 64KB characters long. The text can be formatted using format pictures in the Format cell. For example, "metric", "'The units are '@'"" results in "The units are metric." |
| 1 | Fixed list, a list of items displayed in a drop-down combo box; only one item may be selected from the list. The list of items is stored in the Format cell as a string with semicolon delimiters; for example, "Small; Smaller; Smallest." |
| 2 | Number, such as an integer, dimensions, angles, date, time, duration, and currency; the format of the number is specified by format pictures in the Format cell. For example, "# #/4 uu" displays a fraction to the nearest 1/4-inch, such as 5 1/4 inches. |
| 3 | Boolean, which is either TRUE or FALSE; the values are selected from a drop-down list box in the Custom Properties dialog box. |

| Type | Meaning |
|---|---|
| 4 | Variable list, a list of items displayed in a drop-down combo box; one item may be selected from the list, or the user may type a different value. The list of items is stored in the Format cell as a string with semicolon delimiters; for example, "Good; Better; Best." |
| 5 | Date or time value, displayed as day-month-year, or seconds-minutes-hours, or both. The text can be formatted using format pictures in the Format cell. For example, DateTime("8/25/56 12:34"),"C" displays Saturday, September 25, 1956 12:34:00 PM. |
| 6 | Duration value, displayed as elapsed time. The format is specified via a format picture in the Format cell, such as [d] to display elapsed days. |
| 7 | Currency value, which uses the Windows 95 Regional Settings to format the display. To override the format, specify a format picture in the Format cell. For example, UUU results in the currency's three-letter abbreviation, such as 99.00 USD. |

**Format** (default =No Formula) specifies the format of associated custom property value.

**Value** (default =No Formula) specifies the value of the custom property; when the user enters a value in the Custom Properties dialog box, it is stored here.

**SortKey** (default =No Formula) specifies the order in which items are listed in the Custom Properties dialog box. The sort is locale specific, case insensitive, and descending. The sort key is a string, which Visio automatically encloses in quotation marks.

**Caution:**

The formula in the Value cell is overwritten by the value entered by the user in the Custom Properties dialog box; the Guard() function does not protect the Value cell.

**Invisible** (default =No Formula) specifies whether the custom property is visible in the Custom Properties dialog box.

| Invisible | Meaning |
| --- | --- |
| 0 | Custom property is visible |
| not 0 | Custom property is not visible |

**Ask** (default =No Formula) specifies whether the Custom Property dialog box is automatically displayed when the shape is dragged onto the page or is copied.

| Verify | Meaning |
| --- | --- |
| 0 | Do not display the Custom Properties dialog box (default) |
| not 0 | Display the Custom Properties dialog box |

## Tips

➤ Custom properties are known as attributes or tags in CAD software.

➤ Ask does not affect the properties displayed when you select **Shape | Custom Properties** from the menu bar; in this case, all properties are displayed by the Custom Properties dialog box.

➤ Custom properties can be defined and edited by using the Custom Properties Editor or the cells of the Custom Properties section. The value of a shape's custom properties can be set in the Custom Properties dialog box or in the Value cell.

# Format Pictures

Visio allows you to specify the format of text and numbers using format pictures. These are used in the Format cell of the Custom Properties section and as arguments to the **Format()** and **FormatEx()** functions.

## String and Numeric Values

### Digit Placeholders

| | |
|---|---|
| *# or ## or ##.## etc.* | The # displays a digit or nothing. |
| | *Example:* |
| | FORMAT(25.781m.,"#.##u") displays **25.78in**. |

### Zero Digit Placeholder

| | |
|---|---|
| 0 | The 0 displays a digit or nothing; in addition, leading and trailing zeroes *are* displayed. When there are more digits than # placeholders to the right of the decimal point, the fraction is rounded to the number of placeholders. |
| | *Example:* |
| | FORMAT(25.7m.,"0.## u") displays **25.70m**. |

### Fraction Placeholder

| | |
|---|---|
| / | The forward slash (/) displays a number as a rounded fraction. |
| | *Example:* |
| | FORMAT(25.78,"# #/4") displays **25 3/4**. |

### Space Placeholder

| | |
|---|---|
| *space* | Displays the space character. |
| | *Example:* |
| | FORMAT(25 m.,"0. u") displays **25. m**. |

### Decimal Placeholder

| | |
|---|---|
| . | The period (.) controls the number of digits displayed to the left and right of the decimal point. The decimal character (. or ,) is determined by the Windows Regional Settings. |
| | *Example:* |
| | FORMAT(2578 cm.,"0.00 u") displays **2578.00 cm**. |

## Thousands Separator

| | |
|---|---|
| , | When surrounded by the # or 0 digit placeholders, separates thousands from hundreds. The thousands separator can be either a comma (,) or period (.), depending on the Windows Regional Settings. |

## Scientific Format

E– *or* E+ *or* e– *or* e+

The E+ or e+ displays number in scientific notation with a plus sign (+) before positive exponents and a minus sign (–) before negative exponents; the E– or e– limit the sign display to just a minus sign (–) for negative exponents.

*Example*:

FORMAT(12345.67,"###.#e+#") results in .123.5e+2.

## Unit Placeholders

u *or* U

The u or U forces units to be abbreviated to a single character; u specifies lowercase, while U specifies uppercase.

*Example*:

FORMAT(25meters,"#u") displays **25m**.

uu *or* UU

The uu or UU force units to be spelled out in full, such as meters and feet; u specifies lowercase, while U specifies uppercase.

*Example*:

FORMAT(25m,"# # UU") displays **25 METERS**.

uuu *or* UUU

The uuu or UUU force units to be abbreviated to the universal label; u specifies lowercase, while U specifies uppercase.

## *Currency Values*

## Currency Symbol

$

Displays the currency symbol, as defined by the Windows Regional Settings.

**Customizing ShapeSheets**

### Label Placeholders

| | |
|---|---|
| u *or* U | The u or U force the standard symbol for local currency and the three-character symbol for non-local currencies; u specifies lowercase, while U specifies uppercase. For example, **$25.78** is local currency while **25 FRF** is non-local currency for a computer located in the United States. |
| uu *or* UU | Forces the long currency label, such as **United States dollar** and **French franc**; u specifies lowercase, while U specifies uppercase. |
| uuu *or* UUU | Forces the use of the three-character currency, such as **25.78 USD** and **25 FRF**; u specifies lowercase, while U specifies uppercase. |

## *Text*

### Literal Displays

| | |
|---|---|
| \ | Displays the next character literally (as it is); for the backslash character, use two backslashes \\.<br><br>*Example:*<br><br>"text" or 'text'   Displays the text within the quotes. |

### Text Substitution

| | |
|---|---|
| @ | Replaces the @ with a string of text.<br><br>*Example:*<br>FORMAT("Visio", "Advanced @'" ) results in **"Advanced Visio"**. |
| @+ | Replaces the @+ with a string of text; forces all uppercase text.<br><br>*Example:*<br>FORMAT("Visio", "Advanced @+" ) results in **"Advanced VISIO"**. |
| @- | Replaces the @- with a string of text; forces all lowercase text.<br><br>*Example:*<br>FORMAT("Visio", "Advanced @-" ) results in **"Advanced visio"**. |

## *Date and Time Values*

### Date-Time Separators

| | |
|---|---|
| / | Separates the components of a date; uses the date separator as defined by Windows Regional Settings. |

| | |
|---|---|
| **Date-Time Separators (cont.)** | |
| : | Displays the time as defined by the Windows Regional Settings. |
| T | General time format. |
| **Elapsed Date-Time Placeholder** | |
| [ ] | When used with the h, mm, d, ww, and other placeholders, displays the elapsed time or dates. |
| | *Examples*: |
| | **[h]** is elapsed hours and **[ww]** is elapsed weeks. |
| **Date-Time Placeholders** | |
| c *or* C | **C** specifies the long date format; **c** specifies the short date format; both display the general time format. |
| | *Examples*: |
| | Format(DateTime("9/25/56 11:37"),"C") displays **Saturday, September 25, 1956 11:37:00 PM**. |
| | Format(DateTime("Sep. 25, 1956"),"c") displays **9/25/56**. |
| **Date Placeholders** | |
| d | Displays the day as a number, without leading zero, in the range of **1** to **31**. |
| dd | Displays the day as a number, with leading zero, in the range from **01** to **31**. |
| ddd *or* w | Displays the day of the week by its three-letter abbreviation, in the range from **Sun** to **Sat**. |
| dddd *or* ww | Displays the full name of the day of the week, in the range of **Sunday** to **Saturday**. |
| ddddd | Displays the date in the short form, as defined by the Windows Regional Settings. |
| dddddd | Displays the date in the long form, as defined by Windows Regional Settings. |
| M | Displays the month by its number, without a leading zero, in the range from **1** to **12**. |
| MM | Displays the month by its number, with leading zero, in the range from **01** to **12**. |

| **Date Placeholders (cont.)** | |
|---|---|
| MMM | Displays the month abbreviated to three letters, in the range from **Jan** to **Dec**. |
| MMMM | Displays the full month name, in the range from **January** to **December**. |
| yy | Displays the year by its last two digits, in the range from **00** to **99**. |
| yyyy | Displays the full year number, in the range from **1900** to **2078**. |
| **Time Placeholders** | |
| h | Displays the hour without leading zero, in 12-hour format, such as **0** and **12**. |
| hh | Displays the hour with leading zero, in 12-hour format, such as **00** and **12**. |
| H | Displays the hour without leading zero, in 24-hour format, such as **0** and **24**. |
| HH | Displays the hour with leading zero, in 24-hour format, such as **00** and **24**. |
| m | Displays minutes without leading zero, such as **0** and **59**. |
| mm | Displays minutes with leading zero, such as **00** and **59**. |
| s | Displays seconds without leading zero, such as **0** and **59**. |
| ss | Displays seconds with leading zero, such as **00** and **59**. |
| **AM/PM Designations** | |
| t | Displays the AM or PM abbreviation as defined by the Windows Regional Settings, such as **a** or **p**. |
| tt | Displays the full AM or PM as defined by the Windows Regional Settings, such as **AM** or **PM**. |

## *Document Properties (new in Visio 2000)*

Controls preview quality, scope, and output format of the document (drawing).

### *Cells*

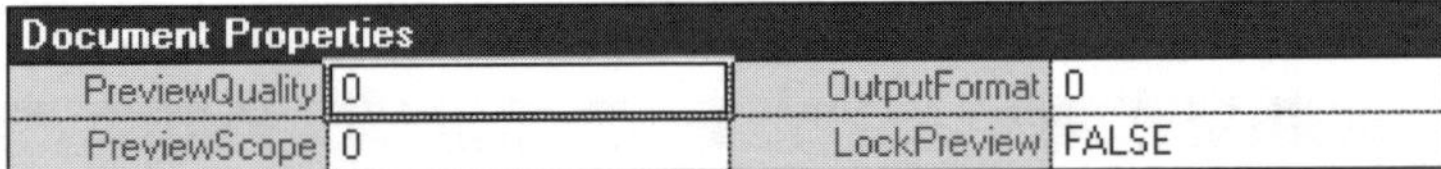

**OutputFormat** specifies the output format for a drawing.

| OutputFormat | Meaning |
| --- | --- |
| 0 | Printing |
| 1 | PowerPoint slide show |
| 2 | HTML or GIF output |

**LockPreview** specifies whether a new preview is saved each time the drawing is saved. TRUE locks the preview to prevent changing the preview image; FALSE saves a preview each time the drawing is saved.

**PreviewQuality** specifies the quality of the drawing preview. 0 is draft mode; 1 is quality mode.

**PreviewScope** specifies the number of previewed pages.

| PreviewScope | Meaning |
| --- | --- |
| 0 | Preview of first page only |
| 1 | No preview image |
| 2 | Preview of all pages in document |

### *Tips*

➤ Some of these values are set via the File | Properties dialog box.

➤ To access the Document Properties ShapeSheet, right-click the drawing's filename in the Document Explorer, and select **Show ShapeSheet** from the shortcut menu.

# Events

Contains formulae for controlling the shape when an event occurs. Event cells are evaluated only when the event occurs, not upon formula entry.

## Cells

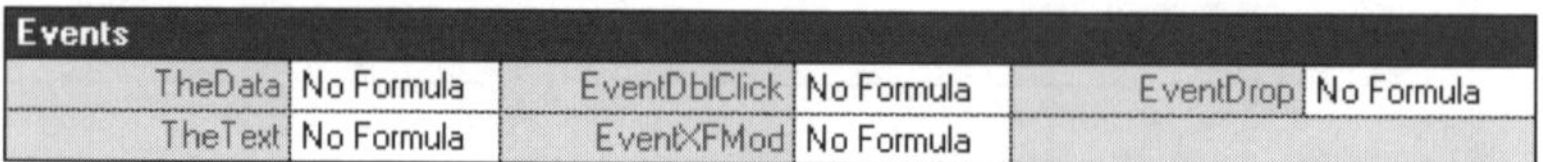

**TheData** (default =No Formula) is reserved for a future version of Visio.

**TheText** (default =No Formula) associates an event with changes to a shape's text. Whenever a change occurs to the text in the shape, Visio evaluates the formula in this cell.

**EventDblClick** (default =OpenSheetWin()) associates an event with a double-click.

**EventXFMod** (default =No Formula) associates an event with transformation to the shape, such as a change in its position and orientation.

**EventDrop** (default =No Formula) associates an event with a shape when it is dragged onto the page, is duplicated, or is pasted.

## Tips

➤ Event cells (**TheText**, **EventDblCick**, **EventXFMod**, and **EventDrop**) are evaluated when the event occurs; they are not activated when you enter a value for them during formula entry.

➤ The cell of one shape can contain an event trigger for another shape, prefix a reference to another shape on the same page.

➤ Use the **TheText** cell to recalculate the text width and height with the **TextWidth( )** and **TextHeight( )** functions.

➤ XF is short for *transformation*, as in the **EventXFMod** cell.

## *Fill Format*

Contains the current fill properties for the shape and its drop shadow.

### *Cells*

| Fill Format | | | | | |
|---|---|---|---|---|---|
| FillPattern | 1 | FillForegnd | 0 | FillBkgnd | 1 |
| ShdwPattern | 0 | ShdwForegnd | 0 | ShdwBkgnd | 1 |

**FillBkgnd** (default =0) specifies the background color. Default is black. See **FillForegnd** for the meaning of the color numbers.

**FillPattern** (default =1) specifies the fill pattern for the shape. Default is solid color fill.

| FillPattern | Meaning |
|---|---|
| 0 | No fill (object appears transparent) |
| 1 | Solid foreground color |
| 2-24 | Various line and shade fill patterns |
| 25-40 | Gradient fill patterns |

**FillForegnd** (default =1) specifies the foreground color. Default is white.

| Color | Meaning |
|---|---|
| 0 | Black |
| 1 | White |
| 2 | Red |
| 3 | Green |
| 4 | Blue |
| 5 | Yellow |
| 6 | Magenta |
| 7 | Cyan |
| 8 | Dark Red |
| 9 | Dark Green |
| 10 | Dark Blue |
| 11 | Dark Yellow |

| Color | Meaning |
|-------|---------|
| 12 | Dark Magenta |
| 13 | Dark Cyan |
| 14 | Gray |
| 15-23 | Shades of gray, ranging from light to dark gray |
| 24 | A custom color specified by the RGB(r,g,b) function, such as RGB(64,128,128) |

**ShdwBkgnd** (default =1) specifies the background color of the shape's drop shadow fill pattern. Default is white. See FillForegnd for the meaning of the color numbers.

**ShdwPattern** (default =0) specifies the fill pattern for the shape's drop shadow. Default is none. See FillPattern for the meaning of fill pattern numbers.

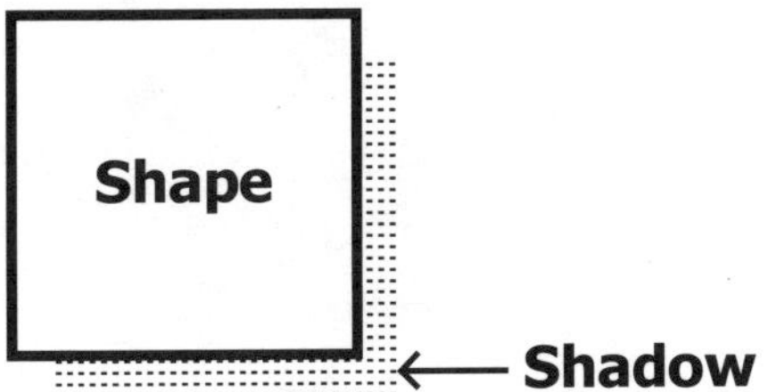


**ShdwForegnd** (default =0) specifies the foreground color of the shape's drop shadow fill pattern. Default is black. See FillForegnd for the meaning of the color numbers.

### Tips

➤ Employ the USE function in the **FillPattern** and **ShdwPattern** cells to specify a custom fill pattern.

➤ A value of 24 or higher specifies a custom color created by the **RGB()** function.

## Foreign Image Info

Contains the width and height of any non-Visio object inserted in the page, typically from another Windows application.

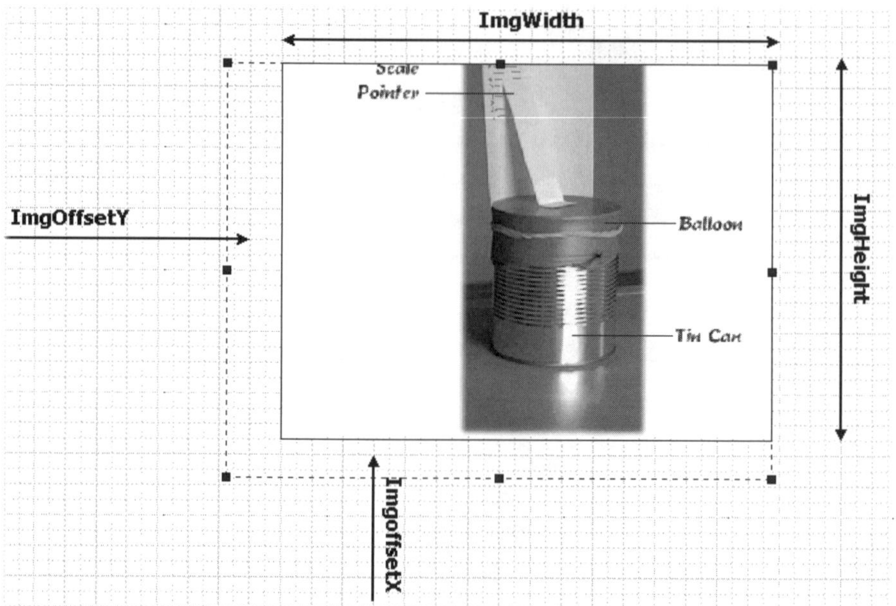


## Cells

| Foreign Image Info | | | | |
|---|---|---|---|---|
| ImgWidth | Width*1 | ImgOffsetX | ImgWidth*0 | |
| ImgHeight | Height*1 | ImgOffsetY | ImgHeight*0 | |

**ImgWidth** (default =Width*1) specifies the width of the object within its border. This formula changes when you crop the object.

**ImgHeight** (default =Height*1) specifies the height of the object within its border. This formula changes when you crop the object.

**ImgOffsetX** (default =ImgWidth*0) specifies the horizontal offset distance from the object's origin. This formula changes when you pan the object with the Crop Tool.

**ImgOffsetY** (default =ImgHeight*0) specifies the vertical offset distance from the object's origin. This formula changes when you pan the object with the Crop Tool.

### Tip

➤ The Image Info section was renamed Foreign Image Info with Visio 2000.

## Geometry

Contains the coordinates of the vertices for the lines and arcs that make up the shape. If the shape has more than one path, there is a Geometry section for each path. To add this section, use the Insert Section command. Visio 2000 supports these objects:

➤ Arc

➤ Ellipse (new to Visio 2000)

➤ Elliptical arc

➤ Infinite line (new to Visio 2000)

➤ Line

➤ NURBS (non uniform rational B-spline; this was a NUBS in earlier versions of Visio)

➤ Spline

➤ Polyline (new to Visio 2000)

Other objects are made from these. For example, a rectangle consists of four lines; a circle is made from a round ellipse.

### Cells

| Geometry 1 | | | | | | | |
|---|---|---|---|---|---|---|---|
| Geometry1.NoFill | TRUE | Geometry1.NoLine | FALSE | Geometry1.NoShow | FALSE | Geometry1.NoSnap | FALSE |
| **Name** | **X** | **Y** | **A** | **B** | **C** | **D** | **E** |
| 1 | MoveTo | Width*0 | Height*0 | | | | |
| 2 | LineTo | Width*0 | Height*1 | | | | |
| 3 | LineTo | Width*1 | Height*1 | | | | |

Cells common to all geometry:

**MoveTo** specifies the x- and y-coordinates of the first vertex (not necessarily the begin point) for the shape (this cell was known as Start in earlier versions of Visio).

| MoveTo | Meaning |
| --- | --- |
| X | Starting x-coordinate |
| Y | Starting y-coordinate |

**NoFill** specifies whether or not the shape can be filled. When TRUE, the shape cannot be filled because it is open; when FALSE, it can be filled because the path is closed (this cell was known as A in earlier versions of Visio).

**NoLine** toggles the visibility of the path. TRUE does not display the path of the boundary of a filled region; FALSE draws the path (new in Visio 2000).

**NoShow** specifies whether or not the shape is displayed on the page. When TRUE, the shape is hidden; when FALSE, the shape is displayed (this cell was known as **B** in earlier versions of Visio).

**NoSnap** toggles whether other shapes snap to the path. TRUE prevents other shapes from snapping to the path; FALSE allows snapping (new in Visio 2000).

Additional cell found in line geometry:

**LineTo** specifies the x-and y-coordinates of the ending vertex.

| LineTo | Meaning |
| --- | --- |
| X | Ending x-coordinate |
| Y | Ending y-coordinate |

# Line

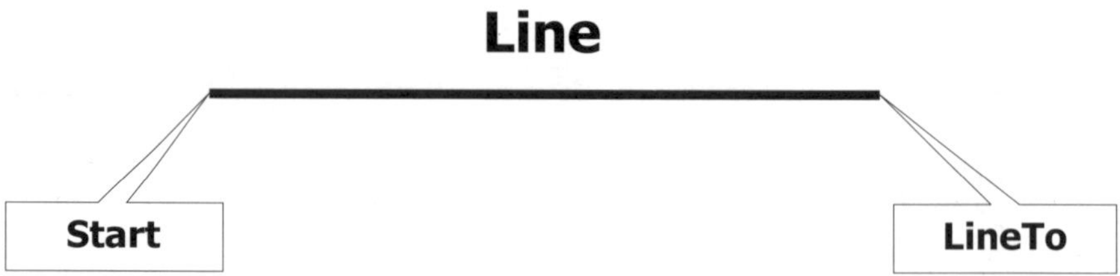


Additional cell found in arc geometry:

**ArcTo** specifies the x- and y-coordinates and bow of a circular arc.

| ArcTo | Meaning |
|---|---|
| X | Ending vertex's x-coordinate |
| Y | Ending vertex's y-coordinate |
| A | Distance from the arc's bisector to the *bow point* (the point halfway along the arc's beginning vertex and ending vertex) |

## Arc

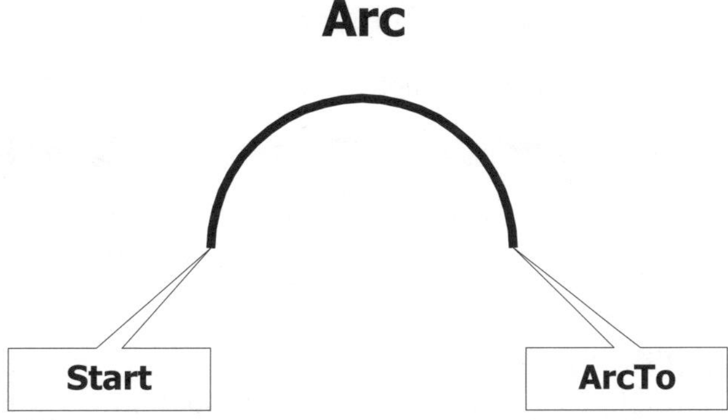



> **Caution:**
>
> Arcs are rarely used in Visio; the only shape that uses ArcTo is the **Center Drag Circle** shape in the **Basic Shapes** stencil. The reason is because a circular arc does not transform. Stretching a shape containing a circular arc should make it elliptical; an ArcTo row, however, does not become elliptical.

Additional cell found in ellipse geometry:

| Geometry 1 | | | | | | | |
|---|---|---|---|---|---|---|---|
| Geometry1.NoFill | FALSE | Geometry1.NoLine | FALSE | Geometry1.NoShow | FALSE | Geometry1.NoSnap | FALSE |
| **Name** | X | Y | A | B | C | D | E |
| 1 | Ellipse | Width*0.5 | Height*0.5 | Width*1 | Height*0.5 | Width*0.5 | Height*1 |

**Ellipse** specifies an ellipse, which can also be used to draw a circle (new to Visio 2000). The ellipse is defined by x,y-coordinates of its center point and two other points on the elliptical curve.

| Ellipse | Meaning |
|---|---|
| X | X-coordinate of the ellipse's center point |
| Y | Y-coordinate of the center point |
| A | X-coordinate of one point on the ellipse |
| B | Y-coordinate of one point on the ellipse |
| C | X-coordinate of another point on the ellipse |
| D | Y-coordinate of another point on the ellipse |

Additional cell found in elliptical arc geometry:

| Geometry 1 | | | | | | | |
|---|---|---|---|---|---|---|---|
| Geometry1.NoFill TRUE | | Geometry1.NoLine FALSE | | Geometry1.NoShow FALSE | | Geometry1.NoSnap | FALSE |
| **Name** | **X** | **Y** | **A** | **B** | **C** | **D** | **E** |
| 1 | MoveTo | Width*0 | Height*0 | | | | |
| 2 | EllipticalArcTo | Width*1 | Height*0 | Width*0.4328 | Height*1 | _ELLIPSE_ | _ELLIPSE_ECC(0.9505,0.7143,2.15 |

**EllipticalArcTo** specifies the x- and y-coordinates, control points, angle of eccentricity, and ratio of major and minor axes of an elliptical arc.

| EllipticalArcTo | Meaning |
|---|---|
| X | Ending vertex x-coordinate |
| Y | Ending vertex y-coordinate |
| A | Control point x-coordinate (point through which the curve of the arc passes) |
| B | Control point y-coordinate |
| C | Angle of the arc's major axis relative to the page (set to 0 when arc is not rotated) |
| D | Ratio of the arc's major axis to its minor axis (when set to 1, the elliptical arc is a circular arc) |

## Elliptical Arc

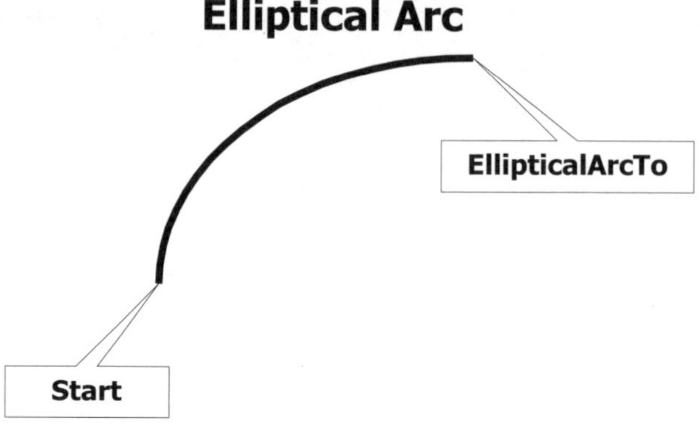

Additional cell found in infinite line geometry:

| Geometry 1 | | | | | | | |
|---|---|---|---|---|---|---|---|
| Geometry1.NoFill | TRUE | Geometry1.NoLine | FALSE | | Geometry1.NoShow | FALSE | Geometry1.NoSnap | FALSE |
| **Name** | X | Y | A | B | C | D | E |
| 1 InfiniteLine | Width*0 | Height*0.5 | IF(Width>0,Width,1 in.) | Height*0.5 | | | |

**InfiniteLine** specifies an infinite line, which is also used to create guidelines (new to Visio 2000). The infinite line is defined by two pairs of x,y-coorinates.

| *InfiniteLine* | *Meaning* |
|---|---|
| X | X-coordinate of one point on the infinite line |
| Y | Y-coordinate of one point on the infinite line |
| A | X-coordinate of another point on the infinite line |
| B | Y-coordinate of another point on the infinite line |

Additional cells found in **NURBS** geometry:

| Geometry 1 | | | | | | | |
|---|---|---|---|---|---|---|---|
| Geometry1.NoFill | TRUE | Geometry1.NoLine | FALSE | Geometry1.NoShow | FALSE | Geometry1.NoSnap | FALSE |
| **Name** | X | Y | A | B | C | D | E |
| 1 MoveTo | Width*0 | Height*0.1356 | | | | | |
| 2 NURBSTo | Width*1 | Height*0.1356 | 25.6859 | 1 | 0 | 1 | NURBS(28.3784, 3, 0, 0, 0. |

**NURBSTo** draws a non-uniform rational B-spline (changed from a NUBS in Visio 2000).

| *NURBSTo* | *Meaning* |
|---|---|
| X | X-coordinate of the last control point |
| Y | Y-coordinate of the last control point |
| A | Second last knot |
| B | Last weight |
| C | First knot |
| D | First weight |
| E | NURBS formula |

Additional cells found in polyline geometry:

**PolylineTo** defines a multi-segment line (new Visio 2000).

| *PolylineTo* | *Meaning* |
| --- | --- |
| X | X-coordinate of the ending vertex |
| Y | Y-coordinate of the ending vertex |
| A | Formula |

**SplineStart** specifies the x- and y-coordinates of a NURBS' second control point.

| *SplineStart* | *Meaning* |
| --- | --- |
| X | X-coordinate of the NURBS' second control point |
| Y | Y-coordinate of the NURBS' second control point |
| A | Specifies the position of the second knot on the NURBS |
| B | Specifies the position of the first knot on the NURBS |
| C | Specifies the position of the last knot on the NURBS |
| D | Specifies the degree of the NURBS; an integer from I to 9 |

**SplineKnot** specifies the x- and y-coordinates of the NURBS knots.

| *SplineKnot* | *Meaning* |
| --- | --- |
| X | X-coordinate of the control point |
| Y | Y-coordinate of the control point |
| A | Specifies the location of the third or following NURBS knots |

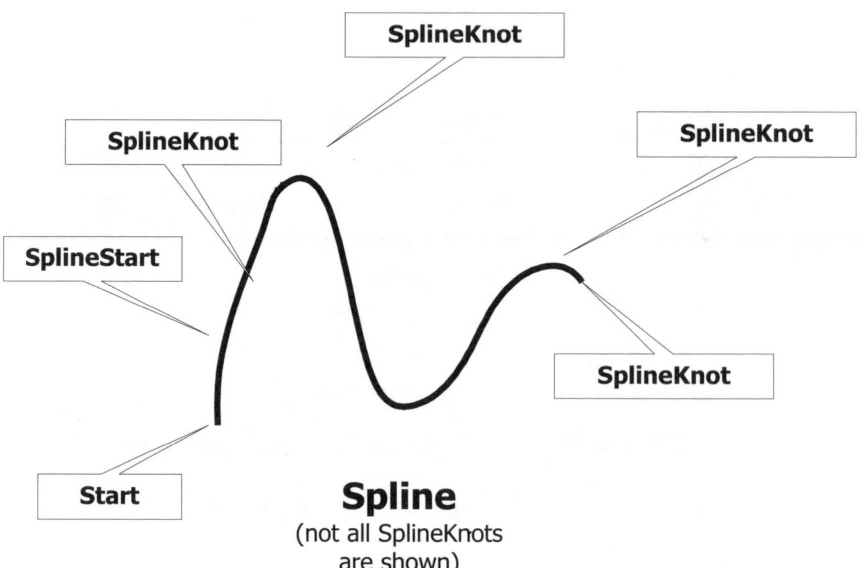


**Spline**
(not all SplineKnots
are shown)

### Tips

➤ When an arc is first drawn, it is an elliptical arc and not a circular arc. If you want to change an elliptical arc to a circular arc, use the Change Row Type command to change EllipticalArcTo to ArcTo.

➤ Do not set the ratio of the elliptical arc's major axis to its minor axis to less than 0, equal to 0, or greater than 1000.

➤ Splines in Visio are drawn with NUBS (non-uniform B-spline) and should not be confused with NURBS (non-uniform rational B-spline), which is more common in CAD software.

➤ The **GeometryN.A1** cell is actually **GeometryN.NoFill** and was called **GeometryN.X0** in earlier versions of Visio. The cell can be called either **GeometryN.NoFill** or **GeometryN.X0**.

➤ Visio 2000 adds the infinite line (which replaces guidelines), ellipse (which also draws a circle), and the polyline (which defines two or more straight line segments).

## Glue Info

Contains data about gluing a 1D shape to other shapes.

### Cells

**BegTrigger** (default =No Formula) specifies the trigger formula (generated by Visio). This formula determines whether the begin point of the 1D shape should move to maintain its connection to another shape.

**EndTrigger** (default =No Formula) specifies the trigger formula (generated by Visio). This formula determines whether the end point of the 1D shape should move to maintain its connection to another shape.

**GlueType** (default =0) specifies whether the 1D shape uses static or dynamic glue when glued to another shape. When GlueType = 3, Visio will write formulae in the **BegTrigger** and **EndTrigger** cells.

| GlueType | Meaning |
| --- | --- |
| 0 | Use static glue (point to point); the default |
| 1 | Unassigned in this version of Visio |
| 2 | Unassigned in this version of Visio |
| 3 | Use dynamic glue (shape to shape) |

**WalkPreference** (default =0) specifies whether the endpoint of a 1D shape moves to a horizontal or vertical connection point; only applies to ambiguous positions when using dynamic glue.

| WalkPreference | Meaning |
| --- | --- |
| 0 | Side-to-side connection: begin and end points move to horizontal connection points |
| 1 | Top-to-side and bottom-to-side connections: begin point moves to vertical connection point; end point moves to horizontal connection point |
| 2 | Side-to-top and side-to-bottom connections: begin point moves to horizontal connection point; end point moves to vertical connection point |
| 3 | Top-to-bottom connections: begin and end points move to vertical connection points |

## Tip

➤ When a 1D shape is glued to another shape with dynamic glue, the BegTrigger and EndTrigger cells refer to the EventXFMod cell of the other shape.

## *Group Properties (new in Visio 2000)*

Contains cells for a group of shapes. The cells specify how shapes are added and moved, and how the group is selected.

### *Cells*

| Group Properties | | | | | |
|---|---|---|---|---|---|
| SelectMode | 1 | IsTextEditTarget | TRUE | IsDropTarget | FALSE |
| DisplayMode | 2 | IsSnapTarget | TRUE | DontMoveChildren | FALSE |

**SelectMode** specifies how a group is selected.

| SelectMode | Meaning |
|---|---|
| 0 | Select the group shape only |
| I | Select the group shape first; second pick selects a member of the group |
| 2 | Select a member of the group first; second pick selects the group |

**DisplayMode** specifies how the group shape and text are displayed.

| Display Mode | Meaning |
|---|---|
| 0 | Hides the group shape and text |
| I | Displays the group shape behind member shapes |
| 2 | Displays the group shape in front of member shapes |

**IsTextEditTarget** toggles how text is added to the group. TRUE means the text is added to the group shape; FALSE means the text is added to the shape at the top of the stacking order.

**IsSnapTarget** toggles whether the group or shapes can be snapped to. TRUE means that shapes in the group can be snapped to; FALSE means that the group is snapped to.

**IsDropTarget** toggles whether a shape can be added to a group by dropping the shape on the group. TRUE enables; FALSE disables the feature.

**DontMoveChildren** toggles the dragability of shapes in the group. TRUE prevents shapes from being dragged; FALSE allows shapes to be dragged with the cursor.

### Tips

> ➤ For IsDropTarget to work, the same behavior must be set for the group and the shape being dropped on the group. Enable the behavior for the shape via the Miscellaneous section's IsDropSource cell.

> ➤ DontMoveChildren only affects dragging member of a group using the cursor (mouse). When set to TRUE, shapes in the group can still be flipped, rotated, resized, and repositioned.

> ➤ The value of DontMoveChildren is set to TRUE for groups in masters created in versions prior to earlier than Visio 2000.

**Note:**

The Guide Info section was removed in Visio 2000. It has been replaced by the InfiniteLine row of the Geometry section.

## Hyperlinks

Contains cells for creating a link between the shape (or page) and another Visio page or file on your computer, the network your computer is connected to, or on the Internet. After creating the hyperlink, the Visio cursor changes to a three-link chain; click to make the jump.

### Cells

| Hyperlinks | Description | Address | SubAddress | ExtraInfo | Frame | NewWindow | Default |
|---|---|---|---|---|---|---|---|
| Hyperlink.Row_1 | No Formula | No Formula | No Formula | No Formula | No Formula | No Formula | No Formula |

**Description** (default ="") specifies a string of text that describes the hyperlink. The description only appears in the Hyperlink dialog box and the Hyperlink section.

**Address** (default ="") specifies the URL (short for Uniform Resource Locator) or filename to which the hyperlink will jump.

**SubAddress** (default ="") specifies an anchor location within the target document.

**Frame** (default ="") specifies the name of the frame to target when Visio is open as an ActiveX document in an ActiveX container.

**ExtraInfo** (default ="") specifies a string containing extra information for the URL, such as the coordinates of an image map, such as "x=12&y=34."

**NewWindow** (default =FALSE) specifies whether the hyperlink opens a new window.

**Default** (default ="") specifies the string that consists of additional data used by a URL (this cell was known as **ExtraInfo** in earlier versions of Visio).

### Tips

➤ A hyperlink can be added to any shape, group, page, or object in the drawing.

➤ In Visio 2000, more than one hyperlink can be added to an object.

➤ URL is short for Uniform Resource Locator and is the universal file naming system used by the Internet. Examples of URLs include:

| URL | Meaning |
| --- | --- |
| http://www.upfrontezine.com | Author Ralph Grabowski's Web site. |
| www.visio.com | Visio's Web site (the http:// portion is optional). |
| ftp://ftp.name.com | An FTP (file transfer protocol) site. |

➤ The SubAddress cell can target the page of a Visio drawing, such as **"Page-1"**; the anchor within an HTML document, such as **"advanced"**; or the range of cells in a spreadsheet, such as **"Sheet1!A1:A210"**.

> ➤ The Hyperlink section was renamed Hyperlinks in Visio 2000.

## Image Properties (new in Visio 2000)

Controls some aspects of bitmap images placed on page.

### Cells

| Image Properties | | | | | |
|---|---|---|---|---|---|
| Contrast | 50 % | Gamma | 1 | Sharpen | 0 % |
| Brightness | 50 % | Blur | 0 % | Denoise | 0 % |

**Contrast** changes the contrast of the bitmap image. Decrease the contrast with a value between 0% and 49%; increase the contrast with a value between 51% and 100%.

**Brightness** changes the brightness of the bitmap image. Darken the image with a value between 0% and 49%; brighten the image with a value between 51% and 100%.

**Gamma** stretches the difference between dark and light areas of the bitmap image when increased beyond the default value of 1.0.

**Blur** softens the bitmap image when changed from the default value of 0%.

**Sharpness** sharpens a bitmap image, increasing the contrast of adjacent pixels.

**Denoise** removes *noise*, which are pixels with random color levels, when changed from the default of 0%.

### Tips

> ➤ A bitmap is an image that consists of pixels.

> ➤ This section is available only for bitmap images.

> ➤ The values in this section are not available via a dialog box.

## *Layer Membership*

Contains a single row with a single cell that specifies the layer reference number(s), which refer to layers assigned to the shape.

### *Cells*

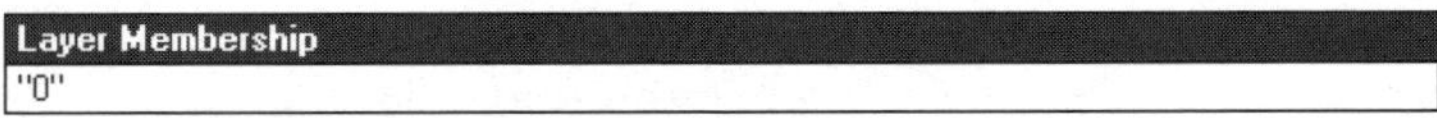


**LayerMember** (default ="0") is the sole cell which specifies the layer name(s). When the shape is assigned to more than one layer, the layers are separated by a semicolon, such as **"0;1;2"**.

### *Tips*

➤ This section lists the layer reference number, not the layer names themselves. The first layer name in the Layer Properties dialog box is layer 0, the second is layer 1, etc.

➤ Unlike in CAD software, Visio shapes can be assigned to more than one layer.

➤ To refer to this cell in a formula, use the name **LayerMember**.

➤ Select **Format | Layer** from the drawing menu bar to select the layer(s) to which the shape should belong.

## *Layers*

Contains all of the layers defined in this page and their properties.

### *Cells*

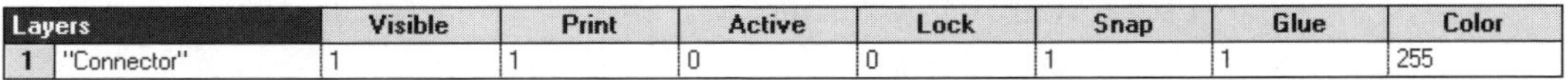

| Layers | | Visible | Print | Active | Lock | Snap | Glue | Color |
|---|---|---|---|---|---|---|---|---|
| 1 | "Connector" | 1 | 1 | 0 | 0 | 1 | 1 | 255 |

**Visible** (default =1) specifies whether shapes are visible. When a shape is on more than one layer, the shape is still visible when at least one of its layers has Visible still turned on (set to 1).

| Visible | Meaning |
| --- | --- |
| 0 | Shapes are hidden |
| *not 0* | Shapes are visible (default) |

**Print** (default =1) specifies whether shapes are printed.

| Print | Meaning |
| --- | --- |
| 0 | Shapes cannot be printed |
| *not 0* | Shapes can be printed (default) |

**Active** (default =0) specifies whether the layer is *active*, which means that a shape without a preassigned layer is placed on the active layer(s) when dragged onto the page.

| Active | Meaning |
| --- | --- |
| 0 | Not an active layer (default) |
| *not 0* | Active layer |

**Lock** (default =0) specifies whether the shapes are *locked*, which means the shapes cannot be edited or selected. When a shape is on more than one layer, then it is locked when at least one of its layers is locked.

| Lock | Meaning |
| --- | --- |
| 0 | Shapes are not locked (default) |
| *not 0* | Shapes are locked |

**Snap** (default =1) specifies whether shapes snap to the grid.

| Snap | Meaning |
| --- | --- |
| 0 | Shapes do not snap to grid |
| *not 0* | Shapes snap to grid (default) |

**Glue** (default =1) specifies whether shapes can be glued. When off (set to 0), shapes cannot be *glued* (do not remain connected together when one shape is moved).

| Glue | Meaning |
| --- | --- |
| 0 | Glue is disabled |
| *not 0* | Glue is enabled (default) |

**Color** (default =255) specifies the color displayed by shapes on that layer.

| Color | Meaning |
| --- | --- |
| 255 | Shape keeps its own color (default) |
| 0-24 | All shapes on this layer take on the same color |

### Tips

➤ This section only appears in the ShapeSheet of a page.

➤ To find out which layer(s) are assigned to a shape, select the shape, then view the Layer Membership section in the shape's ShapeSheet.

## Line Format

Contains the current line format properties for the shape.

### Cells

| Line Format | | | | | |
| --- | --- | --- | --- | --- | --- |
| LinePattern | 1 | BeginArrow | 0 | BeginArrowSize | 2 |
| LineWeight | 0.24 pt. | EndArrow | 0 | EndArrowSize | 2 |
| LineColor | 0 | LineCap | 0 | Rounding | 0 in. |

**LinePattern** (default =1) specifies the pattern for the lines making up the shape; default is a continuous line.

| | | |
| --- | --- | --- |
| 0 (none) | 1 | 2 |
| 3 | 4 | 5 |
| 6 | 7 | 8 |
| 9 | 10 | 11 |
| 12 | 13 | 14 |
| 15 | 16 | 17 |
| 18 | 19 | 20 |
| 21 | 22 | 23 |

| LinePattern | Meaning |
| --- | --- |
| 0 | No line pattern; invisible line |
| I | Solid line (continuous); no pattern |
| 2-24 | Various line patterns consisting of dot, dash, and gap patterns |

**LineWeight** (default =0.72 pt.) specifies the width of the line. You can specify a unit for the line weight; if no unit is specified, the current units are used.

| LineWeight | Meaning |
| --- | --- |
| I | 0.72 pt. or 0.01 in. |
| 3 | 2.16 pt. or 0.03 in. |
| 5 | 3.60 pt. or 0.05 in. |
| 9 | 6.48 pt. or 0.09 in. |
| 13 | 9.36 pt. or 0.13 in. |
| 17 | 12.24 pt. or 0.17 in. |

**LineColor** (default =0) specifies the color of the line color of the shape; default color is black.

| Color | Meaning |
| --- | --- |
| 0 | Black |
| I | White |
| 2 | Red |
| 3 | Green |
| 4 | Blue |
| 5 | Yellow |
| 6 | Magenta |
| 7 | Cyan |
| 8 | Dark Red |
| 9 | Dark Green |
| 10 | Dark Blue |
| II | Dark Yellow |
| 12 | Dark Magenta |
| 13 | Dark Cyan |
| 14 | Gray |
| 15-23 | Shades of gray, ranging from light to dark gray |

| 24 | A custom color specified by the RGB(r,g,b) function, such as RGB(64,128,128) |
|---|---|

**BeginArrow** (default =0) specifies whether a line has an arrowhead at the line's beginning; note that the size of the arrowhead is specified by the ArrowSize cell. Default is no arrowhead.

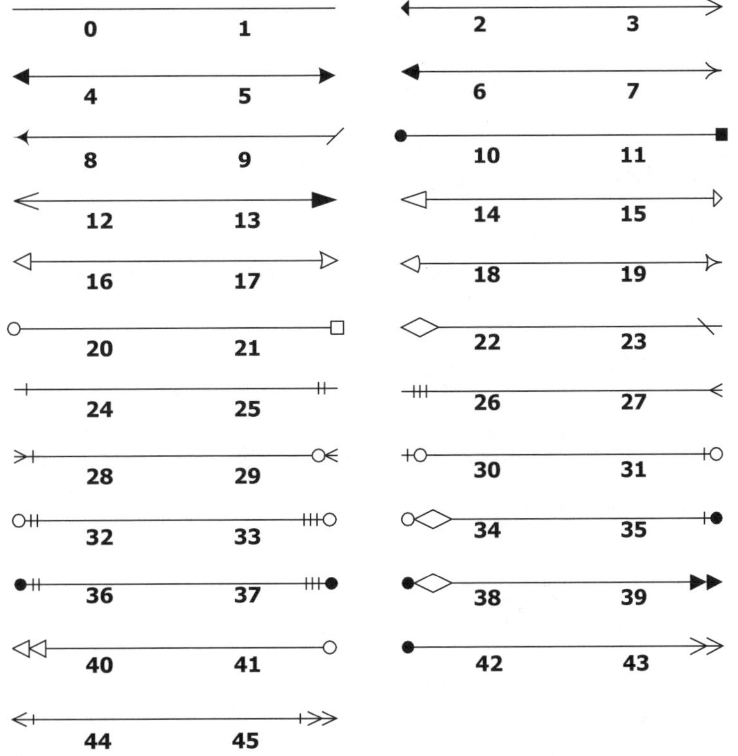

| BeginArrow | Meaning |
|---|---|
| 0 | No arrowhead (default) |
| 1-27 | Single arrowhead styles |
| 28-45 | Double arrowhead styles |

**EndArrow** (default =0) specifies whether a line has an arrowhead at the line's ending; note that the size of the arrowhead is specified by the ArrowSize cell. Default is no arrowhead.

**LineCap** (default =0) specifies whether the line has round (the default) or square corners and endcaps of the lines.

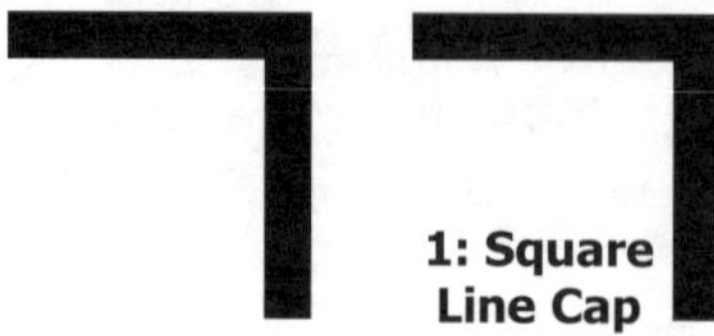



| LineCap | Meaning |
|---------|---------|
| 0 | Round ends and corners (default) |
| I | Square ends and corners |

**BeginArrowSize** (default =1) specifies the size of the begin arrowhead.

**EndArrowSize** (default =1) specifies the size of the end arrowhead.

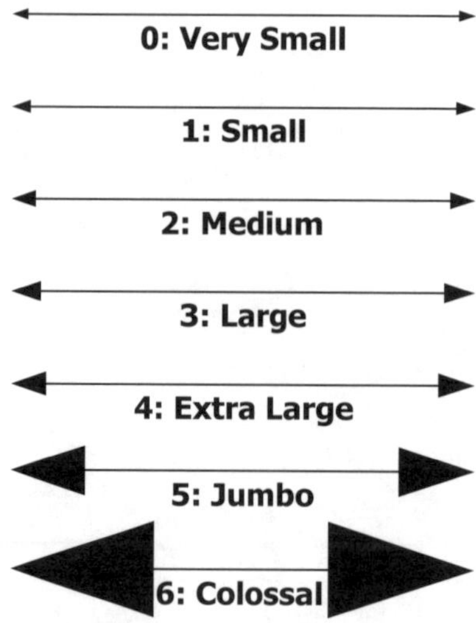



(These two cells were a single cell called ArrowSize in earlier versions of Visio).

| ArrowSize | Meaning |
|---|---|
| 0 | Very small |
| 1 | Small (default) |
| 2 | Medium |
| 3 | Large |
| 4 | Extra large |
| 5 | Jumbo |
| 6 | Colossal |

**Rounding** (default =0 in.) specifies the radius of the fillet (rounding arc) at the intersection of two lines.

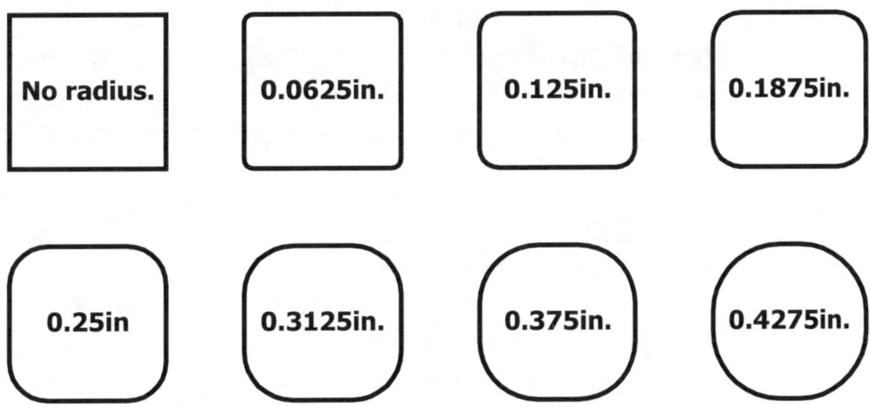




## Tips

➤ To display a custom line pattern, employ the USE function in the LinePattern cell.

➤ To display a custom arrowhead, employ the USE function in the BeginArrow and EndArrow cells.

➤ The Rounding cell is used to create a rectangle with rounded corners.

## Miscellaneous

Contains miscellaneous properties for a shape, such as the visibility of its handles, alignment box, and dynamic feedback.

### Cells

| Miscellaneous | | | | | |
|---|---|---|---|---|---|
| NoObjHandles | FALSE | HideText | FALSE | ObjType | 2 |
| NoCtlHandles | FALSE | UpdateAlignBox | FALSE | IsDropSource | FALSE |
| NoAlignBox | TRUE | DynFeedback | 2 | Comment | "" |
| NonPrinting | FALSE | NoLiveDynamics | TRUE | | |

**NoObjHandles** (default =FALSE) toggles the display of *selection handles* (the green boxes that appear when an object is selected); when not zero, the selection handles do not display when you select the shape.

| NoObjHandles | Meaning |
|---|---|
| 0 | Selection handles are displayed |
| *not 0* | Selection handles are not displayed when shape is selected |

**NoCtlHandles** (default =FALSE) toggles the display of control handles; when non-zero, the control handles do not display when you select the shape.

| NoCtlHandles | Meaning |
|---|---|
| 0 | Control handles are displayed |
| *not 0* | Control handles are not displayed when shape is selected |

**NoAlignBox** (default =FALSE) toggles the display of the *alignment box* (the green dotted line that appears when you select a shape) or *alignment line* of a 1D shape. When non-zero, the alignment box does not display when you select the shape.

| NoAlignBox | Meaning |
|---|---|
| 0 | Alignment box (or line) is displayed |
| *not 0* | Alignment box (or line) is not displayed when shape is selected |

**NonPrinting** (default =FALSE) specifies whether the shape is printed or not. When TRUE (or 1), the shape is displayed but not printed.

| NonPrinting | Meaning |
| --- | --- |
| 0 | Printing enabled |
| not 0 | Printing disabled |

**HideText** (default =FALSE) specifies whether the text is displayed. When TRUE (or 1), the text is not displayed and does not print.

| HideText | Meaning |
| --- | --- |
| 0 | Text is not hidden |
| not 0 | Text is hidden |

**UpdateAlignBox** (default =FALSE) specifies whether the alignment box is recalculated as the control handle is moved. Leave off for faster performance on slower computers.

| UpdateAlignBox | Meaning |
| --- | --- |
| 0 | Alignment box is not updated |
| not 0 | Alignment box is updated |

**DynFeedback** (default =0) specifies the visual feedback when a connector is dragged; does not apply to routable connectors.

| DynFeedback | Meaning |
| --- | --- |
| 0 | Connector remains straight; no legs are displayed |
| 1 | Connector shows three legs while dragged |
| 2 | Connector shows five legs while dragged |

**NoLiveDynamics** specifies the interaction style in a connected diagram, if the shape is placeable or routable. This value is always 0 for a placeable and routable shape; a non-zero value causes unpredictable behavior. TRUE means the shape does not dynamically update; FALSE means the shape updates dynamically.

**ObjType** (default =No Formula) specifies how the shape should be treated; No Formula is equivalent to 0, which allows Visio to determine whether the shape is placeable.

| ObjType | Meaning |
| --- | --- |
| 0 | Visio decides based on the drawing context |
| 1 | Shape is placeable |
| 2 | Shape is routable |
| 3 | Unassigned in this version of Visio |
| 4 | Shape is not placeable nor routable |
| 8 | Object is a group (new in Visio 2000) |

**IsDropSource** toggles whether you can add the shape to a group by simply dragging it onto the group. TRUE means this behavior is enabled; FALSE disables the behavior (new in Visio 2000).

**Comment** contains comment text for a shape (new in Visio 2000).

## Tips

➤ For the toggle cells, 0 is the same as FALSE; 1 is the same as TRUE. You may enter either the number (0 or 1) or the word (FALSE or TRUE).

➤ The ObjType value of a shape, such as a rectangle, is initially 0 (let Visio decide). When it is connected to another shape (via the Tools | Connect Shapes command or the Dynamic Connector tool from the Standard toolbar), the value of ObjType changes to 1 (placeable).

➤ Creating hidden text with the HideText cell could be used as a simple form of *watermarking*, which specifies the source and copyright of the page.

➤ Setting NonPrinting to FALSE is useful for including documentation in the page, such as how to print.

➤ For IsDropSource to work with a group, the IsDropTarget cell of the Group Behavior section must also be set to TRUE.

➤ In Visio 2000, the Shape Layout section's ShapeFixedCode and ShapePermeablePlace cells replace the ObjInteract cell of the Miscellaneous section found in Visio 5.x.

## Page Layout (new in Visio 2000)

### Cells

| Page Layout | | | | | |
|---|---|---|---|---|---|
| PlaceStyle | 0 | BlockSizeX | 0.25 in. | LineToNodeX | 0.125 in. |
| PlaceDepth | 0 | BlockSizeY | 0.25 in. | LineToNodeY | 0.125 in. |
| PlowCode | 0 | AvenueSizeX | 0.375 in. | LineToLineX | 0.125 in. |
| ResizePage | FALSE | AvenueSizeY | 0.375 in. | LineToLineY | 0.125 in. |
| DynamicsOff | FALSE | RouteStyle | 1 | LineJumpFactorX | 0.6667 |
| EnableGrid | FALSE | PageLineJumpDirX | 0 | LineJumpFactorY | 0.6667 |
| CtrlAsInput | FALSE | PageLineJumpDirY | 0 | LineJumpCode | 1 |
| LineAdjustFrom | 0 | LineAdjustTo | 0 | LineJumpStyle | 0 |

**PlaceStyle** specifies how shapes are placed on the page when automatically laid out.

| PlaceStyle | Meaning |
|---|---|
| 0 | Radial (default) |
| 1 | Top to bottom |
| 2 | Left to right |
| 3 | Radial |
| 4 | Bottom to top |
| 5 | Right to left |
| 6 | Circular |

**PlaceDepth** specifies the type of layout.

| PlaceDepth | Meaning |
|---|---|
| 0 | Page default |
| 1 | Medium |
| 2 | Deep |
| 3 | Shallow |

**PlowCode** determines whether placeable shapes move away when you drop a placeable shape nearby. Zero (0) means shapes are not moved; 1 means shapes are moved.

**ResizePage** specifies whether the page is enlarged after shapes are automatically laid out. TRUE enlarges the page; FALSE does not enlarge the page.

**DynamicsOff** toggles whether placeable shapes move, and whether connectors reroute around other shapes and connectors. TRUE disables dynamics; FALSE enable dynamics.

**EnableGrid** toggles whether shapes are laid out on an invisible grid. The grid is defined by the block and avenue specifications. TRUE uses the internal grid; FALSE does not use the grid.

**CtrlAsInput** toggles the *parent* shape. The shape with the control handle is the parent. TRUE means the shape that has the control handle is the parent.

**LineAdjustFrom** specifies which dynamic connectors are spaced apart if they route on top of each other.

| LineAdjustFrom | Meaning |
| --- | --- |
| 0 | Unrelated lines |
| 1 | All lines |
| 2 | No lines |
| 3 | Routing style default |

**BlockSizeX** specifies the horizontal block size (area in which all shapes must fit) when automatically laid out.

**BlockSizeY** specifies the vertical block size (area in which all shapes must fit) when automatically laid out.

**AvenueSizeX** specifies the horizontal space between shapes when automatically laid out.

**AvenueSizeY** specifies the vertical space between shapes when automatically laid out.

**RouteStyle** specifies the routing style and direction for all connectors on the page, except those that don't have a local routing style.

| RouteStyle | Meaning | Direction |
| --- | --- | --- |
| 0 | Default; right angle | None |
| 1 | Right angle | None |
| 2 | Straight | None |
| 3 | Organization chart | Top to bottom |
| 4 | Organization chart | Left to right |

| RouteStyle | Meaning | Direction |
| --- | --- | --- |
| 5 | Flowchart | Top to bottom |
| 6 | Flowchart | Left to right |
| 7 | Tree | Top to bottom |
| 8 | Tree | Left to right |
| 9 | Network | None |
| 10 | Organization chart | Bottom to top |
| 11 | Organization chart | Right to left |
| 12 | Flowchart | Bottom to top |
| 13 | Flowchart | Right to left |
| 14 | Tree | Bottom to top |
| 15 | Tree | Right to left |
| 16 | Center to center | None |
| 17 | Simple | Top to bottom |
| 18 | Simple | Left to right |
| 19 | Simple | Bottom to top |
| 20 | Simple | Right to left |
| 21 | Simple Horizontal-Vertical | None |
| 22 | Simple Vertical-Horizontal | None |

**PageLineJumpDirX** specifies the direction of line jumps on horizontal dynamic connectors that don't have a local jump direction.

| PageLineJumpDirX | Meaning |
| --- | --- |
| 0 | Left (or page's setting) |
| 1 | Up |
| 2 | Down |

**PageLineJumpDirY** specifies the direction of line jumps on vertical dynamic connectors that don't have a local jump direction.

| PageLineJumpDirY | Meaning |
| --- | --- |
| 0 | Up (or page's setting) |
| 1 | Left |
| 2 | Right |

**LineAdjustTo** specifies which dynamic connectors line up on top of each other.

| LineAdjustTo | Meaning |
| --- | --- |
| 0 | Routing style default |
| 1 | Lines that are close to each other |
| 2 | No lines |
| 3 | Related lines |

**LineToNodeX** specifies the horizontal clearance between connectors and shapes on the page.

**LineToNodeY** specifies the vertical clearance between connectors and shapes on the page.

**LineToLineX** specifies the horizontal clearance between connectors on the page.

**LineToLineY** specifies the vertical clearance between connectors on the page.

**LineJumpFactorX** specifies the size of line jumps on horizontal dynamic connectors, relative to the value of the **LineToLineX** cell. Value ranges between 0 and 1.

**LineJumpFactorY** specifies the size of line jumps on vertical dynamic connectors, relative to the value of the **LineToLineY** cell. Value ranges between 0 and 1.

**LineJumpCode** specifies the connectors to which jumps are added.

| LineJumpCode | Meaning |
| --- | --- |
| 0 | None |
| 1 | Horizontal lines only |
| 2 | Vertical lines only |
| 3 | Last routed line only |
| 4 | Last displayed line (top shape in display order) |
| 5 | First displayed line (bottom shape in display order) |

**LineJumpStyle** specifies the line jump style for all connectors on the page wihtout a local line jump style.

| LineJumpStyle | Meaning |
| --- | --- |
| 0 | Use page default |
| 1 | Arc |
| 2 | Gap |
| 3 | Square |
| 4 | Two sides |
| 5 | Three sides |
| 6 | Four sides |
| 7 | Five sides |
| 8 | Six sides |
| 9 | Seven sides |

### Tip

➤ Dynamic grid uses avenue size.

## Page Properties

Contains the properties of the page.

### Cells

| Page Properties | | | | | |
| --- | --- | --- | --- | --- | --- |
| PageWidth | 8.5 in. | PageScale | 1 in. | ShdwOffsetX | 0.125 in. |
| PageHeight | 11 in. | DrawingScale | 1 in. | ShdwOffsetY | -0.125 in. |
| DrawingSizeType | 0 | DrawingScaleType | 0 | InhibitSnap | FALSE |

**PageWidth** (default =8.5 in.) specifies the width of the page, in current drawing units.

**PageHeight** (default =11 in.) specifies the height of the page, in current drawing units.

**DrawingSizeType** (default =0) specifies how the drawing is sized. If you are not concerned with the scale, then select 1 to fit the entire drawing to the page.

| DrawingSizeType | Meaning |
| --- | --- |
| 0 | Same as printer |
| 1 | Fit page to drawing contents |
| 2 | Standard |
| 3 | Custom page size |

| DrawingSizeType | Meaning |
| --- | --- |
| 4 | Custom scaled drawing size |
| 5 | Metric or ISO (International Organization for Standardization) |
| 6 | ANSI engineering |
| 7 | ANSI architectural |

**PageScale** (default =1 in.) specifies the value of the page's unit, in current drawing units.

**DrawingScale** (default =1 in.) specifies the value of the drawing unit.

**DrawingScaleType** (default =0) specifies the drawing scale type.

| DrawingScaleType | Meaning |
| --- | --- |
| 0 | No scale |
| I | Architectural scale |
| 2 | Civil engineering scale |
| 3 | Custom scale |
| 4 | Metric |
| 5 | Mechanical engineering scale |

**ShdwOffsetX** (default =0.125 in.) specifies the horizontal offset of the page's drop shadow.

**ShdwOffsetY** (default =-0.125 in.) specifies the vertical offset of the page's drop shadow.

**InhibitSnap** specifies whether shapes on the foreground page snap to other shapes. TRUE disables snap, except to the ruler and grid; FALSE enables snap.

## Tip

➤ Hold down the **Ctrl** key, then drag the edges of the page to make it smaller or larger.

## Paragraph

Contains the paragraph formatting attributes for the shape's text, including indents, line spacing, and horizontal alignment of paragraphs.

### Cells

| Paragraph | IndFirst | IndLeft | IndRight | SpLine | SpBefore | SpAfter | HAlign | Bullet | BulletString |
|---|---|---|---|---|---|---|---|---|---|
| 0 | 0 in. | 0 in. | 0 in. | -120 % | 0 pt. | 0 pt. | 1 | 0 | "" |

**IndFirst** (default =0 in.) specifies the indentation distance for the first line of each paragraph.

**IndLeft** (default =0 in.) specifies the left indentation distance for all lines of text in each paragraph.

**IndRight** (default =0 in.) specifies the right indentation distance for all lines of text in each paragraph.

**SpLine** (default =–120%) specifies the distance between lines of text; can be expressed in (positive = absolute) units or as a (negative = relative) percentage, where 100% is the height of one text line. For example, the default value of –120% adds a spacing of 20% between lines of text.

| SpLine | Meaning |
|---|---|
| >0 | Absolute spacing in current units |
| =0 | Spacing is 100% of type size |
| <0 | Relative spacing, expressed as a percentage of type size |

**SpBefore** (default =0 pt.) specifies the spacing after a paragraph (not between lines of text) in the shape's text block. Note that the spacing is added to SpLine, as well as TopMargin (if the first paragraph in a text block).

**SpAfter** (default =0 pt.) specifies the spacing after a paragraph (not between lines of text) in the shape's text block. Note that this spacing is added to SpLine, as well as BottomMargin (if the last paragraph in a text block).

**HAlign** (default =1) specifies the horizontal alignment of text within the text block. Other cells can refer to this cell as **Para.HorzAlign**.

| HAlign | Meaning |
| --- | --- |
| 0 | Left alignment; ragged right |
| 1 | Centered |
| 2 | Right alignment; ragged left |
| 3 | Justified; all lines of text, except the last line, are justified |
| 4 | Force justified; all lines of text, including the last line, are justified |

**Bullet** specifies the style of bullet (new to Visio 2000).

| Bullet | Meaning |
| --- | --- |
| 0 | No bullet (default) |
| 1 | ● |
| 2 | ◆ |
| 3 | ■ |
| 4 | ❑ |
| 5 | ❖ |
| 6 | ➢ |
| 7 | ✓ |

**BulletString** specifies a custom bullet as a string, such as "Item" (new to Visio 2000).

## Tips

➤ The Paragraph section does not include a cell for tab settings. To set tabs for a shape's text, use the Text command.

➤ The values of IndFirst, IndLeft, IndRight, SpBefore, and SpAfter are independent of the drawing's scale.

➤ When SpLine is less than 100%, the lines of text will overlap.

➤ The value of SpLine is independent of the scale of the drawing.

➤ The text itself cannot be accessed in any section.

# Protection

Contains the current setting of locks. The **Protection** section protects a formula from being changed by Visio. The Protection section displays more settings than the Protection dialog box. The default value of all cells in this section is **0** (off).

## Cells

| Protection | | | | | |
|---|---|---|---|---|---|
| LockWidth | 0 | LockBegin | 0 | LockTextEdit | 0 |
| LockHeight | 1 | LockEnd | 0 | LockVtxEdit | 0 |
| LockAspect | 0 | LockDelete | 0 | LockCrop | 0 |
| LockMoveX | 0 | LockSelect | 0 | LockGroup | 0 |
| LockMoveY | 0 | LockFormat | 0 | LockCalcWH | 1 |
| LockRotate | 0 | | | | |

**LockWidth** (default =0) prevents the width of the shape from changing.

| LockWidth | Meaning |
|---|---|
| 0 | Width is not locked |
| *not 0* | Width is locked |

**LockHeight** (default =0) prevents the height of the shape from changing.

| LockHeight | Meaning |
|---|---|
| 0 | Height is not locked |
| *not 0* | Height is locked |

**LockAspect** (default =0) prevents the aspect ratio of the shape from changing; shape is resized proportionally.

| LockAspect | Meaning |
|---|---|
| 0 | Aspect ratio is not locked |
| *not 0* | Aspect ratio is locked |

**LockMoveX** (default =0) prevents the shape from moving horizontally.

| LockMoveX | Meaning |
|---|---|
| 0 | Horizontal position is not locked |
| *not 0* | Horizontal position is locked |

**LockMoveY** (default =0) prevents the shape from moving vertically.

| LockMoveY | Meaning |
|---|---|
| 0 | Vertical position is not locked |
| *not 0* | Vertical position is locked |

**LockRotate** (default =0) prevents a 2D shape from rotating; does not affect 1D shapes.

| LockRotate | Meaning |
|---|---|
| 0 | Shape can be rotated |
| *not 0* | Shape cannot be rotated |

**LockBegin** (default =0) prevents the beginning point (BeginX and BeginY) of the shape from changing; specific to 1D shapes and does not affect 2D shapes.

| LockBegin | Meaning |
|---|---|
| 0 | BeginX and BeginY points are not locked |
| *not 0* | Beginning point is locked |

**LockEnd** (default =0) prevents the ending point (EndX and EndY) of the shape from changing; specific to 1D shapes and does not affect 2D shapes.

| LockEnd | Meaning |
|---|---|
| 0 | Ending point is not locked |
| *not 0* | Ending point is locked |

**LockDelete** (default =0) prevents the shape from being deleted. Upon attempting to delete the shape, Visio displays a dialog box stating, "Shape protection and/or layer properties prevent complete execution of this command."

| LockCalcWH | Meaning |
|---|---|
| 0 | Shape can be deleted |
| *not 0* | Shape cannot be deleted |

**LockSelect** (default =0) prevents a shape from being selected; has no effect unless the Shapes option is turned on via the **Tools | Protect Document** command.

| LockSelect | Meaning |
| --- | --- |
| 0 | Shape can be selected |
| not 0 | Shape cannot be selected |

**LockFormat** (default =0) prevents a 2D shape from being formatted.

| LockFormat | Meaning |
| --- | --- |
| 0 | Formatting can be changed |
| not 0 | Formatting cannot be changed |

**LockTextEdit** (default =0) prevents the text in a shape from being edited; does not prevent the text from being formatted.

| LockTextEdit | Meaning |
| --- | --- |
| 0 | Text can be edited |
| not 0 | Text cannot be edited |

**LockVtxEdit** (default =0) prevents the vertices of a shape from being edited.

| LockVtxEdit | Meaning |
| --- | --- |
| 0 | Vertices can be edited |
| not 0 | Vertices cannot be edited |

**LockCrop** (default =0) prevents an object from being cropped (made smaller without scaling); the object is usually an object inserted from another application.

| LockCrop | Meaning |
| --- | --- |
| 0 | Shape can be cropped |
| not 0 | Shape cannot be cropped |

**LockGroup** (default =0) prevents a group from being edited; has no effect on individual shapes.

| LockGroup | Meaning |
| --- | --- |
| 0 | Group can be edited |
| not 0 | Group cannot be edited |

**LockCalcWH** (default =0) prevents a shape's selection rectangle from being recalculated when: (1) a vertex is changed; or (2) a row type is changed in the Geometry section.

| LockCalcWH | Meaning |
| --- | --- |
| 0 | Width and height can be recalculated |
| not 0 | Width and height cannot be recalculated |

### Tips

➤ The following locks are available in the Protection section but not the Protection dialog box: LockCrop, LockVtxEdit, LockTextEdit, LockFormat, LockGroup, and LockCalcWH.

➤ To prevent a 1D shape from being rotated, set LockWidth to 1 instead of LockRotate.

➤ The Layer Properties dialog box allows you to lock objects on a layer; however, the Protection dialog box provides greater protection against changes than does locking by layer.

## Ruler & Grid

Contains the current setting of the page's ruler and grid.

### Cells

| Ruler & Grid | | | | | |
| --- | --- | --- | --- | --- | --- |
| XRulerOrigin | 0 in. | XGridOrigin | 0 in. | XGridSpacing | 0 in. |
| YRulerOrigin | 0 in. | YGridOrigin | 0 in. | YGridSpacing | 0 in. |
| XRulerDensity | 32 | XGridDensity | 8 | | |
| YRulerDensity | 32 | YGridDensity | 8 | | |

**XRulerOrigin** (default =0 in) specifies the distance from the lower-left corner of the page to 0.0 point on the x-axis ruler.

**YRulerOrigin** (default =0 in) specifies the distance from the lower-left corner of the page to 0.0 point on the y-axis ruler.

**XRulerDensity** (default =32) specifies the density of horizontal subdivisions on the x-axis ruler.

| XRulerDensity | Meaning |
| --- | --- |
| 8 | Coarse density, eight divisions per inch at 100% zoom |
| 16 | Normal density, sixteen divisions per inch |
| 32 | Fine density (default), thirty-two divisions per inch |

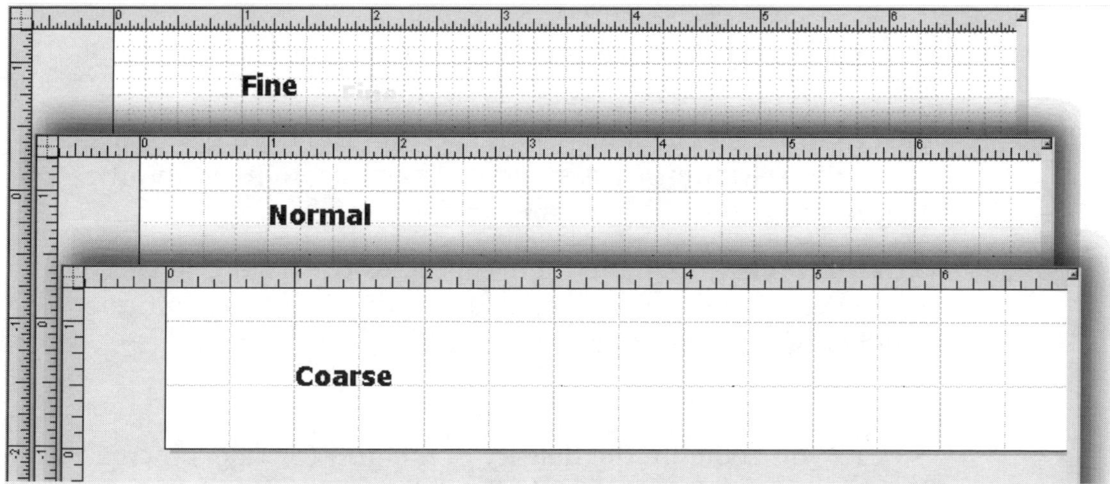


**YRulerDensity** (default =32) specifies the density of horizontal subdivisions on the x-axis ruler.

| YRulerDensity | Meaning |
| --- | --- |
| 8 | Coarse density |
| 16 | Normal density |
| 32 | Fine density (default) |

**XGridOrigin** (default =0 in) specifies the distance from the lower-left corner of the page to 0.0 point of the x-grid.

**YGridOrigin** (default =0 in) specifies the distance from the lower-left corner of the page to 0.0 point of the y-grid.

**XGridDensity** (default =8) specifies the density of the grid in the horizontal direction.

| XGridDensity | Meaning |
| --- | --- |
| 0 | Fixed; the grid does not change density |
| 2 | Coarse density; 2 grid lines per inch at 100% zoom |
| 4 | Normal density; 4 grid lines per inch |
| 8 | Fine density (default); 8 grid lines per inch |

**YGridDensity** (default =8) specifies the density of the grid in the vertical direction.

| YGridDensity | Meaning |
| --- | --- |
| 0 | Fixed |
| 2 | Coarse density |
| 4 | Normal density |
| 8 | Fine density (default) |

**XGridSpacing** (default =0 in) specifies the fixed grid spacing when the XGridDensity is set to 0. As you zoom in or out, the number of grid lines does not change.

**YGridSpacing** (default =0 in) specifies the fixed grid spacing when the YGridDensity is set to 0. As you zoom in or out, the number of grid lines does not change.

## Tips

➤ As you zoom in, the density of the grid (or ruler) increases, so that you see more grid lines; as you zoom out, the density of the grid decreases, so that you see fewer lines. At zoom level of 100%, the default grid density is eight grid lines per inch. Zoom to 200%, and the grid density increases to sixteen grid lines per inch.

➤ Using the fixed grid spacing makes Visio act like CAD software.

➤ Entering an invalid value for some of these settings causes Visio to impose the following values:

| Cell | Default Value |
| --- | --- |
| XRulerDensity | 16 |
| YRulerDensity | 16 |
| YGridDensity | 4 |
| YGridDensity | 4 |

## Scratch

Contains rows of cells for user-defined formulae and constants, which are referred to by other cells, roughly akin to the User-defined Cells section. Cells in the **Scratch** section, however, make specific use of the cells in each row. The **X** and **Y** cells are typically specific to actions related to x- and y-coordinates, while cells **A** through **D** are useful for any purpose.

### Cells

| Scratch | X | Y | A | B | C | D |
|---|---|---|---|---|---|---|
| 1 | No Formula | No Formula | No Formula | No Formula | No Formula | No Formula |

**X** specifies a formula that affects the x-coordinate or height of a shape; uses drawing units.

**Y** specifies a formula affecting the y-coordinate or width of a shape; uses drawing units.

**A-D** (default =**No Formula**) specify any value; unitless.

### Tips

➤ Use the X and Y cells to derive x- and y-coordinate.

➤ The Visio documentation provides the following example: A point in Visio is a single data package for an (x,y) coordinate. When a formula returns a point value, that value is interpreted in one of three ways, depending on the ShapeSheet cell the formula is in.

1. Cells that relate to x-coordinates (for example, PinX, or cells in the X column of a Geometry section) extract just the x-coordinate part of a point value.

2. Cells that relate to y-coordinates extract just the y-coordinate part of a point value.

3. A unitless cell extracts the distance from 0,0 to the point.

For this reason, Visio treats the formula **PNT(3,4)** in three ways:

| Scratch Cell | Formula | Treated As | Result |
|---|---|---|---|
| X | Pnt(3,4) | PntX(Pnt(3,4)) | 3 |
| Y | Pnt(3,4) | PntY(Pnt(3,4)) | 4 |
| A | Pnt(3,4) | Sqrt(3 $^\wedge$ 2+4 $^\wedge$ 2) | 5 |

## Shape Layout (new in Visio 2000)

Controls the placement of shapes, and the routing of connectors.

### Cells

| Shape Layout | | | | | |
|---|---|---|---|---|---|
| ShapePermeableX | FALSE | ShapePermeableY | FALSE | ShapePermeablePlace | FALSE |
| ShapeFixedCode | 0 | ShapePlowCode | 0 | ShapeRouteStyle | 0 |
| ConLineJumpDirX | 0 | ConLineJumpDirY | 0 | ConFixedCode | 0 |
| ConLineJumpCode | 0 | ConLineJumpStyle | 0 | | |

**ShapePermeableX** specifies whether a connector routes horizontally through a shape. TRUE enables; FALSE disables.

**ShapeFixedCode** specifies behavior for a placeable shape.

| ShapeFixedCode | Meaning |
|---|---|
| 1 | Do not move shape during the Lay Out Shapes command. |
| 2 | Do not move shape when other placeable shapes are placed nearby. |
| 128 | Glue to the shape's alignment box, instead of shape's perimeter. |

**ConLineJumpDirX** specifies the line jump direction on horizontal dynamic connectors.

| ConLineJumpDirX | Meaning |
|---|---|
| 0 | As specified by page |
| 1 | Up |
| 2 | Down |

**ConLineJumpCode** specifies when a connector jumps.

| ConLineJumpCode | Meaning |
| --- | --- |
| 0 | As specified by page |
| 1 | Never |
| 2 | Always |
| 3 | Other connector jumps |
| 4 | Neither connector jumps |

**ShapePermeableY** specifies whether a connector routes vertically through a shape. TRUE enables; FALSE disables.

**ShapePlowCode** specifies whether a placeable shape moves away from another placeable shape.

| ShapePlowCode | Meaning |
| --- | --- |
| 0 | As specified by page |
| 1 | Do not plow |
| 2 | Plow all shapes |

**ConLineJumpDirY** specifies the line jump direction on vertical dynamic connectors.

| ConLineJumpDirY | Meaning |
| --- | --- |
| 0 | As specified by page |
| 1 | Left |
| 2 | Right |

**ConLineJumpStyle** specifies the line jump style for dynamic connectors.

| ConLineJumpStyle | Meaning |
| --- | --- |
| 0 | As specified by page |
| 1 | Arc |
| 2 | Gap |
| 3 | Square |
| 4 | Two sides |
| 5 | Three sides |
| 6 | Four sides |
| 7 | Five sides |
| 8 | Six sides |
| 9 | Seven sides |

**ShapePermeablePlace** specifies whether a placeable shape can be placed on top of a shape during the Lay Out Shapes command. TRUE allows a shape to be placed on top of another; FALSE disables the feature.

**ShapeRouteStyle** determines the routing style and direction for a connector on the page.

| ShapeRouteStyle | Routing style | Direction |
|---|---|---|
| 0 | Default; right angle | None |
| 1 | Right angle | None |
| 2 | Straight | None |
| 3 | Organization chart | Top to bottom |
| 4 | Organization chart | Left to right |
| 5 | Flowchart | Top to bottom |
| 6 | Flowchart | Left to right |
| 7 | Tree | Top to bottom |
| 8 | Tree | Left to right |
| 9 | Network | None |
| 10 | Organization chart | Bottom to top |
| 11 | Organization chart | Right to left |
| 12 | Flowchart | Bottom to top |
| 13 | Flowchart | Right to left |
| 14 | Tree | Bottom to top |
| 15 | Tree | Right to left |
| 16 | Center to center | None |
| 17 | Simple | Top to bottom |
| 18 | Simple | Left to right |
| 19 | Simple | Bottom to top |
| 20 | Simple | Right to left |
| 21 | Simple Horizontal-Vertical | None |
| 22 | Simple Vertical-Horizontal | None |

**ConFixedCode** specifies when a connector reroutes.

| ConFixedCode | Meaning |
| --- | --- |
| 0 | Reroute freely |
| 1 | Reroute as needed |
| 2 | Never reroute |
| 3 | Reroute on crossover |

### Tips

➤ In Visio 2000, the ShapeFixedCode and ShapePermeablePlace cells replace the ObjInteract cell of the Miscellaneous section found in Visio 5.x.

➤ The Page Layout section's PageLineJumpDirX and PageLineJumpDirY cells specify the default direction for all connector jumps on a page.

➤ The Page Layout section's LineJumpStyle cell specifies the default style for all connector jumps on the page.

## Shape Transform

Contains the shape's positioning data, including its width, height, angle, center of rotation, flip status, and group resize mode.

### Cells

| Shape Transform | | | | | |
| --- | --- | --- | --- | --- | --- |
| Width | GUARD(EndX-BeginX) | PinX | GUARD((BeginX+EndX). | FlipX | GUARD(FALSE) |
| Height | GUARD(EndY-BeginY) | PinY | GUARD((BeginY+EndY). | FlipY | GUARD(FALSE) |
| Angle | GUARD(0 deg.) | LocPinX | GUARD(Width*0.5) | ResizeMode | 0 |
| | | LocPinY | GUARD(Height*0.5) | | |

**Width** specifies the width of the selected shape in drawing units.

**Height** specifies the height of the shape in drawing units.

**Angle** (default =0 deg) specifies the shape's angle of rotation; this angle is relative to its immediate parent, such as the page or a group.

**PinX** specifies the x-coordinate of the shape's center of rotation; this coordinate is the relative distance from the origin of the shape's immediate parent, such as the page or a group. The *pin* refers to the shape's center of rotation.



233

**PinY** specifies the y-coordinate of the shape's center of rotation; this coordinate is the relative distance from the origin of the shape's immediate parent, such as the page or a group.

**LocPinX** (default =Width*0.5) specifies the x-coordinate of the shape's center of rotation relative to the shape's origin (lower left corner).

**LocPinY** (default =Height*0.5) specifies the y-coordinate of the shape's center of rotation relative to the shape's origin (lower left corner).

**FlipX** (default =0) specifies horizontal flipping (mirroring) of the shape.

| FlipX | Meaning |
| --- | --- |
| 0 | The shape has not been flipped |
| not 0 | The shape has been flipped |

**FlipY** (default =0) specifies vertical flipping (mirroring) of the shape.

| FlipY | Meaning |
| --- | --- |
| 0 | The shape has not been flipped |
| not 0 | The shape has been flipped |

**ResizeMode** (default =0) specifies the group resize mode (see the Behavior command).

| ResizeMode | Meaning |
| --- | --- |
| 0 | Use the setting of group (default) |
| 1 | Reposition only; do not resize |
| 2 | Resize with the group |

## Tips

➤  The *pin* refers to the shape's center of rotation.

➤  The following formulae are the default values for 1D shapes:

| Cell | Default Formula |
|------|-----------------|
| Width | =SQRT((EndX-BeginX) ^ 2 + (EndY-BeginY) ^ 2) |
| Height | 0 |
| Angle | =ATAN2(EndY-BeginY,EndX-BeginX) |
| PinX | (BeginX + EndX)/2 |
| PinY | (BeginY + EndY)/2 |

## Style Properties (new in Visio 2000)

Specifies whether styles are applied to text, lines, and fills—related to the Define Styles dialog box.

### Cells

**EnableTextProps** toggles whether the style applies to text. TRUE to enable; FALSE to disable.

**EnableLineProps** toggles whether the style applies to lines. TRUE to enable; FALSE to disable.

**EnableFillProps** toggles whether the style applies to fill. TRUE to enable; FALSE to disable.

**HideForApply** specifies where the style is shown. TRUE shows the style in the Drawing Explorer and Define Styles dialog box; FALSE shows the style in the Drawing Explorer, Define Styles dialog box, Styles dialog box, and the All Styles list on the Format toolbar.

## Tabs (new in Visio 2000)

Controls the tab position and alignment.

### Cells

| Tabs | Position | Alignment | Position | Alignment | Position | Alignment | P |
|---|---|---|---|---|---|---|---|
| 0 | | | | | | | |

**Position** specifies the position of a tab stop.

**Alignment** specifies the tab alignment.

| Alignment | Meaning |
|---|---|
| 0 | Left |
| 1 | Center |
| 2 | Right |
| 3 | Decimal |

### Tips

➤ The tab position is independent of the drawing scale.

➤ To set a tab stop for specific characters, select the text, then set the tab stop. Visio adds a row to the ShapeSheet; the name of the row represents the number of characters of the tab stop.

## Text Block Format

Contains the vertical alignment, margins, and background color of the text within a shape's text block. A shape may have only one text block. The text itself cannot be accessed in any section.

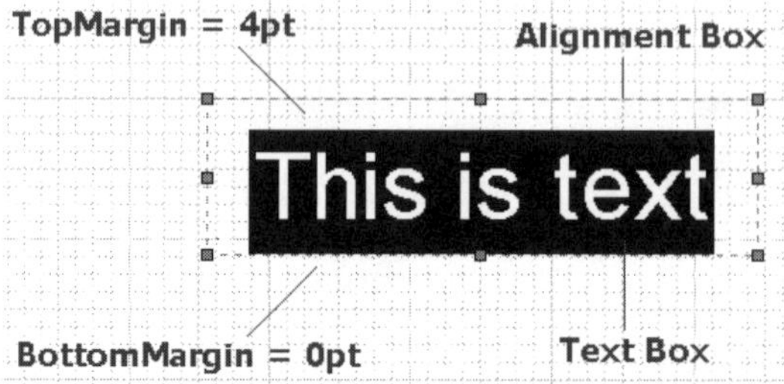

## Cells

<table>
<tr><td colspan="6">Text Block Format</td></tr>
<tr><td>LeftMargin</td><td>4 pt.</td><td>TopMargin</td><td>4 pt.</td><td>TextDirection</td><td>0</td></tr>
<tr><td>RightMargin</td><td>4 pt.</td><td>BottomMargin</td><td>4 pt.</td><td>TextBkgnd</td><td>2</td></tr>
<tr><td>VerticalAlign</td><td>1</td><td>DefaultTabStop</td><td>0.5 in.</td><td></td><td></td></tr>
</table>

**LeftMargin** (default =4 pt) specifies the distance between the left border of the text block and the text area.

**RightMargin** (default =4 pt) specifies the distance between the right border of the text block and the text area.

**VerticalAlign** (default =1) specifies one of three vertical alignments of the text within the text block.

| VerticalAlign | Meaning |
| --- | --- |
| 0 | Top |
| 1 | Middle (default) |
| 2 | Bottom |

**TopMargin** (default =4 pt) specifies the distance between the top of the text block and the top of the text area.

**BottomMargin** (default =4 pt) specifies the distance between the bottom border of the text block and the bottom of the text area.

**DefaultTabStop** specifies the distance between default tab stops; default 0.5 inches (new in Visio 2000).

**TextDirection** specifies the direction of the characters in a text block. Zero (0) means horizontal text, while 1 means vertical text (new in Visio 2000).

**TextBkgnd** (default =0) specifies the background color for the text block.

| TextBkgnd | Meaning |
| --- | --- |
| 0 | Transparent background (default) |
| 1-24 | Black, white, red, etc. |
| 25-254 | Black |
| 255 | Transparent background (no fill color) |

**TextBkgnd** also specifies the text background color for the shape. Range is 1 to 24; 0 and 255 specify a transparent text background; values 25 to 254 specify a custom color via the RGB or HSL function (new in Visio 2000).

### Tips

➤ The text itself can be accessed with the ShapeText(*shapename*,TheText,[*flag*]) functions, which returns the text from *shapename*. The optional *flag* determines how hyphens and tabs are handled.

➤ The value of all the margins is independent of the drawing's scale. When the scale of the drawing changes, the margin measurement does not change.

➤ Use the Text Transform section to specify the angle, width, and height of the text block.

➤ The value of the color in the TextBkgrnd cell is slightly different from Visio's standard color palette numbering. To set a color value, add one to the Color Palette value. For example, black is color #0 in the Color Palette but is color #1 in the TextBkgrnd cell.

➤ The VerticalText cell of the Miscellaneous section in the Japanese version of Visio 5.x has been replaced by the TextDirection cell in all versions of Visio 2000.

## Text Fields

Contains the custom formula added to the shape's text using the Insert | Field command. You can insert more than one field in a shape. Each field is represented by a row in the ShapeSheet.

## Cells

**Format** specifies the format of the custom property using a format picture. This cell applies to custom properties that are defined by the Type cell as a string (type 0), number (2), date/time (5), duration (6), or currency (7) .

**Value** specifies the function of the field; see the list of functions at the end of this chapter.

## Tips

➤ The Text Fields section is not normally displayed by the ShapeSheet. To add this section, select **Insert | Section** from the ShapeSheet menu bar. When the Insert Section dialog box appears, select **Text Fields** and click **OK**.

➤ The Visio documentation incorrectly states that the following cells are found in this section: EditMode, UICategory, UICode, UIFormat, and Type.

➤ Row numbers cannot be renamed (as with rows in User-defined Cells section).

➤ Use the Insert | Field command to create text that automatically updates, such as a date-and-time stamp and associative dimensions. The following formula displays the width of the shape in the current units.

    **=Format(Width,"0.00 u")**

➤ The cells were known by number, such as **1**, **2**, **3**, etc., in earlier versions of Visio.

➤ It is possible for a number to represent a dimension, a scalar number, an angle, a date, a time, or currency. To interpret correctly the number as date, time, or currency, use the DateTime and CY functions in the Format cell instead of a format picture.

Customizing ShapeSheets

## Text Transform

Contains data that positions the text block found with the shape. The *text block* is not the text itself, but the alignment box of the text. A shape can have only one text block. The **Text Transform** section is not normally displayed to save space in the ShapeSheet. The text itself cannot be accessed in any section.

### Cells

| Text Transform | | | | | |
|---|---|---|---|---|---|
| TxtWidth | MAX(TEXTWIDTH(TheText),5*Char.Size) | TxtPinX | Width*0 | TxtLocPinX | TxtWidth*0.5 |
| TxtHeight | TEXTHEIGHT(TheText,TxtWidth) | TxtPinY | Height*0.8676 | TxtLocPinY | TxtHeight*0.5 |
| TxtAngle | 0 deg. | | | | |

**TxtWidth** (default =Width*1) specifies the width of the text block. The default formula makes the text block the same width as the shape's alignment box (defined in the Shape Transform section).

**TxtHeight** (default =Height*1) specifies the height of the text block. The default formula makes the text block the same height as the shape's alignment box (defined in the Shape Transform section).

**TxtAngle** (default =0deg) specifies the angle of the text block. The angle of rotation in measured relative to the x-axis of the shape.

**TxtPinX** (default =Width*0.5) specifies the text block's x-coordinate for the center of rotation. This distance is relative to the origin of the shape (usually the lower-left corner). The default formula of **=Width*0.5** centers the text block within the shape.

**TxtPinY** (default =Height*0.5) specifies the text block's y-coordinate for the center of rotation. This distance is relative to the origin of the shape (usually the lower-left corner). The default formula of **=Height*0.5** centers the text block within the shape.

**TxtLocPinX** (default =TxtWidth*0.5) is similar to the TxtPinX cell but defines the x-coordinate of the center of rotation relative to the origin of the text block itself (not of the shape). The default formula of **=TxtWidth*0.5** centers the text in the text block.

**TxtLocPinY** (default =TxtHeight*0.5) is similar to the TxtPinY cell but specifies the y-coordinate of the center of rotation relative to the origin of the text block itself (not of the shape). The default formula of **=TxtHeight*0.5** centers the text in the text block.

### Tips

➤ The Text Transform section is not normally displayed by the ShapeSheet. To add this section, select **Insert | Section** from the ShapeSheet menu bar. When the Insert Section dialog box appears, select **Text Transform** and click **OK**.

➤ Be aware of the difference between these similar looking cell names: TxtPinX is the center of rotation relative to the shape, while TxtLocPinX is relative to the text block.

➤ The text itself cannot be accessed in any section.

➤ To add text to a shape, select the shape, and then type.

## User-defined Cells

Contains an area for formulae that are referred to by other cells, roughly akin to the Scratch section. You may enter, however, any valid formula or constant value in the Value cell and document it in the Prompt cell.

### Cells

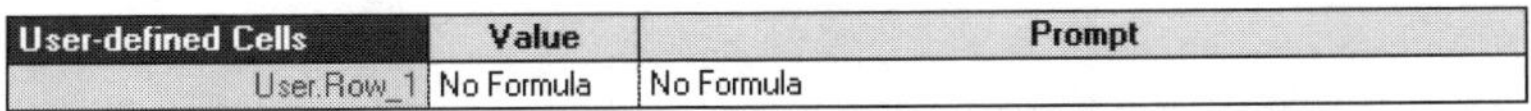

| User-defined Cells | Value | Prompt |
|---|---|---|
| User.Row_1 | No Formula | No Formula |

**User.Row_**_n_ specifies the name of the row. By default, Visio names the rows **User.Row_1**, **User.Row_2**, etc. When you enter a name, such as **MinOffset**, Visio renames the row **User.MinOffset**.



**241**

**Value** (default =No formula) specifies a formula or constant. Other cells can access this formula or constant by its row label, **User.Row_1**.

**Prompt** (default =No formula) specifies a description (or comment) of the user-defined cell (it does not actually prompt the user). Since this is a string, Visio automatically surrounds the text with quotation marks. The Prompt cell need not contain text: prefix a formula or constant with the equal sign ( = ) and Visio evaluates the formula (remember to leave out the quotation marks!).

### Tips

➤ The User.Row_*n* cell names must be unique within the User-Defined cells section.

➤ Although the Prompt cell is meant for documenting the formula in the Value cell, Visio allows you to also place a formula in the Prompt cell: prefix the formula or constant with the equal sign (=) and Visio evaluates the formula (remember to leave out the quotation marks!).

➤ To add a **User-defined cells** section to a shape, right-click in the ShapeSheet window. Select **Insert|Section** from the menu. When the Insert Section dialog box appears, select **User-defined Cells** and click **OK**.

➤ To add additional rows, right click an existing **User-defined Cells** section and select **Insert|Row** from the menu.

# Summary of ShapeSheet Functions

Shapesheet functions can be used in shapesheet cells. The Scratch and User-defined Cells sections are particularly useful for carrying out calculations. The result can be transferred to any other cell, as required. The function reference uses the following syntax:

| | |
|---|---|
| **Ref** | The name of the function is not case-sensitive. Visio recognizes REF(), Ref(), and ref(). |
| **( )** | Arguments are always enclosed in parentheses, such as BLUE(*expression*). |
| **" "** | String (or text) arguments are enclosed in quotation marks, such as OpenFile("*filename*"). |
| **,** | When a function accepts more than one argument, the arguments are separated by a comma, such as Gravity(*angle*, *limit1*, *limit2*). |
| **[ ]** | The square brackets surround arguments that are optional. For example, CY(*value* [ , *currency* \| *code* ] ) means that the CY function requires only the *value* argument. |
| **\|** | The vertical bar separates selectable arguments. For example, CY(*value* [ , *currency* \| *code* ] ) means the CY function accepts a *currency* or a *code* argument but not both. |
| **!** | The exclamation mark separates two parts of a name, such as *filename***!***section*. In *rectangle***!theText**, **theText** has special meaning; it refers to all text within the shape named **shapename**. |
| **arg1, arg2, ....** | The function can have one or more similar aguments. Visio expressions can have up to fourteen arguments. For example, MIN(*number1*, *number2*, ..., *number14*) accepts one, two, or up to fourteen arguments. |

Real numbers have up to fifteen decimal places, such as 3.1415926535898. The largest and smallest real numbers are 922,337,203,685,477.5807 and –922,337,203,685,477.5808.

Order of evaluation, from first to last:

| Operator | Meaning |
|---|---|
| + (unary) | Positive |
| – (unary) | Negative |
| % | Percent |
| ^ | Exponent |
| * | Multiply |
| / | Divide |

| Operator | Meaning |
|---|---|
| + | Add |
| – | Subtract |
| & | String concatenate, such as "draw" & "ing" results in "drawing" |
| > | Greater than |
| => | Greater than or equal to |
| < | Less than |
| <= | Less than or equal to |
| = | Equal |

Use parentheses to change the order of evaluation. Expressions within the innermost parentheses are evaluated first, from left to right.

The following functions are new in Visio 2000:

| | | |
|---|---|---|
| AngleToLoc | DocLastPrint | MasterName |
| AngleToPar | DocLastSave | Name |
| BkgPageName | FieldPicture | Nurbs |
| Category | FileName | PageCount |
| Company | GetRef | PageName |
| Creator | GetVal | Polyline |
| Data1 | HyperlinkBase | ShapeText |
| Data2 | Id | StrSame |
| Data3 | Keywords | StrSameX |
| DecimalSep | ListSep | Subject |
| Description | LocToLoc | Title |
| Directory | LocToPar | Type |
| DocCreation | Manager | TypeDesc |

| Arithmetic Functions | Meaning |
|---|---|
| + | Indicates a positive number, such as +19 |
| – | Indicates a negative number, such as –19 |
| % | Indicates a percentage value, such as 19% |
| ^ | Calculates the exponent, such as $19 \char94 2$ results in 361 |
| * | Multiplies, such as 19*2 results in 38 |
| / | Divides, such as 19/2 results in 9.5 |

| *Arithmetic Functions* | *Meaning* |
| --- | --- |
| + | Adds, such as 19+2 results in 21 |
| − | Subtracts, such as 19–2 results in 17 |

| *Geometric Functions* | *Meaning* |
| --- | --- |
| **AngleToLoc**(*angle, ref, dst*) | Converts *angle* from local coordinates in the source shape to the local coordinates in a destination shape. *Ref* is a reference to a cell in the source object. *Dst* is a reference to a cell in the destination object. |
| **AngleToPar**(*angle, ref, dst*) | Converts *angle* from local coordinates in the source shape to the parent coordinates in a destination shape. *Ref* is a reference to a cell in the source object. *Dst* is a reference to a cell in the destination object. |
| **Gravity**(*angle, limit1, limit2*) | Calculates the angle to keep a text block from turning upside-down; used with the **TxtAngle** cell. Returns 180 degrees when angle is *limit1* and *limit2*; otherwise, returns 0 degrees. *Limit1* and *limit2* default to 90 and 270 degrees. |
| **IntersectX**(*pinx, piny1, angle1, pinx2, piny2, angle2*) | Returns the x-coordinate of the point where two lines intersect. *Pinx1* and *piny1* are the x- and y-coordinates of a point on the first line, while *angle1* is the value of the angle cell. *Pinx2* and *piny2* are the x- and y-coordinates of a point on the second line, while *angle2* is the value of the angle cell. Returns DIV BY 0 error when the lines do not intersect. |
| **IntersectY**(*pinx, piny1, angle1, pinx2, piny2, angle2*) | Returns the y-coordinate of the point where two lines intersect. *Pinx1* and *piny1* are the x- and y-coordinates of a point on the first line, while *angle1* is the value of the angle cell. *Pinx2* and *piny2* are the x- and y-coordinates of a point on the second line, while *angle2* is the value of the angle cell. Returns DIV BY 0 error when the lines do not intersect. |
| **LocToLoc**(*point, ref, dst*) | Returns a transformed *point* in local coordinates in the destination coordinate system. *Ref* is a reference to a cell in the source object. *Dst* is a reference to a cell in the destination object. |

| Geometric Functions | Meaning |
| --- | --- |
| **LocToPar**(*point, ref, dst*) | Returns a transformed *point* in parent coordinates in the destination coordinate system. *Ref* is a reference to a cell in the source object. *Dst* is a reference to a cell in the destination object. |
| **NURBS**(*knot, degree, xType, yType, x, y, knot1, weight1, ...*) | Returns a non-uniform rational B-spline (NURBS). *Knot* is the last knot. *Degree* is the spline's degree. *X* is an x-coordinate. *Y* is a y-coordinate. *Knot1* is a knot on the B-spline. *Weight1* is the corresponding weight on the B-spline. *xType* and *yType* specify how to interpret the x and y input data: |

| x- or yType | Meaning |
| --- | --- |
| 0 | Input is interpreted as a percentage of Width (for xType) or Height (for yType). |
| 1 | Input is interpreted as a local coordinate. |

| Geometric Functions | Meaning |
| --- | --- |
| **Polyline**(*xType, yType, x1, y1...*) | Returns a polyline. *X1* is an x-coordinate. *Y1* is a y-coordinate. *xType* and *yType* specify how to interpret the x and y input data: |

| x- or yType | Meaning |
| --- | --- |
| 0 | Input is interpreted as a percentage of Width (for xType) or Height (for yType) |
| 1 | Input is interpreted as a local coordinate |

| Geometric Functions | Meaning |
| --- | --- |
| **RectSect**(*width, height, x, y, option*) | Draws a pair of imaginary diagonal lines across the rectangle defined by *width* and *height*, which divide it into four sectors and a center point. Returns the sector of a rectangle associated with *x* and *y*: |

| Sector | Meaning |
| --- | --- |
| 0 | Center point of rectangle |
| 1 | Right sector |
| 2 | Top sector |
| 3 | Left sector |
| 4 | Bottom sector |

When a point falls on the diagonal lines, includes:

| Option | Meaning |
| --- | --- |
| 0 | Left and right sectors |
| 1 | Top and bottom sectors |

| *Geometric Functions* | *Meaning* |
| --- | --- |
| **ShapeText**(*shapename*, TheText, [*flag*]) | Returns the text from *shapename*. **TheText** refers to the **TheText** cell of the shape. The optional *flag* specifies the format of the text: |

| *Flag* | *Meaning* |
| --- | --- |
| 0 | Return text exactly as displayed by shape |
| 1 | Include discretionary hyphens |
| 2 | Do not include expanded text in fields |
| 4 | Convert tabs to a single space |
| 8 | Convert tabs to spaces |
| 16 | Convert carriage returns and line feeds to spaces |
| 32 | Convert typographer quotes to straight quotes |
| 64 | Convert adjacent white space to a single space |

| *Window Management Functions* | *Meaning* |
| --- | --- |
| **GotoPage**("*pagename*") | Causes the page named *pagename* to be displayed by the current window |
| **OpenFile**("*filename*") | Opens the Visio document *filename*; transfers focus to this document window |
| **OpenGroupWin**( ) | Opens the Group window with the group |
| **OpenPage**("*pagename*") | Displays *pagename* in new window |
| **OpenSheetWin**( ) | Opens the ShapeSheet window in a new window |
| **OpenTextWin**( ) | Opens the shape's text block; this allows the text to be edited |

| *Color and Pattern Functions* | *Meaning* |
| --- | --- |
| **Blue**(*expression*) | Returns the value of a color's blue component in the range 0 to 255. When *expression* is invalid, returns 0 (black). |
| **Green**(*expression*) | Returns the value of a color's green component in the range 0 to 255. When *expression* is invalid, returns 0 (black). |

**Customizing ShapeSheets**

| Color and Pattern Functions | Meaning |
| --- | --- |
| **HSL**(*hue, saturation, luminosity*) | Returns an index value, based on the document's color palette. The color is specified by *hue* (0 to 239), *saturation* (0 to 240), and *luminosity* (0 to 240). |
| **Hue**(*expression*) | Returns the value of a color's hue component in the range 0 to 239. If *expression* is invalid, returns 0 (black). |
| **Lum**(*expression*) | Returns the value of a color's luminosity component in the range 0 to 240. If *expression* is invalid, returns 0 (black). |
| **Red**(*expression*) | Returns the value of a color's red component in the range 0 to 255. When *expression* is invalid, returns 0 (black). |
| **RGB**(*red, green, blue*) | Returns an index value, based on the document's color palette. The color is specified by its *red, green,* and *blue* components (0 to 255 for each). |
| **Sat**(*expression*) | Returns the value of a color's saturation component in the range 0 to 240. If *expression* is invalid, returns 0 (black). |
| **Use**("*name*") | Applies *name* (a line pattern, fill pattern, or line end) to the shape; *name* must be a valid master name. Always returns 254. Used only in the LinePattern, FillPattern, BeginArrow, and EndArrow cells. |

| Date and Time Functions | Meaning |
| --- | --- |
| **Date**(*year, month, day*) | Returns the date (based on *year, month,* and *day*), such as 6/7/97. Format can be specified with format picture. |
| **DateTime**("*datetime*" \| *expression* [ , *lcid* ] ) | Returns the date and time value retrieved from *datetime* or *expression*. *Datetime* is any recognizable date and time, or cell reference. *Expression* is any expression yielding a date and time. *Lcid* is optional and specifies the locale identifier for evaluating a nonlocal datetime. Format can be specified with format picture. |
| **DateValue**("*datetime*" \| *expression* [ , *lcid* ] ) | Returns the date value retrieved from *datetime* or *expression*. *Datetime* is any recognizable date and time, or cell reference. *Expression* is any expression yielding a date and time. *Lcid* is optional and specifies the locale identifier for evaluating a nonlocal datetime. Format can be specified with format picture. |

| Date and Time Functions | Meaning |
| --- | --- |
| **Day**("*datetime*" \| *expression* [ , *lcid* ] ) | Returns an integer (1 to 31) representing the day of the month retrieved from *datetime* or *expression*. *Datetime* is any recognizable date and time, or cell reference. *Expression* is any expression yielding a date and time. *Lcid* is optional and specifies the locale identifier for evaluating a nonlocal datetime. Format can be specified with format picture. |
| **DayOfYear**("*datetime*" \| *expression* [ , *lcid* ] ) | Returns an integer (1 to 366) representing the day of the year (366 = December 31 during a leap year) retrieved from *datetime* or *expression*. *Datetime* is any recognizable date and time, or cell reference. *Expression* is any expression yielding a date and time. *Lcid* is optional and specifies the locale identifier for evaluating a nonlocal datetime. Format can be specified with format picture. |
| **Hour**("*datetime*" \| *expression* [ , *lcid* ] ) | Returns an integer (0 to 23) representing the hour of the day in international and military format (23 = 11:00 pm) retrieved from *datetime* or *expression*. *Datetime* is any recognizable date and time, or cell reference. *Expression* is any expression yielding a date and time. *Lcid* is optional and specifies the locale identifier for evaluating a nonlocal datetime. Format can be specified with format picture. |
| **Minute**("*datetime*" \| *expression* [ , *lcid* ] ) | Returns an integer (0 to 59) representing the minute of the hour, retrieved from *datetime* or *expression*. *Datetime* is any recognizable date and time, or cell reference. *Expression* is any expression yielding a date and time. *Lcid* is optional and specifies the locale identifier for evaluating a nonlocal datetime. Format can be specified with format picture. |
| **Month**("*datetime*" \| *expression* [ , *lcid* ] ) | Returns an integer (1 to 12) representing the month of the year (1 = January), retrieved from *datetime* or *expression*. *Datetime* is any recognizable date and time, or cell reference. *Expression* is any expression yielding a date and time. *Lcid* is optional and specifies the locale identifier for evaluating a nonlocal datetime. Format can be specified with format picture. |
| **Now**( ) | Returns the current date and time, such as 6/17/98 10:25:00 AM. Format can be specified with format picture. |

| Date and Time Functions | Meaning |
| --- | --- |
| **Second**("*datetime*" \| *expression* [ , *lcid* ] ) | Returns an integer (0 to 59) representing the seconds of the current minute, retrieved from *datetime* or *expression*. *Datetime* is any recognizable date and time, or cell reference. *Expression* is any expression yielding a date and time. *Lcid* is optional and specifies the locale identifier for evaluating a nonlocal datetime. |
| **Time**(*hour, minute, second*) | Returns the time in hours, minutes, and seconds, such as 10:28:00 AM. Format can be specified with format picture. |
| **TimeValue**("*datetime*" \| *expression* [ , *lcid* ] ) | Returns the time value, such as 10:30 AM, retrieved from *datetime* or *expression*. *Datetime* is any recognizable date and time, or cell reference. *Expression* is any expression yielding a date and time. *Lcid* is optional and specifies the locale identifier for evaluating a nonlocal datetime. Format can be specified with format picture. |
| **Weekday**("*datetime*" \| *expression* [ , *lcid* ] ) | Returns an integer (1 to 7) representing the day of the week (1 = Monday). *Datetime* is any recognizable date and time, or cell reference. *Expression* is any expression yielding a date and time. *Expression* may also be a single number representing the number of days since December 31, 1899. *Lcid* is optional and specifies the locale identifier for evaluating a nonlocal datetime. Format can be specified with format picture. |
| **Year**("*datetime*" \| *expression* [ , *lcid* ] ) | Returns an integer representing the year, such as 1998. *Datetime* is any recognizable date and time, or cell reference. *Expression* is any expression yielding a date and time. *Lcid* is optional and specifies the locale identifier for evaluating a nonlocal datetime. Format can be specified with format picture. |

| Text Functions | Meaning |
| --- | --- |
| **Char**(*number*) | Returns the ANSI character for *number* (range is 1 and 255), such as char(65) returns A. |

| Text Functions | Meaning |
|---|---|
| **EvalText**(*shapename*!TheText) | Evaluates the text in the shape named *shapename*; expects the text to be a formula; returns the result. **TheText** specifies all the text in the shape's text block. Returns 0 if *shapename* contains no text; returns error if the text cannot be evaluated. |
| **Format**(*expression*, "*formatpicture*") | Formats *expression* according to *formatpicture*. |
| **FieldPicture**(*code*) | Returns Visio's internal text field format picture. For example, **FieldPicture**(0) returns "0.0 u". |
| **FormatEx**(*expression*, "*formatpicture*", [ *inputunit*, ] [ *outputunit* ] ) | Formats *expression* according to *formatpicture*. *Inputunit* applies a unit if *expression* has no units. *Outputunit* applies units to the result. |
| **Lower**("*string*") | Converts text to all lowercase, such as Lower("Visio") returns "visio". |
| **StrSame**("*string1*", "*string2*", [*flag*]) | Returns TRUE when two strings are the same; returns FALSE when they are not. *String1* is the first string. *String2* is the second string to compare. The optional *flag* is either TRUE to ignore the case, or FALSE (default) to compare the case. |
| **StrSameX**("*string1*", "*string2*"[,*lang*] [,*flag*]) | Returns TRUE when two strings are the same; returns FALSE when they are not. *String1* is the first string. *String2* is the second string to compare. *Lang* is an optional argument that specifies the language for the string: 0 for local language; 750 for universal language. The optional *flag* is: |

| Flag | Meaning |
|---|---|
| 1 | Ignore case |
| 2 | Ignore non-spacing characters |
| 4 | Ignore symbols |
| 4096 | Treat punctuation the same as symbols |
| 65536 | Do not differentiate between Hiragana and Katakana characters. |
| 131072 | Do not differentiate between a single-byte character and the same character as a double-byte character. |

| *Text Functions* | *Meaning* |
| --- | --- |
| **TextHeight**(*shapename*! TheText, *maximumwidth*) | Returns the height of text in the shape *shapename*, where no text line exceeds *maximumwidth*. The height includes: the text height, plus the space before, the space after, line spacing, the top margin, and the bottom margin. Use this function to make text fit the height of the shape. **TheText** specifies all the text in the shape's text block. |
| **TextWidth**(*shapename*!TheText, *maximumwidth*) | Returns the width of text in the shape *shapename*, where no text line exceeds *maximumwidth*. Use this function to make text fit width of the shape. **TheText** specifies all the text in the shape's text block. |
| **Upper**("*string*") | Converts text to all uppercase, such as Upper("Visio") returns "VISIO". |

| *Event Functions* | *Meaning* |
| --- | --- |
| **CallThis**("*procedure*", ["*project*"] , [ *arg1*, *arg2*, ...] ) | Calls procedure in VBA *project* using *arg1*, *arg2*, etc. When *project* is missing, Visio runs the procedure found in the current document. |
| **DefaultEvent**( ) | Performs the default event associated with the object: |

| *Object* | *Default Event* |
| --- | --- |
| Shape | Edit the shape's text |
| Group | Open Group window and display the group |
| OLE | Do primary verb |
| Other | Do nothing |

| | |
| --- | --- |
| **DependsOn**(*cellref* [ , *cellref2*, ... ] ) | Creates a cell reference dependency. This function always returns FALSE. When used in the Event row or Action cell, this function has no effect. |
| **DoOleVerb**("*verb*") | Executes the *verb* of the OLE object. For example, dooleverb("edit") displays the embedded object in a form that lets you edit it. |
| **GetRef**(*cell*) | References *cell*; does not recalculate the formula when *cell* changes. |
| **GetVal**(*cell*) | Returns the value of *cell*; does not recalculate the formula when *cell* changes. |

| Event Functions | Meaning |
| --- | --- |
| **RunAddon**("*string*") | Causes Visio runs the add-on program named *string*. If the document contains a VBA project, Visio passes *string* to the VBA project (in this case, the string must be VBA code). |
| **RunAddonWArgs**("*filename*", "*arg1, arg2 ...*") | Passes the *arguments* as command-line parameters to the program *filename* and runs the program. Argument should be less than fifty-one characters. |
| **SetF**("*cell*", *formula*) | The result of *formula* becomes the new formula in *cell*. When "*formula*" is surrounded by quotation marks, it is written to *cell*. When """*formula*""" is surrounded by three pairs of quotation marks, it is written to *cell* as a string. |

The following functions return data from the Properties dialog box (File | Properties):

| Properties Functions | Meaning |
| --- | --- |
| **Category**() | Returns the text from the Category field |
| **Company**() | Returns the text from the Company field |
| **Creator**() | Returns the text from the Creator field |
| **Description**() | Returns the text from the Description field |
| **Directory**() | Returns the full path of the folder in which the drawing is saved; returns an empty string "" when the drawing hasn't been saved |
| **DocCreation**() | Returns the date and time the drawing was created, as a serial value; format the value with the **Format** function |
| **DocLastPrint**() | Returns the date and time the drawing was last printed, as a serial value; format the value with the **Format** function |
| **DocLastSave**() | Returns the date and time the drawing was last saved, as a serial value; format the value with the **Format** function |
| **Filename**() | Returns the drawing's filename |
| **HyperlinkBase**() | Returns the text from the Hyperlink Base field |
| **Keywords**() | Returns the text from the Keywords section |
| **Manager**() | Returns the text from the Manager section |

| Properties Functions | Meaning |
| --- | --- |
| **Subject**() | Returns the text from the Subject field |
| **Title**() | Returns the text from the Title field |

The following functions return data from the Special dialog box (Format | Special):

| Data Functions | Meaning |
| --- | --- |
| **Data1**() | Returns the text from the Data 1 field |
| **Data2**() | Returns the text from the Data 2 field |
| **Data3**() | Returns the text from the Data 3 field |

| Miscellaneous Functions | Meaning |
| --- | --- |
| **BkgPageName**(*lang*) | Returns the name of the background page. *Lang* is an optional argument that specifies the language for the string: 0 for local language; 750 for universal language. |
| **CY**(*value* [ , *currency* \| *code* ] ) | Returns *value* as a formatted currency. *CurrencyID* and *code* specify the type of currency. Visio recommends that for better precision with a very large currency *value*, use a string argument, such as 3.6 trillion. For example, CY(12.43) returns $12.43. |
| **DecimalSep**( ) | Returns the decimal separator string for the current locale. |
| **Guard**(*expression*) | Protects *expression* from change when the user moves, resizes, or groups shapes in the drawing window. |
| **Help**("*filename.hlp!keyword* \| *number*") | Displays the help file *filename*. Either displays the Search dialog box with the *keyword* or displays help topic *number*. |
| **Hyperlink**("*address*" [ , "*subaddress*", "*extrainfo*", *window*, "*frame*" ] ) | Displays the document found at *address*, which can be a DOS filename, network UNC, or an Internet URL. *Subaddress* specifies a location within address, such as a page name in a Visio file, range in a spreadsheet, or anchor in a HTML page. *Extrainfo* is a string that might be helpful to the address. *Window* specifies whether the hyperlink is opened in a new window and has a value of TRUE or FALSE. *Frame* is the name of an ActiveX frame. |

| Miscellaneous Functions | Meaning |
| --- | --- |
| **Id**() | Returns the shape's internal ID as a number. |
| **Index**(*index, list* [ , [ *delimiter* ] [ , [ *errorvalue* ] ] ] ) | Returns the substring beginning at *index* in the *list*. Returns -1 if string is not found. The *index* is zero-based, meaning the first character position is #0. *Delimiter* defines the delimiter character(s); default is the semicolon ( ; ). *Errorvalue* is returned when *index* is out of range; when *errorvalue* is missing, Visio returns an empty string. For example, index(1,"stefan;heidi;katrina") returns "heidi". |
| **ListSep**() | Returns the list separator string for the current locale. |
| **Lookup**(*key, list* [ , *delimiter* ] ) | Returns an index number indicating the beginning of *key* in the *list*. Returns -1 if string is not found. The **index** is zero-based, meaning the first position is #0. *Delimiter* defines the delimiter character(s); default is the semicolon ( ; ). For example, Lookup("heidi","sfefan;heidi;katrina") returns 1. |
| **LotusNotes**(*"field"*) | Returns the most recent data read from Lotus Notes. |
| **Magnitude**(*constantA, A, constantB, B*) | Returns the result of:<br>$$SQRT((constantA * A)^2 + (constantB * B)^2)$$<br>where:<br>*constantA* is the intersection with y-axes<br>*A* is the rise, the difference in y-direction<br>*constantB* is the intersection with x-axes<br>*B* is the run, the difference in x-direction |
| **MasterName**(*lang*) | Returns the sheet's master name as a string; returns "<no name>" when the sheet has no name. *Lang* is an optional argument that specifies the language for the string: 0 for local language; 750 for universal language. |
| **Name**(*lang*) | Returns the sheet's name as a string; returns "<no master>" when the sheet has no master. *Lang* is an optional argument that specifies the language for the string: 0 for local language; 750 for universal language. |
| **PageCount**() | Returns the number of foreground pages in the drawing. |
| **PageName**(*lang*) | Returns the name of the page. *Lang* is an optional argument that specifies the language for the string: 0 for local language; 750 for universal language. |

| Miscellaneous Functions | Meaning |
| --- | --- |
| **PlaySound**("*filename*" \| "*alias*", *isAlias, doBeepOnFail, synch*) | Plays the *filename* or the system sound *alias* (when *isAlias* is non-zero). Visio beeps when *doBeepOnFail* is non-zero. When *synch* is 0, Visio continues while the sound is played. |
| **Type**( ) | Returns an object's internal type as a number: |

| Number | Meaning |
| --- | --- |
| 70 | Page |
| 71 | Group |
| 72 | Shape |
| 74 | Style |
| 77 | Guide |
| 78 | Foreign |
| 79 | Document |

| | |
| --- | --- |
| **TypeDesc**( ) | Returns a string describing the object's internal type: "Page Sheet", "Group", "Shape", "Style", "Guide", "Metafile", "Bitmap", "OLE Linked Object", "OLE Embedded Object", "Control", "Document Sheet", or "Shape". |
| **UserUI**(*state, defaultexpression, userexpression*) | Evaluates *defaultexpression* when *state* is 0; evaluates *userexpression* when *state* is 1. |

| Statistical Functions | Meaning |
| --- | --- |
| **Max**(*number1, number2, ..., number14*) | Returns the number with the maximum value of the list. For example, max(7,10,11,41,42) returns 42. |
| **Min**(*number1, number2, ..., number14*) | Returns the number with the minimum value of the list. For example, min(7,10,11,41,42) returns 7. |

| Mathematical Functions | Meaning |
| --- | --- |
| **Abs**(*number*) | Returns the absolute value of number. For example, Abs(-17) returns 17. |
| **Ceiling**(*number* [, *multiple*]) | Rounds the *number* up to the nearest *multiple*. When *multiple* is missing, rounds up to the next integer like Int(). For example, Ceiling(11.26,0.5) returns 11.5. |

| Mathematical Functions | Meaning |
| --- | --- |
| **Floor**(*number* [, *multiple*]) | Rounds the *number* down to the nearest *multiple*. When multiple is missing, rounds down to the next integer like Int(). For example, Floor(11.26,0.5) returns 11. |
| **Int**(*number*) | Rounds the *number* down to the nearest integer. For example, Int(11.76) returns 11. |
| **IntUp**(*number*) | Rounds the *number* up to the nearest integer. For example, Intup(11.76) returns 12. |
| **Ln**(*number*) | Returns the natural logarithm of *number*. Returns error value #NUM if *number* is negative. For example, Ln(42) returns 3.7377. |
| **Log10**(*number*) | Returns the logarithm of *number*. Returns error value #NUM if *number* is negative. For example, Log10(42) returns 1.6232 |
| **Modulus**(*number, divisor*) | Returns the remainder after *number* is divided by *divisor*. Returns #DIV/0! error when divisor is 0. For example, Modulus(56,10) returns 0.6. |
| **Pi**( ) | Returns 3.1415926535898. |
| **Pow**(*number, exponent*) | Returns *number* raised to the power of *exponent*. For example, Pow(2,3) returns 8. |
| **Rand**( ) | Returns a random number in the range of 0 to 1 to 5 digits of precision. |
| **Round**(*number, numberofdigits*) | Rounds *number* to the number of decimal places specified by *numberofdigits*. When numberofdigits is 0, number becomes an integer. You can use a negative value for *numberofdigits* to perform rounding to the left of the decimal point, *such* as Round(4321,-2) returns 4300. |
| **Sign**(*number* [, *fuzz*]) | Returns 1 if *number* is positive, 0 if zero, and -1 if negative. *Fuzz* avoids floating-point roundoff errors when calculations are near zero. When *fuzz* is missing, Visio uses 0.000000001. For example, Sign(0.01,0.1) returns 0. |
| **Sqrt**(*number*) | Returns the square root of *number*. Returns #NUM! error when *number* is negative. For example, Sqrt(2) returns 1.4142. |
| **Sum**(*number1,*<br>*number2...number14*) | Adds up all *numbers*. For example, Sum(7,10,11,41,42) returns 111. |

Customizing ShapeSheets

| Mathematical Functions | Meaning |
| --- | --- |
| **Trunc**(*number, numberofdigits*) | Truncates *number* to *numberofdigits*. This function does not round up or round down. You can use a negative value for *numberofdigits* to perform rounding to the left of the decimal point, such as Trunc(4321,-2) returns 4300. |

| Trigonometric Functions | Meaning |
| --- | --- |
| **ACos**(*number*) | Returns the arccosine of *number*. *Number* must be in the range -1 to 1 with the result in the range 0 to 90 degrees. For example, Acos(0) results in 90deg. |
| **Ang360**(*angle*) | Reduces the angle to the range between 0 and 360 degrees. If units are not specified, the angle is in radians. For example, Ang360(375deg) results in 15deg. |
| **ASin**(*number*) | Returns the arcsine of *number*. |
| **ATan**(*number*) | Returns the arctangent of *number*. |
| **ATan2**(*y, x*) | Returns the arctangent of the *y,x*-point. |
| **Cos**(*angle*) | Returns the cosine of *angle*. |
| **CosH**(*angle*) | Returns the hyperbolic cosine of *angle*. |
| **Deg**(*angle*) | Converts *angle* from radians to degrees. |
| **Loc**(*point*) | Returns the x,y-distance of *point* (an x,y-coordinate) as measured from the lower-left corner of the shape's selection rectangle. |
| **Par**(*point*) | Returns the x,y-distance of *point* (an x,y-coordinate) in the coordinate system of the shape's parent. |
| **Pnt**(*x, y*) | Combines x and y to create an x,y-coordinate. |
| **PntX**(*point*) | Returns the x-distance of *point* (an x,y-coordinate) measured from the lower-left corner of the shape's selection rectangle. |
| **PntY**(*point*) | Returns the y-distance of *point* (an x,y-coordinate) measured from the lower-left corner of the shape's selection rectangle. |
| **Rad**(*angle*) | Converts *angle* from degrees to radians. |
| **Sin**(*angle*) | Returns the sine of *angle*. |
| **SinH**(*angle*) | Returns the hyperbolic sine of *angle*. |

| *Trigonometric Functions* | *Meaning* |
| --- | --- |
| **Tan**(*angle*) | Returns the tangent of *angle*. |
| **TanH**(*angle*) | Returns the hyperbolic tangent of *angle*. |

| *Comparison Functions* | *Meaning* |
| --- | --- |
| > *or* **_GT_** | Greater than, such as 19 > 2 results in TRUE. |
| < *or* **_LT_** | Less than, such as 19 < 2 results in FALSE. |
| >= *or* **_GE_** | Greater than or equal to, such as 19 >= 2 results in TRUE. |
| <= *or* **_LE_** | Less than or equal to, such as 19 <= 2 results in FALSE. |
| = *or* **_EQ_** | Equal to, such as 19 = 2 results in FALSE. |
| <> *or* **_NE_** | Not equal to, such as 19 <> 2 results in TRUE. |

The symbol operators (such as > and <) perform fuzzy comparisons and are more likely to return the result you expect.

The alternative operators (such as _GT_ and _LT_) perform a comparison to fifteen digits of precision.

When text strings are compared, Visio attempts to convert the string to a value, such as "19.2 in." becomes 19.2.

If a string, such as "Desk", cannot be converted to a value, the result is 0.

| *Logical Functions* | *Meaning* |
| --- | --- |
| **And**(*logicalexpression1*, *logicalexpression2*, ...) | Returns 1 when all *logicalexpressions* are true (non-zero). Otherwise, returns 0. |
| **BitAnd**(*binarynumber1*, *binarynumber2*) | Returns a binary number. A bit is set to 1 when the bit in *binarynumber1* and *binarynumber2* is 1. Otherwise, the bit is set to 0. |
| **BitNot**(*binarynumber*) | Returns a binary number. A bit is set to 1 when the bit in *binarynumber* is 0. Otherwise, the bit is set to 0. |
| **BitOr**(*binarynumber1*, *binarynumber2*) | Returns a binary number. A bit is set to 1 when the bit in *binarynumber1* or *binarynumber2* is 1. Bit is set to 0 only when both *binarynumber1* and *binarynumber2* are set to 1. |
| **BitXOr**(*binarynumber1*, *binarynumber2*) | Returns a binary number. A bit is set to 1 when the bit in either *binarynumber1* or *binarynumber2* is 1 but not both. Otherwise, the bit is set to 0. |

| Logical Functions | Meaning |
| --- | --- |
| **If**(*logicalexpression, valueiftrue, valueiffalse*) | Returns *valueiftrue* if *logicalexpression* is true. Otherwise, returns *valueiffalse*. |
| **Not**(*logicalexpression*) | Returns 1 if *logicalexpression* is false. Otherwise, returns 0. |
| **Or**(*logicalexpression1, logicalexpression2, ...*) | Returns 1 when any *logicalexpression* is true (non-zero). Otherwise, returns 0. |

| Error Handling Functions | Meaning |
| --- | --- |
| **IsErr**(*cell*) | This function is used with formulae that refer to another cell. Returns true when the value of *cell* is any error type. Returns false with error #N/A. |
| **IsErrNa**(*cell*) | This function is used with formulae that refer to another cell. Returns true when the value of *cell* is #N/A. Returns false with any other error type. |
| **IsError**(*cell*) | This function is used with formulae that refer to another cell. Returns true when the value of *cell* is any error type. Returns false if no error exists. |
| **IsErrValue**(*cell*) | This function is used with formulae that refer to another cell. Returns true when the value of *cell* is error #VALUE. Returns false with any other error. |
| **NA**( ) | Returns error #NA. |
| **Ref**( ) | Returns error #REF. |

| Error Types | Meaning |
| --- | --- |
| #DIV/0! | Number was divided by 0. |
| #VALUE! | Wrong type of argument or operand. |
| #REF! | A cell was referenced that does not exist. |
| #NUM! | The result is an invalid number, such as taking the square root of a negative number. |
| #N/A! | Value is not available. Use the na() function in a cell that's missing information, which prevents the cell's default value from being used. |

# Chapter Review

In this chapter you learned detailed information about each ShapeSheet section and received an introduction to ShapeSheet functions.

The next section introduces database links.

# *Customizing Databases*

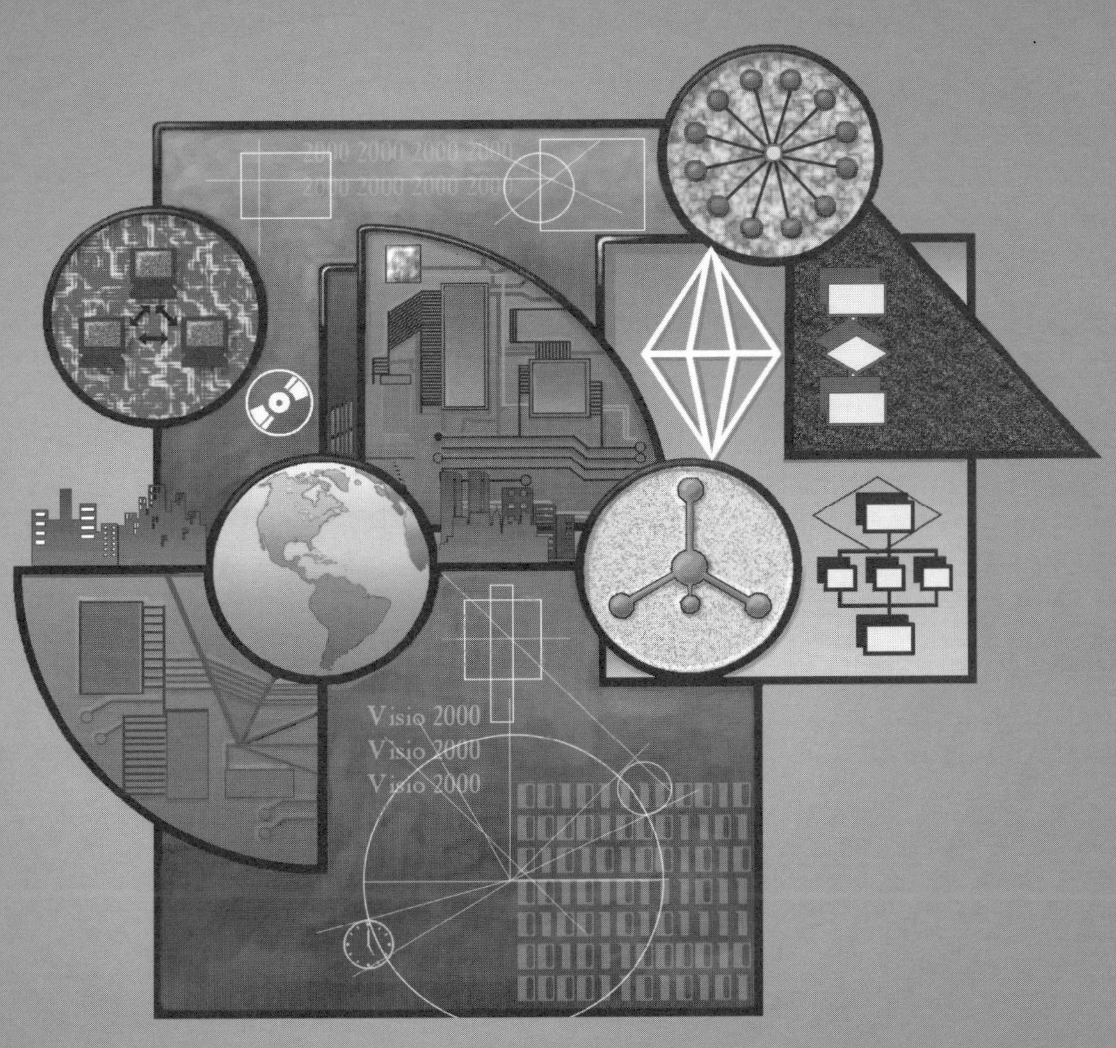

# Chapter 9

# Introduction to Database Links

In this chapter, you are introduced to linking Visio drawings with an external database. This is useful for automatically generating Visio drawings or for sharing data stored in a Visio drawing. In particular, you learn:

- What a database is
- ODBC, the open database connectivity standard
- How Visio connects with a database file
- Visio's limited data types

By the end of the chapter, you should understand what a database is and what it can do for you, and have a basic understanding of how Visio links shapes with records and fields in a database table.

## What is a Database?

A database stores information and lets you retrieve the information. As you read that sentence, you might be thinking to yourself, "My word processor does that; my spreadsheet does that." And you would be right. Word processors and spreadsheets have simple database features, such as the ability to sort a table by its columns.

Database software, however, is capable of advanced sorting and data output. For example, you could ask the database software to produce a list of all employees with a birthday in August, sort the list by dates, then print the list of names by date. The data can be output to the screen, the printer, a file on disk, or another program, such as Visio.

When it comes right down to it, a database consists simply of rows of data (called *records*). Every record contains exactly the same types of data (called *fields*) in precisely the same order. For example, here are three records, each containing four fields:

| Stefan | Vancouver | $1,234.45 | No |
| Heidi | Vancouver | $2,345.67 | No |
| Katrina | Vancouver | $3,456.78 | Yes |

By looking at these records, you can guess that field #1 contains a name. Field #2 contains a location. Field #3 contains an amount, perhaps the monthly salary. Field #4 contains a toggle (yes or no), perhaps indicating whether the person has access to the executive bathroom.

I present to you the table again, this time adding in the database structure:

| Field # | 1 | 2 | 3 | 4 |
|---|---|---|---|---|
| *Field Name* | *Name* | *Location* | *Amount* | *Executive Bathroom Privileges* |
| **Record #1** | Stefan | Vancouver | $1,234.45 | No |
| **Record #2** | Heidi | Vancouver | $2,345.67 | No |
| **Record #3** | Katrina | Vancouver | $3,456.78 | Yes |

If you are familiar with spreadsheets, then you may notice that this database table looks very much like a spreadsheet, with its rows and columns.

| | A | B | C | D |
|---|---|---|---|---|
| 1 | Name | Location | Amount | Executive Bathroom Privileges |
| 2 | Stefan | Vancouver | $1,234.45 | No |
| 3 | Heidi | Vancouver | $2,345.67 | No |
| 4 | Katrina | Vancouver | $3,456.78 | Yes |
| 5 | | | | |
| 6 | | | | |
| 7 | | | | |

Indeed, recall from Section II of this book that Visio uses a spreadsheet-like interface to display its shape data in ShapeSheets. Keep the similarities in mind: only the terminology is different. The ShapeSheet rows are called *records* in the database; the ShapeSheet cells are called *fields* in the database; the ShapeSheet itself is known as the *table* in the database.

One other important term you need to know is *key*. The primary key is a field that uniquely identifies each record. In the table above, you might use **Name** as the key.

If you are familiar with database software, then you should know about Visio's limitations. Visio sees only a flat table of rows and columns of data; it cannot make relational database queries. Visio has only three data types, as discussed at the end of this chapter. Visio cannot execute SQL commands directly; it is possible to do this indirectly. Visio is limited to connecting one record to one shape; it cannot connect two or more records to a shape. A future version of Visio may eliminate these restrictions.

# Reasons for Making the Connection

Why would you want to connect Visio with a database? Readers of my Visio books have e-mailed me their needs. Here are some of them:

"I am documenting an old mainframe system, so I load information into a database and show the flowchart of jobs/programs/files in Visio."

"I am using a database to create a network diagram in Visio."

"I connected Visio to my database because I needed a more efficient way to document database development projects."

Other examples include facilities management (keeping track of furniture and other corporate assets) and centralized master generation. You can probably think of your own examples.

Perhaps the most important thinking you need to do is whether to store the data in the Visio drawing or in the external database. Here is the difference: you store the data in the external database when the data needs to be shared among other users and other software applications.

The Visio-database connection is more powerful than showing data graphically. You can control the database from Visio, such as adding and deleting records. You can even create new database files from Visio. This is pretty exciting stuff!

# Visio and ODBC

Once a Visio shape is connected to a database record, Visio and the database can pass information back and forth, and keep the two versions of the data synchronized. The mechanism for doing this is called ODBC, short for *open database connectivity*. This is a standard, written by Microsoft, for sharing database information between applications under Windows. It lets a software program access, view, and modify data from a database. Get used to the abbreviation ODBC, because you'll be seeing it a lot.

Before the advent of ODBC, a software program, such as Visio, needed an interface driver for every database program. A *driver* is a piece of software that lets a program communicate with another program or hardware. (You are probably familiar with hardware drivers that let Windows communicate with your computer's graphics board, CD-ROM, network card, etc.) Pre-ODBC you would have one database driver for dBase, another database driver for Sybase, another database driver for Paradox, and on and on. It was a pain for software developers to write a driver for every database program, then have to update every driver each time the software was upgraded.

For this reason, Microsoft invented ODBC. Pretty much all Windows-based database programs convert their proprietary data format to ODBC format. Examples include Paradox, Oracle, Access, dBase, Alpha Four, SQL Server, and Sybase. Excel contains a limited form of ODBC; for example, Excel cannot be made to delete a record via ODBC. Visio says they've heard of one customer who managed to get ODBC working between Visio running under Windows and dBase II running on a mainframe computer!

Similarly, a number of non-database Windows applications have ODBC, such as AutoCAD, MicroStation, Lotus Notes, and Visio. These programs can read ODBC data and can control ODBC-compatible databases.

**Caution:**

ODBC might not be installed on your computer. The appropriate ODBC components and database drivers are only installed if you choose the **Complete** option when installing Visio. All editions of Visio, including Visio 2000 Standard Edition, support ODBC.

# Which Database Program?

With all this talk about database connectivity, you may be wondering, "Which database program is best for me?" The list of database programs includes Paradox, Fox Pro, Oracle, Access, dBase, Alpha Four, SQL Server, Sybase, Excel, etc. The short answer is, "None!"

You heard right: to connect a Visio drawing with a database file, you *don't* need a database program. That's because Visio includes everything you need to create the database file from within Visio. Visio has an option to create an Access-compatible database file. It is only when you want to access (pardon the pun) the database file from outside of Visio that you might need the database program.

If you want, however, to dabble with an actual database program, you have several low-cost choices. If you have Microsoft Office, you can begin with the Excel spreadsheet program. Microsoft Office Professional includes the Access database



Customizing Databases

program. Otherwise, there are a number of low-cost database programs that are dBase II-compatible, such as Alpha Four. Some of these are available in free demo versions, which limit only the size of database you are allowed to create.

# How Visio Connects with the Database

When you connect Visio with a database file, you connect the *cells* in the ShapeSheet to *fields* in the database table. It's as simple as that. Visio does the hard work of keeping track of which cells are linked to which fields. ODBC does the hard work of transferring data and commands back and forth.

If you are unfamiliar with databases—even perhaps afraid of the thought of dealing with database—relax, because Visio has the Database Wizard, which walks you through the process of linking shapes in a drawing with database records.

To help set the concept (cells = fields) in concrete in your mind, let's look at a practical example. A network diagram describes all resources on the network (computers, printers, etc.) and how the resources are connected (the network cabling).

A common shape in a network diagram is the computer. Let's see if we can come up with properties that describe that computer:

➤ Size and position of the computer shape

➤ Color of the computer shape

➤ Asset information, such as the type of computer, when it was purchased, and asset ID number

➤ Name of the computer shape

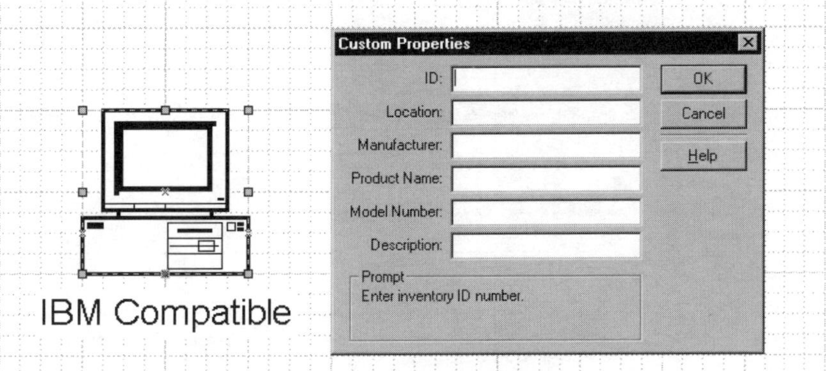


From the knowledge of the ShapeSheet gained in Part II of this book, we know the data is stored in these sections and cells:

➤ Size and position of the shape is stored in the Shape Transform section. Size is determined by the Height and Width cells; the PinX and PinY cells determine the position.

➤ Color of the shape is stored in the Line Format and Fill Format sections. The Line Format section defines the properties of lines that make up the shape, such as width in the LineWeight cell, pattern in the LinePattern cell, and color in the LineColor cell. The Fill Format section defines the properties of the shape's fill and drop shadow.

➤ Asset information is stored in the Custom Properties section. There is one row of cells for every item displayed by the Custom Properties dialog box. One row for ID, another row for Location, etc.

➤ For database purposes, the name of the shape must be stored in the Custom Properties section.

It turns out that the Custom Properties section becomes the catchall: just about anything that cannot be stored in one of the predefined section cells is stuffed into a Custom Properties row. There is an exception. Visio uses the User-defined Cells section to store information about the database link:

| User-defined Cells | Value | Prompt |
|---|---|---|
| User.ODBCDataSource | "Visio Database Samples" | "The ODBC data source to which the shape is linked |
| User.ODBCQualifier | "" | "Qualifier cell.  This cell contains the name of t |
| User.ODBCTable | "Network - Computers" | "The database table to which the shape is linked." |
| User.ODBCKeyField1 | "MachineSN" | "Key field link.  This cell stores the name of a c |
| User.ODBCKeyCell1 | "Prop.MachineSN" | "Key cell.  This cell contains the name of a custo |
| User.ODBCKeyMirror1 | "SN10000004" | "Key field mirror cell.  This cell contains the mo |
| User.ODBCLink1 | "PinX==XLocation==1" | "A link field.  Specifies which cell in the shape |
| User.ODBCMirror1 | "1343 in." | "A mirror field.  Stores the most recently retriev |
| User.ODBCLink2 | "PinY==YLocation==1" | "A link field.  Specifies which cell in the shape |
| User.ODBCMirror2 | "1177 in." | "A mirror field.  Stores the most recently retriev |
| User.ODBCLink3 | "Prop.Cost==Cost==111" | "A link field.  Specifies which cell in the shape |
| User.ODBCMirror3 | "2000" | "A mirror field.  Stores the most recently retriev |
| User.ODBCLink4 | "Prop.HardDiskSpace==Hard Disk S| | "A link field.  Specifies which cell in the shape |
| User.ODBCMirror4 | "850" | "A mirror field.  Stores the most recently retriev |
| User.ODBCLink5 | "Prop.MachineType==Machine Type| | "A link field.  Specifies which cell in the shape |

| Cell Name | Meaning |
|---|---|
| **ODBCTable** | Contains the name of the database table to which the shape is linked, such as "Network - Computers." |
| **ODBCDataSource** | Contains the name of the ODBC data source to which the shape is linked, such as "Visio Database Samples." |
| **ODBCLink1...n** | Specifies which cell in the shape is associated with a particular field in the database table, such as "PinX==XLocation==1" or "Prop.MachineTypecode==Machine Type code==32" or "Prop.Cost==Cost==111." There is one row in ODBCLink*n* per field. Also specifies whether Visio evaluates data retrieved from a field as a string or a number and the units of measurement. The end of this chapter contains the complete list of codes. |
| **ODBCKeyCell1...5** | Contains the name of the Custom Properties row that stores the value for the key field named by the ODBCKeyFields*n* cells, such as "Prop.MachineSN." There is a maximum of five ODBCKeyCell*n* cells. |

| Cell Name | Meaning |
| --- | --- |
| **ODBCKeyField1...5** | Contains the name of the cell that contains the value for a database key field, such as "MachineSN." The primary key is a field that uniquely identifies each record. There is a maximum of five ODBCKeyField*n* cells. |
| **ODBCKeyMirror1...5** | Contains the most recently retrieved value for a linked database field, such as "1343 in." Visio uses these cells to determine the record that the shape was linked to when its key value(s) was changed. There is a maximum of five ODBCKeyMirror*n* cells. |
| **ODBCMirror1...*n*** | Contain the last valid values retrieved from database fields. There is one row in ODBCMirror*n* per field. Visio uses these cells to determine whether the values have changed since the last synchronization. |
| **ODBCQualifier** | Contains the name of the database with the table. Note: This cell is used only when a single data source can support multiple databases. |

# Visio Data Types

A database file consists of rigorous fields of data stored in rows of records. Earlier, I noted that each field contained a specific type of data, such as text, number, or toggle. It turns out that Visio supports a very few specific data types. Specifically, these three:

| Data Type | Meaning |
| --- | --- |
| **Number** | When a cell contains a number, it is always a double-precision real number. Formatting makes the number appear to be an integer, such as 100, or a number with units, such as 12.3 ft. |
| **Text** | A cell can contain up to 252 characters. (It would be 254 but two characters are always the surrounding " marks). |



Customizing Databases

| Data Type | Meaning |
| --- | --- |
| **Data1...3** | These fields can contain up to 64KB of each. There are three Data*n* fields per shape. In Visio, you can only access the Data*n* fields via the Format \| Special command or through VBA programming; this data is not accessible via the ShapeSheet. |

Normally, the database file expects to receive its information with data formatted into the correct data types. Most database programs require you to specify whether a field consists of an integer number, a real number, a single character, a text string, a Boolean (true or false value), a date, etc.

Fortunately for us, Visio interprets the information, and makes a best guess at its data type. For example, Visio is able to interpret the string "12.1 in." as the number 12.1 with the units of inches. Still, this might lead to the occasional unexplained error when a data type is converted incorrectly.

To define the units of a number, Visio uses the following convention. The units are stored in the ODBCLink*n* cells of the User-defined Cells section, using a format that looks like this:

$$=\text{"Prop.Cost}==\text{Cost}==111\text{"}$$

This means that the Custom Properties row called Prop.Cost stores the Cost data of the shape. The cost data is formatted in currency units (unit code 111). The complete list of unit codes is as follows:

| Code | Meaning |
| --- | --- |
| 0 | String value |
| 1 | String formula |
| 32 | Non-dimensional number |
| 40 | Date |
| 48 | Number with no explicit units |
| 50 | Points (72 points per inch) |
| 51 | Picas (6 picas per inch) |
| 53 | Didots (67 didots per inch) |
| 54 | Ciceros (12 ciceros per didot) |

| Code | Meaning |
|------|---------|
| 63 | Use default units, as specified by the page |
| 64 | Use drawing's default units |
| 65 | Decimal inches |
| 66 | Feet |
| 67 | Feet and inches |
| 68 | Decimal miles |
| 69 | Centimeters |
| 70 | Millimeters |
| 71 | Meters |
| 72 | Kilometers |
| 73 | Fractional inches |
| 74 | Fractional miles |
| 75 | Yards |
| 80 | Angle with no explicit units |
| 81 | Angle in decimal degrees |
| 82 | Angle in degrees, minutes, and seconds |
| 83 | Angle in radians |
| 84 | Angle in minutes and seconds |
| 85 | Angle in seconds |
| 111 | Currency |
| 252 | Leaves number in current units |

# Chapter Review

This chapter provided you with an introduction to linking Visio with an external database file. You learned some database terminology, the importance of ODBC, and how cells are linked to fields. You saw the importance of understanding the ShapeSheet before tackling advanced Visio topics.

In the next chapter, you use the Database wizard to link shapes in a drawing with a database file.

**Customizing Databases**

# Chapter 10

# Exporting Drawings to Database Files

Visio can export the data stored in its ShapeSheet cells to an external file. A database program (such as Access or dBase) can read the external file, as can a spreadsheet program (such as Quattro Pro or Excel) or any other program that can read formatted data files. In this chapter, you learn about:

➤ Visio's database wizards and commands

➤ Exporting a drawing to a database file for the first time

➤ Exporting an updated drawing

➤ Selecting a different export format

By the end of this chapter, you should be able to use the Database Export wizard to export cell data to an Excel spreadsheet file and an ASCII text file.

## Visio Database Wizards and Commands

Visio exports the data stored in its ShapeSheet cells to an external database file. To assist you in the process, Visio includes a number of database wizards and commands. These are:

➤ **Database Export Wizard**   A wizard that leads you through the steps of selecting a database file format and exporting cell data to the file.

> **Database Wizard**   A wizard that leads you through the steps of creating a two-way connection between shape cells and database fields.

> **Database Refresh**   A command that updates Visio cells to match database fields.

> **Database Update**   A command that updates database fields to match Visio cells.

> **Database Settings**   A dialog box that lets you specify settings for automatically updating drawings and database files.

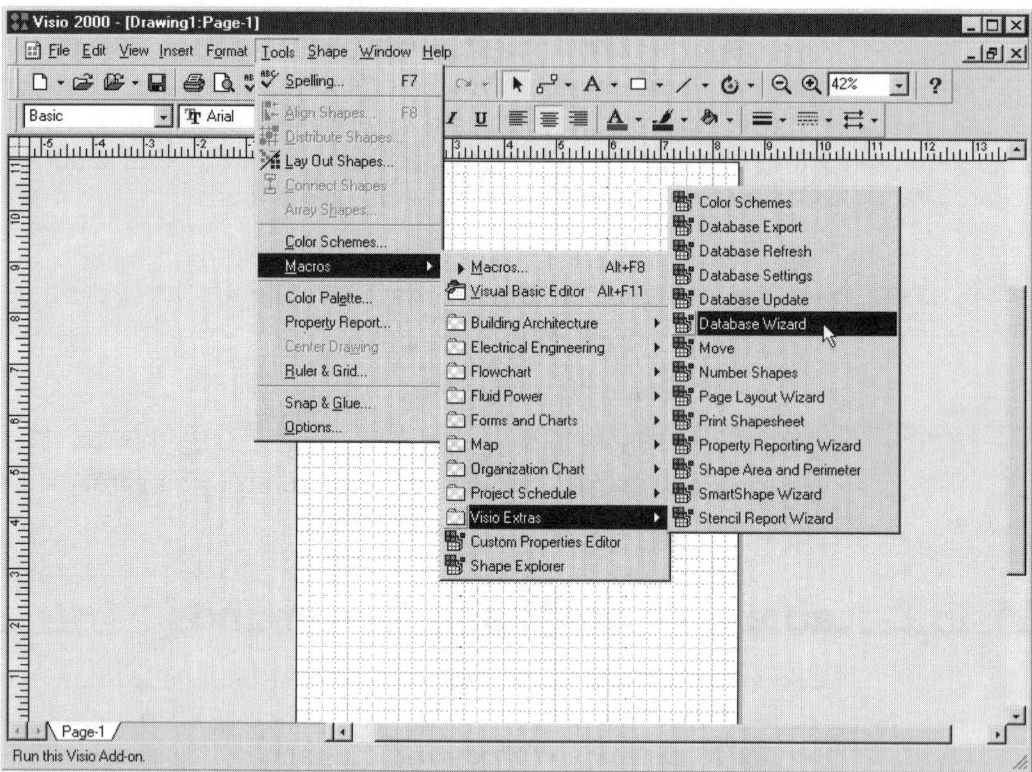


The wizards are found by selecting **Tools | Macros | Visio Extras** from the menu bar.

In this chapter, you learn about the Database Export wizard (in the next chapter, you learn about the Database wizard). The Database Export wizard performs two tasks: (1) it helps you select the shapes and cells to export; and (2) it helps you select the ODBC driver and the format of the database file.

Visio uses the ODBC (short for *open database connectivity*) standard, which lets software programs communicate with many different database programs. Because so many different database programs are available on the market, this chapter concentrates on the two most common: the Excel spreadsheet program and plain ASCII text files. You do *not* need a copy of Excel for this chapter but it helps for viewing the resulting XLS file; versions as old as Excel v3 work just fine.

This chapter consists primarily of tutorials that walk you through the Database Export wizard three times. In the first tutorial, you learn how to export the data found in Visio shape cells to an XLS Excel database file. In the second tutorial, you make changes to the drawing, then learn how to export the updated data. In the third tutorial, you learn how to change the export format, namely to a CDF (short for *comma-delimited format*) text file.

# Exporting a Drawing for the First Time

In the following tutorial, you learn how to export the data found in Visio shape cells to an XLS Excel database file. Later, in the second tutorial, you make changes to the drawing, then learn how to export the updated data. Finally, in the third tutorial, you learn how to change the export format.

**Tip:**

Some Visio database tutorials require you to first work with the ODBC data source administrator, found in the Windows Control Panel. You do *not* need to select **Start | Settings | Control Panel | OBDC** to use the ODBC Data Source Administrator dialog box to set up the

**Customizing Databases**

> parameters. This tabbed dialog box makes it hard to know what to do when. Fortunately, Visio's database wizards takes you to the right dialog boxes in the correct order. Visio's database wizards (and there are more than just this export wizard) do the work for you in setting up the ODBC parameters.

1. Start Visio with **Chapter7.Vss**, the stencil file you created in Chapter 7.

2. Create a simple floor plan with the **Furniture** master. The plan shown in the figure contains these furniture objects:

| Furniture | Width | Depth | Number of shapes in drawing |
|---|---|---|---|
| Rug | 10" | 10" | 1 |
| Couch | 6" | 1.5" | 1 |
| Chair | 1.5" | 1.5" | 3 |
| Desk | 3.6" | 2.4" | 1 |

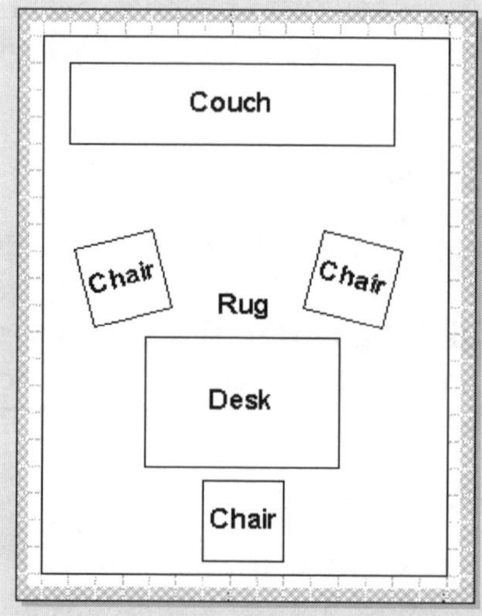


3. Select **Tools | Macros | Visio Extras | Database Export** from the menu bar. Notice that Visio displays the Database Export wizard.

4.  Click **Next** in the first three dialog boxes to accept the defaults. For example, the second dialog box lets you choose the drawing (it's the one you've already opened) and the page (this drawing has only one page). The third dialog box lets you choose the shape (you want to export all shapes).

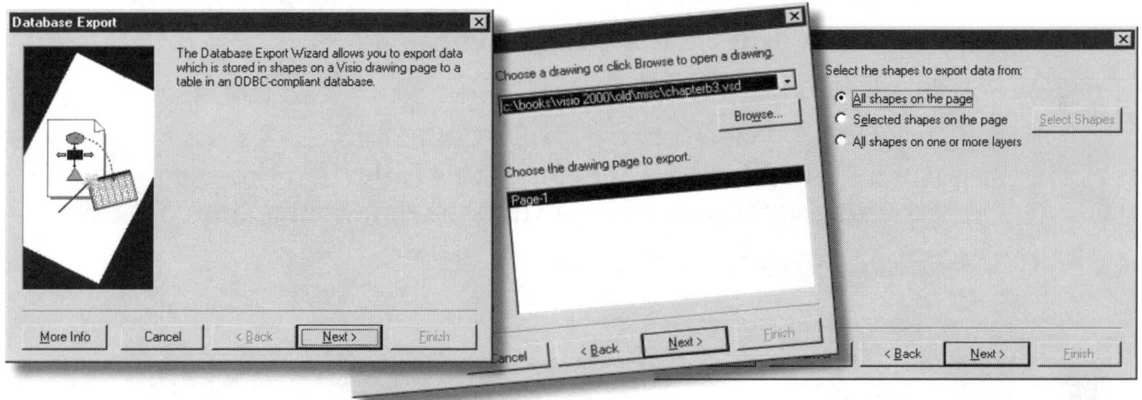

5.  When you get to "Select the Visio data you wish to export," I'll show you a shortcut. In this dialog box, you select the cells you want stored as fields in the database file. In the **Visio Cells and Fields** column, Visio displays all of the cell names, which you might want at some point in your career, but not today.

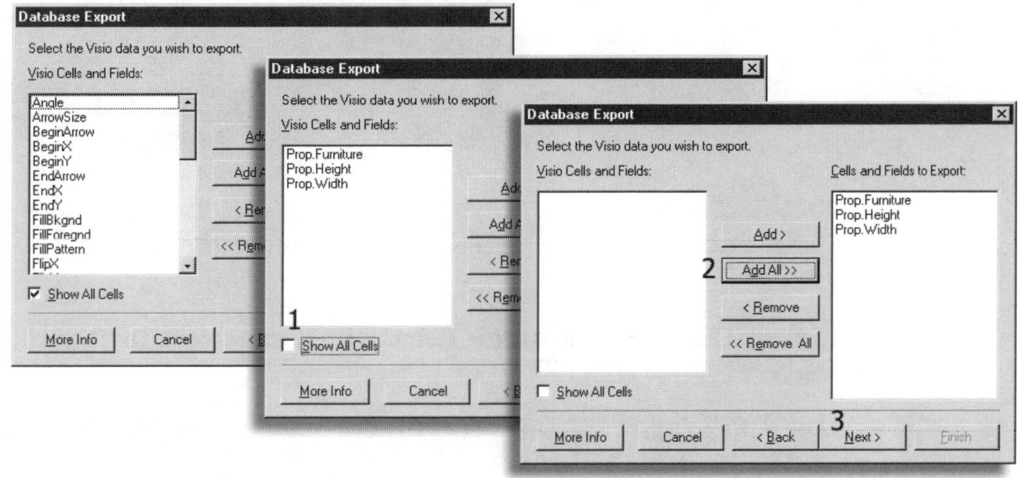

Customizing Databases

➤ Click **Show All Cells** to turn off the option (no check mark). Notice that the wizard displays only the cells found in the Custom Properties section, which are the ones we want.

➤ Click **Add All**. Notice that the remaining cell names, Prop.Furniture, Prop.Height, and Prop.Width, appear in the **Cells and Fields to Export** column.

➤ Click **Next**.

6.  In this step, you select the ODBC Data Source. This is a fancy name for the database file. Since this is the first time you are exporting data from this drawing, the data source does not exist.

    Click **Create Data Source**.

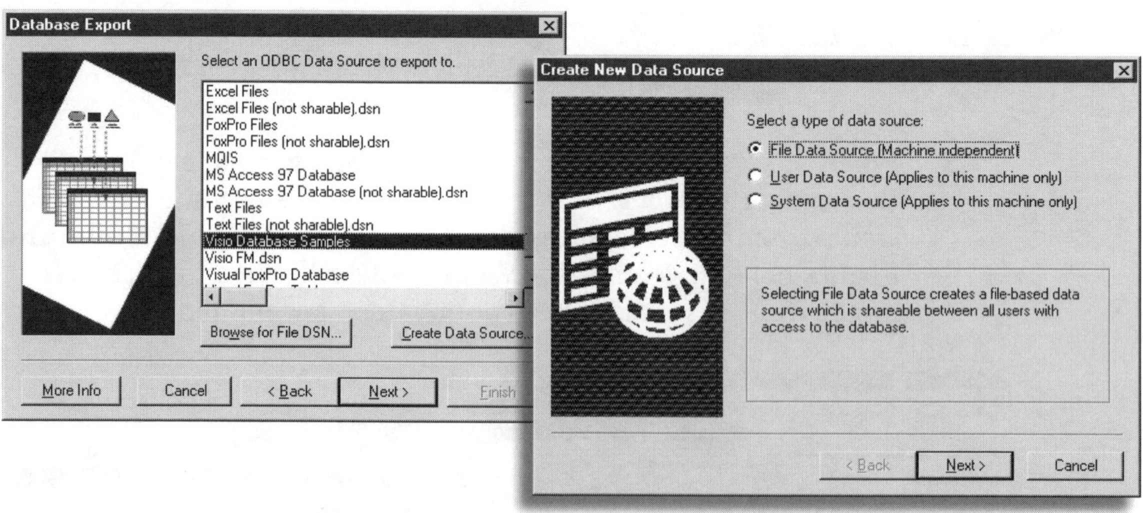


7.  In this step you select a type of data source. Visio provides you with three choices, which determine where the database is stored.

    Select **File Data Source (Machine independent)**, and click **Next**.

8.  Here you select the database driver, which determines the database file format. The list of formats will vary, since it depends on the ODBC drivers installed on your computer. The illustration

shows these drivers are installed on my computer. Some of the names include dBase, Excel, Oracle, Paradox, and Text.

Select **Microsoft Excel Driver**, and click **Next**.

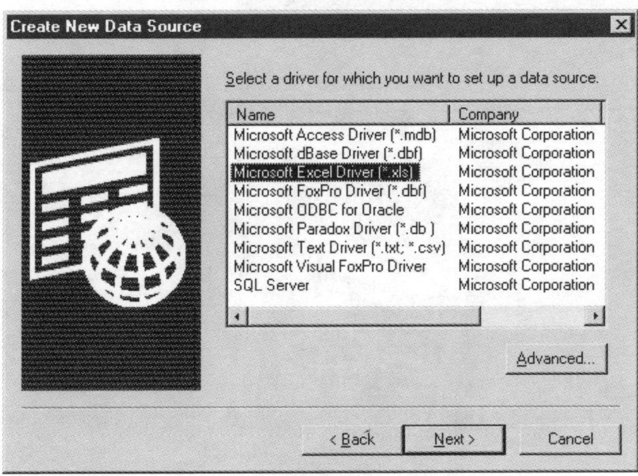


9.  You must specify the name of the DSN file. The DSN file (short for *data source name*) stores parameters that you specify in this wizard. The format of the DSN file is very similar to an INI (initialization) file used by many Windows programs. The first few lines of the DSN file looks like this:

```
[ODBC]
DRIVER=Microsoft Excel Driver (*.xls)
UID=admin
UserCommitSync=Yes
Threads=3
```

I find it is a good idea to use a name that describes the database file format you want Visio to create. For example, specify "Excel.Dsn" for a spreadsheet file, or "Access.Dsn" if you happen to use that particular database program. (If you want to store the DSN file in another folder, click **Browse** and select the folder.)

Type **Excel** and click **Next** or **Save**, then click **Next** again if you clicked the Browse button. Visio automatically adds the .DSN extension.

10. Visio displays a summary of the export options you selected. Even though this dialog box displays the Finish button, you're not finished yet! As the dialog box warns, "The driver may prompt you for more information."

    Click **Finish**.

11. As I warned, the ODBC driver intervenes. It displays the ODBC Microsoft Excel Setup dialog box. With it, you specify the setup for using Excel as the database program.

    In the **Database** section, select the version of Excel that you have on your computer. I happen to use Excel 97, and selected **Excel 97-2000** from the **Version** list box.

    If necessary, uncheck **Use Current Directory** to prevent ODBC from using its own default directory (which can make it hard to find the database file).

Click **Select Workbook**, and select the same folder you chose earlier for the DSN file. That ensures all files are together in the same subdirectory.

Click **Options**. Notice that the dialog box becomes longer to display additional options:

Uncheck **Read Only**; otherwise Visio will not be able to write to the Excel file.

Click **OK**.

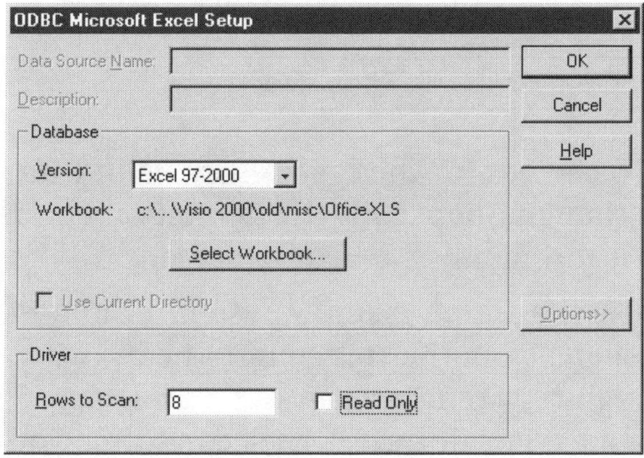

12.  Notice that Visio has returned to the Database Export dialog box. I find the terms used by this dialog box confusing. For example, **Database** is not the name of the database file but the folder that the database file is stored in.

Type **MyOffice** in the **Table Name** text entry box. This is not the name of the table; rather, this is the name of the spreadsheet file, MyOffice.Xls in this case. Since you are working with a spreadsheet, you can only have a single table name. If you were working with a database program, you would be able to have one or more table names.

The **Key Field** is the first field in the database file. It identifies each shape by a unique identification number. Here you specify the name for the field; it is safe to keep the default of **ShapeKey**.

Select **Guid** from the **Key Type** list box.

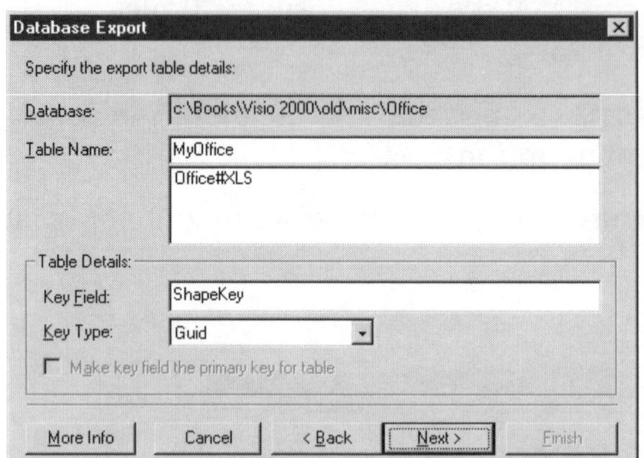

You have two choices for the type of key field: **ShapeID** or
**Guid**. Even though ShapeID is the default and easier to understand, Guid is ultimately the better choice:

➤ **ShapeID** is a simple naming system Visio uses when you
   drag a shape from the stencil into the drawing. When you
   drag the Furniture master into the drawing, Visio names the
   first instance Furniture.1. The second time you drag the
   master into the drawing, Visio names the second instance
   Furniture.2, and so on. The ShapeID is easy to understand,
   since you can get an idea of what the shape is in the database file. The drawback is that the name is not permanent.
   When you erase a shape and drag another shape into the
   drawing, Visio reuses the ShapeID. Erase the shape identi-
   fied as Furniture.1, then drag in another Furniture master, it
   gets the name Furniture.1.

➤ **Guid** is a unique number assigned to the shape when it is
   exported to the database file. The number is thirty-nine digits long, and looks similar to:

   {BC2640C3-06B0-11D2-8E9D-00AA00201DF7}

Click **Next**.

13. This dialog box expects you to specify the "export mapping
    details." I recommend you don't, especially as a first-time user. I

have found that making changes causes the wizard to fail later when it attempts to write the database file. Nevertheless, I'll give a short tour of this dialog box:

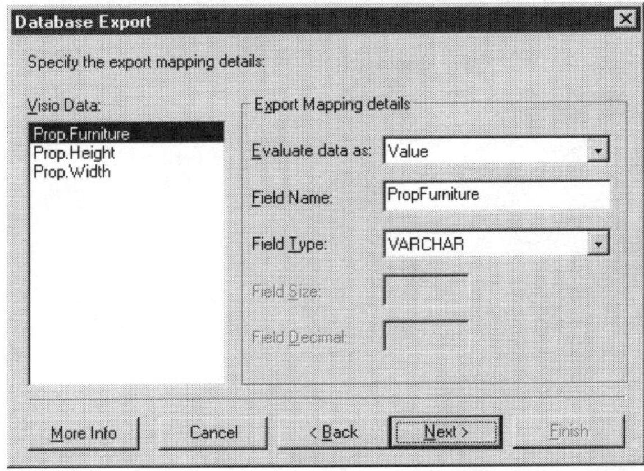

➤ The **Visio Data** column lists the cell names you selected earlier. As you select each cell name, you can specify the format in which the data should be exported in the **Export Mapping details** area.

➤ **Evaluate data as** lets you select one of Visio's data formats, such as Number or Inches. Keep the default value of **Value**.

➤ **Field Name** lets you change the name of the field. By default, the field name is the same as the cell name, minus the dot. There usually is no reason to change the field name.

➤ **Field Type** lists the data formats recognized by the database program. In the case of Excel, the list is quite short: Currency, Datetime, Logical, Number, and Text. Once again, leave the default value of **Text**.

➤ **Field Size** is used only when you select a field type that allows you to specify its width (number of characters or digits). Similarly, **Field Decimal** becomes available only when you select a real-number file type that lets you specify the number of decimal places.

I repeat: Make no changes to this dialog box. *Trust me.*

Click **Next**.

14. The next dialog box has a single option: "Add export right mouse action to the drawing page." This option adds an item, called **Database Export Table**, to the shortcut menu.

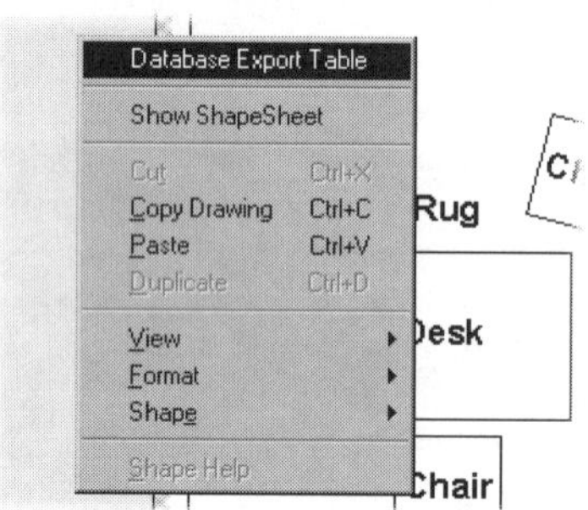


As shown by the illustration, this item appears on the shortcut menu when you right-click the drawing. It acts as a shortcut so that you can more quickly export the drawing to the database file.

Check the option, and click **Next**.

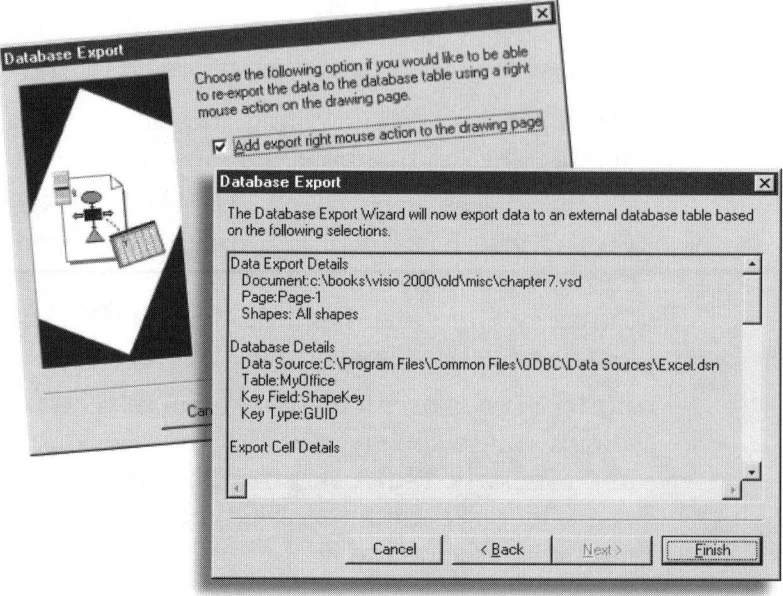

**15.** For the second time, Visio displays a summary box of the options you choose. For the second time, click **Finish**.

This time you are truly finished. Depending on the speed of your computer, it may take a few seconds or a minute to export the cell data for each shape and write the data to the spreadsheet file. While Visio is working, it displays the database wait icon, which looks like a tiny spreadsheet and hourglass.

**16.** Start Excel and open the **MyOffice.Xls** file. If necessary, adjust the column width to see all the text. You should see:

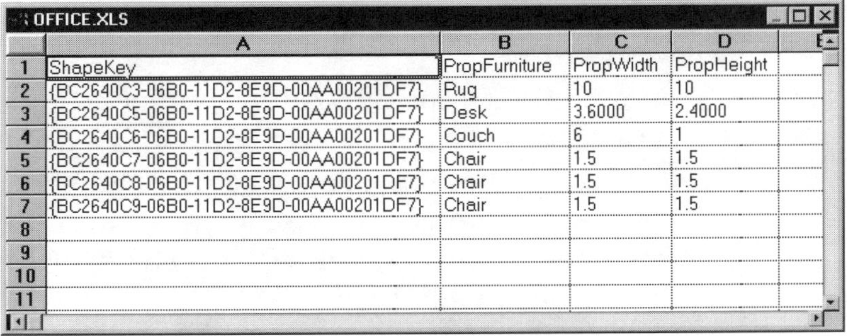

| | A | B | C | D | E |
|---|---|---|---|---|---|
| 1 | ShapeKey | PropFurniture | PropWidth | PropHeight | |
| 2 | {BC2640C3-06B0-11D2-8E9D-00AA00201DF7} | Rug | 10 | 10 | |
| 3 | {BC2640C5-06B0-11D2-8E9D-00AA00201DF7} | Desk | 3.6000 | 2.4000 | |
| 4 | {BC2640C6-06B0-11D2-8E9D-00AA00201DF7} | Couch | 6 | 1 | |
| 5 | {BC2640C7-06B0-11D2-8E9D-00AA00201DF7} | Chair | 1.5 | 1.5 | |
| 6 | {BC2640C8-06B0-11D2-8E9D-00AA00201DF7} | Chair | 1.5 | 1.5 | |
| 7 | {BC2640C9-06B0-11D2-8E9D-00AA00201DF7} | Chair | 1.5 | 1.5 | |
| 8 | | | | | |
| 9 | | | | | |
| 10 | | | | | |
| 11 | | | | | |

➤ One column for the ShapeKey field, followed by one column for each cell name you selected earlier.

➤ One row for the field names, followed by one row for each shape exported from the drawing.

Congratulations! You have exported the shape data in the Visio drawing to a database file. Now that the data is stored in a file, you can manipulate it.

It may have seemed laborious to go through these 16 steps just to export a few shapes to a database file. I have some good news for you. You go through these steps only the first time you create the connection between the drawing and the database file. In the next section of this chapter, I show you how to export an updated drawing, a process that goes much, much faster.



Customizing Databases

# Exporting an Updated Drawing

You have linked the Visio drawing to a database file. At some point, you make changes to the drawing, and then you want to export the changed data to the database file, a process that updates the database. Fortunately, the process is much faster the second time around.

In this tutorial, you make changes to the drawing, then learn how to export the updated data.

**Caution:**

Visio updates a spreadsheet by writing over it. (Visio does *not* mark deleted rows with a deleted message, as stated by Visio's documentation.) If you want to protect the earlier spreadsheet file from loss, specify a different table name, or copy the XLS file to another folder.

**I.** Make some changes to the floor plan, such as adding a side desk and removing a chair.

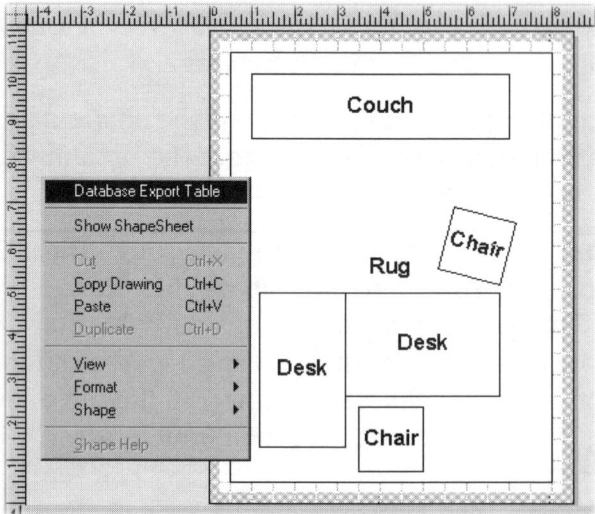

2. Right-click the page and select **Database Export Table** from the shortcut menu.

3. Notice the icon. It shows the miniature spreadsheet and hourglass. This indicates Visio is busy working with a database file. In particular, notice the small red arrow: it is pointing to the spreadsheet. This indicates Visio is exporting data to the spreadsheet or database file.

4. Notice that Visio displays a warning dialog box:

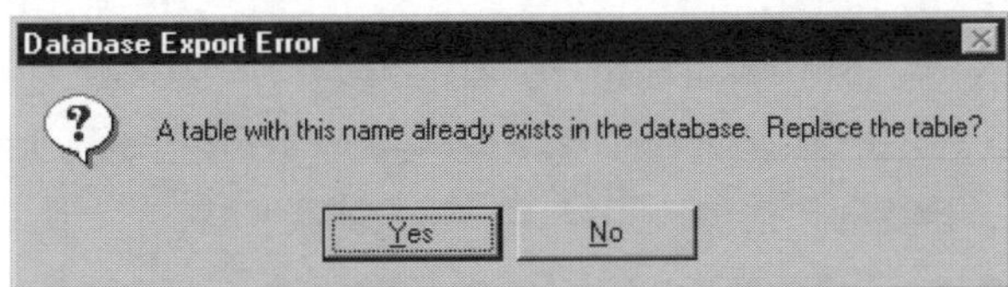


   ➤ Click **No**, and Visio stops the database export process.

   ➤ Click **Yes**, and Visio continues exporting the data. This action overwrites the existing XLS file.

   There is, unfortunately, no option to save the data to another filename.

5. Visio indicates it has finished by returning the cursor back to its normal, pointer state.

6. Open the newly rewritten XLS file in Excel. Notice the changes (two desks and two chairs).

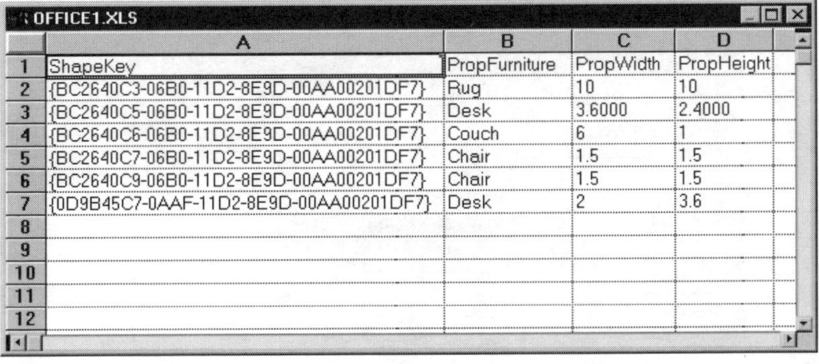

| | A | B | C | D |
|---|---|---|---|---|
| 1 | ShapeKey | PropFurniture | PropWidth | PropHeight |
| 2 | {BC2640C3-06B0-11D2-8E9D-00AA00201DF7} | Rug | 10 | 10 |
| 3 | {BC2640C5-06B0-11D2-8E9D-00AA00201DF7} | Desk | 3.6000 | 2.4000 |
| 4 | {BC2640C6-06B0-11D2-8E9D-00AA00201DF7} | Couch | 6 | 1 |
| 5 | {BC2640C7-06B0-11D2-8E9D-00AA00201DF7} | Chair | 1.5 | 1.5 |
| 6 | {BC2640C9-06B0-11D2-8E9D-00AA00201DF7} | Chair | 1.5 | 1.5 |
| 7 | {0D9B45C7-0AAF-11D2-8E9D-00AA00201DF7} | Desk | 2 | 3.6 |
| 8 | | | | |
| 9 | | | | |
| 10 | | | | |
| 11 | | | | |
| 12 | | | | |

**Customizing Databases**

# Selecting a Different Export Format

Earlier this chapter, you exported the Visio drawing to an Excel spreadsheet file. Sometimes you may want to change the file format. Other times, you may want to add some more cell names to the export list and change the field names to more meaningful wording.

In the following tutorial, you learn how to export the data to a text file. A similar technique applies when you want to switch from Excel to a database program, such as dBase or Paradox.

1. Start Visio with **Chapter10.Vss**—the stencil file and the floorplan you created earlier in this chapter.

2. Select **Tools | Macros | Visio Extras | Database Export** from the menu bar.

3. As before, click **Next** three times. Notice "Select the Visio data you want to export" in the dialog box and the list of cell names under **Visio Cells and Fields**. (Click **Show All Cells** if you do not see a list of many cell names.)

4. Scroll through the list and think about which cell names might be useful to export. For example, PinX and PinY provide the x- and y-coordinates of the shape.

   Select **PinX** in the Visio Cells and Fields column. Click **Add** to add PinX to the Cells and Fields to Export column.

   Repeat for **PinY**.

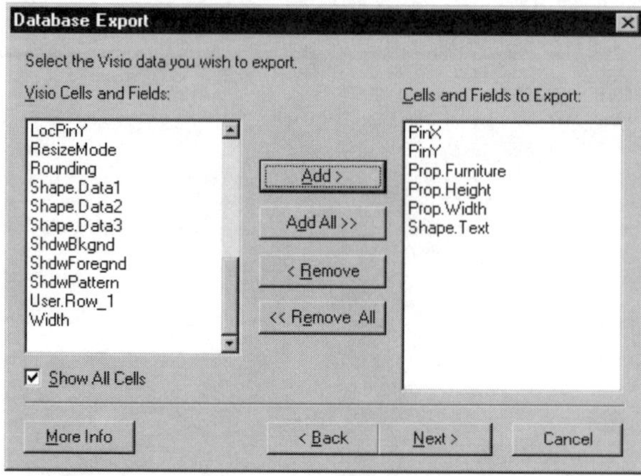

Click **Next**.

5. Click **Create Data Source** when "Select an ODBC Data Source to export to" appears in the wizard. You need to create a new data source, since you are not reusing the settings for Excel.

6. Select **File Data Source** as the type of data source, as before.

   Click **Next**.

7. Select **Microsoft Text Driver** as the data source driver. The text driver outputs the cell data to a plain ASCII text file in comma or tab-separated format. This is the best option when your computer has no other database or spreadsheet program installed.

   Click **Next**.

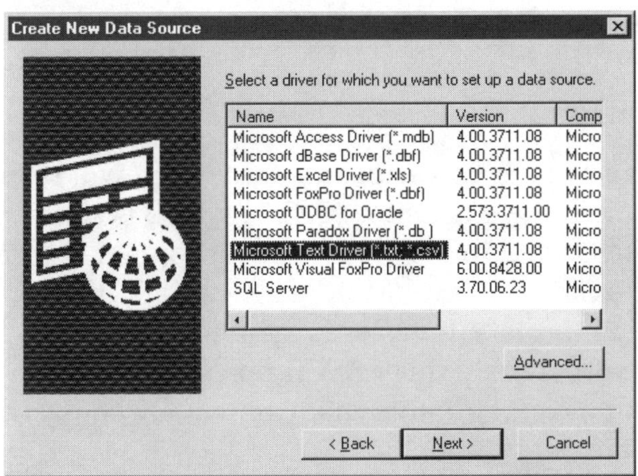

8. Type **Text.Dsn** for the data source filename. (To store the DSN file in another folder, click the **Browse** button and select the folder.)

   Click **Next**.

9. Click **Finish** and continue on to the **ODBC Text Setup** dialog box.

10. Uncheck **Use Current Directory** to prevent ODBC from using its own default directory.



**293**

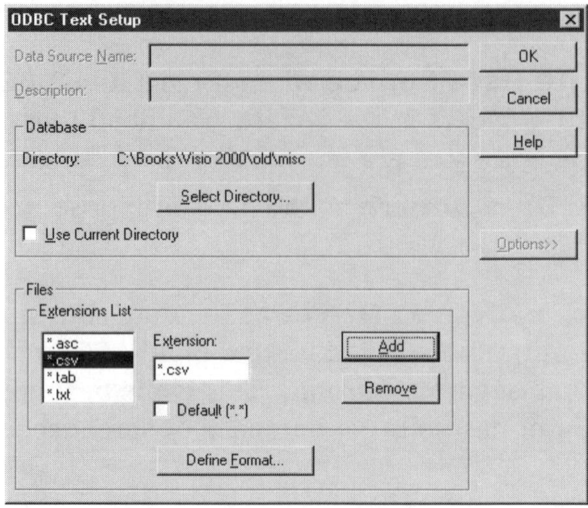

Click **Select Directory**, and select the same folder you chose earlier for the DSN file.

Click **Options**.

Click ***.csv** under **Extensions List**. Visio will save the cell data to a file with the extension of .CSV, which is short for *comma-separated value*. This means a comma separates each field. The filename extension really doesn't matter; Visio provides this option to make it easier for you to identify the file. Some software programs expect ASCII text files to have a specific filename extension, although that can usually be overridden. Your choices are:

➤   ***.asc** is short for ASCII file.

➤   ***.csv** is short for comma-separated file.

➤   ***.tab** is short for tabulation, and is meant for tab-separated files.

➤   ***.txt** is short for text file.

Click **Add**.

11.   Click **Define Format**. Notice the Define Text Format dialog box. (As with Excel files, an ASCII text file does not support multiple tables.)

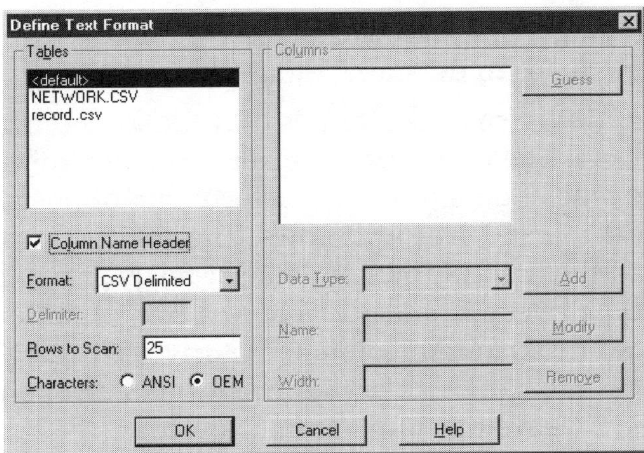

> The **Column Name Header** check box adds a row at the beginning of the file, which contains the names of the fields (or columns). Check this option if you want the convenience of the field names at the top of the file. Uncheck this option if the software you work with expects only data. Some software programs include an option that lets you skip the first line of a data file.

> The **Format** list box lets you select the separator character. The *separator character* separates fields from each other. For example, the comma separates the fields shown below:

> "2.1875 in.","3.1125 in.","Desk","2","3.6"

> When a database or spreadsheet program reads the separator character, it knows that a new field has begun. A spreadsheet, for example, places each field into its own cell. The most common separators are comma and tab, but sometimes other characters are used. Most software that reads data files has the option to use the comma (called CSV or comma delimited) or the tab (called tab delimited) characters. ODBC lets you use the comma, the tab, or any other character.

> The **Delimiter** text box becomes available when you select **Custom Delimited** as the **Format**. Here you may type



**295**

any single or group of characters that ODBC will use to separate fields in the database file.

➤ The **Rows to Scan** item is only found in the Text and Excel drivers. The ODBC driver scans this many rows to guess at the type of data found in each column of fields. The default for the Text driver is 25 rows. This means the driver will read the first 25 rows of data (or fewer, if the file is shorter). If the driver finds that a field in a column differs from all the other fields in that column, the driver reports an error message. You can think of this as a form of error checking. It is best to leave this number unchanged.

➤ The **Characters** options of ANSI and OEM are not critical. They may make a difference if you are working with a non-English version of Visio. In that case, select **OEM**.

12. Click **OK** twice. Notice that Visio returns to the Database Export wizard. This means you have completed the ODBC portion of the configuration.

13. Click **Browse for File DSN** if the Text.Dsn filename does not appear in the "Select an ODBC Data Source to export to" list. Click **Next**, if necessary.

14. Visio displays "Specify the export table details" in the wizard. There is probably no need to make any changes here; Visio remembers the options you selected earlier with the Excel setup. Click **Next**.

15. When "Specify the export mapping details" appears in the wizard, change the field names so that they are more informative. Click **PinX** and change the **Field Name** from **PinX** to **X Coordinate**.

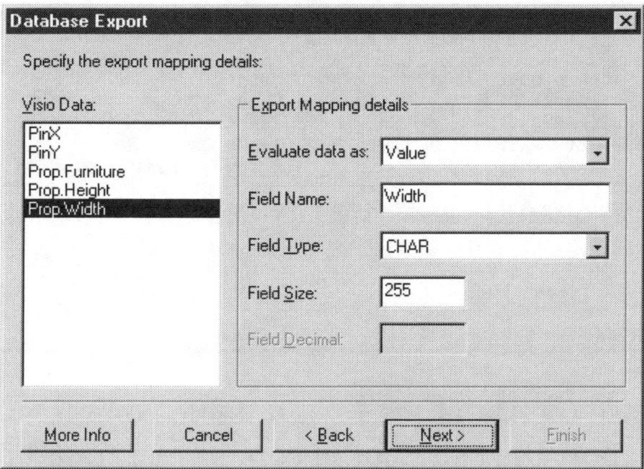


Similarly, change:

➤ PinY to Y Coordinate

➤ Prop.Furniture to Furniture Type

➤ Prop.Height to Depth

➤ Prop.Width to Width

As before, *do not change* any other setting, such as the Field Type or Field Size. Otherwise, the export process will fail!

Click **Next**.

16. Check **Add export right mouse action to the drawing page**. If you uncheck this option, Visio removes Database Export Table from the shortcut menu, even if it was there earlier.

    Click **Next**.

    And click **Finish**.

17. Wait a few seconds, then use Notepad to examine the contents of Office. (A bug in Visio leaves out the extension.) You should see one row with the modified field names, followed by one column for each shape whose cell data was exported. Notice the comma that separates each field name. The quotation marks surround every field because Visio treats the data as text.

```
Office - Notepad                                                      _ □ ✕
File  Edit  Search  Help
"ShapeKey","XCoordiante","YCoordinate","FurnitureType","Width","Depth"
"{BC2640C3-06B0-11D2-8E9D-00AA00201DF7}","4.25 in.","5.5 in.","Rug","10","10"
"{BC2640C5-06B0-11D2-8E9D-00AA00201DF7}","4.9875 in.","3.7 in.","Desk","3.6000","2.4000"
"{BC2640C6-06B0-11D2-8E9D-00AA00201DF7}","4 in.","9.25 in.","Couch","6","1"
"{BC2640C7-06B0-11D2-8E9D-00AA00201DF7}","4.25 in.","1.5 in.","Chair","1.5","1.5"
"{BC2640C9-06B0-11D2-8E9D-00AA00201DF7}","6.25 in.","6 in.","Chair","1.5","1.5"
"{0D9B45C8-0AAF-11D2-8E9D-00AA00201DF7}","2.1875 in.","3.1125 in.","Desk","2","3.6"
```

When you use the Database Export Table command from now on, Visio will export the cell data in comma-separated format and overwrites the text file named Office, at least until you change the ODBC settings again.

# Chapter Review

In this chapter, you learned how to use the Database Export wizard to export the data stored in ShapeSheet cells to an external file. You exported the cell data to an Excel spreadsheet file and an ASCII text file.

In the next chapter, you learn how to create a two-way link between the Visio drawing and the database file. With the link in place, you can make changes to the database file and they will be reflected in the Visio drawing, and vice versa.

# Chapter 11

# Creating Drawings from Text Files

Earlier in this book, you learned how to store data in the Custom Properties section, then export the data with the Property Reporting wizard.

Visio can work in reverse: it can take the data stored in a text file and create a diagram. This is like creating gold from lead.

Visio's *Using Visio Products* manual covers this important subject in a mere two pages. In this chapter, you learn all there is to know about converting text to diagrams:

➤ The format of text files

➤ The format of records

➤ Manual and automatic shape positioning

➤ Valid record names and formats

➤ Required and optional records

➤ Record and field reference

By the end of this chapter, you should know how to format a text file to create a Visio drawing.

## The Format of Text Files

In order for Visio to be able to convert a text file into a drawing, the text file must be written carefully in a structured manner. (We're not talking about converting a letter you wrote to your mother into a diagram suitable for a greeting card.)

Since Visio imports text files via the File | Open command, it is possible to be mistaken, as I was initially, that the Text Files option is for the mass importation of text into diagrams. Not at all; this option causes Visio to read the text file and determine two things: (1) the order in which to select shapes from a stencil; and (2) which shapes to connect together.

The text file must be in one of two file formats:

**CSV** (short for *comma-separated value*) separates each field with a comma, like this:

    shape,katrina,furniture,,4.25,5.5

**TXT** (short for *text* but really should be *tab-separated value*) separates each field with a tab (the ⊠ symbol indicates a tab), like this:

    shape ⊠ katrina ⊠ furniture ⊠ ⊠ 4.25 ⊠ 5.5

The documentation provided by Visio, the corporation, says you must use commas in text files that end in .CSV and tabs in text files that end in .TXT. It turns out that Visio, the software, isn't that fussy. While the file extension must be CSV or TXT, the field separator can be a comma, or a tab, or a semicolon. (During importation, Visio displays a dialog box that lets you specify.) If you use a file extension other than CSV or TXT, Visio will complain variously "File not found" and "File is corrupt."

## The Text File Format

To create the text file, you must use a rigidly defined format that consists of words separated by commas (or tabs). Here is a summary of the text file format; later, we'll get into a tutorial and the details:

➤ Each line in the text file is either *record* or a comment line. The file can have blank lines to aid the readability of the text file.

➤ Each record line must conform to a specific format. The format is one record name followed by one or more fields, like this:

> record-name,field-value,field-value,field-value

➤ The number of fields depends on the record. For example, the **Template** record has a single field, but the **Shape** record can have as many as seven or more fields.

➤ Some fields are optional. If you are allowed to omit a field, simply type the comma (or tab), such as:

> master,,circle,basic.vss

You don't need a comma (or tab) after the last field with an entry. For example, the Shape record can have seven or more fields. You can type shape,,,,,,,,, or shape. Either form of the record draws a 1"x0.5" rectangle in the center of the drawing.

➤ You can add a comment to the text file by prefixing the text with a semicolon (the default), as follows:

> ; This is a comment.

The comment does not appear in the Visio diagram; it remains in the text file to help document contents of the file.

As an alternative, you may use these other punctuation marks: hash mark (#), exclamation (!), slash (/), or backslash (\). During importation, Visio displays a dialog box that lets you specify which character indicates the start of a comment line.

➤ Every record-name and field-value must be separated from the next by a comma in a CSV file, or by a tab in a TXT file.

➤ Quotation marks are optional. Visio interprets everything in quotation marks, whether text or number, as text. You may use double (") or single (') quotation marks; during importation, Visio displays a dialog box that lets you specify. If you don't use quotation marks, Visio interprets text as text and numbers as numbers.

**Customizing Databases**

**301**

Visio recognizes twelve record names in the text file. These are: Master, Shape, Link, AvenueSize, BlockSize, Gridding, LineToLineClearance, NodeToLineClearance, PlacementStyle, RoutingStyle, Property, and Template.

Some records are required in the text file. They must be used in the text file in this order:

**Master** specifies the VSS stencil file holding the masters.

**Shape** specifies the master to use and assigns a unique name to the shape.

**Link** specifies the names of shape pairs that have a link drawn between them.

All Master records should occur before all Shape records; all Shape records should occur before all Link records. That's because Visio has to load the stencil file (VSS) holding the masters before it can place the shapes. And Visio has to place the shapes before it can link them.

The figure below shows these three elements: two shapes are linked with a connector:

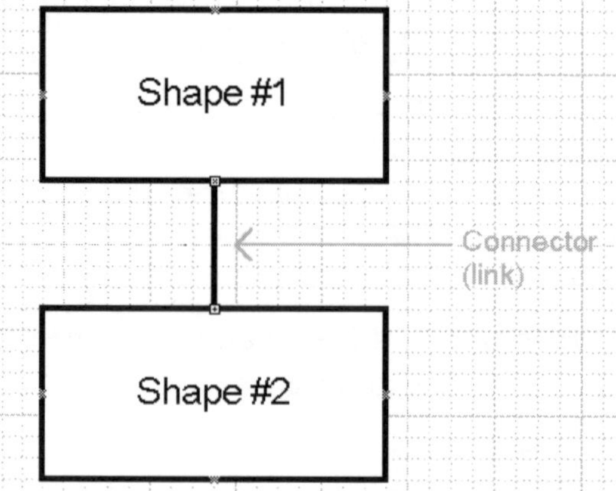

**Note:**

At the very minimum, the text file contains a single Shape record. When the master record is left out, or cannot be found, Visio draws shapes as plain rectangles.

The remaining records fall into two groups; all are optional. One group of records specifies parameters for the Lay Out Shapes grid (more details coming up soon); the second group of records has nothing to do with the grid. The grid-related records are:

**Gridding** specifies whether to turn on the Lay Out Shapes grid. Visio automatically turns on the grid when you do not provide x,y-coordinates for the shapes.

**NodeToLineClearance** specifies the minimum distance between shape (nodes) and connectors by the Lay Out Shapes grid.

**AvenueSize** specifies the width and height of avenues in the Lay Out Shapes grid.

**BlockSize** specifies the block size in the Lay Out Shapes grid.

**LineToLineClearance** specifies the minimum distance between connectors in the Lay Out Shapes grid.

**PlacementStyle** specifies the layout style for the Lay Out Shapes grid.

**RoutingStyle** specifies the connector routing style for the Lay Out Shapes grid.

And these records have nothing to do with the grid:

**Property** defines (or redefines) custom properties for a master.

**Template** specifies the name of a Visio template file (VST) that defines the drawing's defaults, such as the size of page, the grid spacing, and number formats. A text file must contain only one Template record.

# The Format of Records

To make it easier to understand what a record consists of, let's look at something you should be fairly familiar with by now: a shape. The Shape record is used for any shape that is not a connector (you use the Link record for connectors). This is the format of the record that defines a shape:

*shape,shapeid,mastername,shapetext,shapex,shapey,width,height, property1,property2,...,propertyn*

Let's examine this record, bit by bit, to see what it means. As we work through the fields of the Shape record, I will progressively add fields to an example record. We will end up with:

    shape,katrina,furniture,,4.25,5.5,,,Desk,5,2.5

**ShapeID** is a name you give the shape. It can be as simple as the name of the person in an organizational chart. The only catch is that the name must be unique. For example, you could call the shape "Katrina" and there must be: (1) only one Shape record in the entire file with the ID of Katrina; and (2) only one shape in the entire drawing called Katrina. For example:

    shape,katrina

**MasterName** refers back to the name defined in the Master record. The Master record does three things: (1) lets you select the VSS stencil file; (2) lets you select the master in the stencil; and (3) lets you give a name to that master. When this field is blank or Visio cannot find the master, Visio draws the shape as a rectangle. For example:

    shape,katrina,furniture,

**ShapeText** is text that gets displayed in the shape, just as if you were to double-click the shape and type some text. This text can be anything you want and might be the name of the desk's occupant. For example:

    shape,katrina,furniture,Katrina Nicole,

**ShapeX** and **ShapeY** are the shape's x- and y-coordinates. These are equivalent to the PinX and PinY cells of the ShapeSheet. The x- and y-distances are measured from the page's lower-left corner to the center (typically but not always) of the shape's alignment box. To place a shape at the center of a standard 8-1/2"x11" page, specify 4.25 and 5.5. For example:

shape,katrina,furniture,Katrina Nicole,4.25,5.5,

If you don't want to spend the time figuring out the correct x,y-coordinates of each and every shape, simply leave these two fields blank—and let Visio do the work. When the two fields are blank, Visio sets up the Lay Out Shapes grid to automatically position the shapes. For example:

shape,katrina,furniture,Katrina Nicole,,,

**Width** and **Height** define the width and height of the shape's alignment box. You can leave either or both of these fields empty, in which case Visio uses the default sizes. For example:

shape,katrina,furniture,Katrina Nicole,4.25,5.5,,,

**PropertyN** is optional. It defines one or more values for the Custom Properties section of the shape. In the previous chapter, we defined a furniture shape with three custom properties: Type, Width, Depth. You use this field to specify those properties, such as:

shape,katrina,furniture,,4.25,5.5,,,Desk,5,2.5

By now you should be able to read the meaning of that line of text: place a shape (with the user-defined name of katrina) using the Furniture master with no text (,,) at location x=4.25, y=5.5 on the page, using its default width and height (,,,), and filling in the Custom Properties cells with the Desk label, 5 wide, and 2.5 deep. Recall that the Furniture master's custom properties define the text label and the size of the furniture. For this reason, I left the ShapeText, Width, and Height fields empty in this record.

Earlier in this chapter, I noted that either shape,,,,,,,,,, or shape draws a 1"x0.5" rectangle in the center of the drawing. Now you know why.

Let's work through a tutorial that places the Furniture shape:

1. Open the Notepad text editor.

2. Type the following:

   **master,desk525,furniture,C:\books\advancedvisio\ furniture.vss**

   **shape,katrina,furniture,,4.25,5.5,,,Desk,5,2.5**

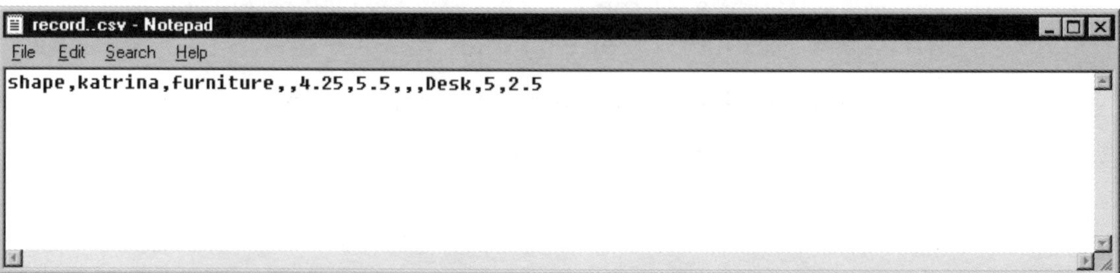

The Master record specifies the user-defined name of desk525 of the Furniture stencil in the Furniture.vss file (which you find on the CD-ROM provided with this book). Replace **C:\books\advancedvisio\furniture.vss** with the location and name of the stencil you saved in Chapter 7.

3. Select **File | Save As**. Type **record.csv** for the filename. Select a convenient folder in which to store the file. Click **Save**.

4. Open Visio. When the Choose a Drawing Template dialog box appears, click **Cancel**.

5. Select **File | Open**.

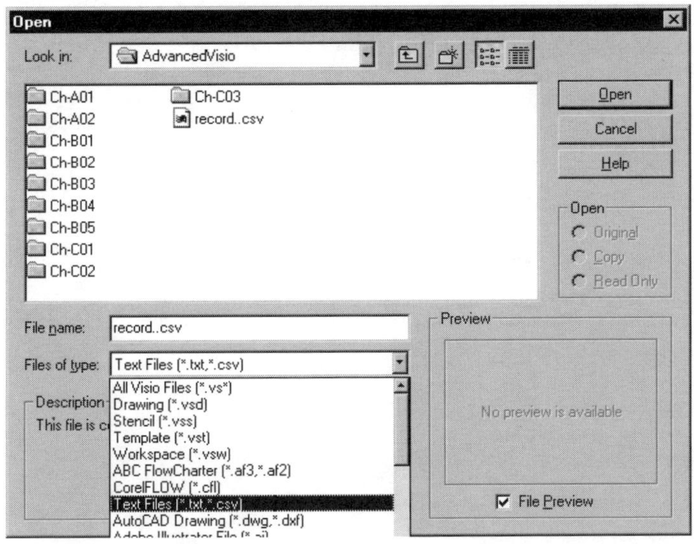

6. Select **Text Files (*.txt, *.csv)** from **Files of type**. If necessary, select the correct folder from **Look in**. Notice that this displays all files ending with .CSV and .TXT in that folder.

7. Double-click **Record.csv**. Notice that Visio displays the Visio File Converter dialog box. This lets you choose the character that separates fields, identifies strings, and prefixes comment lines. There is no need to change the defaults. The **Merge into current drawing** option is available when a drawing is already open.

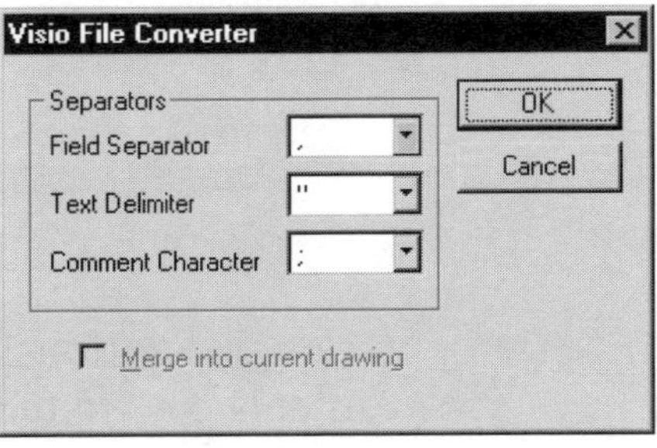

8. Click **OK**. Notice that Visio spends a busy half-minute or so loading the default template file, the master file, and draws the desk for Katrina in the center of the page.



**Customizing Databases**

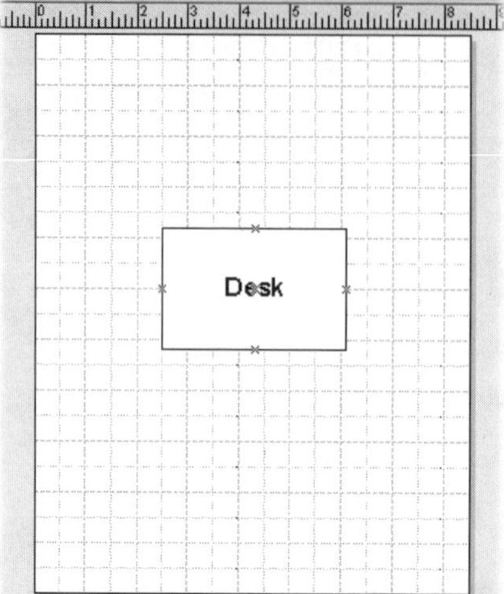

9.  Click **OK**. If there is an error in processing the text file, Visio displays an error message, as shown at the right, below. Visio provides a hint only about the first error it found in the text file.

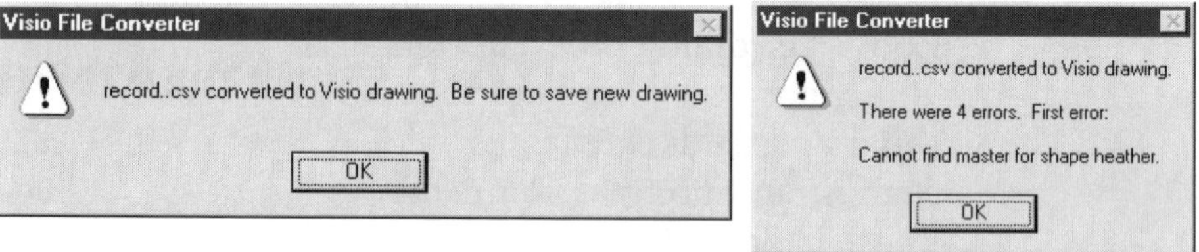



Congratulations! You created a Visio drawing from a simple text file. Next, we tackle the problem of placing more than one shape and connecting them.

# Manual and Automatic Shape Positioning

By now, you may be thinking, "If I have more than one shape, the drawing's going to become a jumble of overlapping shapes! How does Visio know where to place the shapes?" Visio provides two methods for positioning shapes: manual and automatic.

In the manual method, you provide the x,y-coordinates in the text file. The coordinates define the location of each shape. The coordinates measure the x,y-distance from the page origin (0,0 is the lower-left corner) to the center of the shape's alignment box.

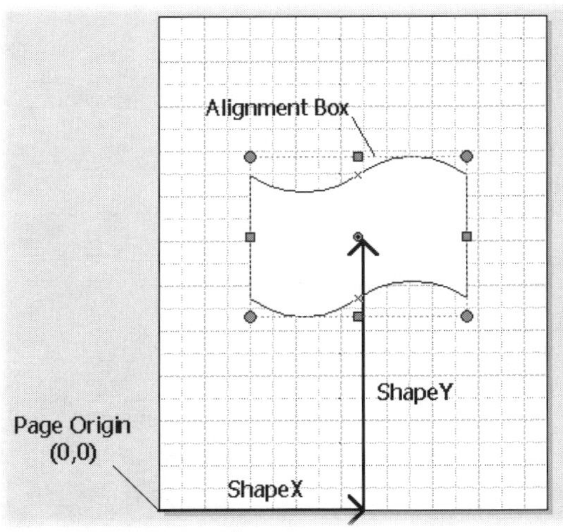


Here is where the x,y-coordinates are found in the Shape record:

*shape,shapeid,mastername,shapetext,shapex,shapey,width,height,
property1,property2,...,propertyn*

Since it can get tedious trying to figure out the correct x,y-coordinates for every single shape in the drawing, Visio provides an automated method for positioning the shapes. The Tools | Lay Out Shapes command is designed for use with connected drawings, such as flowcharts, organization charts, network diagrams, and other drawings that use connectors. For drawing without connectors, the shapes are arranged in an array.

There are three ways to use this command: (1) leave out the shapex and shapey fields of the Shape record and Visio automatically executes the Lay Out Shapes function to automatically position the shapes; (2) specify the related records in the text file, such as BlockSize and LineToLineClearance; or (3) use the Tools | Lay Out Shapes command on the shapes after importing the text file.

The Lay Out Shapes dialog box allows you to specify many aspects of laying out shapes automatically, such as:

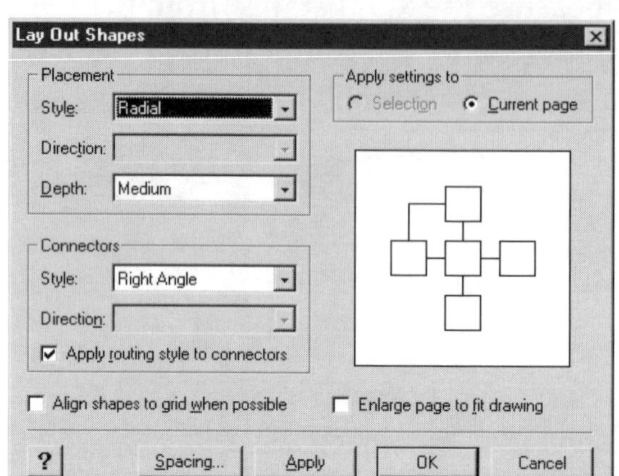

**Align shapes to grid when possible** lays out the shapes on an invisible grid, which is not the same as the grid lines you see on the page. This is a grid of *avenues* and *blocks*, like a city road system, that positions shapes. You specify the grid settings with the **Spacing** button. Visio's documentation warns to not use this grid when the drawing contains shapes of different sizes, or shapes that are larger than the grid. This option matches the Gridding record.

**Style** specifies the direction in which Visio places the shapes. **Flowchart/Tree** is best for drawings with a direction, such as organization charts and process flow diagrams. **Radial** is better for undirected drawings, such as network diagrams. This option in the dialog boxes matches the PlacementStyle record.

**Enlarge page to fit drawing** determines whether the drawing page gets larger to accommodate shapes. When writing a text file, you cannot specify the depth.

# Required and Optional Records

Some records are *required* in the text file. And they *must* be written in this order:

1. Master specifies the VSS stencil file holding the masters.

2. Shape specifies the master to use and assigns a unique name to the shape.

3. Link specifies the names of shape pairs that have a link drawn between them.

All Master records should occur before all Shape records; all Shape records should occur before all Link records. That's because Visio has to load the stencil file (VSS) holding the masters before it can place the shapes. And Visio has to place the shapes before it can link them.

At the very minimum, the text file contains just Shape records. When the master record is left out or cannot be found, Visio draws the shapes as a plain rectangle. As well, you may have shapes in a drawing without links.

The remaining records are optional and fall into two groups. Some records specify parameters for the Lay Out Shapes command:

**PlacementStyle** specifies the layout style for the Lay Out Shapes grid.

**RoutingStyle** specifies the connector routing style for the Lay Out Shapes grid.

**Gridding** specifies whether to turn on the Lay Out Shapes grid. Visio automatically turns on the grid when you do not provide x,y-coordinates for the shapes.

**LineToLineClearance** specifies the minimum distance between connectors in the Lay Out Shapes grid.

**NodeToLineClearance** specifies the minimum distance between shape (nodes) and connectors by the Lay Out Shapes grid.



Customizing Databases

**AvenueSize** specifies the width and height of avenues in the Lay Out Shapes grid.

**BlockSize** specifies the block size in the Lay Out Shapes grid.

And these records have nothing to do with the grid:

**Property** defines (or redefines) custom properties for a master.

**Template** specifies the name of a Visio template file (VST) that defines the drawing's defaults, such as the size of page, the grid spacing, and number formats. A text file must contain only one Template record.

# Linked Diagram Tutorial

With all this information under your belt, it's time to make good use of it. In the following tutorial, we'll write up a network diagram in a text file. The diagram will link four computers and a printer to a server. In this tutorial, we go through three stages: (1) examine the master shapes to find out their names and custom properties, if any; (2) write the text file using a spreadsheet; and (3) import the text file into Visio to create the network diagram.

We will work with the **Basic Network** stencil file found in the **\Visio 2000\Solutions\Network Diagram** folder. You will need to know the exact location of the file (i.e., the full path and file name).

## *Examine the Master Shapes*

When Visio imports the text file, Visio is very fussy. It wants every *t* crossed and every *i* dotted. A single spelling error causes Visio to create something less than you are expecting. For this reason, you need to carefully inspect the masters that you will be working with.

1. Using the Windows File Explorer or File Manager, record by writing down:

➤ The filename of the stencil file containing the masters:

Stencil file: _________________________________________.VSS

For this tutorial, we are using Basic Network Shapes.Vss. It's okay to work with two or more stencils, if you need to.

➤ The folder (or subdirectory) containing the VSS stencil file:

Stencil folder: _________________________________________

On my computer, it is C:\CAD\Visio 2000\Solutions\Network Diagram\ , so that's what you'll be seeing in this tutorial.

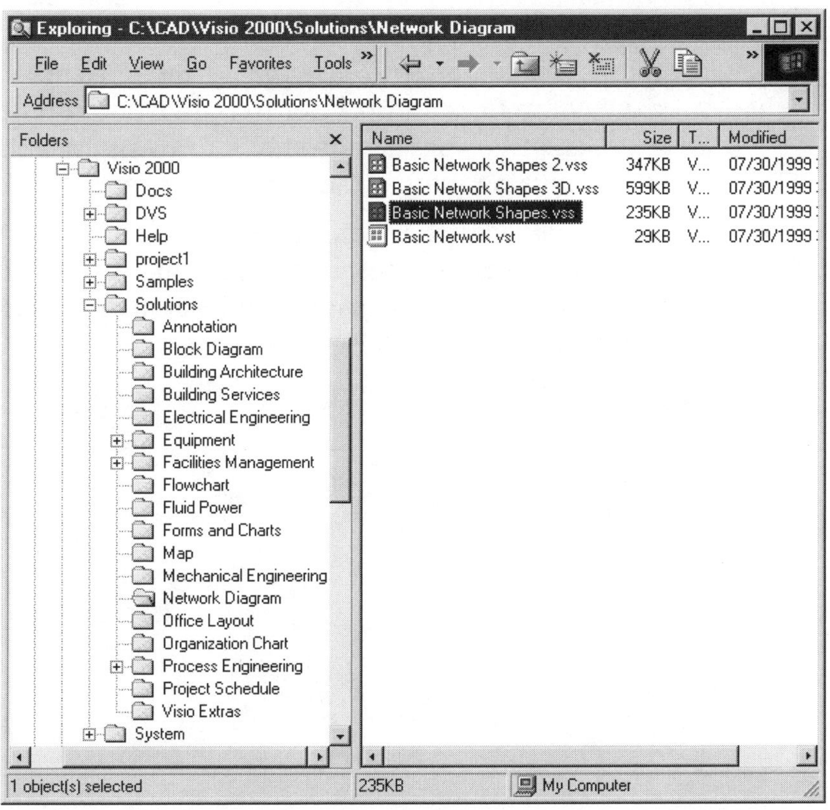


**2.** Start Visio. Select **Network Diagram** in the Choose a Drawing Type dialog box. Double-click **Basic Network Shapes**.

3.  Decide which masters you will be using in the drawing. Write down their names:

    _______________________________

    _______________________________

    _______________________________

    For this tutorial, you'll be using these masters:

    > Desktop PC
    > Server/Tower
    > Printer 3

    Although it is tempting to use one of the network shapes to connect the computers and printer together, avoid Ethernet, Straight Bus, etc. In order for the automatic drawing creation to work, you will be using plain straight lines for the connectors.

4.  Drag the masters you'll be using into the drawing. You do this to examine their custom properties. For this tutorial, drag the **Desktop PC**, **Server/Tower**, and **Printer 3** masters into the drawing.

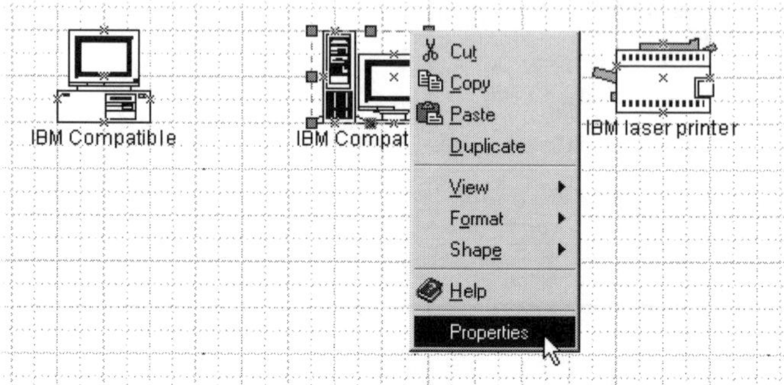

**5.** Right-click a shape. Select **Properties** from the shortcut menu. Record the custom properties:

_______________________________________

_______________________________________

_______________________________________

_______________________________________

_______________________________________

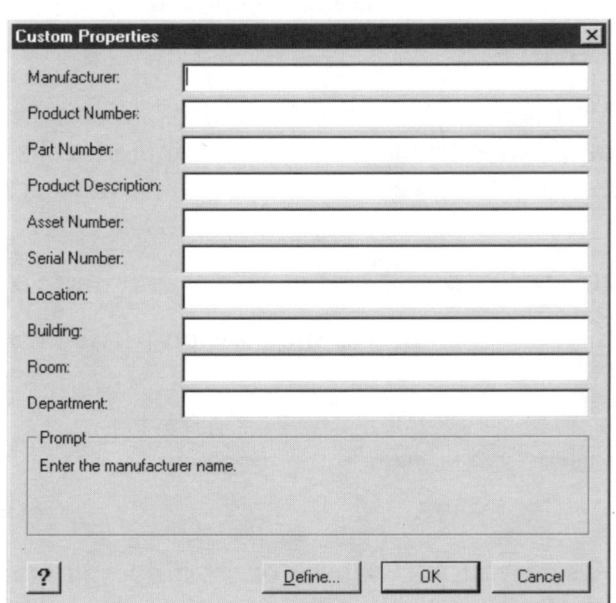


For this tutorial, we'll use the following subset of custom properties:

> Manufacturer
> Product Number
> Part Number
> Product Description
> Asset Number



**315**

6. The custom properties are the same for all three shapes. Exit Visio, since you have all the information you need.

## Write the Text File

I find it is easier to write a complex text file using a spreadsheet. (If you do not have access to a spreadsheet, then you can use the Notepad text editor.)

1. Open the spreadsheet.

2. I find it handy to reserve the first two rows of the spreadsheet for my documentation. In the first row, enter comments that document the format of the **Master** record. In cell A1, type:

   ***;master***

   Recall that the semicolon tells Visio this is a comment line. I apply **bold italic** formatting to the comment cells, to help differentiate them from cells containing data. In cells A2 through A4 type:

   ***masterName | masterid | stencilName***

   The vertical bar | indicates the division between spreadsheet cells.

   | | A | B | C | D |
   |---|---|---|---|---|
   | 1 | *;master* | *masterName* | *masterid* | *stencilName* |
   | 2 | | | | |

3. A few rows down (half a dozen or so, it doesn't really matter since you can always add and delete rows as required), type the comment line documenting the shape records:

   ***;shape | shapeid | masterName | shapeText | shapeX | shapeY | width | height | properties 1...n***

   Starting under **properties 1...n**, add the following text in each cell:

   ***; | | | | | | | Manufacturer | Product Number | Part Number | Product Description | Asset Number***

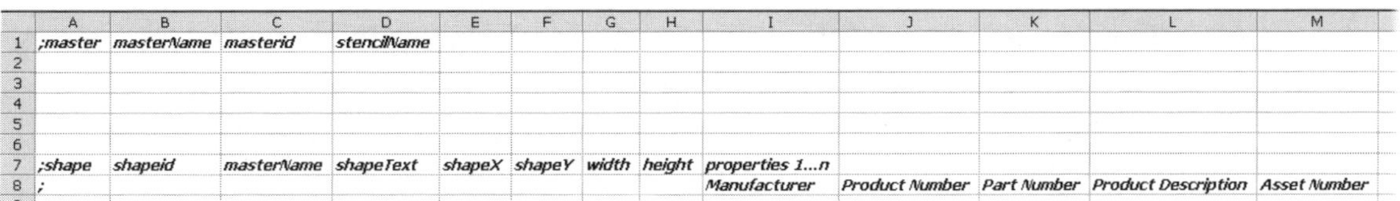

| | A | B | C | D | E | F | G | H | I | J | K | L | M |
|---|---|---|---|---|---|---|---|---|---|---|---|---|---|
| 1 | ;master | masterName | masterid | stencilName | | | | | | | | | |
| 2 | | | | | | | | | | | | | |
| 3 | | | | | | | | | | | | | |
| 4 | | | | | | | | | | | | | |
| 5 | | | | | | | | | | | | | |
| 6 | | | | | | | | | | | | | |
| 7 | ;shape | shapeid | masterName | shapeText | shapeX | shapeY | width | height | properties 1…n | | | | |
| 8 | ; | | | | | | | | Manufacturer | Product Number | Part Number | Product Description | Asset Number |

Notice that I took two rows to document the Shape record. The first comment row contains the names of the fields. The second comment row contains the names of the custom properties, which we recorded earlier.

 **Note:**

Don't forget that semicolon in the first cell of all comment rows!

4. In a similar manner, add comment lines to document the **Links** and **PlacementStyle** records:

   *;link  |  shapeid  |  masterid  |  text  |  from  |  to  |  properties 1…n:*

   *;placementStyle  |  style*

| | A | B | C | D | E | F | G | H | I | J | K | L | M |
|---|---|---|---|---|---|---|---|---|---|---|---|---|---|
| 1 | ;master | maste | masterid | stencilName | | | | | | | | | |
| 2 | | | | | | | | | | | | | |
| 3 | | | | | | | | | | | | | |
| 4 | | | | | | | | | | | | | |
| 5 | | | | | | | | | | | | | |
| 6 | | | | | | | | | | | | | |
| 7 | ;shape | shape | masterName | shapeText | shapeX | shapeY | width | | height | properties 1…n | | | |
| 8 | ; | | | | | | | | Manufacturer | Product Number | Part Number | Product Description | Asset Number |
| 9 | | | | | | | | | | | | | |
| 10 | | | | | | | | | | | | | |
| 11 | | | | | | | | | | | | | |
| 12 | | | | | | | | | | | | | |
| 13 | | | | | | | | | | | | | |
| 14 | | | | | | | | | | | | | |
| 15 | | | | | | | | | | | | | |
| 16 | ;link | shape | masterid | text | | from | to | properties 1…n: | | | | | |
| 17 | | | | | | | | | | | | | |
| 18 | | | | | | | | | | | | | |
| 19 | | | | | | | | | | | | | |
| 20 | | | | | | | | | | | | | |
| 21 | | | | | | | | | | | | | |
| 22 | | | | | | | | | | | | | |
| 23 | ;placementStyle | style | | | | | | | | | | | |

5. With the documentation complete, this is probably a good time to save the spreadsheet file so that you don't lose your valuable work. Select **File | Save As** from the menu bar.



**Customizing Databases**

6. This is crucial: you must not save the drawing in spreadsheet format, such as WKS or XLS. You must save it in CSV format. The method will vary, depending on the brand and version of spreadsheet you are using. On mine, which happens to be Excel 97, select **CSV (Comma delimited) (*.csv)** from the **Save as type** list. (In Excel v3, click **Options**, select **CSV** as the file format, and click **OK**.) Enter **Network.Csv** for the filename, and click **OK**.

Excel v3

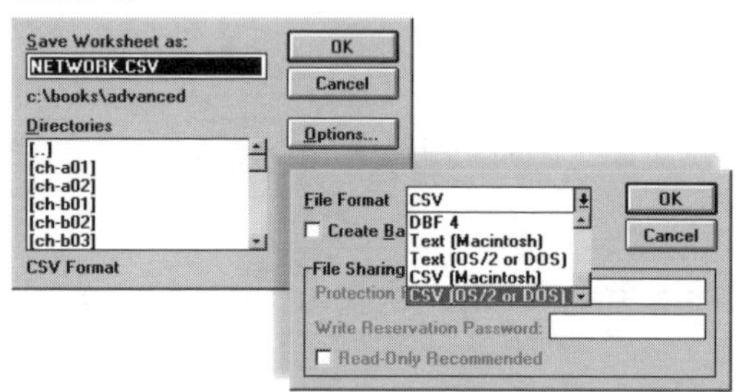

Excel 97

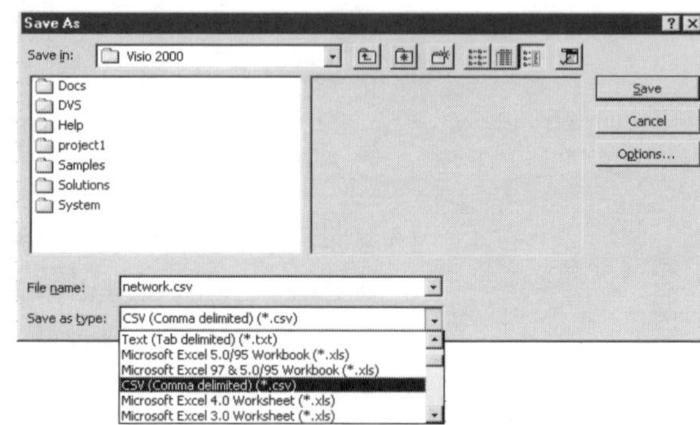

7. Now it is time to enter the data. This can be tedious, but if you make good use of your spreadsheet's **Edit | Copy** and **Edit | Paste** command, the time will pass quicker. For the master section, enter the following data:

| master | masterName | masterid | stencilName |
| --- | --- | --- | --- |
| master | deskpc | Desktop PC | d:\cad\visio 2000\solutions\network diagram\basic network shapes.vss |
| master | server | Server / Tower | d:\cad\visio 2000\solutions\network diagram\basic network shapes.vss |
| master | cable | Dynamic Connector | d:\cad\visio 2000\solutions\network diagram\basic network shapes.vss |
| master | printer | Printer 3 | d:\cad\visio 2000\solutions\network diagram\basic network shapes.vss |

Recall that MasterName is the user-definable name that makes it easier for you to identify the master in the text file's shape and link sections. You can assign any unique name you prefer.

MasterID is the name of the master, which we recorded earlier in Stage 1. StencilName is the path and filename of the stencil file containing the network shapes.

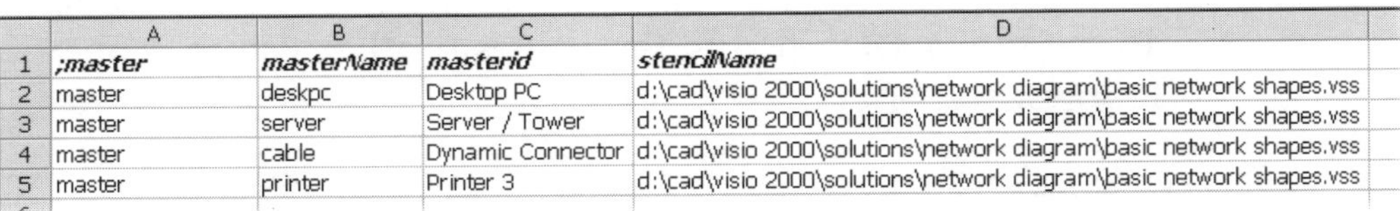

| | A | B | C | D |
|---|---|---|---|---|
| 1 | *;master* | *masterName* | *masterid* | *stencilName* |
| 2 | master | deskpc | Desktop PC | d:\cad\visio 2000\solutions\network diagram\basic network shapes.vss |
| 3 | master | server | Server / Tower | d:\cad\visio 2000\solutions\network diagram\basic network shapes.vss |
| 4 | master | cable | Dynamic Connector | d:\cad\visio 2000\solutions\network diagram\basic network shapes.vss |
| 5 | master | printer | Printer 3 | d:\cad\visio 2000\solutions\network diagram\basic network shapes.vss |
| 6 | | | | |

**8.** For the shape section, enter the following data (leave the ShapeX, ShapeY, Width, Height, and Properties fields empty):

| shape | shapeid | masterName | shapeText | shapeX | shapeY | width | height | properties 1…n: |
|---|---|---|---|---|---|---|---|---|
| shape | katrina | deskpc | Katrina | | | | | |
| shape | stefan | deskpc | Stefan | | | | | |
| shape | heidi | deskpc | Heidi | | | | | |
| shape | heather | deskpc | Heather | | | | | |
| shape | servers | server | Server | | | | | |
| shape | printers | printer | Laser Printer | | | | | |

| | A | B | C | D | |
|---|---|---|---|---|---|
| 1 | *;master* | *masterName* | *masterid* | *stencilName* | |
| 2 | master | deskpc | Desktop PC | d:\cad\visio 2000\s | |
| 3 | master | server | Server / Tower | d:\cad\visio 2000\s | |
| 4 | master | cable | Dynamic Connector | d:\cad\visio 2000\s | |
| 5 | master | printer | Printer 3 | d:\cad\visio 2000\s | |
| 6 | | | | | |
| 7 | *;shape* | *shapeid* | *masterName* | *shapeText* | s/ |
| 8 | *;* | | | | |
| 9 | shape | katrina | deskpc | Katrina | |
| 10 | shape | stefan | deskpc | Stefan | |
| 11 | shape | heidi | deskpc | Heidi | |
| 12 | shape | heather | deskpc | Heather | |
| 13 | shape | servers | server | Server | |
| 14 | shape | printers | printer | Laser Printer | |
| 15 | | | | | |

Recall that leaving the ShapeX and ShapeY fields empty forces Visio to automatically lay out the shapes, saving you a lot of work!

The ShapeID is just like the MasterName: a user-defined name to help you identify the shapes later in the links section. Notice how each shape makes reference back to the MasterName.

The ShapeText is the text that will appear in the shape's text block. You can enter any wording you prefer.

**9.** To the shape section, add the values for the custom properties, as follows:

| Manufacturer | Product Number | Part Number | Product Description | Asset Number |
|---|---|---|---|---|
| Touch PC | XD684 | 10023 | 486DX | 951111 |
| Touch PC | XS684 | 10045 | 486SX | 951213 |
| Touch PC | P1-685 | 10067 | Pentium | 970215 |
| Touch PC | PM-685 | 10089 | Pentium MMX | 980317 |
| Touch PC | PX-685 | 10135 | Pentium Xeon | 990618 |
| Lexmark | Optra Rx+ | 20012 | 16ppm | 961012 |

| *t* | *properties 1...n* | | | | |
|---|---|---|---|---|---|
| *Manufacturer* | *Product Number* | *Part Number* | *Product Description* | *Asset Number* |
| Touch PC | XD684 | 10023 | 486DX | 951111 |
| Touch PC | XS684 | 10045 | 486SX | 951213 |
| Touch PC | P1-685 | 10067 | Pentium | 970215 |
| Touch PC | PM-685 | 10089 | Pentium MMX | 980317 |
| Touch PC | PX-685 | 10135 | Pentium Xeon | 990618 |
| Lexmark | Optra Rx+ | 20012 | 16ppm | 961012 |

**10.** Now comes the part where you have to think harder: the links section. The Links record requires that you specify which shapes should be connected. For this network diagram, we want the printer and all desktop computers connected to the server, like this:

| link | shapeid | masterId | text | from | to | properties 1...n: |
|---|---|---|---|---|---|---|
| link | cable1 | cable | | katrina | servers | |
| link | cable2 | cable | | stefan | servers | |
| link | cable3 | cable | | heidi | servers | |
| link | cable4 | cable | | heather | servers | |
| link | cable5 | cable | | printers | servers | |

| 15 | | | | | | | |
|---|---|---|---|---|---|---|---|
| 16 | *;link* | *shapeid* | *masterid* | *text* | *from* | *to* | *properties 1...n:* |
| 17 | link | cable1 | cable | | katrina | servers | |
| 18 | link | cable2 | cable | | stefan | servers | |
| 19 | link | cable3 | cable | | heidi | servers | |
| 20 | link | cable4 | cable | | heather | servers | |
| 21 | link | cable5 | cable | | printers | servers | |
| 22 | | | | | | | |

As before, the ShapeID is the user-definable name you give to each of the links. You can assign any unique name you prefer.

The MasterID column makes reference to the Dynamic Connector shape that we defined in the master section.

The Text column is for the connectors text block, which we leave blank for this tutorial. Similarly, we leave the Properties field blank.

The definition of the links takes place in the From and To fields. Each of the desktop computer shapes (katrina, stefan, etc.) and the printer shape (printers) is linked to the server shape (servers). Notice how we are using the user-definable names to identify the instances of master shapes.

11. We have one record left to go. The PlacementStyle record tells Visio how to automatically lay out the shapes. When the Style field contains 1, Visio uses a radial pattern, which is appropriate for a network diagram. Enter this data now:

| *placementStyle* | *Style* |
| --- | --- |
| placementstyle | 1 |

12. Save the file one more time, making sure you are saving it in CSV format.

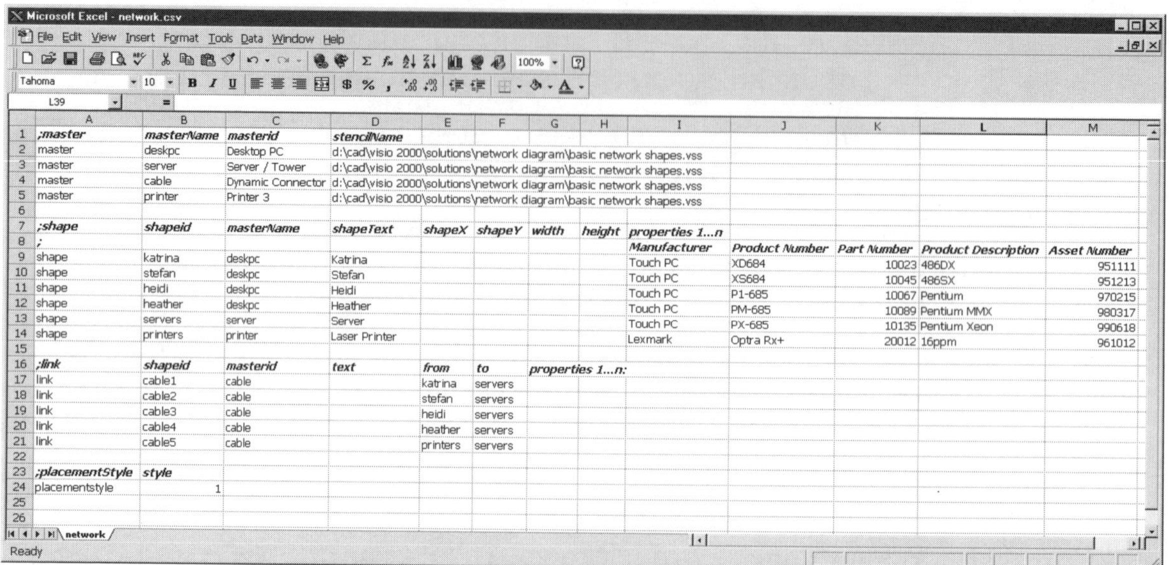

If you were using Notepad, the result looks like the not-very-pretty illustration below. Note that this is what the Network.Csv file looks like.

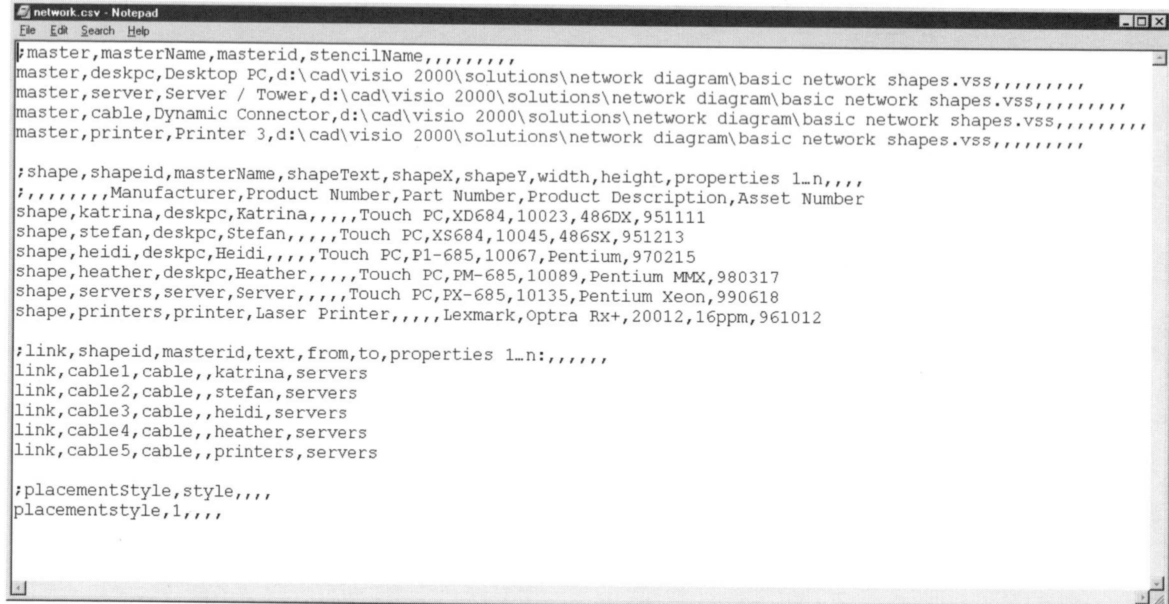

**13.** Exit the spreadsheet or the text editor.

## Import into Visio

You now create the drawing by importing the text file into Visio. The final part of this tutorial is similar to the earlier tutorial.

1. Open Visio and click **Cancel** in the **Welcome to Visio 2000** dialog box.

2. Select **File | Open**. Select **Text Files ( *.txt,*.csv)** from **Files of type**. If necessary, select the correct folder from **Look in**. Double-click **Network.Csv**. If Visio will not open the file, it could be because you did not exit Excel.

3. In the **Visio File Converter** dialog box, enter these values for these fields:

   ➤ Field Separator          ,

   ➤ Text Delimiter           "

   ➤ Comment Character      ;

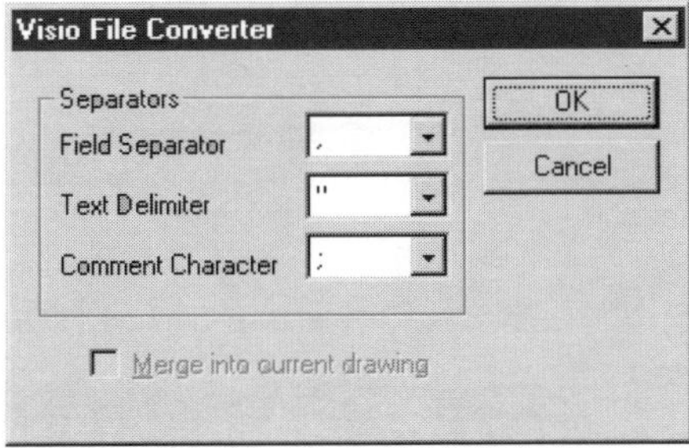

   Click **OK**.

4. Select **Tools | Center Drawing** to center the drawing on the page.

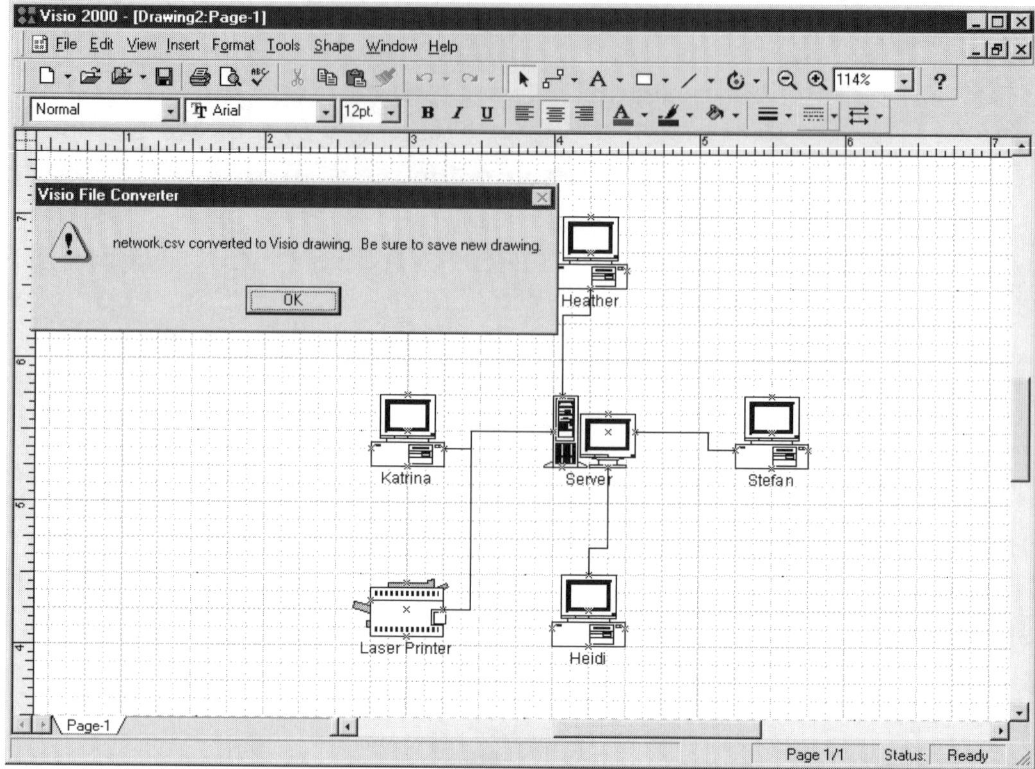

5.  Select a shape and right-click. Select Properties from the shortcut menu. Notice that Visio correctly filled in all the custom properties in the Custom Properties dialog box.

6.  Select **File | Save As** to save the drawing.

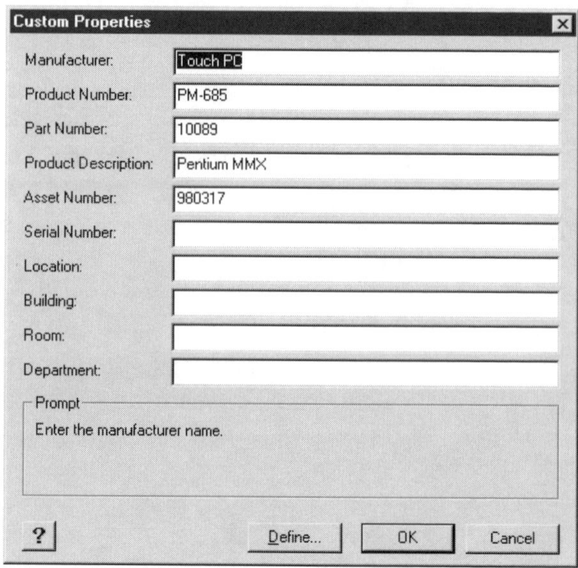

# Record and Field Reference

## *AvenueSize*

(*Optional*) Specifies the width and height of avenues in the Lay Out Shapes grid.

Format:

avenuesize,*width,height*

Example:

avenuesize,0.5,0.5

| Field | Meaning |
| --- | --- |
| Width | Specifies the avenue width, in inches. |
| Height | Specifies the avenue height, in inches. |

## *BlockSize*

(*Optional*) Specifies the block size in the Lay Out Shapes grid.

Format:

blocksize,*width,height*

Example:

blocksize,1,1

| Field | Meaning |
| --- | --- |
| Width | Specifies the block width, in inches. |
| Height | Specifies the block height, in inches. |

## *Gridding*

(*Optional*) Specifies whether to turn on the grid used by Lay Out Shapes. This invisible grid is not the same as the grid lines you see on the page; rather, this is a grid of *avenues* and *blocks,* like a city road system, used by the Lay Out Shapes command to position shapes. Visio warns to not use the grid when the drawing contains shapes of different sizes or shapes that are larger than the grid.

Format:

> gridding,*usegrid*

Example:

> gridding,1

| Field | Meaning |
| --- | --- |
| UseGrid | Specifies whether to use the Lay Out Shapes grid; 0 = turn off the Lay Out Shapes grid. I (or non-zero) = turn on the grid. |

## LineToLineClearance

(*Optional*) Specifies the minimum distance between connectors in the Lay Out Shapes grid.

Format:

> linetolineclearance,*horizontal,vertical*

Example:

> linetolineclearance,0.125,0.125

| Field | Meaning |
| --- | --- |
| Horizontal | Specifies the horizontal space, in inches. |
| Vertical | Specifies the vertical space, in inches. |

## Link

Defines a 1D shape that connects two 2D shapes. Visio recommends that you use the Dynamic Connector shape because it connects shapes with dynamic glue. This allows Visio to automatically reposition connectors when you move the shapes to ensure connectors do not cross other shapes.

Format:

> link,*shapeid,mastername,text,from,to,property1,property2, ...,propertyn*

Example:

link,link101,flowchart,,shape10,shape11

| Field | Meaning |
|---|---|
| ShapeID | (*Optional*) Defines the user-definable name, which allows you to refer to the connector by its unique name. |
| MasterName | (*Optional*) Specifies the master shape to use for the connector, which is defined via the MasterName field of the Master record. When this field is empty or Visio cannot find the master, the link is created with the Layout Connector shape. |
| Text | (*Optional*) Specifies the text displayed by the connector's text block. |
| From | Specifies the ShapeID name of the shape from which the link begins. |
| To | Specifies the ShapeID name of the shape where the link ends. |
| Property*n* | (*Optional*) Specifies one or more values, if the connector has Custom Property cells. |

## Master

Defines the master shape and the VSS stencil file containing the master; assigns a user-definable name to the master. When Visio cannot locate the master, it uses the rectangle shape.

Format:

master,*mastername,masterid,stencilname*

Example:

master,shape12,card,c:\visio\stencils\flowchart.vss

| Field | Meaning |
|---|---|
| MasterName | (*Optional*). Defines a user-definable name that you assign the master. This lets the Shape and Link records reference this master by the name. The name must be unique within a drawing. |

| Field | Meaning |
|-------|---------|
| MasterID | Specifies the name of the master in the VSS stencil file. When Visio cannot locate the master, it uses the rectangle shape. |
| StencilName | (*Optional*) Specifies the name of the Visio VSS stencil file that contains the master. You may include the full DOS path, such as C:\Visio\Support\Filename.Vss. When Visio cannot locate the master, it uses the rectangle shape. You may leave this field empty when you include the Template record and the master is on the template file's stencil. |

## NodeToLineClearance

(*Optional*) Specifies the minimum distance between shape (nodes) and connectors by the Lay Out Shapes grid.

Format:

> nodetolineclearance,*horizontal,vertical*

Example:

> nodetolineclearance,0.125,0.125

| Field | Meaning |
|-------|---------|
| Horizontal | Specifies the horizontal spacing, in inches. |
| Vertical | Specifies the vertical spacing, in inches. |

## PlacementStyle

(*Optional*) Specifies the layout style for the Lay Out Shapes grid.

Format:

> placementstyle,*style*

Example:

> placementstyle,1

| Field | Meaning |
| --- | --- |
| Style | Specifies the style of laying out shapes:<br>0 = Radial<br>1 = Top to Bottom<br>2 = Left to Right |

## Property

(*Optional*) Defines (or redefines) custom properties for a master.

**Caution:**

This record replaces the shape's existing custom properties.

Format:

> property,*master,rowname,label,prompt,type,format,value,*
> *hidden,ask*

Example:

> property,shape12,,Card,"Enter card type",,,,1,0

| Field | Meaning |
| --- | --- |
| Master | (*Optional*) Specifies the name of the master shape define (or redefine) custom properties. Use the same name in this field as you used in the MasterName field of the Shape and Link records. When blank, this custom property is assigned to all masters in the drawing. |
| RowName | (*Optional*) Specifies the row of the Custom Property section in the ShapeSheet. When blank, Visio uses the generic name Row_n. |
| Label | (*Optional*) Specifies the label that appears in Label cell of the Custom Properties section. When blank, Visio uses the generic label of Row_n. |
| Prompt | (*Optional*) Specifies the text that appears in the Prompt cell of the Custom Properties section. |
| Type | (*Optional*) Specifies the integer that defines the custom property type and appears in the Type cell. See the previous chapter for the complete list of types. |

| Field | Meaning |
|---|---|
| Format | (*Optional*) Specifies the format string that appears in the Format cell of the Custom Properties section. See the previous chapter for the complete list of types. |
| Value | (*Optional*) Specifies the default value of the custom property and appears in the Value cell of the Custom Properties section. The value must agree with the Type field. |
| Hidden | (*Optional*) Determines whether the custom property is displayed by the Custom Properties dialog box:<br>0 (or blank) = Custom property is displayed.<br>1 = Custom property is not displayed. |
| Ask | (*Optional*) Determines whether the custom property is displayed by the Custom Properties dialog box when the shape is created or copied:<br>0 (or blank) = Custom property is displayed.<br>1 = Custom property is not displayed. |

For more details, see the Custom Properties section in Chapter 7.

## RoutingStyle

(*Optional*) Specifies the connector routing style for the Lay Out Shapes grid.

Format:

    routingstyle,*style*

Example:

    routingstyle,5

| Field | Meaning |
|---|---|
| Style | Specifies the routing styles:<br>1 = Right angles<br>5 = Flow chart |

## Shape

(*Required*) Used for shapes that are not connectors. It identifies the master used to draw the shape, and it contains shape text, size and position data, and custom property values. (For connectors, see the Link record type.)

Format:

> shape,*shapeid,mastername,shapetext,shapex,shapey,width,*
> *height,property1,property2,...,propertyn*

Example:

> shape,shape09,shape12,,4.5,5.5,1.5,0.5

| Field | Meaning |
|---|---|
| ShapeID | (*Optional*) Defines a user-defined name that identifies the shape; must be unique within the drawing. |
| MasterName | (*Optional*) Specifies the master that creates this shape; this is the same name as used in the MasterName field of the Master record. When this field is left blank or Visio cannot find the master, the shape is drawn as a rectangle. |
| ShapeText | (*Optional*) Specifies the text displayed by the shape's text block. |
| ShapeX | (*Optional*) Specifies the shape's x-coordinate; when blank, Visio uses the Lay Out Shapes command to automatically position the shape. |
| ShapeY | (*Optional*) Specifies the shape's y-coordinate; when blank, Visio uses the Lay Out Shapes command to automatically position the shape. |
| Width | (*Optional*) Specifies the width of shape. When empty, Visio uses the default width defined by the master. |
| Height | (*Optional*) Specifies the height of shape. If this field is empty, Visio uses the default height for the master. |
| Property*n* | (*Optional*) Specifies one or more values, if the master has custom properties. |

### *Template*

(*Optional*) Specifies a Visio template upon which the drawing is based. Each text file can contain only one template record. Used to establish defaults for drawing parameters such as page size, date formats, grid and ruler settings, and so on, when a new drawing is created.

Format:

> template,*filename*

Example:

> template,c:\visio 2000\drawings\template.vst

| Field | Meaning |
|---|---|
| FileName | Specifies the name of the VST Visio template file; may include a DOS path name, such as C:\Visio 2000\ Drawings\Filename.Vst. |

## Chapter Review

In this chapter, you learned how to get Visio to create a drawing from a carefully structured text file. You learned the syntax of records and fields, how to specify masters, shapes, and connectors, and how to automatically position shapes.

In the next chapter, you learn how to create a two-way link between a Visio drawing and a database file.

# Chapter 12

# *Linking Drawings with Databases*

In the previous two chapters, you learned how to export and import shapes to and from database files. The process, however, was one-way. Visio provides the Database wizard to create a two-way link between the drawing and the database, which can be automatically or manually updated. The Database wizard creates linking information between the shapes and records (or rows) in the database file. In this chapter, you learn how to:

➤ Create masters from a database file

➤ Examine the database link information contained in cells

By the end of the chapter, you should be able to understand how the Database wizard creates a master that is linked to an external database file.

## Creating Masters from a Database

In the previous two chapters, you worked unidirectionally. In Chapter 10, "Exporting Drawings to Database Files," you used the Database Export wizard to export the shapes to a database file. In Chapter 11, "Creating Drawings from Text Files," you used the File | Open command to import a database file, and create shapes.

Both of these actions are *static*. You create a "picture" of what the drawing or the database looks like in an instant of time. When the database changes, the drawing doesn't, and vice versa. In some cases, this may be precisely what you may want.

**Customizing Databases**

Other times, you may want the drawing and the database to accurately reflect each other at all times. Visio makes this happen by creating a link between the shapes in the drawing and the records in the database file. The link information is stored in the User-defined Cells section of each shape.

| User-defined Cells | Value | Prompt |
|---|---|---|
| User.Row_1 | No Formula | No Formula |
| User.ODBCConnection | "ODBCDataSource=C:\Program Files\Common Files\ODBC\Data Sources\Excel.dsn\|ODBCQualifier=\|ODBCTable=Office#XLS\|1 | "This cell contains the link information for the Database Wizard." |
| User.ODBCChecksum | "d370bc89" | "This cell contains a checksum of the database record." |

Visio provides the Database wizard to perform important tasks, like select the database file format; create the User-defined Cells cells; and store the linking information. Using the Database wizard will not be an entirely new experience. In some parts of this wizard, you will recognize dialog boxes you encountered in the Database Export wizard.

> **Caution:**
>
> Before you begin this tutorial, ensure you have the following files on your computer:
>
> Furniture.Vss
> Excel.Dsn
> MyOffice.Xls

These are used in the following tutorial. The files were created earlier in Chapter 10, "Exporting Drawings to Database Files" and are available on the CD-ROM included with this book.

1. Open Visio, and click **Cancel** in the **Welcome to Visio 2000** dialog box.

2. From the menu bar, select **Tools | Macros | Visio Extras | Database Wizard**.

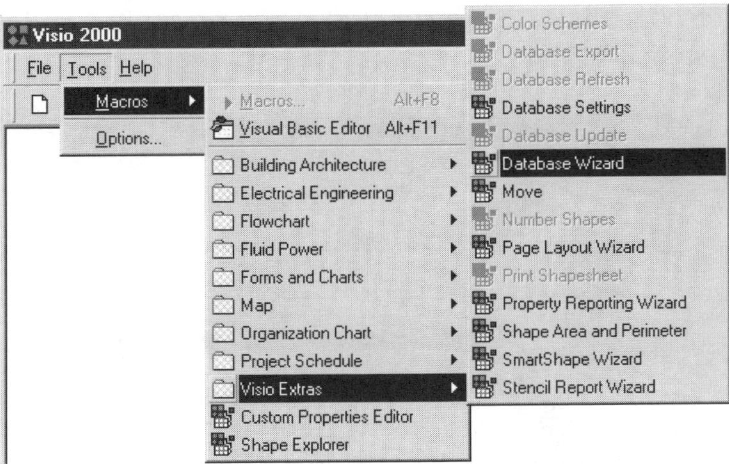

3. Click **Next** in the Database wizard's initial dialog box.

4. Select **Generate new masters from a database** and click **Next**. You will be creating a new stencil file containing masters that are linked to an external database file.

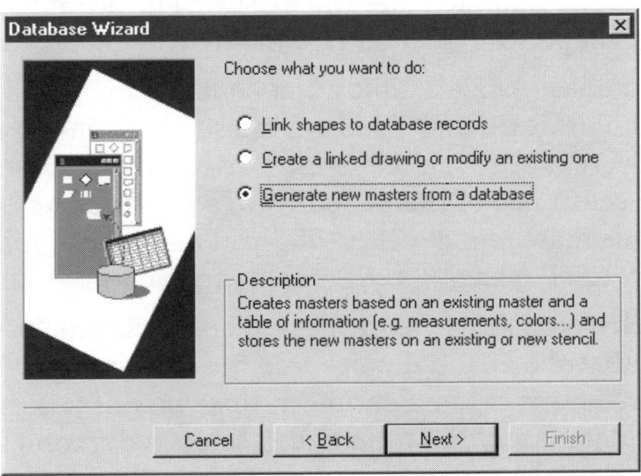

5. Click **Browse**, and select **Furniture.Vss** from the folder the stencil file is stored in. This stencil was created during a tutorial in Chapter 10, "Exporting Drawings to Database Files." (You can also find this file on the CD-ROM provided with this book.)

Notice that Visio opens the Furniture.Vss file, and displays the stencil in Visio.

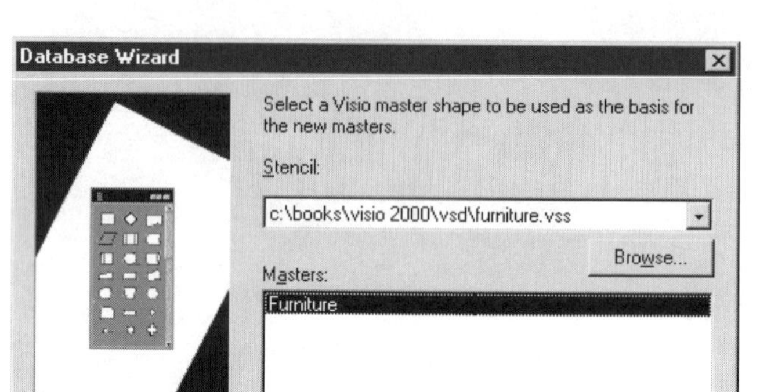

Visio uses the existing stencil and its masters as a prototype for creating a new stencil with new masters that contain the database linking data. Neither the existing Furniture.Vss file, nor its master shape, will be modified in any way by this wizardry.

6.  The Database Wizard dialog box contains the name of a single master, Furniture under Masters (also found in the stencil). If there were more than one master listed under Masters, you would select *one* of them. To create a database link with more than one master in a stencil file, you must rerun this Database wizard. Click **Next**.

7.  Click **Browse for File DSN**, and select **Excel.Dsn** from the folder that the ODBC data source file is located in. This data source file was created earlier in this book. If you prefer to work with a database other than Excel, select a different DSN file, or create a new one, corresponding to that database program.

    The DSN file instructs Visio's Database wizard how to work with the ODBC driver. In the case of Excel, the Excel.Dsn file provides the parameters needed for interfacing Visio with Excel XLS files via ODBC.

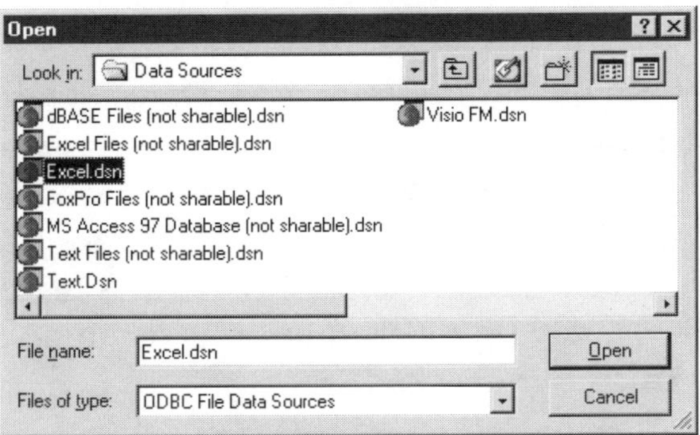

8. The wizard prompts "Choose a database object to connect to."
   *Database object* is a fancy term for database file. If a database file
   contains more than one table or view, then these, too, are consid-
   ered database objects. The point is that Visio want you to select a
   single table. Simple database files, such as those created by
   Excel, contain a single table only: in this case, you select the XLS
   file itself. Other info in this dialog box has this meaning:

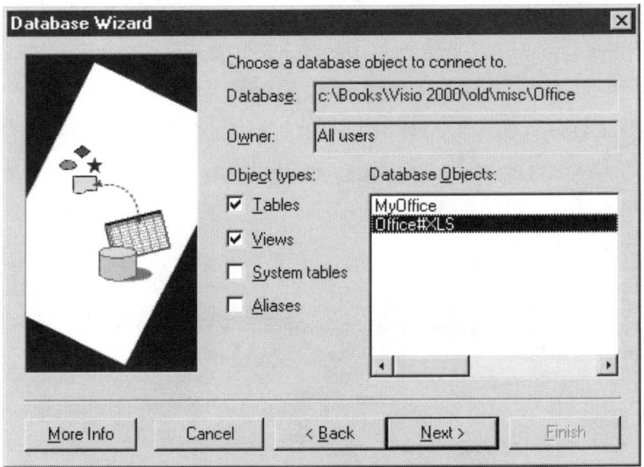

> ➤ **Database** refers to the subdirectory the DNS file points to.
>   This option is usually grayed out. It applies only to database
>   programs that allow access to multiple databases.

> ➤ **Owner** is usually grayed out. It becomes available when
>   you use a database, such as SQL Server, that allows you to

specify an object creator. Often, the object creator contains a subset of database objects.

➤ **Object types** refers to how the database data is structured. Advanced databases have tables, and views, and systems tables, and aliases. A simple Excel database has only a *table*, which in reality is the filename of an XLS file containing the data. Views may be checked but it is meaningless for Excel. Ensure **Tables** is checked.

➤ **Database Objects** is the list of XLS filenames (in the case of this tutorial) but could list the names of tables and views found in a more complex database file.

➤ Ensure Tables is checked. Select **Office#XLS** from the list of Database Objects. Once again, this file (Office.xls, in reality) was created in an earlier chapter of this book.

Click **Next**.

9. The wizard asks you to "Choose the number of fields that comprise the primary key for the selected table." The *primary key* is how Visio keeps track between the shape in the Visio drawing and record (or row) in the database file. Here, you tell Visio how many primary keys you will be using (1 is the recommended number); in the following dialog box, you select the cell that becomes the primary key.

Accept the default of **1** and click **Next**.

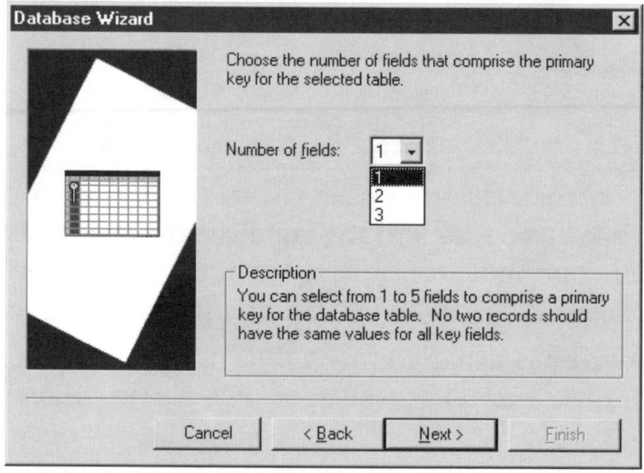

**10.** For the primary key, select **Prop.Furniture** in the **Field** list.

As we saw in the previous step, Visio lets you have as many as *five* primary keys. Last in the list, under Field, is *ShapeKey*. The ShapeKey consists of a unique 32-digit identifier consisting of both numbers and the letters of the alphabet. Visio invents this identifier when a shape is created. Here is an example:

BC2640C6-11D2-8E9D-00AA00201DF7

Because the ShapeKey is unique, it could be an ideal candidate for being the primary key. Being a 32-digit computer-generated number, however, the ShapeKey is not particularly descriptive; in fact, it is downright meaningless to humans. For this reason, we tend to choose a different field to be the primary key, such as Prop.Furniture.

Click **Next**.

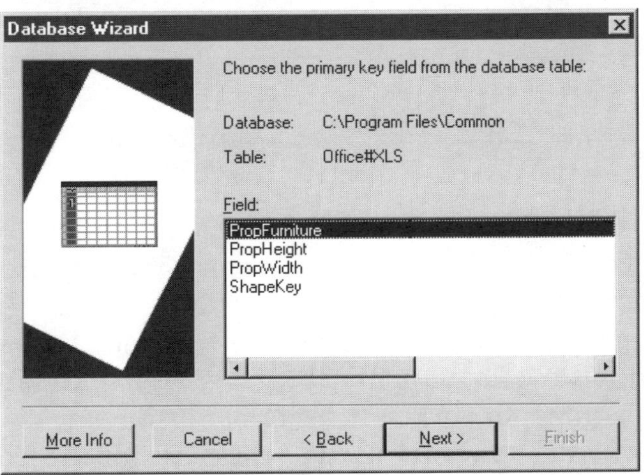


**11.** Click **Keep database links in new master** to turn on the option (check mark). Even though the default is off, you need this option turned on. Here is what happens when on:

➤ Visio maintains the link between the master and the database file.



Customizing Databases

➤ You will be able to add database-related commands to the shortcut menu of shapes (this happens in the next step of this wizard).

➤ You will be able to instruct Visio to keep the shapes synchronized with the database file.

I think those are all pretty good reasons for saying "Yes!" to **Keep database links in new masters**.

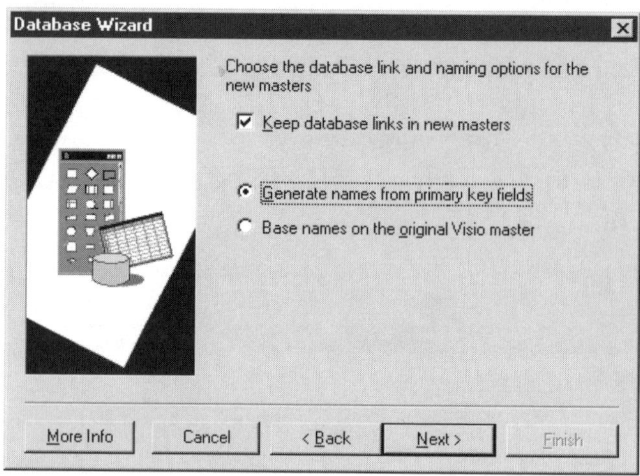


**12.** In the same dialog box, you have a choice of how Visio will name the new masters. Recall how the icons (that represent the masters) appear in the stencil window: you've got the (usually) square icon, with a name underneath. Later, at the end of this wizard, Visio will automatically generate names for the icons. In the meantime, to get ready for the big moment, Visio would like to know what you want used as the basis for the icon names. Here are your two choices:

Choice #1: Generate names from primary key fields. Visio will take whatever is in the primary key, and generate the name. (If you had selected ShapeKey in the earlier step, then Visio will generate this horrid name that's 32 letters l-o-n-g, as shown by the illustration.)

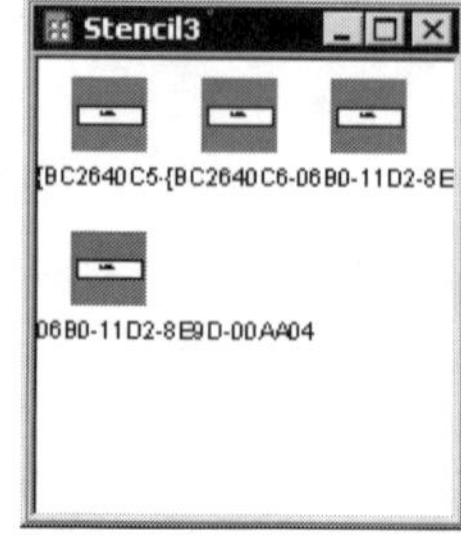

On the other hand, if you selected a primary key that was more descriptive, such as based on the Prop.Furniture cell, then this is a good option. The icon names, in our case, will be Desk, Chair, Couch, and Rug, as shown by the illustration.

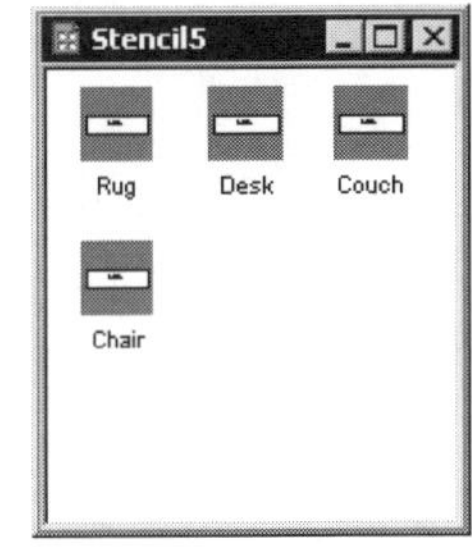

If you choose two primary key fields, Visio uses both in the form of:

Desk_BC2640C6-11D2-8E9D-00AA00201DF7

although most of the name is overwritten by the name of the adjacent icon, as shown by the illustration.

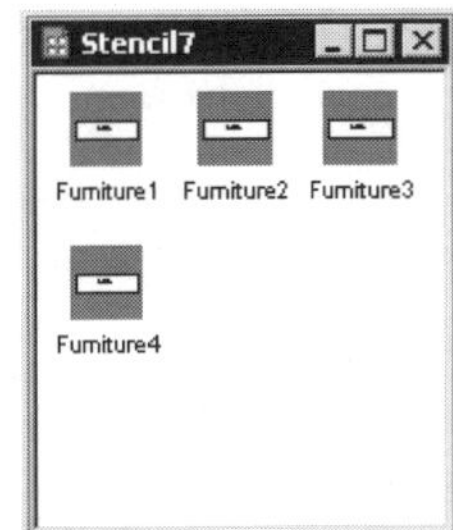

Choice #2: Base names on the original Visio master. In our case, the original master is called Furniture. Visio will generate names for the master that look like Furniture1, Furniture2, etc., essentially creating (in our case) four identical masters.

Select **Generate names from primary key fields** and click **Next**.

13. Here you select actions that take place when the master is dropped on the page, as well as select the commands to display in the shape's shortcut menu:

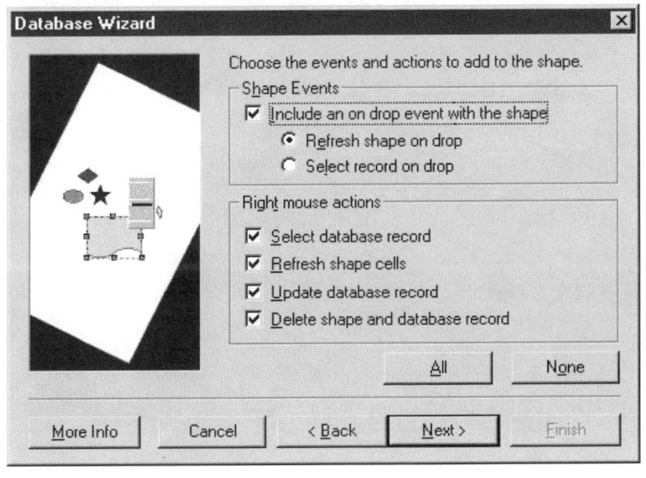

**Include an on drop event with the shape**   When this option is turned on (as it is, by default), Visio will carry out one of the two following actions. Recall that *on drop* means dragging a master from the stencil onto the drawing page.

➤ **Refresh shape on drop**   This option automatically updates the cells in the instanced shape of masters linked to the database file.

➤ **Select record on drop**   Consider this the manual version of the previous option. When you drop the master on the page, Visio opens the **Select Database Record** dialog box that lets you select a record via its primary key. If you use ShapeKey as the primary key, you'll see the dialog box listing incomprehensible numbers, as shown below:

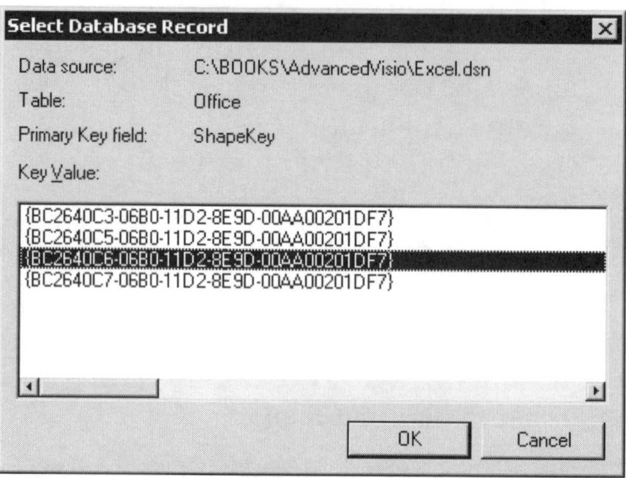


If you use another cell, such as Prop.Furniture, as the primary key, you'll see this in the dialog box, instead:

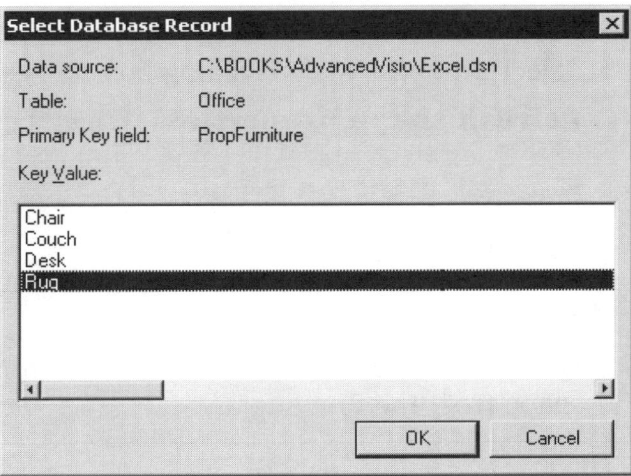

Visio then draws the shape based on the contents of the record, and not based on the master you dragged from the stencil. This is useful to you for overriding a shape with a record.

**Right mouse actions**   Each option listed here shows up as a command on the shape's shortcut menu. All options are selected for you, which is good when you want to have control over the shape's relationship with the database. Turn off these commands when you don't want other users performing unauthorized acts with your shapes.

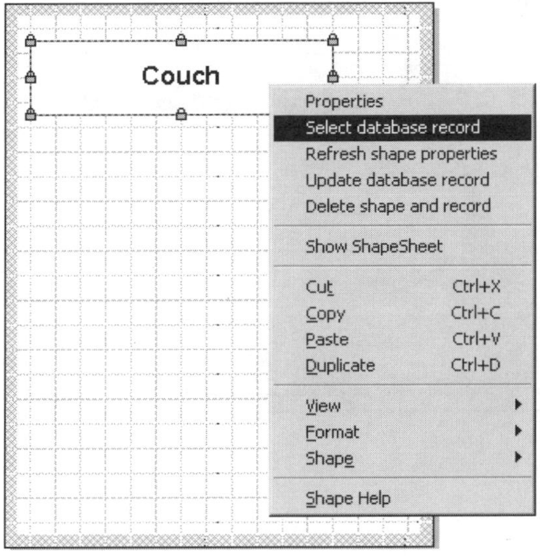

> ➤ **Select database record**   This command displays the Select Database Record dialog box, as described earlier.

> ➤ **Refresh shape properties**   When a change has occurred in the database file, select this command to refresh the drawing.

> ➤ **Update database record**   When a change has occurred to the drawing, select this command to update the database file.

> ➤ **Delete shape and record**   This command erases the shape from the drawing and its associated record in the database file.

> These commands are stored in the Action section of the cell's ShapeSheet.

> Click **Next**.

14. Select the name of the cell in which to store the primary key field. A good choice is the one that Visio presents as the default, Prop.PropFurniture, in our case. The value is stored in the PropFurniture cell of the Custom Properties section of the ShapeSheet.

    Click **Next**.

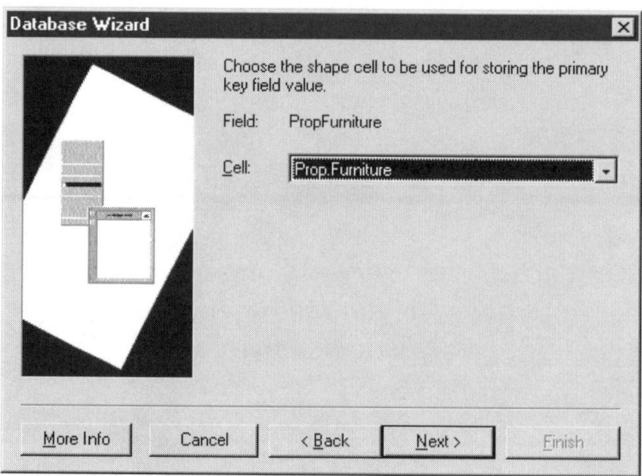

**15.** Often the names of fields in the database file bear no relation to the names of ShapeSheet cells. In our case, the names do match, because we had generated the database file from the Visio drawing. This dialog box lets you match names between cells and fields manually or automatically. This is how Visio knows to match the data between the drawing and the external file.

The manual method takes three steps: (1) select a cell name from the list under Cells; (2) select a field name from the list under Database Fields; and (3) click Add. Visio puts the two together in a format that looks like Angle==Rotation.

The automatic method takes one step: click **Automatic**. In our case, this works wonderfully, since the cell and field names match.

Click **Automatic** and **Next**.

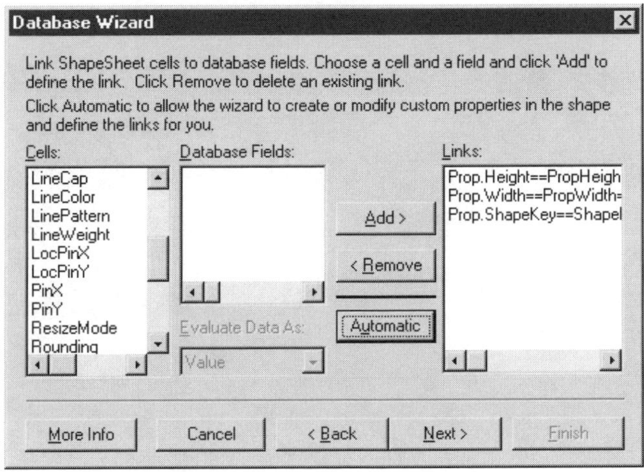



**16.** We have reached the last decision screen. In this dialog box, you can choose to have the database-generated master stored in a new stencil file, an existing stencil file, or in a copy of an existing stencil file.

Click **Create a new stencil**, and **Next**.

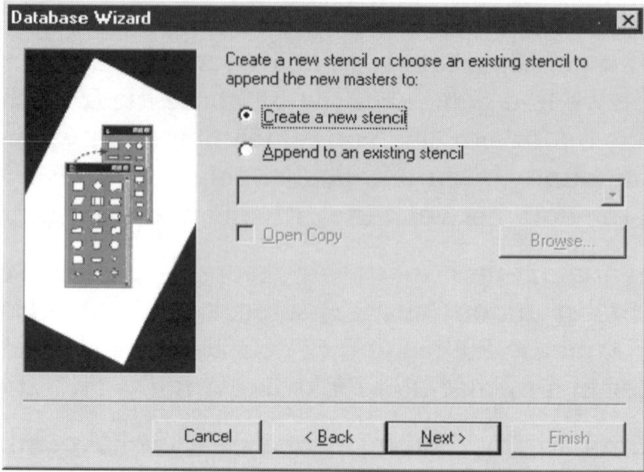

**17.** We're done! Visio lists a summary of your selections of the last sixteen steps. Click **Finish** to complete the task. If the Database wizard reports an ODBC error, the most likely cause is that you selected an incorrect file in steps 5, 7, or 8.

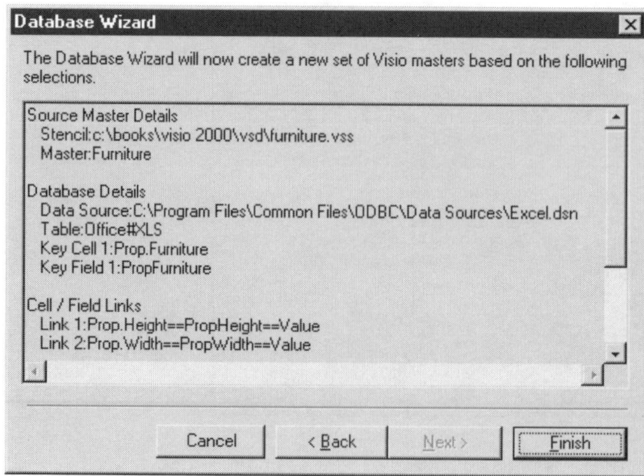

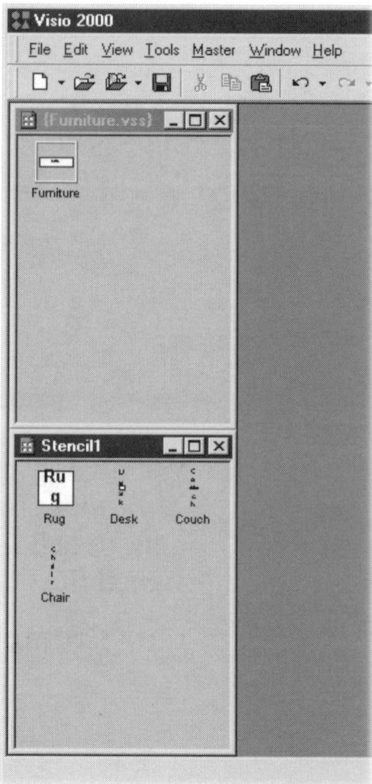

Notice that Visio creates a new stencil file, containing one master for every record in the database file. If you like, edit the look of the icons. Save the stencil as **Database.Vss** with the File | Save As command.

# Examining the Database Link

Now that you've created a link between Visio and a database file, let's take a look at what the Database wizard did to the cells of the ShapeSheet.

Open a new drawing. Drag a master, such as Rug, from the new Stencil1.Vss stencil onto the page. Select **Window | Show ShapeSheet** to open the ShapeSheet window.

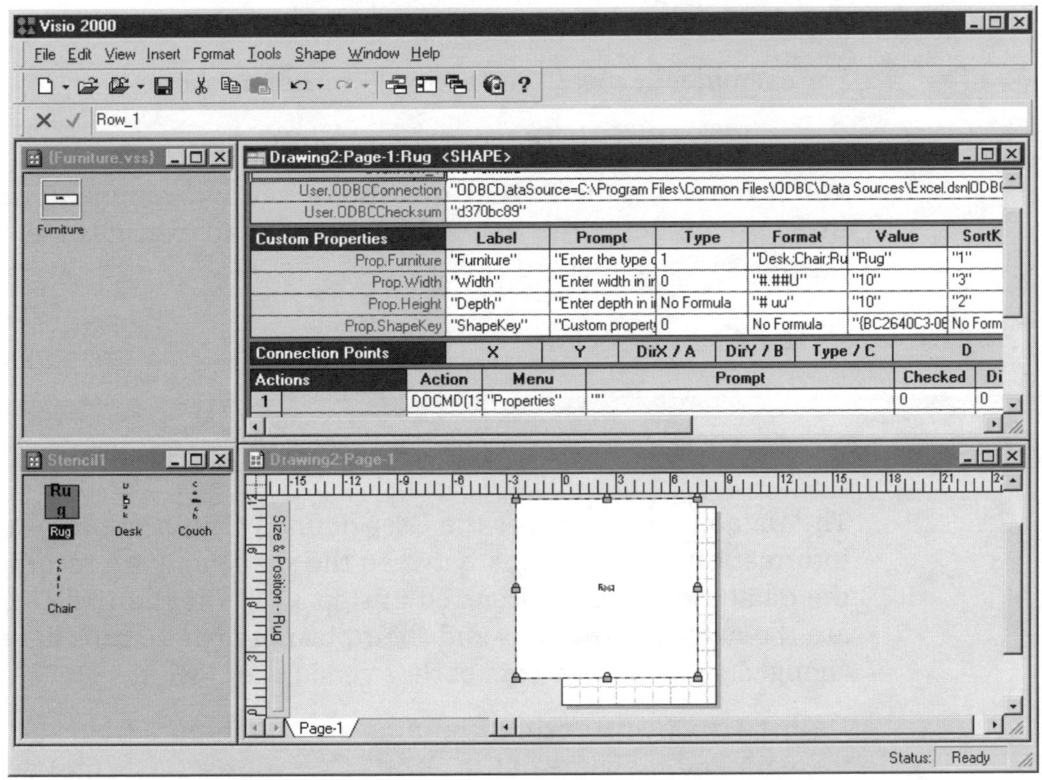

Notice that the Database wizard made changes to several sections of the ShapeSheet: Actions, Custom Properties, User-defined Cells, and Events. Let's look at each of them.

## The Actions Section

| Actions | | Action | Menu | Prompt | Checked | Disabled |
|---|---|---|---|---|---|---|
| 1 | | DOCMD(1312) | "Properties" | "" | 0 | 0 |
| 2 | | RUNADDON("Database Select Record") | "Select database record" | "Select a record from the database table." | 0 | 0 |
| 3 | | RUNADDON("Database Refresh Shape") | "Refresh shape properties" | "Refresh linked shape cells using values from the database record." | 0 | 0 |
| 4 | | RUNADDON("Database Update Record") | "Update database record" | "Update linked record in database table with shape cell values." | 0 | 0 |
| 5 | | RUNADDON("Database Delete Shape") | "Delete shape and record" | "Delete the selected shape and the associated record in the database." | 0 | 0 |

During step 14 of the Database wizard tutorial, you had the option to have database-related commands added to the shape's shortcut menu. Visio adds these commands to rows 2 through 5 of the Actions section.

For example, in row 2, the action is to run a macro:

RUNADDON("Database Select Record")

When you select the **Select database record** command from the shortcut menu, the **RunAddOn** command executes the "Database Select Record" macro.

## The User-defined Cells Section

| User-defined Cells | Value | Prompt |
|---|---|---|
| User.Row_1 | No Formula | No Formula |
| User.ODBCConnection | "ODBCDataSource=C:\Program Files\Common Files\ODBC\Data Sources\Excel.dsn|ODBCQualifier=|ODBCTable=Office#XLS|1 | "This cell contains the link information for the Database Wizard." |
| User.ODBCChecksum | "d370bc89" | "This cell contains a checksum of the database record." |

The Database wizard uses the User-defined Cells section to store information about the link between the shape and the record in the database file. This occurred in step 11 of the tutorial. Here are the names of the cells and their meaning (these cells have changed significantly from earlier versions of Visio):

**User.ODBCConnection** contains the link information, such as the path and filename of the ODBC data source (DSN file) and table name. For the Rug shape connected to the Excel spreadsheet file, the data is:

="ODBCDataSource=C:\Program Files\Common Files\ODBC\Data Sources\Excel.dsn|
ODBCQualifier=|ODBCTable=Office#XLS|1|PropFurniture=Prop.Furniture|3|
PropHeight=Prop.Height=0|PropWidth=Prop.Width=0|ShapeKey=Prop.ShapeKey=0|"

This is not documented by Visio Corp. Parsing the statement at each vertical bar, the statement becomes easier to read:

```
ODBCDataSource=C:\Program Files\Common Files\ODBC\Data
Sources\Excel.dsn
ODBCQualifier=
ODBCTable=Office#XLS
1
PropFurniture=Prop.Furniture
3
PropHeight=Prop.Height=0
PropWidth=Prop.Width=0
ShapeKey=Prop.ShapeKey=0
```

Let's look at each of these in turn:

**ODBCDataSource=C:\Program Files\Common Files\ODBC\Data Sources\Excel.dsn** specifies the path and filename of the ODBC data source (DSN file).

**ODBCQualifier=** specifies whether the database contains more than one table.

**ODBCTable=Office#XLS** specifies the name of the linked data source table or view. In step 8 of the tutorial, you selected the Office.xls spreadsheet file as the table; Excel does not support views.

The number 1 specifies the number of tables.

**PropFurniture=Prop.Furniture** specifies the names of the primary key field(s) in the database file and can have up to five key fields. In step 10 of the tutorial, you selected Prop.Furniture as the key field.

The number 3 specifies the number of cells that correspond to data source table fields.

**PropHeight=Prop.Height=0** specifies the names of the cells that correspond to data source table fields. There is one row of cells per linked field. In step 15 of the tutorial, you specified which fields should match which cell names. One of the field-cell associations is:

**"Prop.PropHeight==PropHeight==0"**

This means the Prop.PropHeight cell corresponds to the PropHeight field. The 0 is a code that tells Visio to evaluate the data as a string (when the data is copied from the field to the cell). The possible codes are:

| Code | Meaning |
| --- | --- |
| 0 | String (text) |
| 1 | Formula string |
| 32 | Non-dimensional number |
| 40 | Date |
| 48 | Unitless number |
| 50 | Points |
| 51 | Picas |
| 53 | Didots |
| 54 | Ciceros |
| 63 | Default page units |
| 64 | Default drawing units |
| 65 | Decimal inches |
| 66 | Decimal feet |
| 67 | Feet and inches |
| 68 | Decimal miles |
| 69 | Centimeters |
| 70 | Millimeters |
| 71 | Meters |
| 72 | Kilometers |
| 73 | Fractional inches |
| 74 | Fractional miles |
| 75 | Yards |
| 80 | Angle with no explicit units |
| 81 | Angle in decimal degrees |
| 82 | Angle in degrees, minutes, seconds |
| 83 | Angle in radians |
| 84 | Angle in minutes, seconds |

| Code | Meaning |
|------|---------|
| 85 | Angle in seconds |
| 111 | Currency |
| 252 | Keep in current units |

**PropWidth=Prop.Width=0** and **ShapeKey= Prop.ShapeKey=0** specify the field name matched with the cell name.

**User.ODBCChecksum** contains a number that confirms that data transaction was made correctly.

## The Custom Properties Section

| Custom Properties | Label | Prompt | Type | Format | Value | | SortKey | Invisible | Ask |
|---|---|---|---|---|---|---|---|---|---|
| Prop.Furniture | "Furniture" | "Enter the type of furniture, such as Desk or Chair." | 1 | "Desk;Chair;Rug;Couch" | "Rug" | | "1" | 0 | 1 |
| Prop.Width | "Width" | "Enter width in inches." | 0 | "#.##U" | "10" | | "3" | 0 | 1 |
| Prop.Height | "Depth" | "Enter depth in inches." | No Formula | "# uu" | "10" | | "2" | 0 | 1 |
| Prop.ShapeKey | "ShapeKey" | "Custom property generated from database field ShapeKey." | 0 | No Formula | "{BC2640C3-06B0-11D2-8E9D-00AA00201DF7}" | | No Formula | No Formula | No Formula |

In this chapter, we have been looking at how a shape can be linked to a record in a database file. Recall that a *record* is like a row in a spreadsheet. A record contains *fields* of data, where each field is like a cell in a spreadsheet row. Recall also that Visio is limited to linking one record per shape. In step 16 of the tutorial, you determined which fields correspond to cell names.

The Database wizard stores the record in the Custom Property section. Each field gets one row in this section. In the tutorial, the database fields are called PropFurniture, PropHeight, PropWidth, and ShapeKey. The Database wizard prefixes each field name with "Prop." since that is Visio's convention for identifying row names in the Custom Properties section.

The Label column contains the field name. The Value column contains the field value. The Type column contains a code number identical to the list shown earlier in the User-defined Cells description. For example, the "PropFurniture" field contains the value of "Couch" and should be treated as a string (**0**).

Since the value in the Invisible column is No formula (which is equivalent to 0), these fields show up in the Custom Properties dialog box. Right-click the shape and select Properties:

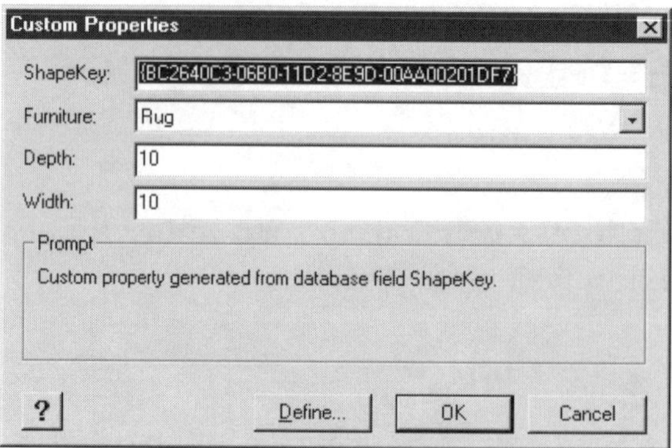

If you prefer these fields not be displayed by the Custom Properties dialog box, change the value in the Invisible column to 1.

## The Events Section

The Events section contains a single addition by the Database wizard. In step 13 of the tutorial, you requested that an on-drop event be added to the master. For this reason, the EventDrop cell contains the macro command:

RUNADDON("Database Refresh Shape")

This causes Visio to refresh the shape based on the contents of the database file. If the file has been changed, the shape will be changed.

***Tip:***
To learn more about the jargon used by ODBC, read the help file for ODBC installed on your computer. To access the help file: from the Windows task bar, select **Start | Settings | Control Panel**. In the Control Panel window, double-click **ODBC Data Source (32-bit)**. In the ODBC Data Source Administrator, click the **Help** button. In the ODBC Help window, click **Index** and select **Glossary** from the list.

# Chapter Review

You should now understand how the database wizard creates a master that is linked to an external database file.

# *Index*

database link, examining, 347-353
database object, 337
Database Refresh command, 278
Database Settings dialog box, 278
Database Update command, 278
Database wizard, 278, 334-346
data*n* data type, 274
date functions, 248-250
Define Styles dialog box, 48, 53
deselecting objects, 5
document object, 12
Document Properties section, 187
double-click behavior, changing, 104-105
drawing tools, 8-9
driver, 268
drop shadow, customizing, 39-40
DSN file, 283
duplicating shapes, 6

**E**
Ellipse tool, 9
error handling functions, 260-261
error types, 261
event functions, 252-253
Events section, 96, 188
export format, selecting, 292-298
exporting
    custom property data, 128
    data, 16-17, 150-151
    drawings, 279-289
    updated drawings, 290-291

**F**
fields, 266, 267
    linking with cells, 345
Fill Format section, 96, 189-191
fill pattern,
    applying custom, 56-57
    creating custom, 53-56
fill style, creating custom, 57-58
Foreign Image Info section, 191-193
foreign object, 12
Format cell, 140-143
format pictures, 141, 182-186
formula, 151
formulae, writing, 151-152
Freeform tool, 9
functions,
    arithmetic, 244-245

color and pattern, 247-248
comparison, 259
data, 254
date, 248-250
error handling, 260-261
event, 252-253
geometric, 245-247
logical, 260
mathematical, 257-258
miscellaneous, 254-256
new in Visio 2000, 244
properties, 253-254
statistical, 257
text, 250-252
time, 248-250
trigonometric, 258-259
window management, 247

**G**
geometric functions, 245-247
geometry, 7
Geometry 1 section, 96
Geometry section, 193-199
global coordinate system, 20
Glue Info section, 96, 199-200
Gridding, 325-326
Group command, 28
group,
    adding shapes to, 26, 27
    removing shapes from, 27
    selecting, 27
group data, 28
group object, 11
Group Properties section, 201-202
grouping shapes, 25-26
guide object, 11

**H**
handles, 103
Hyperlinks section, 202-204

**I**
ID number, 153-154
Image Properties section, 96, 204
importing data, 16-17
infinite line, 9
instances, 147
Invisible cell, 133-135
invisible cells, 175

# I don't have time for learning curves.

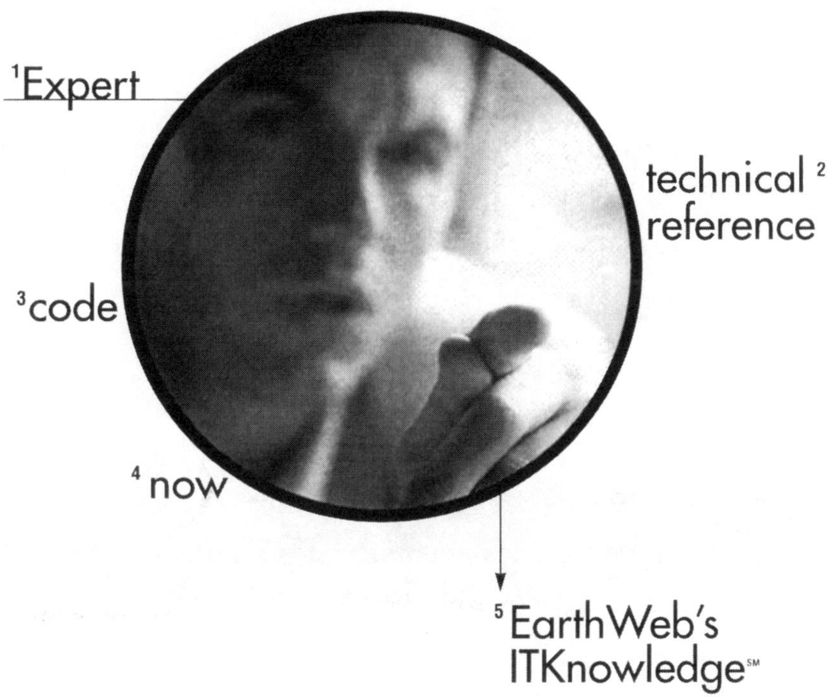


They rely on you to be the **❶** expert on tough development challenges. There's no time for learning curves, so you go online for **❷** technical references from the experts who wrote the books. Find answers fast simply by clicking on our search engine. Access hundreds of online books, tutorials and even source **❸** code samples **❹** now. Go to **❺** EarthWeb's ITKnowledge, get immediate answers, and get down to it.

Get your FREE ITKnowledge trial subscription today at <u>itkgo.com</u>.
Use code number 026.

# About the CD

The companion CD contains examples of the working files used in the exercises throughout this book.

Use the Windows Explorer to copy the files from the CD to your hard drive.

Opening the CD package makes this book non-returnable.